W9-AOZ-076

Personal Epistemology and Teacher Education

Routledge Research in Education

For a full list of titles in this series please visit www.routledge.com

Personal Epistemology and Teacher Education

Edited by Jo Brownlee, Gregory Schraw and Donna Berthelsen

Routledge
Taylor & Francis Group
New York   London

First published 2011
by Routledge
711 Third Avenue, New York, NY 10017

Simultaneously published in the UK
by Routledge
2 Park Square, Milton Park, Abingdon, Oxon OX14 4RN

Routledge is an imprint of the Taylor & Francis Group, an informa business

Typeset in Sabon by IBT Global.
Printed and bound in the United States of America on acid-free paper by IBT Global.

Library of Congress Cataloging-in-Publication Data

Personal epistemology and teacher education / edited by Jo Brownlee, Gregory Schraw, and Donna Berthelsen.
    p. cm.—(Routledge research in education ; 61)
Includes bibliographical references and index.
1. Teachers—Training of. 2. Knowledge, Theory of. I. Brownlee, Jo.
II. Schraw, Gregory J.   III. Berthelsen, Donna.
LB1707.P47 2011
370.71'1—dc22
2011005046

ISBN: 978-0-415-88356-6 (hbk)
ISBN: 978-0-203-80661-6 (ebk)

Contents

PART II:
Inservice Teachers and Teaching

Conclusion

Tables

Figures

Introduction

1 Personal Epistemology and Teacher Education

An Emerging Field of Research

Jo Brownlee, Gregory Schraw, and Donna Berthelsen

ABSTRACT

A growing body of personal epistemology research shows that personal epistemologies influence student learning, particularly in academic contexts. However, we know little about how personal epistemologies relate to teaching, and even less about teacher education. This introductory chapter sets the stage for this book which brings together a range of international researchers in the field of personal epistemology, teaching, and teacher education. This introductory chapter explores personal epistemology as a construct in the field of teaching and teacher education. In particular, it focuses on teacher education as one contextual influence on personal epistemologies by exploring the nature of teachers' personal epistemologies, teachers' personal epistemologies and learning, teachers' personal epistemologies and teaching, and changing personal epistemology in teacher education programs.

INTRODUCTION

Our changing, complex world has necessitated an evolution in how we think about knowledge, knowing, and the nature of teaching. Social constructivist theories in teaching and teacher education are now considered effective ways to theorize teaching and learning. This means that teachers are expected to facilitate student-centered learning by helping students to construct knowledge in social contexts; engage in higher order thinking rather than reproducing knowledge; address real world ill-structured problems; and engage in collaborative learning (Elen & Clarebout, 2001; Yang, Chang, & Hsu, 2008). The current focus on learners as active agents in their own learning has emerged because we now have a better understanding of how teaching and learning take place in social contexts and how knowledge construction is mediated by tools of technology (Windschitl, 2002).

Even though social constructivist approaches to teaching are advocated as good practice, many teachers are challenged by these approaches to teaching (Rosenfield & Rosenfield, 2006) and traditional, teacher-centered approaches often remain the default teaching practice (see e.g., Windschitl, 2002; Yang, Chang, & Hsu, 2008). This is hardly surprising if we consider that Western education contexts, in general, reflect objectivist epistemologies in which teaching and learning are conceived of as transmission and reception of knowledge respectively (Windschitl, 2002). Whereas it might be agreed that teachers need to engage in constructivist teaching practices, what is also important is that they have beliefs that support these approaches to teaching (Windschitl, 2002). We argue that a specific type of teacher belief is of interest here. These are the beliefs teachers hold about the nature of knowledge and knowing which are referred to as personal epistemology.

Theory and research related to personal epistemology is one way in which we can better understand teaching and learning (Kang, 2008), in particular the current focus on social constructivist approaches. Much of the personal epistemology research to date has taken place in academic contexts (Schraw & Sinatra, 2004) and there is a robust body of research that shows how personal epistemologies influence student learning. However, very little research has investigated the relationship between personal epistemologies and teaching (Kang, 2008), and even less in the specific field of teacher education. This book brings together a range of international researchers in the field of personal epistemology, teaching, and teacher education, with a view to addressing this gap in the research.

The gap seems to be evident in the area of personal epistemologies and teaching practice at all levels—early years, elementary, secondary, and tertiary teaching with research into teacher education even more limited (Feucht, 2009). Recently Hofer (2010) expressed concern that we still lack research evidence in the area of personal epistemologies and teaching practice. She argues that challenges in the field lie in how broader contexts impact personal epistemologies and practice. These contextual influences may influence how teachers view the role of authority in knowledge building, the certainty of knowledge, and how knowledge is justified. This suggests that links between personal epistemologies and practice may be moderated by the broader teaching and learning environments (Johnston, Woodside-Jiron, & Day, 2001; Kang & Wallace, 2005). This book takes up Hofer's challenge to further explore personal epistemology as a construct in the field of teaching and teacher education by addressing the following topics:

- The nature of teachers' personal epistemologies
- Teachers' personal epistemologies and learning
- Teachers' personal epistemologies and teaching
- Changing personal epistemology in teacher education programs

THE NATURE OF TEACHERS' PERSONAL EPISTEMOLOGIES

Personal epistemology is philosophy at the individual level and reflects how we think about knowledge and knowing (Hofer, 2010). In general, the term *Personal epistemology* is more widely used than *epistemological beliefs* because it reflects the individual, rather than philosophical, nature of these beliefs (Kitchener, 2002; Sandoval, 2005). Whereas there is still no definitive view about whether personal epistemology as a construct reflects beliefs, attitudes, knowledge, ways of knowing, or reasoning skills, there is overall support for the notion that personal epistemology involves an individual's cognition about knowing and knowledge (Pintrich, 2002). It is not surprising then, that in addition to the variety of perspectives about what constitutes personal epistemology, a range of paradigms is evident in the field. These paradigms, including *epistemological development, epistemological beliefs, epistemological theories, epistemic metacognition, and epistemological resources* (Hofer, 2004a, 2004b), have provided us with rich understandings about how to promote effective learning, and to a lesser extent, effective teaching in a range of education contexts. It informs the first main topic that this book seeks to address: *What is the nature of teachers' personal epistemologies?* Figure 1.1 provides an overview of the chapters in this book which address this topic.

In the first paradigm, *Epistemological development*, much of the research has examined how a range of education contexts influence the development of personal epistemology (Hofer, 2004a). These unidimensional, stage-like views of change in personal epistemologies are reflected in the seminal work of Perry (1970) and King and Kitchener (1994). This early work showed that individuals may move from simple, black and white views through to complex evidenced-based ways of knowing. A considerable body of recent evidence has also reflected similar developmental trajectories. For example, Kuhn and Weinstock (2002) reported changes in personal epistemology from absolutist (absolute view of knowledge), to *subjectivist* (personal opinions count) to *evaluativist* (tentative, evidenced based knowledge). Individuals with *Absolutist* personal epistemologies view knowledge as either right or wrong, and so there is little need to be reflective or evaluate knowledge. As individuals begin to understand that knowledge is tentative, they may begin to conceive of knowledge and knowing as a personal construction. Here *subjectivist* beliefs value personal opinions, but knowledge still remains largely unexamined. In the final position, the *evaluativist* understands that knowledge is constructed, but that some knowledge is "better" than others. This means that knowledge claims need to be made on the basis of evaluating a range of perspectives and then coming to the "best" evidenced based response. From this perspective knowledge is tentative, perspectival, and constructed. The research related to personal epistemology commonly uses the terms *naive* and *sophisticated* to refer to this range of personal epistemologies (Pintrich, 2002).

Another paradigm which has found prominence in the field of personal epistemology relates to *Epistemological Beliefs*. This paradigm stands in contrast to the developmental paradigm because it focuses on how personal epistemology is comprised of independent, multidimensional beliefs which influence learning (Hofer, 2004a). Schommer was the first to describe personal epistemologies as a set of independent beliefs (Schommer-Aikens, 2004). This means that individuals may hold a range of beliefs that may or may not be aligned to a particular personal epistemological stance. For example, an individual may simultaneously hold naïve beliefs in the certainty of knowledge and yet also believe that knowledge is personally constructed. A large body of research over the last 30 years has drawn on Schommer's epistemological beliefs as a way to further understand learning in secondary and higher education contexts.

Other research in the field considers personal epistemology as more than a collection of independent beliefs. Research which draws on the paradigm of *Epistemological Theories* involves a view that individuals may have a general theory of knowledge and the domain-specific theories in relation to, for example, science (Hofer, 2004b). This approach considers personal epistemology to be comprised of theories about the nature of knowing and the nature of knowledge. Hofer has built on this paradigm to describe an emerging field related to *Epistemic Metacognition* (Hofer, 2004a; Kitchener, 1983). From this perspective personal epistemology is conceived of as a "set of beliefs, organized into theories, operating at the metacognitive level. Such theories develop in interaction with the environment, are influenced by culture and education . . . operate at both the domain-general and domain-specific level, are situated in practice and are activated in context" (p. 46).

Finally, *Epistemological Resources* refer to the notion of personal epistemology as context-specific epistemological resources, rather than developmental stages, beliefs, or theories (Louca, Elby, Hammer, & Kagey, 2004).

How do we conceptualize personal epistemology?

In Chapter 2, Yadav and his colleagues provide a comprehensive overview of how we conceptualize personal epistemology in teacher education. For research that draws on the paradigm of *Epistemological development* take a look at Chapter 5 (Brownlee et al.) and Chapter 12 (Tabak & Weinstock). The paradigm related to *Epistemological beliefs* is reflected in Chapter 13 (Valanides & Angeli) and Chapter 14 (Schwartz & Jordan). *Epistemological theories* are used to inform the research reported in Chapter 4 (Strømsø & Bråten), Chapter 7 (Bendixen & Corkhill), Chapter 11 (Weinstock & Roth), and Chapter 16 (Lee & Tsai). Other chapters use a combination of paradigms namely epistemological beliefs and epistemological theories (Chapter 6, Walker et al.; Chapter 15, Feucht).

Figure 1.1   How do we conceptualize personal epistemology?

They believe that children as well as adults can have multiple ways of knowing the world that may vary depending on the learning context.

Pintrich (2002) summarized these various paradigms into three broader ways of researching personal epistemology: cognitive developmental (*Epistemological development*), cognitive (*Epistemological beliefs, Epistemic metacognition, Epistemological theories*), and contextual (*Epistemological resources*) approaches. In this chapter, we refer to personal epistemology in the context of teaching and teacher education and take personal epistemology to mean the teachers' cognition about knowing and knowledge, regardless of the paradigm on which the research is based.

TEACHERS' PERSONAL EPISTEMOLOGIES AND LEARNING

Personal epistemologies are considered to be activated during the process of learning and influence the extent to which we make meaning and engage in complex problem solving (Hofer, 2002). This is of critical importance when we consider that the core business of teachers is learning and managing complex environments with multiple stakeholders. Teachers with sophisticated personal epistemologies are more likely to be able to engage in ill-structured problem solving, and argue based on evidence for a "best" solution. This is an important skill for any workplace environment, but especially in teaching contexts. However, whereas sophisticated personal epistemologies may be an important goal for teacher education programs, often undergraduates who finish their courses and enter the profession still hold relatively naïve personal epistemologies. Clearly, in these circumstances, teacher education programs are not helping preservice teachers to develop more sophisticated personal epistemologies needed for effective teaching (White, 2000).

To date, we have strong evidence to show that an individual's personal epistemology influences learning strategies and learning outcomes in preservice teachers (Muis, 2004). Personal epistemologies may filter how preservice teachers experience learning in teacher education courses and engage in meaningful approaches to learning (Yadav & Koehler, 2007; Many, Howard, & Hoge, 2002; Muis, 2004; Peng & Fitzgerald, 2006). These meaningful approaches to learning can be described as deep-holistic learning strategies (Ramsden, 2003, in Thomas, Pilgrim, & Oliver, 2005). Such strategies focus on building personal meaning and organizing ideas so that links are made to prior knowledge, connecting ideas and evaluating a range of evidence (critical thinking). On the other hand, surface-atomistic strategies focus on the surface or textual meaning with few interconnections made between topics and theories. Often this results in rote learning (Ramsden, 2003, in Thomas, Pilgrim, & Oliver, 2005). The deep-holistic and surface-atomistic approaches to learning reflect what Windschitl (2002) described as *strong* and *weak* acts of constructivism. When students engage in *strong* acts of construction, they use deep-holistic approaches to learning whereas *weak* approaches to constructivism involve the use of surface-atomistic approaches to learning. In essence, Windschitl's account of constructivism means that all learners engage in some form of constructivism, although the depth of meaning-making may vary.

A number of studies have shown that sophisticated personal epistemologies are related to meaningful approaches to learning. Bondy et al. (2007) investigated how personal epistemologies were related to approaches to learning by interviewing 14 preservice teachers. They found that students with sophisticated personal epistemologies (knowledge is uncertain and integrated) were more likely to be open to multiple perspectives and to see the interconnections between ideas. Brownlee, Berthelsen, and Boulton-Lewis (2004) also found similar relationships in a group of child care workers in Australia. Caregivers who described evaluativistic patterns of beliefs also described deeper approaches to learning in which connections were made between new and prior knowledge. Some research also suggests that personal epistemologies may be related to levels of critical thinking, which is a dimension of meaningful approaches to learning. Bråten and Strømsø (2006b) showed that 1st year Norwegian preservice teachers' personal epistemologies about the speed of knowledge acquisition influenced their capacity to engage in critical thinking in the context of evaluating Web-based resources. Muis (2004) described these personal epistemologies as *availing*, rather than sophisticated, because such personal epistemologies were supportive or availing of meaningful, strong constructivist approaches to learning.

Meaningful approaches to learning may also be related to goal setting. Some studies show that personal epistemologies may influence goal setting, which then impacts on the approach to learning that is used. Ravindran, Greene, and DeBacker (2005) investigated the links between achievement goals, personal epistemology, learning approaches, and how learning was applied in other contexts. One hundred and one preservice teachers were asked to complete an 84-item achievement goals (learning and performance goals) questionnaire, a personal epistemology survey, and learning approaches survey (meaningful/shallow approaches). The results showed that goals and personal epistemology predicted the approaches students took to learning. This suggests that more sophisticated personal epistemologies were linked to meaningful approaches to learning and mastery goals. Bråten and Strømsø (2006c) also investigated the relationship between personal epistemologies, achievement goals, and theories of intelligence. In a sample of both teacher education and business students in Norway, they found that students who believed in quick learning were less likely to adopt mastery goals, which focus on meaningful approaches to learning. Further, students who believed that knowledge was absolute and passively received were also not likely to use mastery goals in their learning.

Whereas some studies show the links between personal epistemologies and approaches to learning, other research shows how sophisticated personal epistemologies can lead to *meaningful learning outcomes*. For example, Bråten and

Strømsø (2006a) investigated text comprehension and personal epistemologies in 39 Norwegian preservice teachers. Their findings showed that students with sophisticated personal epistemologies demonstrated better comprehension when reading multiple, partly conflicting texts about Attention Deficit Hyperactivity Disorder. Preservice teachers with more naïve personal epistemologies however were better able to understand text, when engaged with single texts that did not offer conflicting information. In a later study with 135 Norwegian preservice teachers Bråten, Strømsø, and Samuelstuen (2008) also found links between personal epistemologies and comprehension of science texts. Preservice teachers who thought that knowledge in the area of climate change was complex were better able to understand multiple texts than preservice teachers who viewed climate change as a simple concept. However, it was interesting that students who viewed knowledge as a construction did not do as well as those who thought climate change knowledge could be transferred from authority to learner. Conflicting results were also evident in Peng and Fitzgerald's (2006) study of 60 preservice teachers completing special education courses in four universities in the US. Whereas they found that personal epistemologies about fixed ability were related to difficulties with problem solving, their results did not show that naïve beliefs in the Structure of Knowledge were related to understanding of texts. These studies show how various dimensions of personal epistemologies may differentially influence learning outcomes in terms of text comprehension as a learning outcome.

Collectively, these studies demonstrate that personal epistemologies influence learning in terms of approaches to learning and learning outcomes. This is clearly an important body of research for understanding how preservice teachers navigate their teacher education courses and develop a sound body of knowledge and skills for entry into the teaching profession. The weak and strong constructivist acts of learning articulated by Windschitl (2002) are especially important for understanding learning strategies and outcomes in teacher education. We can also distinguish between weak and strong approaches to constructivist teaching and how these are related to personal epistemology. See Figure 1.2 for an overview of the chapters which address the topic of personal epistemologies and learning for preservice teachers.

How are preservice teachers' personal epistemologies related to learning?

Take a look at Chapter 4 (Strømsø & Bråten), Chapter 6 (Walker et al.), and Chapter 13 (Valanides & Angeli) to find out more about how teachers' personal epistemologies might be related to their approaches to learning in teacher education contexts.

Figure 1.2 How are preservice teachers' personal epistemologies related to learning?

TEACHERS' PERSONAL EPISTEMOLOGIES AND TEACHING

When teachers promote *strong* acts of construction in their students, they help students to use deep-holistic approaches to learning (Ramsden, 2003, in Thomas, Pilgrim, & Oliver, 2005) and to build personal meaning. Such teachers focus on what matters to the student, helping them to make connections to their own experiences. They try to use real world experiences in which students are encouraged to weigh up different types of evidence, thus engaging in higher order thinking rather than reproducing knowledge and often this is done collaboratively with the teacher and their peers (Elen & Clarebout, 2001; Yang, Chang, & Hsu 2008). Teachers who promote *weak* approaches to constructivism, on the other hand, create learning conditions that promote surface-atomistic approaches to learning. These teaching approaches are teacher-centered and didactic in nature, and often focus on learners reproducing information without necessarily demonstrating personal understanding. When we acknowledge teaching as promoting weak or strong constructivist learning approaches, it is evident that all teachers engage in some form of constructivist teaching. There is evidence in the literature that personal epistemologies are related to this range of constructivist teaching practices for both inservice and preservice teachers.

Personal Epistemologies and Teaching: Inservice Teachers

Maggioni and Parkinson (2008) completed a review of studies which investigated teaching practice and personal epistemology. With a focus on inservice teachers rather than preservice teachers, they explored the relationship between personal epistemology and teaching practice. A range of research shows that personal epistemologies are consistent with teaching practices. For example Yang, Chang, and Hsu (2008) showed that Taiwanese secondary earth science teachers' views about personal epistemologies were aligned with instruction in science teaching: Views about constructivist instruction aligned with sophisticated personal epistemologies. Muis (2004) noted that the "types of instruction in which students are immersed parallel the types of beliefs they have" (p. 363). Speed, accuracy, and memorization of rules in math teaching is connected to personal epistemologies that learning is quick, there is one right answer, students need to have ability to succeed, knowledge is absolute in math (and does not change), math knowledge is not interconnected, and the teacher is the ultimate authority.

Brownlee (2000, 2001) also found that personal epistemologies and teaching practice were consistent in early years teachers. Their study showed that child care teachers who held evaluativistic personal epistemologies were more likely to describe child-centered, constructivist approaches to teaching. Child care teachers with more naïve personal epistemologies in which knowledge is considered to be absolute and simplistic were more likely to engage in teaching practices that required children to be less active and rely more on adults to direct their learning. Schraw and Sinatra (2004) also noted that teachers with more sophisticated personal epistemologies are likely to be quite adaptable in terms of teaching strategies and engage more with their students.

Links between personal epistemologies and teaching practice have also been found in special education teachers (Jordan & Stanovich, 2003). Jordan and Stanovich described two main ways of conceptualizing disability: Pathological—endogenous beliefs where teachers do not take responsibility for intervening because disability is not able to be changed; and interventionist—exogenous beliefs where teachers take an active role in supporting children with disabilities to learn. They argue that personal epistemologies influence both beliefs about disability and practices in teaching for diversity. From this perspective, they further argue that changing such practices requires a change in personal epistemologies and beliefs about disabilities, although they also believe that changing practices may ultimately lead to belief change. This line of research is developed in Chapter 14 by Schwartz and Jordan where they demonstrate further the links between personal epistemology, beliefs about ability/disability, and teaching practices. In Chapter 11, Weinstock and Roth's study shows how teachers' personal epistemologies are related to their teaching for student autonomy whereas in Chapter 12, Tabak and Weinstock talk about how teaching practices related to inquiry teaching can cultivate certain personal epistemologies in children. They argued that children need to be encouraged to think beyond a "tolerance" for all perspectives to one in more critical perspectives are encouraged in judging the quality of a response. These studies all demonstrate a consistency between personal epistemologies and practice in teaching. In particular they show that naïve personal epistemologies are related to weaker acts of constructivist teaching whereas more sophisticated personal epistemologies are linked to strong constructivist teaching practices.

Whereas there is evidence that personal epistemologies may be related to teaching practice, some research indicates that beliefs and practice are not always consistent. In Many et al.'s (2002) review of the literature, they reported that whereas there is evidence to suggest that personal epistemologies and teaching practice are often consistent, the broader school contexts, for example school culture, may result in teachers practicing in ways that do not reflect their personal epistemologies. A number of chapters in the book report this lack of consistency between personal epistemologies and practice. See Figure 1.3 for an overview of these chapters. Lee and Tsai (Chapter 16) showed that the more experienced science teachers in his study held personal epistemologies which were not always reflected in their practice. Schraw, Olafson, and VanderVeldt in Chapter 10 also noticed that some of the teachers in their sample did not demonstrate consistent beliefs and practices. They argued that inservice teachers have had more experience in teaching and

How are teachers' personal epistemologies related to inservice teaching?

Many of the chapters in this book have, as their focus, the relationship between personal epistemologies and teaching practice for inservice teachers. Chapter 11 (Weinstock & Roth), Chapter 12 (Tabak & Weinstock), and Chapter 14 (Schwartz & Jordan) report research which shows that teachers' personal epistemologies are consistent with their teaching practices. Conversely Chapter 10 (Schraw & Olafson), Chapter 15 (Fuecht), and Chapter 16 (Lee & Tsai) reflect on how personal epistemologies are not always evident in teaching practice, and demonstrate inconsistencies between beliefs and practices. It seems that this is an area of research in personal epistemology that needs to be addressed in more detail in future research.

Figure 1.3   How are teachers' personal epistemologies related to inservice teaching?

therefore are less likely to adjust their beliefs as the result of short term interventions. Feucht (Chapter 15) also found that the teacher in his case study espoused personal epistemologies that did not match her personal epistemologies about teaching reading. These chapters help us to understand better how personal epistemologies may not be enacted in teaching practice.

Personal Epistemologies and Teaching: Preservice Teachers

Another distinct body of research also investigates personal epistemologies and teaching in preservice teachers. However, we know a great deal more about personal epistemologies and preservice teachers' learning than we do about personal epistemologies and their teaching practices (Kang, 2008). In this section we briefly describe research that has considered personal epistemologies and teaching in preservice teachers by first looking at the links between personal epistemologies and teaching beliefs and then personal epistemologies and teaching practices. A comprehensive review of the research related to preservice teachers is provided by Yadav and his colleagues in Chapter 2. Figure 1.4 provides information about the chapters in this book which deal with preservice teachers' personal epistemologies and teaching.

A number of studies have investigated how preservice teachers' personal epistemologies are related to beliefs/conceptions regarding teaching rather than their actual teaching practice (e.g., Chai, Khine, & Teo, 2006). Cheng, Chan, Tang, and Cheng (2009) used a mixed-method approach to investigate conceptions of teaching and personal epistemologies in a sample of 228 4th year preservice teachers at the University of Hong Kong. The survey measured personal epistemology using the Epistemological Beliefs Questionnaire, whereas the Conceptions of Teaching scale measured beliefs about constructivist/traditional approaches to teaching. A subsample of 31 preservice teachers was selected to be interviewed. Both qualitative and quantitative sets of data showed that a large number of the preservice teachers believed that learning effort was needed for successful learning, were of the view that knowledge evolved over time, and believed it was important to critique knowledge, particularly experts' knowledge. These sophisticated personal epistemologies were found to be related to constructivist conceptions of teaching. Chan (2004) also found similar results in his investigation of personal epistemologies and conceptions of teaching with Hong Kong preservice teachers.

A range of other studies have investigated personal epistemologies and observed teaching practice, rather than beliefs about or conceptions of teaching. For example, Tsai and Liang (2009) investigated 36 early childhood preservice teachers in Taiwan who were studying a science education unit. Each student had to design a science activity for young children and receive feedback on this task from their peers online. Tsai and Liang found that those students with more sophisticated personal epistemologies were able to take on board peer feedback and develop more creative, enjoyable, and science-relevant activities. These data show that it may be important to take account of students' personal epistemologies when designing learning tasks that involve online peer assessment. In Chapter 5, Brownlee and her colleagues also investigated how preservice child care teachers view personal epistemology and the links between such beliefs and their practices. They showed clear links between more sophisticated personal epistemologies and child-centered, constructivist teaching interactions.

How are preservice teachers personal epistemologies related to preservice teaching?

In Chapter 1, Yadav et al. offer a comprehensive overview of personal epistemology in the context of preservice teacher education. This will give you an introduction to the topic. Then take a look at Chapter 3 (Tillema), Chapter 5 (Brownlee et al.), Chapter 7 (Bendixen & Corkhill), Chapter 8 (Fives), and Chapter 9 (Marra & Palmer) to find out more about how personal epistemologies are related to teaching practice for preservice teachers. Also, Chapter 3 (Tillema) and Chapter 4 (Strømsø & Bråten) explore how personal epistemologies are related to teaching practice for Academic staff in preservice teacher education courses.

Figure 1.4   How are preservice teachers' personal epistemologies related to preservice teaching?

CHANGING PERSONAL EPISTEMOLOGY
IN TEACHER EDUCATION PROGRAMS

Higher education, and specifically teacher education, needs to promote the development of sophisticated personal epistemologies not only because of the links between sophisticated personal epistemologies and meaningful learning but also because a knowledge economy requires sophisticated approaches to knowing (Kienhues, Bromme, & Stahl, 2008). In order for teacher educators to support preservice teachers to engage in meaningful learning for effective teaching we need to consider four key issues. Preservice teachers need to be able to: Build knowledge for teaching; have access to knowledge systems; hold personal epistemologies that influence what they gain from teacher education courses; and be able to make decisions in ill-defined contexts (Yadav & Koehler, 2007). A focus on personal epistemologies is a way to address these key issues in teacher education. It is important for teacher educators to understand the nature of preservice teachers' personal epistemologies and the specific teaching and learning strategies and environments that help to promote more sophisticated personal epistemologies (Liu & Tsai, 2008).

A range of research indicates that preservice teachers' personal epistemologies actually influence how they view the nature of instruction in teacher education courses. Many et al. (2002) found that preservice teachers with more naïve personal epistemologies were less able to appreciate the role of critical refection in journal entries and indeed reflected by producing summaries of content rather than critically reflecting on their learning. The effectiveness of teaching strategies used by their teacher educators was influenced by the nature of preservice teachers' personal epistemologies. Yadav and Koehler (2007) also argued that preservice teachers hold personal epistemologies that influence how they perceive their experiences in teacher education courses. They suggested that their personal epistemologies may indeed be quite naïve based on their previous personal experiences of school and this may actually be counterproductive. Silverman (2007) suggests that personal epistemologies are not a focus in teacher education programs for either preservice teachers or teacher educators and yet there is mounting evidence to suggest that personal epistemologies influence teaching beliefs and practices. We now discuss ways in which we might focus on personal epistemologies in teacher education programs, with a view to promoting the development of more sophisticated personal epistemologies.

There is evidence to suggest that explicit reflections on personal epistemologies may encourage changes in such beliefs. In fact most studies of preservice teachers personal epistemologies include, as part of their recommendations for teacher education, that personal epistemologies should become focal in such courses and that students need to be engaged in explicit reflection on such beliefs (Bondy et al., 2007; Cady, Meier, &

Lubinski, 2006; Chai et al., 2006; Chan, 2004; Cheng et al., 2009; Liu & Tsai, 2008; Kang, 2008; Silverman, 2007; Tsai & Liang, 2009; Yilmaz-Tuzun & Topcu, 2008). This explicit reflection suggests what Maggioni and Parkinson (2008) describe as "Epistemological moves" (p. 453) where teachers explicitly "direct students to what counts as knowledge and appropriate ways of obtaining that knowledge in the specific situation" (p. 453).

In other research, personal epistemologies were shown to be affected by explicit reflection on the process of critical thinking (Valanides & Angeli, 2005). Valanides and Angeli implemented teaching interventions with preservice teachers which focused on critical thinking to produce changes in personal epistemologies. The results showed that preservice teachers who were involved in the *Infusion* intervention (discussion of article, prepared outline for a paper on the issue, and reflection on their thinking, short lecture, conversation with researcher) experienced more change in personal epistemologies than the *General* intervention program (lectures and discussion of article for preparation for a paper). Whereas there is overwhelming consensus that preservice teachers need to reflect on personal epistemologies and the nature of critical thinking, it is not clear exactly how this should take place. Recent research into calibration may help to shed some light on how we may be able to achieve effective reflections on personal epistemologies.

Calibration training could be implemented with preservice teachers to help them to increase awareness of beliefs and knowledge in general and the extent to which their teaching practices reflect those beliefs/knowledge. Cunningham et al. (2004) suggested that "teachers' calibration of their knowledge of varying conceptual approaches to a domain is a metacognitive skill" (in Maggioni & Parkinson, 2008, p. 454) which is important for how teachers use their existing knowledge to obtain new knowledge. "Well-calibrated teachers know what they do and do not know and can therefore seek knowledge in areas that need improvement" (p. 454). Cunningham et al. (2004) investigated the knowledge base of 722 early years teachers (K–3) in regard to a range of topics: Children's literature, phonological awareness, and phonics. Teachers then gave themselves a rating on how much they knew about these topics. The results showed that teachers were well-calibrated in the area of children's literature. "Addressing teachers' beliefs without improving their calibration would not be very effective" (Maggioni & Parkinson, 2008, p. 454).

On the other hand, it seems that personal epistemologies may influence calibration (Maggioni & Parkinson, 2008). Stahl et al. (2006) argued that teachers with sophisticated personal epistemologies were more able to "calibrate their goal setting and planning to the difficulty of the task" (in Maggioni & Parkinson, 2008, p. 455). Therefore preservice teachers need to engage in explicit reflection on personal epistemologies to come to understand their own personal epistemologies and then be shown how to calibrate these personal epistemologies to various teaching contexts. "Research suggests that it may be possible to train teachers to calibrate the accuracy of their epistemic cognition and teaching practices for a specific discipline through providing feedback on the difference between believing and doing, thus improving both epistemic and metacognitive monitoring and subsequent strategy use" (Maggioni & Parkinson, 2008, p. 458).

The use of refutational texts also holds promise for supporting changes in personal epistemologies. Refutational text provides information that is meant to offer conflicting information that is supported with evidence. For example, Kienhues, Bromme, and Stahl (2008) randomly assigned German psychology and teacher education students to either an intervention focused on refutational texts or one in which texts were non-challenging. In the refutational text intervention, the concept that DNA fingerprinting is effective was introduced to students, followed by text that presented conflicting information about DNA testing that stressed uncertainty of the research. The non-challenging text intervention presented only facts about DNA fingerprinting with no debates evident. Students with naïve personal epistemologies in the refutational text intervention became more sophisticated in their personal epistemologies regarding complexity and stability of knowledge. Interestingly, students with sophisticated personal epistemologies who experienced the non-challenging text intervention became more naïve in their personal epistemologies. Gill, Ashton, and Algina (2004) randomly allocated 161 preservice teachers in mathematics education to either an intervention group based on augmented activation and refutational text or to a group in which expository text was used. Augmented activation means that students were provided with information that alerted them to the possibly conflicting text and that it was important that they should explicitly focus on the ideas that they might disagree with. Preservice teachers in the augmented activation and refutational text group experienced more changes in personal epistemologies than the traditional text group. These studies show that short-term interventions may influence personal epistemologies and that instruction which induces critical thinking has the potential to impact on personal epistemologies.

Explicit reflection on personal epistemologies, calibration, and refutational texts may all offer possibilities for the development of more sophisticated personal epistemologies in teacher education. Indeed these approaches may be considered to be good examples of ways in which to promote strong constructivist approaches to teaching and learning in teacher education programs. Bondy et al. (2007) argue that such approaches to teaching and learning require teacher educators to create respectful, caring learning environments in which students feel safe be able to reflect, calibrate, and think critically. They also suggest that students who hold more naïve personal epistemologies may need to be carefully supported in processing of information that involves critical analysis of evidence and may need to be helped to make connections between theory and practice. See Figure 1.5.

How do personal epistemologies change?
Each of the chapters in this book provide ideas for how we might intervene in teacher education programs to support the development of more sophisticated personal epistemologies. You will find this information at the end of each of the chapters. You will also notice how most of the authors in this book recognize the role of explicit reflection in promoting changes in personal epistemology.

Figure 1.5   How do personal epistemologies change?

ABOUT THIS BOOK

This book addresses teacher education and personal epistemology for pre-service and inservice teachers in a number of countries, namely The Netherlands, Cyprus, Australia, United States, Canada, Norway, and Taiwan. Within the two main sections of the book which are focused on preservice and inservice teaching, we will discuss theory and practice for early childhood, elementary, secondary, and tertiary teaching.

In the first section of the book, we focus on preservice teachers with implications for teacher education. The first chapter by Yadav provides an overview of epistemic beliefs in the context of teacher education. The next two chapters (Chapter 3, Tillema; Chapter 4, Strømsø) then offer a more in depth look at personal epistemologies of Faculty. The book then provides a cross-sectorial perspective by focusing on preservice teacher education in early childhood (Chapter 5, Brownlee et al. & Chapter 6, Walker et al.); elementary (Chapter 7, Bendixen & Corkhill); and secondary (Chapter 8, Fives; Chapter 9, Marra & Palmer) contexts.

The second section of the book is about inservice teaching. Chapters 10 through to 16 discuss personal epistemology in the context of inservice teaching with implications for teacher education. In Chapter 10 (Schraw et al.), Chapter 11 (Weinstock & Roth), and Chapter 12 (Tabak & Weinstock), the focus is on epistemic beliefs and the links to pedagogy in the classroom. The next three chapters describe research related to problem solving (Chapter 13, Valanides & Angeli), teaching to diversity (Chapter 14, Schwartz & Jordan), teaching reading (Chapter 15, Feucht), and teaching science (Chapter 16, Lee & Tsai).

Collectively, these chapters raise important questions we revisit in the final chapter. One is how to reconcile the three paradigms described by Pintrich (2002) in order to promote the development of a unified model of epistemological beliefs. A second is the extent to which teachers' personal epistemologies are domain-specific versus domain-general. This question is addressed in a number of the chapters in this volume and has important consequences for conceptualizing teaching across a variety of domains and content areas. A third question is about how teachers' personal epistemologies are related to teaching. Again, many of the chapters in this volume address this question, suggesting that constructivist views lead to important differences with respect to curricular and pedagogical decisions. A fourth question relates to how personal epistemologies affect student learning. Several chapters suggest they affect both learning and students' beliefs about the value of learning. The final question addresses how teachers' personal epistemologies change over the short- and long-term. Each of the chapters in this volume comments on this important question, supporting the notion that beliefs change due to greater explicit awareness of the relationship between personal epistemologies and classroom practice. Although the present volume does not answer these questions definitively, it provides valuable insights into how these questions have been addressed in recent research, and provides data that incrementally will help researchers improve and justify theory in future research.

REFERENCES

Bondy, E., Ross, D., Adams, A., Nowak, R., Brownell, M., Hoppey, D., et al. (2007). Personal epistemologies and learning to teach. *Teacher Education and Special Education: The Journal of Teacher Education Division of the Council for Exceptional Children, 30,* 67–82.

Bråten, I., & Strømsø, H. (2006a). Effects of personal epistemology on the understanding of multiple texts. *Reading Psychology, 27,* 457–484.

Bråten, I., & Strømsø, H. (2006b). Epistemological beliefs, interest, and gender as predictors of Internet-based learning activities. *Computers in Human Behaviour, 22,* 1027–1042.

Bråten, I., & Strømsø, H. (2006c). Predicting achievement goals in two different academic contexts: A longitudinal study. *Scandinavian Journal of Educational Research, 50*(2), 127–148.

Bråten, I., Strømsø, H., & Samuelstuen, M. (2008). Are sophisticated students always better? The role of topic-specific personal epistemology in the understanding of multiple expository texts. *Contemporary Educational Psychology, 33,* 814–840.

Brownlee, J. (2000). *An investigation of core beliefs about knowing and peripheral beliefs about learning and teaching in pre-service teacher education students: Implementing a teaching program to develop epistemological beliefs* (Unpublished doctoral dissertation). Brisbane, Qld: Queensland University of Technology.

Brownlee, J. (2001). Knowing and learning in teacher education: A theoretical framework of core and peripheral epistemological beliefs. *Asia Pacific Journal of Teacher Education & Development, 4*(1), 167–190.

Brownlee, J., Berthelsen, D., & Boulton-Lewis, G. (2004). Caregivers' personal epistemologies and practice: Implications for working with toddlers in long day care. *European Early Childhood Education Research Journal, 4*(1), 55–70.

Cady, J., Meier, S., & Lubinski, C. (2006). Developing mathematics teachers: The transition from preservice to experienced teacher. *The Journal of Educational Research, 99*(5), 295–305.

Chai, C. S., Khine, M. S., & Teo, T. (2006). Epistemological beliefs on teaching and learning: A survey among pre-service teachers in Singapore. *Educational Media International, 43*(4), 285–298.

Chan, K. (2004). Preservice teachers' epistemological beliefs and conceptions about teaching and learning: Cultural implications for research in teacher education. *Australian Journal of Teacher Education, 29*(1), 1–13.

Cheng, M., Chan, K., Tang, S., & Cheng, A. (2009). Pre-service teacher education students' epistemological beliefs and their conceptions of teaching. *Teaching and Teacher Education, 25,* 319–327.

Elen, J., & Clarebout, G. (2001). An invasion in the classroom: Influence of an ill-structured innovation on instructional and epistemological beliefs. *Learning Environments Research, 4,* 87–105.

Feucht, F. (2009). The epistemic influence of elementary school teacher beliefs, instruction, and educational materials on reading lessons in elementary classrooms. EARLI Symposium 2009, University of Toledo, Ohio.

Gill, M., Ashton, P., & Algina, J. (2004). Changing preservice teachers' epistemological beliefs about teaching and learning in mathematics: An intervention study. *Contemporary Educational Psychology, 29*(2), 164–185.

Hofer, B. (2002). Personal epistemology as a psychological and educational construct: An introduction. In B. Hofer & P. Pintrich (Eds.), *Personal epistemology: The psychological beliefs about knowledge and knowing* (pp. 3–14). Mahwah, NJ: Lawrence Erlbaum Associates.

Hofer, B. (2004a). Epistemological understanding as a metacognitive process: Thinking aloud during online searching. *Educational Psychologist, 39*(1), 43–55.

Hofer, B. (2004b). Introduction: Paradigmatic approaches to personal epistemology. *Educational Psychologist, 39*(1), 1–3.

Hofer, B. (2010). Personal epistemology in Asia: Burgeoning research and future directions. *The Asia-Pacific Education Researcher, 19*(1), 179–184.

Johnston, P., Woodside-Jiron, H., & Day, J. (2001). Teaching and learning literate epistemologies. *Journal of Educational Psychology, 93*(1), 223–233.

Jordan, A., & Stanovich, P. (2003). Teachers' personal epistemological beliefs about students with disabilities as indicators of effective teaching practices. *Journal of Research in Special Educational Needs, 3*(1), 1–14.

Kang, N. (2008). Learning to teach science: Personal epistemologies, teaching goals, and practices of teaching. *Teaching and Teacher Education, 24,* 478–498.

Kang, N., & Wallace, C. S. (2005). Secondary science teachers' use of laboratory activities: Linking epistemological beliefs, goals, and practices. *Science Education, 89*(1), 140–165.

Kienhues, D., Bromme, R., & Stahl, E. (2008). Changing epistemological beliefs: The unexpected impact of a short-term intervention. *British Journal of Educational Psychology, 78,* 545–565.

King, P. M., & Kitchener, K. S. (1994). *Developing reflective judgment.* San Francisco: Jossey-Bass.

Kitchener, K. S. (1983). Cognition, metacognition, and epistemic cognition. *Human Development, 26,* 222–232.

Kitchener, R. (2002). Folk epistemology: An introduction. *New Ideas in Psychology, 20,* 89–105.

Kuhn, D., & Weinstock, M. (2002). What is epistemological thinking and why does it matter? In B. Hofer & P. Pintrich (Eds.), *Personal epistemology: The psychological beliefs about knowledge and knowing* (pp. 123–146). Mahwah, NJ: Lawrence Erlbaum Associates.

Liu, S., & Tsai, C. (2008). Differences in the scientific epistemological views of undergraduate students. *International Journal of Science Education, 30*(8), 1055–1073.

Louca, L., Elby, A., Hammer, D., & Kagey, T. (2004). Epistemological resources: Applying a new epistemological framework to science instruction. *Educational Psychologist, 39*(1), 57–68.

Maggioni, L., & Parkinson, M. (2008). The role of teacher epistemic cognition, epistemic beliefs, and calibration in instruction. *Educational Psychology Review, 20*(4), 445–461.

Many, J., Howard, F., & Hoge, P. (2002). Epistemology and preservice teacher education: How do beliefs about knowledge affect our students' experiences? *English Education, 34*(4), 302–322.

Muis, K. (2004). Personal epistemology and mathematics: A critical review and synthesis of research. *Review of Educational Research, 74*(3), 317–377.

Peng, H., & Fitzgerald, G. (2006). Relationships between teacher education students' epistemological beliefs and their learning outcomes in a case-based hypermedia learning environment. *Journal of Technology and Teacher Education, 14*(2), 255–285.

Perry, W. G. (1970). *Forms of intellectual and ethical development in the college years.* New York: Holt, Rinehart and Winston.

Pintrich, P. (2002). Future challenges and directions for theory. In B. Hofer & P. Pintrich (Eds.), *Personal epistemology: The psychological beliefs about knowledge and knowing* (pp. 389–414). Mahwah, NJ: Lawrence Erlbaum Associates.

Ravindran, B., Greene, B., & DeBacker, T. (2005). Predicting preservice teachers' cognitive engagement with goals and epistemological beliefs. *Journal of Educational Research, 98*(4), 222–233.

Rosenfield, M., & Rosenfield, S. (2006). Understanding teacher responses to constructivist teaching environments: Challenges and resolutions. *Science Education, 90*, 385–399.

Sandoval, W. (2005). Understanding students' practical epistemologies and their influence on learning through inquiry. *Science Education, 89*(1), 634–656.

Schommer-Aikens, M. (2004). Explaining the epistemological belief system: Introducing the embedded systemic model and coordinated research approach. *Educational Psychologist, 39*(1), 19–29.

Schraw, G., & Sinatra, G. (2004). Epistemological development and its impact on cognition in academic domains. *Contemporary Educational Psychology, 29*(2), 95–102.

Silverman, J. (2007). Epistemological beliefs and attitudes toward inclusion in preservice teachers. *Teacher Education and Special Education: The Journal of the Teacher Education Division of the Council for Exceptional Children, 30*(1), 42–51.

Thomas, G., Pilgrim, A., & Oliver, K. (2005). Self-assessment and reflective learning for first year university geography students: A simple guide or simply misguided? *Journal of Geography in Higher Education, 29*(3), 403–420.

Tsai, C., & Liang, J. (2009). The development of science activities via on-line peer assessment: The role of scientific epistemological views. *Instructional Science, 37*, 293–310.

Valanides, N., & Angeli, C. (2005). Effects of instruction on changes in epistemological beliefs. *Contemporary Educational Psychology, 30*, 314–330.

White, B. (2000). Pre-service teachers' epistemology viewed through the perspectives on problematic classroom situations. *Journal of Education for Teaching, 26*(3), 279–306.

Windschitl, M. (2002). Framing constructivism in practice as the negotiation of dilemmas: An analysis of the conceptual, pedagogical, cultural, and political challenges facing teachers. *Review of Educational Research, 72*, 131–175.

Yadav, A., & Koehler, M. (2007). The role of epistemological beliefs in preservice teachers' interpretation of video cases of early-grade literacy instruction. *Journal of Technology and Teacher Education, 15*(3), 335–361.

Yang, F., Chang, C., & Hsu, Y. (2008). Teacher views about constructivist instruction and personal epistemology: A national study in Taiwan. *Educational Studies, 34*(5), 527–542.

Yilmaz-Tuzun, O., & Topcu, M. (2008). Relationships among preservice science teachers' epistemological beliefs, epistemological world views, and self-efficacy beliefs. *International Journal of Science Education, 30*(1), 65–85.

Part I

Preservice Teachers and Teaching

2 Personal Epistemology in Preservice Teacher Education

Aman Yadav, Mauricio Herron,
and Ala Samarapungavan

ABSTRACT

Teacher educators are confronted with the challenge of creating meaningful learning experiences for would-be teachers that develop them into
knowledgeable, reflective, skillful, and effective practitioners. Of c urse,
this is no easy task, for several reasons. First, teachers need to build up
knowledge systems that are fundamental to teaching, including knowledge
of student thinking and learning, and knowledge of subject matter (Shulman, 1986). Second, teaching is dependent upon highly flexible access to
organized systems of knowledge (Putnam & Borko, 2000). Furthermore,
teachers must use their knowledge and make decisions in a complex, ill-
structured, dynamic environment (Leinhardt & Greeno, 1986). Finally,
research has suggested that preservice teachers bring their own beliefs and
attitudes that influence what they learn from teacher education programs
(Hollingsworth, 1989; Holt-Reynolds, 1992). In addition, beliefs about the
nature of knowledge, that is personal epistemologies, have been found to
be related to learning (Hofer & Pintrich, 1997). In this chapter we discuss
what we know about the role of personal epistemology in teacher education
and the limitations of the current knowledge about personal epistemology
in teacher education.

INTRODUCTION

This chapter presents an overview of the role of personal epistemology in
preparing preservice teachers. It has four main sections—the role of beliefs
in teacher education, personal epistemology, research on personal epistemology and teacher preparation, and future directions in research on teachers' personal epistemologies. The first section introduces how preservice
teachers' prior beliefs influence their experience in a teacher education program. The second section provides a brief synopsis of research on personal
epistemology. The third section discusses the role of personal epistemology
in teacher preparation; specifically, about what we know of the relationship

between preservice teachers' personal epistemology and their learning, metacognition, and teaching strategies. Finally, the fourth section provides directions for future research on personal epistemology.

ROLE OF BELIEFS IN TEACHER EDUCATION

Preservice teachers enter a teacher education program with their own beliefs about teaching and learning which influences what they learn from their teacher education program (Hollingsworth, 1989; Holt-Reynolds, 1992). Even though teaching is a complex enterprise with uncertainties and dilemmas, preservice teachers tend to have more simplistic views of teaching as they fail to see the complexities and ill-structured nature of teaching. These belief structures about teaching and learning have been formed long before they enter teacher education programs and emanate from their own personal experiences of being students, having spent a considerable amount of time over the years as students in classrooms (Ball, 1988; Weinstein, 1990). Lortie (1975) described this as *apprenticeship of observation*, where teacher candidates have formed their own conceptions of what is "good" teaching based on their K–12 experiences as students. Preservice teachers' beliefs about teaching and learning are "robust, idiosyncratic, sensitive to the particular experiences of the holder, incomplete, familiar, and sufficiently pragmatic to have gotten the teacher or student to where they are today" (Clark, 1988, p. 7). Additionally, these beliefs may be erroneous and be discrepant with the beliefs held by teacher educators and therefore interfere with current conceptions in the field. As Holt-Reynolds (1992) put it, "There are, however, times when students' lay concepts are not quite contextualizing, illuminating, and helpful so much as they are powerful, potentially misleading, and unproductive as resources for learning the principles we hope to teach" (p. 327). Furthermore, preservice teachers' beliefs go beyond their teacher education program and have the potential to influence the decisions they make about their own teaching as novice teachers (Hollingsworth, 1989; Weinstein, 1990). Hence, it is vital to take into account the beliefs of preservice teachers to make them better future teachers.

In general, research has suggested that preservice teachers bring their own beliefs to teacher education programs and understanding of those beliefs is fundamental to improving their professional training and teaching practices (Pajares, 1992). In this sense, in order to design teaching preparation programs that can help preservice teachers to develop adequate understandings about teaching and their role in the classroom, teacher educators need to be aware of preservice teachers' prior belief systems, which may jeopardize their learning experiences during the program and, hence, their future teaching practices. Some of the beliefs that preservice teachers bring to teacher preparation programs are related to how they understand the nature of knowledge and knowing (i.e., personal epistemology), and this has became a central issue in educational research. For example in the context of science teaching, the American Association for the Advancement of Science (AAAS, 1998) and the National Research Council (NRC, 1996) want teachers to not only develop content-area and pedagogical content knowledge through their teaching preparation programs, but also an understanding of the nature of knowledge in science.

PERSONAL EPISTEMOLOGY

Hofer and Pintrich (1997) defined personal epistemology as individuals' theories and beliefs about the nature of knowledge and knowing. Over the past 40 years research on personal epistemology has shown that people have varied beliefs about the nature of knowledge and knowing and that these beliefs seem to change with age and with education or expertise (Hofer & Pintrich, 2002). Starting with the results of a longitudinal study published by Perry in 1970, various models have been proposed which map the content, structure, and developmental trajectories of personal epistemology, particularly in adolescents and young adults (Baxter Magolda, 2004; Hammer & Elby, 2002; King & Kitchener, 2002; Kuhn, 1991; Schommer, 1990).

According to Hofer (2001), the study of personal epistemology has been divided into two main lines of research: The first identifying stages of psychological development in personal epistemology, and the second regarding the study of beliefs about the nature of knowledge and knowing as a system of more-or-less independent beliefs. In the first line of research, Perry's characterization of ethical and intellectual development is perhaps the most influential model about personal epistemologies and their development (Moore, 2002). Perry (1970) found that the intellectual development of college students can be explained in terms of 9 sequential "positions" about the nature of knowledge and knowing. These 9 positions have been usually grouped into four larger categories: Dualism, multiplicity, relativism, and commitment within relativism. Briefly, *dualism* is position in which the knowledge is conceived as a matter of right-or-wrong absolutes and relies on authority. *Multiplicity* is a step towards relativism. In this position, the right-or-wrong absolutes start to dissipate and the individual accepts the possibility of multiple, equally right bodies of knowledge. In the third position, *relativism*, knowledge begins to be conceived as contextually-situated and constructed by the individual. Finally, in the later position, *commitment within relativism*, individuals show a commitment with responsibility, engagement, values, careers, relationships, and personal identity (Hofer & Pintrich, 1997). Some have suggested that this transition from dualism to commitment within relativism can be understood in the form of a continuum that goes from absolutism/objectivism to contextualism/relativism

(Cano & Cardelle-Elawar, 2004), and this broader characterization of epistemological development seems to be supported by other models developed in this line of research (Baxter Magolda, 1992; Kuhn, 1991).

Even though this global characterization of development may suggest that there is an agreement among different research programs about the transitional nature of personal epistemologies from absolutist/objectivist positions to relativistic ones, Kuhn and Weinstock (2002) have claimed that the proliferation of various stage-models and conceptualizations about personal epistemology has brought with it many critics regarding a lack of consistency in terms of the epistemological elements that characterize each stage of development. They suggested that this particular issue has constrained the growth of research on personal epistemology and therefore proposed a general conceptualization of development in order to make its study more appropriate for theoretical and empirical analysis. Kuhn and Weinstock argued that the nature of development should be defined by the interaction between the subjective and objective dimensions of knowing. In this sense, the development of personal epistemology is understood as a transition from objectivism to subjectivism and the subsequent coordination of these two positions.

Now turning to the second line of research on personal epistemology, Schommer's (1990, 1994) model suggested that personal epistemology cannot be conceived as a unidimensional construct which develops through fixed stages or positions, but rather it should be seen as a multidimensional construct that needs to be studied according to 5 dimensions. The stability of knowledge (unchanging knowledge versus tentative knowledge), the structure of knowledge (isolated versus integrated), the source of knowledge (omniscient authority versus empirical evidence), the speed of learning (quick versus gradual), and the ability to learn (fixed versus improvable). These dimensions can be thought of as being independent or together, which suggests that individuals' beliefs about knowledge and knowing "do not necessarily develop in synchrony (. . .) [and they] may be pictured as frequency distributions rather than single point of continuum" (Schommer, 1994, p. 302). This model of personal epistemology proposed by Schommer has been challenged in various regards. For example, Hofer and Pintrich (1997) argued that the last two dimensions on Schommer's model, that is the speed of learning and the ability to learn, are problematic because they seem to make reference to beliefs and attitudes towards learning and not to individuals' personal epistemologies.

Although it has been commonly accepted that there are important theoretical and methodological differences between these lines of research, some researchers have attempted to integrate key theoretical elements of both lines of research to develop guiding models for the study of personal epistemology. Recently, Bendixen and Rule (2004) suggested that an integrative model of personal epistemology should take into consideration the following: (a) mechanisms and conditions of change; (b) dimensions that define the nature of personal epistemology; (c) the attainment of advanced personal episte-mology; (d) the role of metacognition on personal epistemology; (e) the role of affective variables in the development of personal epistemology; (f) the influence of peers and individuals' cognitive abilities; (g) the use mechanisms to improve development. Despite this and other efforts to unify research on personal epistemology, there are other important theoretical elements, which suggest some problematic issues for inquiry in this area.

First, there is a large variation concerning how researchers have labeled the concept of beliefs about the nature of knowledge and knowing. Accord-ing to Hofer (2001) researchers have used terms such as personal episte-mology, epistemological beliefs, epistemic assumptions, epistemological resources, ways of knowing, reflective judgments, epistemological reflec-tions, epistemological theories, and the list goes on. Although this issue has made difficult the attainment of a unified model, it seems that recently researchers have begun to agree in using personal epistemology, epistemic cognition, and/or epistemological beliefs to describe beliefs about knowl-edge and knowing.

Second, there is concern among researchers about the extent to which personal epistemologies should be considered as domain-general or domain-specific beliefs. Most of the initial research on personal epistemology con-sidered that people's ideas about the nature of knowledge and knowing are stable, domain-general beliefs (Perry, 1970; Schommer, 1990, 1994). However, recently researchers have suggested that personal epistemol-ogy should be considered as domain-specific (Hofer, 2000; Samarapun-gavan, Westby, & Bodner, 2006) and context-specific (Hammer & Elby, 2002). Furthermore, some have recommended that it is essential to under-stand how general and domain-specific beliefs operate together (Hofer, 2001; Tabak & Weinstock, 2005). Even though there is a growing body of research on domain-specific epistemology in science (Abd-El-Khalick & Akerson, 2009; Schwartz & Lederman, 2008) and mathematics (Gill, Ashton, & Algina, 2004; Hall, 2002; Muis, 2004), there are little or no studies that have attempted to integrate the study of domain-specific with the study of domain-general personal epistemology. Hofer (2001) has sug-gested that research on personal epistemology "can benefit from deeper consideration of how general and discipline-specific beliefs operate together (. . .), enhancing our understanding of beliefs about knowledge and know-ing in educational contexts" (p. 377).

And third, other scholars have criticized the conceptual and episte-mological foundations by which most general models have sketched the dimensions that outline individuals' personal epistemologies. For exam-ple, some researchers have suggested that personal epistemologies should be understood not only in terms of epistemological commitments, but also in terms of ontological ones (Greene, Azevedo, & Torney-Purta, 2008; Schraw & Olafson, 2008). According to Schraw and Olaf-son, epistemic beliefs refer to the origin and acquisition of knowledge, whereas ontological beliefs refer to the nature of reality. Others have also suggested that in order to develop a better conceptualization of what ontological and epistemological dimensions count as part of individuals' personal epistemologies, research needs to establish a closer dialogue with current issues and conceptualizations in philosophy and epistemology (Chinn, Buckland, & Samarapungavan, 2010; Greene et al., 2008). This dialogue could assist researchers in the understanding of which epistemological and ontological dimensions should be considered in the study of personal epistemology.

Despite these and other important issues regarding personal epistemology that are beyond the scope of this chapter, there has been a large body of research that has placed the study of personal epistemology as one of the most promising and influencing areas of research in education. In general, results in the last 25 years have suggested that personal epistemology seems to be related to variables such as gender (Baxter Magolda, 1992), educational background and expertise (Alexander & Dochy, 1995), cultural background (Chan & Elliott, 2000), learning (Brownlee, Purdie, & Boulton-Lewis, 2003), teaching (Hashweh, 1996; Kang, 2008), beliefs about learning and teaching (Chan, 2004), conceptual change (Mason, 2003; Qian & Alvermann, 2000), critical thinking (King & Kitchener, 1994, 2002), and motivation (Hofer, 1994).

Without doubt, this broad investigative landscape in research on personal epistemology in addition to what we know about the role of teachers' beliefs on teacher education, suggests important challenges to our understanding of teachers' and preservice personal epistemologies. These challenges represent new directions not only for research on preservice teachers' personal epistemologies, but also for teaching education. In the next sections we discuss some of these challenges for teaching education and suggest future directions.

PERSONAL EPISTEMOLOGY AND TEACHER PREPARATION

Given that personal epistemologies may influence teaching, it is important to examine its role in preparing future generations of teachers. Previous research has suggested that preservice teachers' personal epistemologies influence teaching conceptions, what they "see" when observing exemplary teaching practices (Yadav & Koehler, 2007), and influence their teaching goals (Kang, 2008). According to Brownlee (2004), preservice teachers with relativist beliefs are more likely to see teaching through a constructivist lens where teachers' goals are to facilitate the learning process rather than transmit knowledge, whereas those holding objectivist/absolutist personal epistemology view teaching as a one-way interaction where learners receive information from the teacher with little focus on making connections with students' prior knowledge. Furthermore, teachers with sophisticated personal epistemology use teaching strategies that detect student misconception and induce conceptual change (Hashweh, 1996) and also use cooperative learning more effectively (Brody & Hill, 1991, as cited in Brownlee, 2001).

Previous research on preservice teachers' personal epistemologies has also suggested that they can hold a more complex set of beliefs that includes sophisticated as well as naïve beliefs (Brownlee, 2001; Kang, 2008). For example, Brownlee interviewed 29 preservice teachers to examine their personal epistemologies. She found that the majority of those preservice teachers held a wide range of beliefs and that there are multiple ways of knowing, with only one participant believing that knowledge was transmitted to students. Kang also found similar results. He concluded that preservice teachers have a complex set of personal epistemologies along the ontological and relational dimensions. The ontological dimension referred to a continuum of beliefs about science as a fixed body of knowledge to science as an evolving body of knowledge, whereas the relational dimension ranged from "learning as receiving school subject knowledge to learning as answering one's own questions" (Kang, 2008, p. 484). By ontological we refer to categories and attributes that define reality. In this sense, Kang's ontological dimension refers to how scientific knowledge is determined by those categories and attributes.

Preservice teachers' personal epistemologies have also been found to be related metacognition (e.g., Brownlee, Purdie, & Boulton-Lewis, 2001). Brownlee and her colleagues developed an intervention program designed to encourage preservice teachers to explicitly reflect on their personal epistemologies. They suggested that if preservice teachers are encouraged to reflect on their epistemologies at a metacognitive level they could attain more sophisticated views about the nature of knowledge (see also Brownlee, 2004). In addition, Abd-El-Khalick and Akerson (2009) designed an intervention program in order to train preservice teachers in the use of metacognitive strategies and found a strong link between preservice teachers' metacognitive awareness and their informed understandings of the nature of science.

Preservice teachers' personal epistemology seem to be also related to their approaches to learning (Brownlee & Berthelsen, 2006; Chan, 2003), teaching goals and strategies (Hashweh, 1996; Kang, 2008), and their teaching practices (Tsai, 2003). For example, Chan found that individuals' beliefs about knowledge transferred by an external authority were positively correlated with surface learning approaches, and negatively correlated with deep learning approaches. Both deep and achieving approaches were positively correlated with the belief that learning requires effort and a process of understanding. In addition, Hashweh found that teachers' personal epistemologies have an impact on their teaching strategies. Specifically, she noticed that teachers with constructivist epistemology tend to use more effective teaching strategies (e.g., teaching for conceptual change).

Similarly, Kang also found that teachers with sophisticated views about science have teaching goals that are congruent with current science education reforms. For example, teachers who believed science as being tentative and evolving utilized teaching goals that encouraged their students to develop critical thinking skills.

However, preservice teachers with sophisticated personal epistemology do not necessarily incorporate more constructivist approaches in their teaching or have constructivist conceptions of teaching (Cheng, Chan, Tang, & Cheng, 2009). Cheng et al. found that even though preservice teachers held sophisticated views about science, they still seemed to conceive learning and teaching from a "traditional" perspective. According to Chai, Khine, and Teo (2006), this disconnect between beliefs about knowing and how they teach might occur for several reasons. First, preservice teachers may be more comfortable in a didactic teaching approach because a constructivist approach would require them to give up their authority and actively engage students' ideas, a task not easy for inexperienced teachers. Second, it is possible that preservice teachers hold two sets of beliefs, one for their personal epistemology and another for teaching. Finally, the school context itself might be prohibitive in implementing more active learning pedagogies.

Kang (2008) also found that school contexts may impede preservice teachers enacting social constructivist teaching to match their personal epistemology. He noted that teaching conditions may lead teachers to regress (i.e., teaching based on less sophisticated epistemology that their initial beliefs) in terms of enacting their personal epistemologies. Kang argued for teacher education programs to develop preservice teachers' skills and provide them with tools to deal with classroom teaching conditions, such as content coverage and large class sizes, which typically encourage traditional teaching practices. Furthermore, teacher education courses should not only provide content knowledge but also afford opportunities for preservice teachers to engage in inquiry oriented pedagogies and discussion of underlying epistemology. Exposing preservice teachers to "inquiry-oriented courses that address subject matter knowledge to be taught in schools will prepare them for reform-oriented teaching" (Kang, 2008, p. 495).

Given the nature of preservice teachers' personal epistemology and their influence on teaching practices, teacher educators need to find ways to influence preservice teachers' view of teaching and learning by emphasizing the relativist nature of education. Specifically, it is important to move preservice teachers from naïve personal epistemology (e.g., dualistic) to more sophisticated beliefs (relativistic) to allow them to incorporate more reformed teaching practices. Brownlee (2001) suggested that teacher education programs "may need to encourage students to reflect in a variety of ways of knowing (increased differentiation of beliefs) and then to find ways to integrate those beliefs" (p. 288). Kang (2008) and Cheng et al. (2009) also argued that reflection on teaching as well as personal epistemology should be promoted within teacher education as a way to refine preservice teachers' personal epistemology. Kang further recommended that this should be a cyclic process that engages preservice teachers in practice, reflection, and deliberation to foster epistemological development. Such an approach would allow preservice teachers to become aware of their own beliefs and understand that some ways of knowledge are more sophisticated than others.

As discussed previously, preservice teachers come to teacher education programs with their own conceptions of teaching and learning; hence, it is important to allow preservice teachers to explore their own beliefs and challenge their ideas. Relational pedagogy, which emphasizes constructivist principles of knowing and learning, such as valuing student as a knower and building upon students' prior experiences, has also been recommended for teacher education programs (Cheng et al., 2009). Within this framework, it is important to create a supportive learning environment within teacher education programs where all opinions/beliefs are explored and allow students to share their ideas without feeling threatened by the instructors or peers. Bondy et al. (2007) suggested that "instructors must carefully consider whether alternate perspectives are represented through readings, and not only supported but protected in class discussions" (p. 79). Preservice teachers' naïve personal epistemology could also be challenged using video case-based systems that showcase alternative teaching practices (Yadav & Koehler, 2007). Specifically, teacher educators could use video cases to activate and challenge preservice teachers' current beliefs and focus their attention on relevant aspects of teaching and learning that conflict with their beliefs.

The research on preservice teachers' personal epistemologies has mainly focused on the nature of their beliefs about the nature of knowledge and knowing and what factors influence those beliefs. Research has suggested that preservice teachers usually hold naïve or inappropriate beliefs about the nature of knowledge and knowing. Preservice teachers' domain-general personal epistemologies seem to change from believing in knowledge as received absolute truths (e.g., individuals passively receive truths from authority that are a direct copy of reality) to knowledge as reasoned constructed truths (e.g., individuals actively create their own truths that are supported by evidence).

In summary, research on preservice teachers' personal epistemology has found that they are related to a broad range of cognitive, behavioral, and contextual variables. Preservice teachers' personal epistemologies may be influenced by their experience in the content area, and the educational context. Furthermore, preservice teachers' personal epistemology seem to be also related to their approaches to learning, teaching goals and strategies, their teaching practices, and what they perceive about teaching and learning from video cases.

FUTURE DIRECTIONS

There are several future challenges that researchers interested in personal epistemology face including the need to develop more robust, nuanced, and diverse measures of personal epistemology and the need to rethink the dimensions/constructs that comprise personal epistemology.

The first and most pressing challenge is to develop robust and nuanced measures of personal epistemology. DeBacker, Crowson, Beesley, Thoma, & Hestevold (2008) analyzed three widely used epistemic questionnaire measures: The Epistemological Questionnaire (Schommer, 1990); the Epistemic Beliefs Inventory (Schraw, Bendixen, & Dunkle, 2002); and the Epistemological Beliefs Survey (Wood & Kardash, 2002), and concluded that they have poor construct validity with inadequately specified and operationalized components, and large error components. Therefore the development of more rigorous measures with items that are operationalized from carefully defined and specific constructs is crucial to the future study of personal epistemology and its impact on teaching and learning.

Apart from a need to develop more robust measures, we also argue that we need to be able to measure personal epistemologies in a more nuanced way at different levels of granularity. Depending on the grain or level of analysis, different facets or dimensions of personal epistemology may become important and new facets may emerge as well. For example, one granularity issue relates to the degree of domain-specificity or domain-generality in the analysis of personal epistemology. Much of the research on personal epistemology in preservice teachers has focused on domain-general personal epistemology, which probably has limited connection to actual classroom practice. One problem with past attempts to examine domain-specificity in personal epistemology such as those of Hofer (2000) may be that researchers use the same items (e.g., those that assess the certainty of knowledge) across domains and hope to find differences in how such dimensions are applied.

To truly measure domain-specific and contextual effects, researchers might need to develop unique sets of items to measure dimensions that may not be shared across domains and contexts. Samarapungavan et al. (2006) noted that enacted domain-specific epistemologies or what principles of knowledge evaluation people apply in practical contexts of judgment may differ from their answers to more general decontextualized questions about the nature of knowledge. Recent work by Guerra-Ramos, Ryder, and Leach (2010) indicates that when questions were grounded in pedagogically relevant contexts, primary teachers showed more sophisticated and nuanced understanding of the nature of science than they typically display in response to questionnaires. More research of this nature will help us distinguish teachers' enacted personal epistemology from more general decontextualized beliefs, both domain-general and domain-specific.

Whereas the need to develop richer and more contextually grounded measures, such as measures of enacted (Samarapungavan et al., 2006) or practical (Sandoval, 2005) epistemology, is important, we argue for the use of more diverse methodological tools. Researchers have also discussed various methodological issues in the study of individuals' personal epistemology (Greene et al., 2008; Hofer & Pintrich, 1997; Wood & Kardash, 2002). One issue is the constructs/dimensions to be measured, what types of measures and data to collect. Hofer and Pintrich noted that, even though the use of free responses (e.g., open-ended interviews) can offer a rich and complex description of individuals' reasoning about the nature of knowledge and knowing, they are extremely time and cost consuming, which makes them difficult to replicate.

Many of the more contextually-grounded approaches require the analyses of participant responses to open-ended questions embedded in practical scenarios. Such contextually-grounded measures preclude the use of large samples (associated with scale studies) because the measures would need to be individually administered and are time consuming. In part, the problems of generalizability could be addressed through replication studies. On the other hand, researchers have also criticized the use of standardized multiple-choice instruments to study personal epistemology because they do not provide an understanding of individuals' construction of meanings nor the complexity of their personal epistemology (Wood, Kitchener, & Jensen, 2002).

As a result of these methodological issues in research on personal epistemology, there is a need for using diverse measures and combining quantitative and qualitative approaches for data collection and analysis (Bendixen & Rule, 2004; Pintrich, 2002). One possible approach is to use open-ended questionnaires to assess individuals' personal epistemology and conduct replication studies to establish stable belief structure. The open-ended responses can then be used to develop scale-based instruments that could be easily administered to a large sample size and establish generalizability. The challenges we describe above are therefore opportunities to move the research on personal epistemology forward towards greater conceptual clarity and ecological validity.

The final important challenge we suggest is the need to rethink the dimensions/constructs that comprise personal epistemology. The social dimension of teachers' epistemological development is one area of contemporary work in personal epistemology that has been under-represented. One example of research into social epistemology is in the work of Goldman (1999, 2006). His work suggests that it is important to examine not just the individual psychological dimensions of epistemology but also the social dimensions of knowledge producing and knowledge regulating communities (e.g., how do knowledge producing communities develop rational systems and reliable processes for generating and evaluating knowledge). There is currently limited research on the influence of teacher preparation programs on preservice teachers' personal epistemology and how they impact their actual classroom instruction but looking at teacher preparation programs as one form of knowledge producing community would allow us to examine the social dimensions of personal epistemology for teachers. We also do not know very much about how these social dimensions of personal epistemology change as teachers progress through their teacher education courses into the first years of teaching. Longitudinal research on the influence of teacher preparation programs on preservice and inservice teachers' personal epistemology is essential. Such research needs to follow preservice teachers into their first years of teaching to examine how their teaching practices and personal epistemologies develop as they negotiate the K–12 classroom landscape.

REFERENCES

Abd-El-Khalick, F., & Akerson, V. (2009). The influence of metacognitive training on preservice elementary teachers' conceptions of nature of science. *International Journal of Science Education, 31*(16), 2161–2184.

Alexander, P. A., & Dochy, F. J. (1995). Conceptions of knowledge and beliefs: A comparison across varying cultural and educational communities. *American Educational Research Journal, 32*(2), 413–442.

American Association for the Advancement of Science (AAAS). (1998). *Blueprints for reform: Science, mathematics, and technology education.* New York: Oxford University Press.

Ball, D. (1988). Unlearning to teach mathematics (Issue Paper # 88–1). East Lansing, MI: National Center for Research on Teacher Education.

Baxter Magolda, M. B. (1992). *Knowing and reasoning in college: Gender-related patterns in students' intellectual development.* San Francisco: Jossey Bass.

Baxter Magolda, M. B. (2004). Evolution of a constructivist conceptualization of epistemological reflection. *Educational Psychologist, 39*(1), 31–42.

Bendixen, L. D., & Rule, D. C. (2004). An integrative approach to personal epistemology: A guiding model. *Educational Psychologist, 39*(1), 69–80.

Bondy, E., Ross, D., Adams, A., Nowak, R., Brownell, M., Hoppey, D., et al. (2007). Personal epistemology and learning to teach. *Teacher Education and Special Education, 30*(2), 67–82.

Brody, C., & Hill, L. (1991). *Cooperative learning and teacher beliefs about pedagogy.* Paper presented at the Annual Meeting of the American Educational Research Association, Chicago, IL.

Brownlee, J., Purdie, N., and Bouthon-Lewis, G. (2001). Changing epistemological beliefs in pre-service teacher education students. *Teaching in Higher Education* 6(2), 247–268.

Brownlee, J. (2001). Epistemological beliefs in pre-service teacher education students. *Higher Education Research and Development, 20*(3), 281–291.

Brownlee, J. (2004). Teacher education students' epistemological beliefs: Developing a relational model of teaching. *Research in Education, 72,* 1–17.

Brownlee, J., & Berthelsen, D. (2006). Personal epistemology and relational pedagogy in early childhood teacher education programs. *Early Years, 26*(1), 17–29.

Brownlee, J., Purdie, N., & Boulton-Lewis, G. M. (2003). An investigation of student teachers' knowledge about their own learning. *Higher Education, 45,* 109–125.

Cano, F., & Cardelle-Elawar, M. (2004). An integrated analysis of secondary school students' conceptions and beliefs about learning. *European Journal of Psychology of Education, 19*(2), 167–187.

Chai, C. S., Khine, M. S., & Teo, T. (2006). Epistemological beliefs on teaching and learning: A survey among pre-service teachers in Singapore. *Educational Media International, 43*(4), 285–298.

Chan, K.-W. (2003). Hong Kong teacher education students' epistemological beliefs and approaches to learning. *Research in Education, 69*, 36–50.

Chan, K.-W. (2004). Preservice teachers' epistemological beliefs and conceptions about teaching and learning: Cultural implications for research in teacher education *Australian Journal of Teacher Education, 29*(1), 1–13.

Chan, K.-W., & Elliott, R. G. (2000). Exploratory study of epistemological beliefs of Hong Kong teacher education students: Resolving conceptual and empirical issues. *Asia-Pacific Journal of Teacher Education, 28*(3), 225–234.

Cheng, M. M. H., Chan, K.-W., Tang, S. Y. F., & Cheng, A. Y. N. (2009). Preservice teacher education students' epistemological beliefs and their conceptions of teaching. *Teaching and Teacher Education, 25*(2), 319–327.

Chinn, C. A., Buckland, L. A., & Samarapungavan, A. (2010). *Expanding the dimensions of research on epistemic cognition: Applying philosophy to psychology and education.* Paper presented at the American Educational Research Association, Denver, CO.

Clark, C. M. (1988). Asking the right questions about teacher preparation: Contributions of research on teacher thinking. *Educational Researcher, 17*(2), 5–12.

DeBacker, T. K., Crowson, H. M., Beesley, A. D., Thoma, S. J., & Hestevold, N. L. (2008). The challenge of measuring epistemic beliefs: An analysis of three self-report instruments. *Journal of Experimental Education, 76*(3), 281–312.

Gill, M. G., Ashton, P., & Algina, J. (2004). Changing preservice teachers epistemological beliefs about teaching and learning in mathematics: An intervention study. *Contemporary Educational Psychology, 29*, 164–185.

Goldman, A. I. (1999). *Knowledge in a social world.* Oxford, UK: Oxford University Press.

Goldman, A. I. (2006). Social epistemology. In E. Zalta (Ed.), *Stanford encyclopedia of philosophy (online)*.

Greene, J. A., Azevedo, R., & Torney-Purta, J. (2008). Modeling epistemic and ontological cognition: Philosophical perspectives and methodological directions. *Educational Psychologist, 43*(3), 142–160.

Guerra-Ramos, T., Ryder, J., & Leach, J. (2010). Ideas about the nature of science in pedagogically relevant contexts: Insights from a situated perspective of primary teachers' knowledge. *Science Education, 94*(2), 282–307.

Hall, R. (2002). An analysis of views of the nature of mathematics by gender. *Philosophy of Mathematics Education Journal, 16*. Retrieved from http://people.exeter.ac.uk/PErnest/pome16/contents.htm

Hammer, D., & Elby, A. (2002). On the form of a personal epistemology. In B. K. Hofer & P. R. Pintrich (Eds.), *Personal epistemolgy: The psychology of beliefs about knowledge and knowing* (pp. 169–190). Mahwah, NJ: Lawrence Erlbaum Associates.

Hashweh, M. (1996). Effects of science teachers' epistemological beliefs in teaching. *Journal of Research in Science Teaching, 33*(1), 47–63.

Hofer, B. K. (1994). *Epistemological beliefs and first-year college students: Motivation and cognition in different instructional contexts.* Paper presented at the Annual Meeting of the American Psychological Association, Los Angeles, CA.

Hofer, B. K. (2000). Dimensionality and disciplinary differences in personal epistemology. *Contemporary Educational Psychology, 25*, 378–405.

Hofer, B. K. (2001). Personal epistemology research: Implications for learning and teaching. *Journal of Educational Psychology Review, 13*(4), 353–383.

Hofer, B. K., & Pintrich, P. R. (1997). The development of epistemological theories: Beliefs about knowledge and knowing and their relation to learning. *Review of Educational Research, 67*(1), 88–140.

Hollingsworth, S. (1989). Prior beliefs and cognitive change in learning to teach. *American Educational Research Journal, 26*(2), 160–189.

Holt-Reynolds, D. (1992). Personal history-based beliefs as relevant prior knowledge in course work. *American Educational Research Journal, 29*(2), 325–349.

Kang, N. (2008). Learning to teaching science: Personal epistemology, teaching goals, and practices of teaching. *Teaching and Teacher Education, 24,* 478–498.

King, P. M., & Kitchener, K. S. (1994). *Developing reflective judgment: Understanding and promoting intellectual growth and critical thinking in adolescents and adults.* San Francisco: Jossey-Bass.

King, P. M., & Kitchener, K. S. (2002). The reflective judgment model: Twenty years of research on epistemic cognition In B. K. Hofer & P. R. Pintrich (Eds.), *Personal epistemology: The psychology of beliefs about knowledge and knowing* (pp. 37–61). Mahwah, NJ: Lawrence Erlbaum Associates.

Kuhn, D. (1991). *The skills of arguments.* Cambridge, England: Cambridge University Press.

Kuhn, D., & Weinstock, M. (2002). What is epistemological thinking and why does it matter? In B. K. Hofer & P. R. Pintrich (Eds.), *Personal epistemology: The psychology of beliefs about knowledge and knowing* (pp. 121–144). Mahwah, NJ: Lawrence Erlbaum Associates.

Leinhardt, G., & Greeno, J. G. (1986). The cognitive skill of teaching. *Journal of Educational Psychology, 78,* 75–95.

Lortie, D. (1975). *Schoolteacher: A sociological study.* Chicago, IL: University of Chicago Press.

Mason, L. (2003). Personal epistemology and intentional conceptual change. In G. Sinatra & P. R. Pintrich (Eds.), *Intentional conceptual change* (pp. 201–238). Mahwah, NJ: Lawrence Erlbaum Associates.

Moore, W. S. (2002). Understanding learning in a postmodern world: Reconsidering the Perry scheme of ethical and intellectual development. In B. K. Hofer & P. R. Pintrich (Eds.), *Personal epistemology: The psychology of beliefs about knowledge and knowing* (pp. 17–36). Mahwah, NJ: Lawrence Erlbaum Associates.

Muis, K. R. (2004). Personal epistemology and mathematics: A critical review and synthesis of research. *Review of Educational Research, 74*(3), 317–377.

National Research Council (NRC). (1996). *National science education standards.* Washington, DC: National Academic Press.

Pajares, M. F. (1992). Teachers' beliefs and educational research: Cleaning up a messy construct. *Review of Educational Research, 62*(3), 307–332.

Perry, W. G. (1970). *Forms of intellectual and ethical development in the college years: A scheme.* New York: Holt, Rinehart & Winston.

Pintrich, P. R. (2002). Future challenges and directions for theory and research on personal epistemology. In B. K. Hofer & P. R. Pintrich (Eds.), *Personal epistemology: The psychology of beliefs about knowledge and knowing* (pp. 389–414). Mahwah, NJ: Lawrence Erlbaum Associates.

Putnam, R. T., & Borko, H. (2000). What do new views of knowledge and thinking have to say about research on teacher learning? *Educational Researcher, 29*(1), 4–15.

Qian, G., & Alvermann, D. (2000). Relationship between epistemological beliefs and conceptual change learning. *Reading and Writing Quarterly, 16,* 59–74.

Samarapungavan, A., Westby, E. L., & Bodner, G. M. (2006). Contextual epistemic development in science: A comparison of chemistry students and research chemists. *Science Education, 90,* 468–495.

Sandoval, W. A. (2005). Understanding students' practical epistemology and their influence on learning through inquiry. *Science Education, 89*(4), 634–656.

Schommer, M. (1990). Effects of beliefs about the nature of knowledge on comprehension. *Journal of Educational Psychology, 82*(3), 498–504.

Schommer, M. (1994). Synthetizing epistemological belief research: Tentative understanding and provocative confusions. *Educational Psychology Review, 6*(4), 293–319.

Schraw, G., Bendixen, L. D., & Dunkle, M. E. (2002). Development and validation of the epistemic belief inventory. In B. K. Hofer & P. R. Pintrich (Eds.), *Personal epistemology: The psychology of beliefs about knowledge and knowing* (pp. 261–275). Mahwah, NJ: Lawrence Erlbaum Associates.

Schraw, G., & Olafson, L. (2008). Assessing teachers' epistemological and ontological worldviews. In M. S. Khine (Ed.), *Knowing, knowledge and beliefs: Epistemological studies across diverse cultures* (pp. 25–44). Dorchert, The Netherlands: Springer Science.

Schwartz, R., & Lederman, N. G. (2008). What scientists say: Scientists' views of nature of science and relation to science context. *International Journal of Science Education, 30*(6), 727–771.

Shulman, L. (1986). Those who understand: Knowledge growth in teaching. *Educational Researcher, 15*(2), 4–14.

Tabak, I., & Weinstock, M. (2005). Knowledge is knowledge is knowledge? The relationship between personal and scientific epistemology. *Canadian Journal of Science, 5*(3), 307–328.

Tsai, C.-C. (2003). Taiwanese science students' and teachers' perceptions of the laboratory learning environments: Exploring epistemological gaps. *International Journal of Science Education, 25*(7), 847–860.

Weinstein, C. S. (1990). Prospective elementary teacher' beliefs about teaching: Implications for teacher education. *Teaching and Teacher Education, 6,* 279–290.

Wood, P., & Kardash, C. (2002). Critical elements in the design and analysis of studies of epistemology. In B. K. Hofer & P. R. Pintrich (Eds.), *Personal epistemology: The psychology of beliefs about knowledge and knowing* (pp. 231–260). Mahwah, NJ: Lawrence Erlbaum Associates.

Wood, P., Kitchener, K. S., & Jensen, L. (2002). Considerations in the design and evaluation of a paper-and-pencil measure. In B. K. Hofer & P. R. Pintrich (Eds.), *Personal epistemology: The psychology of beliefs about knowledge and knowing* (pp. 277–294). Mahwah, NJ: Lawrence Erlbaum Associates.

Yadav, A., & Koehler, M. (2007). The role of epistemological beliefs in preservice teachers' interpretation of video cases of early-grade literacy instruction. *Journal of Technology and Teacher Education, 15*(3), 335–361.

3 Looking into Mirrors
Teacher Educators' Dilemmas in Constructing Pedagogical Understanding about their Teaching

Harm Tillema

ABSTRACT

This chapter explores how teacher educators are committed to understanding their teaching from the perspective of the dilemmas they encounter in practicing their teaching. The focal point of this research is finding ways to assess teacher educators' experienced conflicts between their personal and professional beliefs on teaching and the opportunities they have to prepare their students for teaching. It is argued that teacher educators' personal epistemologies can be interpreted (and assessed) from the dilemmas they encounter. Dilemmas, which represent inconsistencies between personal epistemologies and practices, therefore provide a powerful way in which to measure personal epistemologies and choices the teacher educator makes with regard to teaching actions. In this chapter, we measured teacher educators' personal epistemologies and practices through an instrument that investigated how teacher educators: (a) reconstructed conditions in teaching practice, and (b) re-conceptualized their thinking. The mixed-method approach revealed how the underlying professional dilemmas of teacher educators can be highlighted to reveal their personal epistemologies. It is noted that teacher educators as professionals struggle with practicing what they conceptualize as well as with conceptualizing what they practice.

CAPTURING TEACHER EDUCATORS' PERSONAL VIEWS ON TEACHING

Teacher educators find themselves in increasingly demanding positions, which require them to account for their conceptions of teaching in preparing their students for the teaching profession (Ben-Peretz, 2001). In their daily work as teacher educators, they may experience regulated preconditions of practice and external standards, while also trying to realize their conceptions of teaching (Cochran-Smith & Zeichner, 2006). To understand this sense making process it is important to acknowledge the contextual or embedded nature of personal epistemologies of teacher educators (Baxter Magolda, 2004; Mason, 2003) as they are grounded in the everyday challenges of their teaching practice (Mena Marcos & Tillema, 2006).

Research shows that teacher educators may experience conflict when trying to enact their beliefs in teaching (Borko, 2004; Edwards, Gilroy, & Hartley, 2002; Hasweh, 2005). Several studies (Husu, 2005; Samaras, 2002; Tickle, 2001) have shown that teacher educators may hold positive attitudes and beliefs towards their role in exercising and moderating their teaching practices, however, they may also experience conflicts when trying to enact their beliefs in teaching (Borko, 2004; Edwards et al., 2002; Hasweh, 2005). These studies illustrate that experiencing such conflicts may facilitate changes in thinking which enable them to (re)position their role as teacher educators.

Understanding teacher conflicts may help us to understand the enactment of personal epistemologies. It may be important to unravel these experienced conflicts in the enactment of their professional beliefs in order to reveal personal epistemologies of professionals (Sugrue, 2005). One way to disclose this inner process of reconciling conflicting demands and preferred roles in being a teacher educator is to investigate the dilemmas they experience (Kremer Hayon & Tillema, 1999; Paris & Paris, 2001). Teaching dilemmas represent the explicitly recognized (dis)connections between teacher educators' thinking and their actual teaching practice. They occur when teacher educators have to balance the conditions for teaching with their own thinking on teaching practice (Mayer-Smith & Mitchell, 1997; Woods, Jeffrey, Troman, & Boyle, 1997). Examples of dilemmas are to be found in the many accounts of practitioner research (Darling Hammond & Young, 2002; Lampert, 1997), self studies by individual teacher educators (Samaras, 2002), and teacher biographies (Kelchtermans, 2005).

Whereas a teaching dilemma involves an anomaly, as noted by Billig (1988), between personal epistemology and an actual experience that has to be resolved, it also presents a *reflective argument* involving two or more *alternatives of action* (Merriam Webster dictionary). This leads to *deliberate action* to be taken to resolve the conflict. To describe actual teaching dilemmas, therefore, we propose three elements that need to be evident as part of a teacher educator's dilemma:

(a) Reflection or an understanding of a problem or conflict;
(b) a choice or thoughtful consideration of alternatives; and
(c) deliberate action taken to resolve the matter or a course of steps outlined mindfully.

Hence, teaching dilemmas are not just of interest for the study of dispositions and beliefs of teacher educators, but because of their "embeddedness" in teaching practice, they may provide insight into the actual linkage between professionally held personal epistemologies on the one hand and preferred solutions of daily problems on the other hand (Kane, Sandretto, & Heath, 2002). Studying dilemmas might therefore expose the enactment of a teacher educator's personal epistemology as a pedagogy for teaching (Tsui, 2009; Van Manen, 1995).

Using Dilemmas to Study Personal Epistemologies

Most teacher educators are aware of the inconsistencies they may experience between their beliefs about teaching and their actual classroom practice in teacher education (Borko, 2004; Gallagher & Bailey, 2000). As such, teacher educators may find themselves in ambivalent situations (Paris & Paris, 2001) and having to resolve numerous dilemmas. Developing strategies for dealing with dilemmas calls for high level of professional thinking (i.e., element *a* described above) as it involves weighing several alternatives for action (i.e., element *b*) to be able to decide upon the one which best meets specific needs (i.e., element *c*).

Recognizing dilemmas as such may be a useful trigger for teacher educators' thinking and acting (Bereiter, 2002; Cochran-Smith, 1991; Hasweh, 2005), but also (re)present the experienced difficulties that impede their own teaching activities. In this sense, dilemmas can be regarded as manifestations of personal epistemologies (Mason, 2003), or as epistemologies that are embodied or contextualized in practice. Therefore, we argue that studying the nature of dilemmas and how teacher educators solve dilemmas will help us to consider how their personal views operate in context (Edwards et al., 2002)[1]. In this respect, it is of interest to clarify and measure how teacher educators attribute anomalies, problems, and conflicts that give rise to teaching dilemmas. As far as capturing dilemmas is concerned, it would mean that dilemmas need to disclose *conditions for practice*, while also revealing the professional's *thinking on teaching* practices (Butler, 2005).

In this chapter, we aim to detail how dilemmas can be assessed as representations of personal epistemologies. We are particularly interested in how teacher educators' views on promoting learning in their students (Kane et al., 2002) are evident in the dilemmas they experience. In our studies (Kremer-Hayon & Tillema, 2002; Tillema & Kremer-Hayon, 2005) we found that a major domain in which dilemmas occur is in the context of teacher education when one is learning-to-teach (Tillema, 2005a). On the one hand, teacher educators may be tempted to adopt alternative teaching practices that might better prepare student teachers by offering them greater autonomy and self-regulation over their learning (Zimmerman & Schunk, 2001), whereas on the other hand, teacher educators may feel they have to align with the demands of the practice teaching experience (Grossman, 2005). This may lead to professional dilemmas in learning to teach resulting from apparent conflicts of beliefs and expected action opportunities (Kremer-Hayon & Tillema, 2002; Paris & Paris, 2001).

Assessing Personal Epistemologies on Learning to Teach

Dilemmas about learning to teach are of special interest for the study of the teachers' personal epistemologies because they can disclose some of their inner world on teaching, and provide a glimpse into the linkage between conceptions and preferred solutions to daily teaching problems. Professional dilemmas "mirror the arena of the professional deliberations and choices with respect to the initiation of concrete activities" (Tillema & Kremer-Hayon, 2005, p. 218). As described earlier, dilemmas usually denote a reflective argument that presents a choice between two or more equally justified alternatives for action. It is this tension between alternatives of equally perceived values that calls for a decision to act and can reflect one's personal epistemology (Butler, 2005). This personal and epistemological reasoning involves not only reflective processes of identifying, framing, and finding inherent problems to be solved from multiple conceptual perspectives, but also considering their consequences and possible outcomes for action.

Previous studies (Tillema, 2005b; Windschitl, 2002) reported three different types of dilemmas in learning to teach (see also Brodeur, Deaudelin, & Bru, 2005). One of the most common is the divergence between theory versus practice; that is, the conflict between what is said (or preached) and what is (or needs to be) done (Tillema & Kremer-Hayon, 2005). A second dilemma is related to teachers' teaching orientation or style (Kember, 1997), which typically ranges from traditional, direct-teaching through to a student centered progressive, open-teaching approach. A third dilemma concerns the locus of initiation of learning; that is, whether the teacher or student commences instruction and classroom activity. This pertains to goal selection, assignment distribution, appraisal, and determining sources of information.

Assessing personal epistemologies largely has been done by questionnaires, following Schommer's approach to measuring beliefs about knowledge and knowing (Bendixen, 2002; Schommer, 2004). Her approach has been criticized (Hofer & Pintrich, 2002; Sinatra & Pintrich, 2003) due to the de-contextualized, pre-defined, and highly structured interpretation of personally held beliefs. Others have called for an embedded, context sensitive, and "rich" description of personal beliefs (Kane et al., 2002). Our own approach relies upon a mixed-method design (Burke Johnson & Onwuegbuzie, 2004; Maxwell, 2004), as exemplified in our study on personal epistemologies of teacher educators (Tillema & Orland-Barak, 2006).

Our approach uses a two-step process to assess professional beliefs through a questionnaire and subsequent interviews. The first step in our mixed-method approach is to ask teacher educators to complete a self-report questionnaire called the *Teaching for Professional Learning* (TPL) questionnaire.

THE CURRENT STUDY

Data was collected using this mixed-method approach to capture dilemmas with teacher educators. Twenty nine teacher educators volunteered to participate (from two different teacher education institutions in The Netherlands). All had extensive experience in their profession (over 15 years). Data collection consisted of administering the TPL questionnaire and the *Memorable Events Technique* (MET) interview.

Table 3.1 The Teaching for Professional Learning (TPL) Questionnaire

Please indicate to what degree you would support following statements as applying to your position on professional development as a teacher (educator): 1 = not; 2 = hardly; 3 = moderately; 4 = largely; 5 = highly

Rethinking one's actions (α = . 78)	1	2	3	4	5
Knowing oneself is a prime route towards professionalism in one's teaching	☐	☐	☐	☐	☐
Developing your own style of teaching is at the core of teaching of my student (teacher)s	☐	☐	☐	☐	☐
It is essential to have found a personal way to reflect on one's teaching	☐	☐	☐	☐	☐
It is through collaboration and exchange with colleagues that you learn most	☐	☐	☐	☐	☐
Time to reflect and think over one's teaching is what is needed to manage yourself as a teaching professional	☐	☐	☐	☐	☐
Working towards practical solutions in your teaching needs inquiry and study	☐	☐	☐	☐	☐
You are accountable for your teaching actions	☐	☐	☐	☐	☐
It is in your planning and organizing of your teaching that you show mastery	☐	☐	☐	☐	☐
Being able to select your own goals is what motivates to take hold of one's teaching	☐	☐	☐	☐	☐

Learning from your work is in fact being able to successfully integrate different sources of knowledge

*Restructuring work conditions*α= . 87*	1	2	3	4	5
Organizing your work your way is a continuous problem in a teaching position	☐	☐	☐	☐	☐
There is too little time to do other things than the program requires	☐	☐	☐	☐	☐
One constantly needs to take care that students are actively involved	☐	☐	☐	☐	☐
One has to accept that not all students are interested in what I am teaching	☐	☐	☐	☐	☐
In fact, one cannot teach the way one would	☐	☐	☐	☐	☐
One needs to be pragmatic in one's aspirations as far as goal attainment is concerned	☐	☐	☐	☐	☐
One finds oneself often without support from those in managerial positions	☐	☐	☐	☐	☐
Workshops and discussions with colleagues are 'as good as it gets'	☐	☐	☐	☐	☐

Note. *Item responses for this scale are reversed to arrive at the total score for the questionnaire.

Questionnaire on Beliefs on Professional Learning and Knowledge Construction

An adapted version of Schommer's questionnaire (2004) was applied initially, measuring: Speed, structure, construction of knowledge, next to success of knowledge and professionalism. However, the low scale reliabilities in our study (Tillema & Orland-Barak, 2006), on average having a Cronbach α of .56, brought us to construct a content or topic sensitive questionnaire related to teacher educators' views on teaching. Items are based on earlier construct validation studies we conducted in the field of teacher education representing professionally recognized views on teaching (Tillema, 2000; Tillema & Kremer-Hayon, 2005). The questionnaire instrument is a 2-factor inventory on the epistemology of teaching pedagogy measuring teaching professionals' conceptions about taking ownership and responsibility (i.e., "steering") in becoming a professional teacher. The instrument gauges orientations (factors) on: *Rethinking one's actions* and *Restructuring work conditions* as signifying two sides of the teaching professionals' epistemological position. The two scales of the questionnaire were piloted on homogeneity within two different teaching settings: 103 teachers in higher education and 72 teacher educators. The overall scale reliabilities that were obtained for the two factors are presented in Table 3.1, together with the items of the questionnaire.

Open Interview on Dilemma Formation

In addition to the questionnaire instrument, which looks in particular at the teacher educators' professional beliefs regarding teaching, a semi-structured interview technique was deployed to map the formation of dilemmas during their teaching (i.e., to cover the process of evolving and dealing with dilemmas 'in situ' (Clandinin & Connelly, 2000; Sturges & Klinger, 2005). Whereas most open-interview methods restrict pre-structuring and sequencing of questions, this interview technique, called Memorable Events Technique (MET; Tillema & Orland-Barak, 2006) scaffolds the interviewer to focus on settings or situations that stand out, and are to some degree significant to teacher educators as they signify a conflict or typical problem that was dealt with—successfully or not—in their past.

In the MET approach to interviewing, it is acknowledged that teacher educators build their personal beliefs on the experiences they encounter (both explicitly as well as implicitly) which shape their subsequent actions and that—with aid of the interview method—these experiences can be formulated in a coherent way. The notion that (past) experiences shape (future) action is also employed in other techniques like teacher biographies or self studies; however, the MET instrument specifically addresses the significance and impact of experiences (Maxwell, 2004; Sturges & Klinger, 2005). The MET-instrument gauges the "specialness" of incidents that have affected teaching practices of teacher educators, and in this way are linking action and reflection (Mena Marcos & Tillema, 2006).

The memorable event interview consists of two parts; the first part is meant to describe the event; the second is intended for reflection upon the event. The written part of the MET interview invites participants to write down memorable events based on their recollection.

Written Part of the Memorable Events Instrument

The following questions are used in the Memorable Events Instrument:

> What incidents/events/ instances do you recall as memorable during your past teaching (i.e., year) that affected your thinking about teaching? When writing each incident, please try to consider the following questions:
> A—What was the incident about?
> B—Why is it particularly memorable?
> C—Who participated in it/contributed?
> D—What was your contribution or role during the incident?
> E—How did others relate to your position?
> F—Did you feel challenged/rejected/encouraged etc. by the incident?
> G—What has been the value of the occurrence for professional development?
> Would you encounter a similar incident in the future? (If yes or no, Why?)
> (Do you look back upon it as positive or negative?)

This set of questions produces a text to be analyzed before entering the second, conversation part. The interview or conversation part of the MET includes the following questions about incidents provided by the interviewer.

Conversation Part of the Memorable Events Instrument

After the opening statement in the interview, several focused queries are initiated, utilizing three different lenses:

> *0. Opening question*
> You have described a memorable event. We would like to talk more in depth about it. In what way does the incident give you a new sense of understanding of your teaching practice?

Subsequent probing questions are:

> *1. Lens: Understanding gained*
> 1.1   What about the convictions that you expressed in your account (Pick from A till G), how would you evaluate them?

1.2   Can you think of examples of the things you said that express what you have learned and gained from it?

1.3   Can you identify some ideas expressed that you think contributed to your understanding of the problem at hand?

2. Lens: Perspective (belief) change

2.1   Can you think of examples of things you said in which the beliefs that you expressed were challenged?

2.2   What experiences have changed your way of approaching matters and how have they influenced you?

3. Lens: Impact on future action

3.1   Have the incidents you described in any way affected your thinking? How?

3.2   What kind of consequences would you say you draw as a result of the incident?

3.3   Describe what you regard as outstanding in the memorable incident/event/moment. Why was it memorable for you?

3.4   If you were to think of a metaphor to describe the event, what would you choose and why?

Analysis of the data consists of scoring the conversation part of the interview for each of the three lenses. Text propositions gathered under each lens are rated on the three aspects of dilemma identification as mentioned above, including the presence or mentioning of (a) reflection, as a reference to professional knowledge; (b) deliberate choice, as decisions and weighing of alternatives; (c) action potential as concrete behavioral steps or consequences. For each lens, the degree to which the three aspects of the dilemma are present (by marking and summating the counts) are determined.

FINDINGS

Findings for the TPL questionnaire on both scales indicated a moderate to high level of orientation towards autonomy (self steering) in professional learning present among teacher educators, however there was considerable variance among respondents (i.e., differences). See Table 3.2.

Table 3.2   Orientation Towards Autonomy

Scales	Mean	SD
Rethinking one's actions	4. 01	1. 38
Restructuring one's work conditions*	2. 87	2. 24

Note. *Scale value reversed to indicate high conception on professional learning.

The interviews were used to further clarify these differences among teacher educators. Scoring their MET data with regard to the three defining elements of dilemmas (i.e., reflection, choice, and action) revealed that teacher educators mentioned few (8%) instances of dilemmas having all elements present; that is, illustrated their reasoning by reflection AND choice AND action. In fact, we could better position the accounts given into two alternative ways of reasoning: (1) expressing tension (i.e., accounts with reflection only; 56%); and (2) declaring concern (i.e., specifying reflection AND action; 36%). In our view, the surprisingly low amount of "full-fledged" dilemmas caused us to look in more detail at the given accounts to gauge their content and the phrasings of expressed problems as "pedagogies of practice" to differentiate between high and low orientations on professional learning. At this detailed level, we found only one of the memorable events pertained to life experiences; it referred to a "critical" person in the past that influenced the respondent's professional life up until this day. "My first encounter with practice teaching, my first lesson in a school was with a very fine person who stood in front of the class and I thought in a flash 'that is how I want to become'." A considerable amount of memorable events (8 or 27%) was related to professional experiences (i.e., a particular training course or an exciting dialogue with colleagues). "I have learned a lot from a course I attended on practicing mentoring; I immediately changed my way of talking to students and got very positive response from them."

Most memorable events (69%) referred to identified problems in the actual teaching practice of teacher educators; categorized as: (1) theory versus practice; (2) reflection linked to action; (3) delivery or initiation in instruction; and (4) supervision versus coaching students:

(1) "each time I work with a group of students I keep saying to myself that my main role and purpose lies in keeping my students interested in practicing theory while theorizing practice."
(2) "When I select a format or make assignments for my course I find it of great difficulty to bridge engaging, motivating tasks with relevance to the content I teach; it seems as if the two are in constant contradiction."
(3) "How do you motivate students? How! They are so resigned; how do you involve them; when I prepare my lessons this is constant on my mind."
(4) "The great moments are when you step into a real dialogue with your students and discuss in a mature way what they encountered in their practice teaching, so they will learn from."

The reflective stage (2nd, conversational part) of the MET instrument, intended to explore and unfold these incidents, was used to give further detail to the dilemmas mentioned (in Part A). As noted before most incidents were not fully developed as dilemmas; at best, they could be labeled:

Table 3.3 Dilemmas Encountered in Teaching Student Teachers

Dilemmas specified as:	Low TPL score	High TPL score
Theory versus practice 3.84*	Problems with linkage to content taught	How to give a practical realistic preparation
Reflection versus action 3.01	Not enough time because of demands	How to deal with student differences
Supervision versus mentoring 2.72	How to have more students under control	Improve my skills to promote student learning
Delivery versus initiation 2.32	How to give more focus on independent learning How to prepare for practice demands	More integrated and student based learning Stimulating students

Note. *Scale mean range is 1 to 5.

Reflections on or (be)for(e) action (Mena Marcos, Sanchez, & Tillema, 2009). This is not to say the teacher educators' accounts were not elaborate. On the contrary, teacher educators gave extensive statement of the incidents they experienced (were able "to talk the talk"; Mena Marcos & Tillema, 2006). But as epistemologies of practice they lacked specificity with regard to three lenses specified earlier: (a) gaining professional understanding, or 'knowledge building"; that is reflection; (b) deliberate change in beliefs and perspectives on teaching, that is, choice; and (c) careful consideration of action possibilities to guide future teaching, that is, action.

It was further analyzed whether professional learning orientation (questionnaire ratings) had any influence on experienced dilemmas, that is, considering (work) conditions and rethinking one's teaching practice. Differentiating between the high and low group showed typical dissimilarities between them, as shown in Table 3.3.

CONCLUSION

Overall, our measurement approach indicated that the combined use of the TPL questionnaire and subsequent interview of Memorable Events is able to detect clear and different orientations about a pedagogy of teaching practice by teacher educators. The combined use of both instruments as an approach to exploring dilemmas was found to be a useful way to portray personal epistemologies on pedagogies of teaching. Especially looking into greater depth at the memorable events of teacher educators enabled disclosure of the dilemmas they experienced.

Typical for the combined approach is collecting accounts on professional epistemologies as intended and deliberate actions undertaken, choices that were made between alternatives for action, and the reflective reference made to professional knowledge that could ground or validate teacher educator's actions. The MET interview, in particular, contributed a great deal to the understanding of dilemmas governing the practical reasoning of teacher educators. It needs to be acknowledged that the TPL questionnaire proved to be useful to ascertain certain positions taken in a pedagogy of practice when it comes to orientations of professional learning.

It is worth noting that the accounts of dilemmas given by teacher educators were extensive in nature and 'talked', but they also were not particularly 'knowledge based' or detailed in the 'walked'. In fact, they could be best labeled as 'reflections' in a manner similar to what was noted before by Mena Marcos and Tillema (2006) and Kane et al. (2002). These authors indicate the difficulties teacher educators have in explicating their knowledge base from which they operate in practice and specify their teaching actions in a grounded way. According to our view an account of a professional dilemma would contain three integrated elements: 'Grounded' reflection, considerate choice, and deliberate action; but we did collect mainly reflective accounts from teacher educators (that is, showing not well integrated narrative connecting grounded knowledge with deliberate, i.e., carefully selected action). In representing epistemologies of practice this finding could imply the need for an increased search regarding the "knowledge-ability" of teacher educators' accounts of practice. By this we mean the analysis of deliberate practices in greater depth, and their link with the explication of personal epistemologies at a grounded level (Cobb, 1994). We believe that the context-specific approach in which we studied epistemologies (i.e., as embedded within a particular domain of practice and by means of different instruments) is able to accomplish this detailed search. Determining epistemologies at a grounded level in practice, we contend, is best accomplished by collecting authentic, real life accounts that represent the concerns, knowledge, and beliefs of teacher educators. The memorable events approach assured that the accounts given were personally lived and authentic, and are related to felt problems in the daily work of teacher educators (i.e., are not contrived or "talk"). To be noted is the story-like nature (Clandinin & Connelly, 2000; Nyveldt, 2008) of the detected epistemologies of practice, that is, embedded in a personal context and in a narrative structure (i.e., having a setting, an agent, and a resolution).

IMPLICATIONS

The mixed-method approach in determining personal epistemologies proved to be a valuable instrument to generate reflection about the conditions and thinking of teacher educators at their workplace (Hodkinson & Hodkinson, 2005). As a professional development tool, it has been used on a number of occasions in several teacher education institutes. Teacher educators, working in small group sessions or individually with a "critical friend" (Eraut, 2007), regard the approach as helpful in explicating their implicit views and use it as a tool to reflect upon their work, looking for conditions in their work that could be ameliorated, or otherwise can challenge implicit, routinized thinking. Of special importance, according to interviewed teacher educators, is the 'search for explanations' in their concerns or problems encountered in practice. In this sense, the mixed-method approach can be supportive to workplace learning of (teaching) professionals which, then, could scaffold a "grounded" epistemology of their practice.

NOTES

1. Although this position on epistemologies as being context dependent is under debate in the literature (Schommer, 2004; Hofer & Pintrich 2002; Bendixen, 2004; and Baxter Magolda, 2004); our claim is that personal epistemologies can best be studied in a contextualized way, i.e. , within a certain domain of pedagogy, in order to reveal its specifics.

REFERENCES

Baxter Magolda, M. B. (2004). Evolution of a constructivist conceptualization of epistemological reflection. *Educational Psychologist, 39*(1), 31–43.

Bendixen, L. D. (2002). A process model of epistemic belief change, In B. K. Hofer & P. Pintrich (Eds.), *Personal epistemology: The psychology of beliefs about knowledge and knowing* (pp. 191–201). Mahwah, NJ: Lawrence Erlbaum Associates.

Ben-Peretz, M. (2001). The impossible role of teacher educators in a changing world. *Teacher Education, 52*(1), 48–56.

Bereiter, C. (2002). *Education and mind in the knowledge age.* Mahwah, NJ: Lawrence Erlbaum Associates.

Billig, M. (1988*). Ideological dilemmas.* London: Sage.

Borko, H. (2004). Professional development and teacher learning: Mapping the terrain. *Educational Researcher, 33*(8), 3–15.

Brodeur, M., Deaudelin, C., & Bru, M. (2005). Le developpement professionnel des enseignants, apprendre a enseigner pour soutenir lápprentissasage des eleves. *Revue des sciences de léducation, 31*(1), 5–16.

Burke Johnson, R., & Onwuegbuzie, A. (2004). Mixed method research, a research paradigm whose time has come. *Educational Researcher, 33*(7), 14–27.

Butler, D. L. (2005). Láutoregulation dede lápprentissage et la collaboration dans le developpment professional. *Revue de sciences de léducation, 30*(1), 55–79.

Clandinin, D. J., & Connelly, F. M. (2000). *Narrative inquiry: Experience and story in qualitative research.* San Francisco: Jossey Bass.

Cobb, P. (1994). Where is the Mind? Constructivist and socio-cultural perspectives on mathematical development. *Educational Researcher, 23*(7), 13–20.

Cochran-Smith, M. (1991). Learning to teach against the grain. *Harvard Educational Review, 61*(3), 279–310.

Cochran-Smith, M., & Zeichner, K. (2006). *Studying teacher education.* American Educational Research Association, Washington, DC: Lawrence Erlbaum Associates.

Darling Hammond, L., & Young, P. (2002). Defining high quality teachers: What does scientifically based research actually tell us. *Educational Researcher, 31*(9), 13–25.

Edwards, A., Gilroy, P., & Hartley, D. (2002). *Rethinking teacher education: Collaborative responses to uncertainty.* London: Routledge Falmer Press.

Eraut, M. (2007). Learning from other people in the workplace. *Oxford Review of Education, 33*(4), 403–422.

Gallagher, K., & Bailey, J. (2000). The politics of teacher education reform: Strategic philanthropy and public policy making. *Educational Policy, 14*(1), 11–24.

Grossman, P. M. (2005). Research on pedagogical practices in teacher education. In. M. Cochran-Smith. & K. M. Zeichner (Eds.), *Studying teacher education: Report of the AERA panel on research and teacher education.* Mahwah, NJ: Lawrence Erlbaum Associates.

Hasweh, M. Z. (2005). Teacher pedagogical constructions: A reconfiguration of pedagogical content knowledge. *Teachers and Teaching: Theory and Practice, 11*(3), 273–292.

Hodkinson, H., & Hodkinson, P. (2005). Improving schoolteachers' workplace learning. *Research Papers in Education, 20*(2), 109–131.

Hofer, B., & Pintrich, P. R. (2002). *Personal epistemology, the psychology of beliefs about knowledge and knowing.* Mahwah, NJ: Lawrence Erlbaum Associates.

Husu, J. (2005). Analyzing teacher knowledge in its interactional position. In D. Beyaard, P. Meyer, & H. Tillema (Eds.), *Teacher professional development in changing conditions* (pp. 117–131). Dordrecht: Springer.

Kane, R., Sandretto, S., & Heath, C. (2002). Telling half the story: A critical review of research on the teaching beliefs and practices of University Academics. *Review of Educational Research, 72*(2), 177–228.

Kelchtermans, G. (2005). Professional commitment beyond contract: Teachers' self-understanding, vulnerability and reflection. Bi-annual meeting of the International Study Association on Teachers and Teaching (ISATT). Sydney, Australia.

Kember, D. (1997). A reconceptualisation of the research into university academics, conceptions of teaching. *Learning & Instruction, 7,* 255–276.

Kremer-Hayon, L., & Tillema, H. H. (1999). Self-regulated learning in the context of teacher education. *Teaching & Teacher Education, 15*(5), 507–522.

Kremer-Hayon, L., & Tillema, H. H. (2002). "Practising what we preach"—Teacher educators' dilemmas in promoting self-regulated learning: A cross case comparison. *Teaching & Teacher Education, 18*(5), 593–607.

Lampert, M. (1997). Teaching about thinking and thinking about teaching. In V. Richardson (Ed.), *Constructivist teacher education* (pp. 84–107). London: Falmer Press.

Mason, L. (2003). Personal epistemologies and intentional conceptual change. In G. M. Sinatra & P. R. Pintrich (Eds.), *Intentional conceptual change* (pp. 199–237). Mahwah, NJ: Lawrence Erlbaum Associates.

Maxwell, J. (2004). Causal explanation, qualitative research, and scientific inquiry in education. *Educational Researcher, 33,* 3–11.

Mayer-Smith, J. A., & Mitchell, I. J. (1997). Teaching about constructivism, using approaches informed by constructivism. In V. Richardson (Ed.), *Constructivist teacher education: Building a world of new understandings* (pp. 129–153). London: Falmer Press.

Mena Marcos, J., Sanchez, E., & Tillema, H. (2009). Teachers' reflection on action: What is said (in research) and what is done (in teaching). *Reflective Practice, 10*(2), 191–204.

Mena Marcos, J., & Tillema, H. (2006). Studying studies on teacher reflection and action: An appraisal of research contributions. *Educational Research Review, 1,* 112–132.

Nyveldt, M. (2008). *Validity in teacher assessment, an exploration of judgment processes of assessors* (Doctoral dissertation). Leiden University, The Netherlands.

Paris, S. G., & Paris, A. H. (2001). Classroom applications of research on self regulated learning. *Educational Psychologist, 36*(2) 89–101.

Samaras, A. (2002). *Self study for teacher educators.* New York: Peter Lang.

Schommer, M. (2004). Explaining the epistemological belief system. *Educational Psychologist, 39*(1), 19–31.

Sinatra, G. M., & Pintrich, P. R. (2003). *Intentional conceptual change.* Mahwah, NJ: Lawrence Erlbaum Associates.

Sturges, K., & Klinger, J. (2005). Mapping the process: An exemplar of process and challenge in grounded theory analysis. *Educational Researcher, 34,* 3–13.

Sugrue, C. (2005). Revisiting teaching archetypes. In D. Beyaard, P. Meyer, & H. Tillema (Eds.), *Teacher professional development in changing conditions* (pp. 149–164). Dordrecht: Springer.

Tickle, L. (2001). Professional qualities and teacher induction. *Journal of In-Service Education, 27*(1), 51–64.

Tillema, H. H. (2000). Belief change towards self-directed learning in student teachers: Immersion in practice or reflection on action. *Teaching & Teacher Education, 16,* 575–591.

Tillema, H. H. (2005a). Miroirs de l'Autoregulation de l'Apprentissage: les dilemmas des formateurs d'enseignants. *Revue de Sciences de l' Education, 31*(1), 111–133.

Tillema, H. H. (2005b). Teacher educators' dilemmas: Constructing pedagogical understanding in teaching student teachers. In L.V. Barnes, (Ed.). *Contemporary Teaching and Teacher Issues* (pp. 119–140). New York: Nova Science Publishers.

Tillema, H. H., & Kremer-Hayon, L. (2005). Facing dilemmas: Teacher educators' ways to construct a pedagogy of teacher education. *Teaching in Higher Education, 10*(2), 207–221.

Tillema, H. H., & Orland-Barak, L. (2006). Constructing knowledge in professional conversations: The role of beliefs on knowledge and knowing. *Learning & Instruction 16*(6), 592–608.

Tsui, A. B. M. (2009). Distinctive qualities of expert teachers. *Teachers and Teaching: Theory and Practice, 15*(4), 421–439.

Van Manen, M. (1995). On the epistemology of reflective practice. *Teachers and Teaching: Theory and Practice, 1*(1), 33–50.

Windschitl, M. (2002). Framing constructivism in practice as the negotiations of dilemmas. *Review of Educational Research. 72*(2), 131–177.

Woods, P., Jeffrey, B., Troman, G., & Boyle, M. (1997) *Restructuring schools, reconstructing teachers.* London: Falmer press.

Zimmerman, B. J., & Schunk, D. H. (Eds.). (2001). *Self-regulated learning and academic achievement.* (2nd ed.). New York: Springer-Verlag.

4 Personal Epistemology in Higher Education

Teachers' Beliefs and the Role of Faculty Training Programs

Helge I. Strømsø and Ivar Bråten

ABSTRACT

Through the last decades an increasing number of studies have demonstrated that students' personal epistemologies are related to important aspects of learning in higher education. Still, little is known about how faculty can scaffold the development of more adaptive personal epistemology in their students. In the present chapter, we address this issue with a focus on belief systems among university teachers. Specifically, we will discuss the nature of those belief systems, whether teachers' beliefs about teaching necessarily are related to their personal epistemology, and how belief systems about teaching and about knowledge may be related to teaching practice. Finally, we will sum up this discussion with six tentative recommendations for the design of faculty training programs.

INTRODUCTION

The role of people's beliefs and belief systems has been considered important in the educational domain through several decades. Within the field of educational psychology, a number of different beliefs and belief systems have been studied, with some of the most common concepts being teaching beliefs (e.g., Kane, Sandretto, & Heath, 2002), beliefs about learning (e.g., Brownlee, Walker, Lennox, Exley, & Pearce, 2009), self-efficacy beliefs (Bandura, 1997), and epistemological beliefs (Schommer, 1990). This interest in people's beliefs regarding teaching, learning, and knowledge is due to the assumption that beliefs may affect how people teach and learn. Regarding teaching in higher education, research on university teachers' beliefs has mainly concerned what they think about teaching and learning—teaching beliefs—and to a lesser degree teachers' personal epistemology, that is, personal beliefs about the nature and justification of knowledge (Bråten, 2010; Hofer & Pintrich, 1997). In the present chapter we will discuss whether teaching beliefs and personal epistemology may be related among university teachers. Before we enter that discussion, we will justify our focus on personal epistemology in higher education by introducing research results clearly indicating how personal epistemology is related to learning. The chapter will conclude with several recommendations regarding how university teachers may become more aware of beliefs that may affect teaching and learning.

First, we will briefly look at how the term *beliefs* can be understood in the context of educational psychology. Several researchers in the field make a distinction between beliefs and knowledge. For example, Calderhead (1996) describes beliefs as generally referring to "suppositions, commitments, and ideologies," whereas knowledge refers to "factual propositions and understandings" (p. 715). In addition, Eichenbaum and Bodkin (2000) suggest that beliefs are more resistant to change than knowledge. Not all researchers will support a distinct categorisation of beliefs versus knowledge, and emphasize that the two concepts necessarily overlap (Abelson, 1979; Pajares, 1992), but there seems to be a tendency towards describing beliefs as having stronger affective and evaluative components than knowledge, and assuming that beliefs mainly develop from personal experiences and thereby are more strongly rooted in episodic memory than knowledge (Kane et al., 2002; Nespor, 1987; Pajares, 1992). The more or less episodic origin of beliefs also implies that such mental representations might be less organized and more difficult to articulate and discuss than knowledge but might still guide behavior (Conway, 2008). The assumption that beliefs are more affective, evaluative, and based in episodic memory, will also be our point of departure in the present chapter, and our main concern will be the personal epistemology of university teachers and students in higher education.

PERSONAL EPISTEMOLOGY AND LEARNING IN HIGHER EDUCATION

Though our main concern here is with the role of university teachers' personal epistemology, we first need to justify the importance of personal epistemology in the context of students' learning. During the last two decades there have been a number of studies demonstrating relationships between personal epistemology and learning in higher education. However, several researchers have pointed out that the conceptualizations, instruments, and analyses applied in studies on students' personal epistemology in higher education may represent problems regarding reliability and validity, for example low reliability coefficients and lack of stability in the factor structure across studies (DeBacker, Crowson, Beesley, Thoma, & Hestevold, 2008; Greene, Azevedo, & Torney-Purta, 2010). We agree that students' personal epistemologies have been hard to access in unambiguous and reliable ways. Still, we believe that research in the field has produced convincing indications about the importance of personal epistemology in higher education, such as the relationship between personal epistemology on the one hand and self-regulated learning (Muis, 2007), text-based learning, and motivation on the other (Buehl & Alexander, 2005).

Even if one chooses to neglect the empirical research in the field, there are normative reasons for emphasizing the development of students' personal epistemology; as such beliefs include the perceived criteria and validation processes used to determine the value of knowledge within a discipline. That is, in emphasizing students' personal epistemology we also introduce them to the standards embedded in the discipline they study. Some argue that by doing so we contribute to the development of students' rational thought and intellectual capabilities, and thereby their abilities to "engage purposively" in a complex society (Barnett, 2009, p. 439). Whereas the development of students' personal epistemology obviously is of relevance to more normative and philosophical founded aims in higher education, we will focus here on the results from empirical research in arguing that teachers in higher education should pay attention to such beliefs.

The relationships between learning and students' personal epistemology have been reported in a number of studies and it is not the aim of the present chapter to give a thorough review of this research. However, in order to illustrate why personal epistemology may be of importance to learning in higher education, we will present some examples from our own research. In several studies we have attempted to explore how personal epistemology may be related to students' processing and comprehension of multiple texts about a multifaceted topic. With the texts being partly contradicting and the topic—global warming—being quite complex, the task could be characterized as more ill-structured than well-defined. It is assumed that people's beliefs are more involved in their processing of ill-structured problems where standard processing strategies do not work, than in people's processing of well-structured problems (Nespor, 1987). Students' personal epistemologies were assessed according to the multidimensional framework of Hofer and Pintrich (1997) including two belief dimensions concerning knowledge (certainty and simplicity) and two concerning knowing (source and justification), in the context of beliefs related to the topic at hand (climate change).

With respect to beliefs about knowledge, in particular the certainty dimension, we found that students believing knowledge about climate change to be tentative and evolving were more likely to perform well on an *intertextual* (cross-text) comprehension task than students believing knowledge about the topic to be absolute and unchanging (Strømsø, Bråten, & Samuelstuen, 2008). It also turned out that students considering knowledge to be tentative were more able to profit from challenging argument tasks than students emphasizing the certain nature of knowledge (Bråten & Strømsø, 2010; Gil, Bråten, Vidal-Abarca, & Strømsø, 2010). Regarding the simplicity dimension, results from several of our recent studies (Bråten & Strømsø, in press; Strømsø et al., 2008) indicate that students believing knowledge about climate change to be theoretical and complex score better on both *intratextual* and *intertextual* comprehension tests than students believing such knowledge to consist of a loose collection of facts. Also students' strategic processing of the texts, as evidenced by their note-taking, seemed to be more sophisticated regarding within- and cross-text elaborations when students believed knowledge on climate change to be complex rather than a collection of facts (Hagen, Strømsø, & Bråten, 2009).

As for the dimensions concerning knowing, our results also indicated that those beliefs may be related to students' learning. With respect to the source dimension, we found that students viewing knowledge as transmitted from experts, with this traditionally labeled naïve beliefs, comprehended the document set better than students holding what has traditionally been labeled more sophisticated beliefs, viewing knowledge as constructed by the self (Bråten, Strømsø, & Samuelstuen, 2008; Strømsø et al., 2008). Those results indicate that students need to balance their personal opinion and trust in external authority when they encounter new and complex topics. Results concerning the justification dimension showed that students believing that knowledge claims should be based on rules of inquiry and cross-checking of knowledge sources outperformed students tending to believe that knowledge claims on climate change may be justified through own opinion, firsthand experience, or common sense (Bråten & Strømsø, in press).

In sum, we believe the magnitude of research on personal epistemology and learning in higher education published during the last decades has justified the need for teachers in tertiary education to pay attention to students' beliefs about knowledge and knowing. University teachers also need more knowledge on how to promote the development of students' personal epistemology. However, the research base on this issue is so far very limited. Still, results from some studies indicate possible interventions.

PROMOTING THE DEVELOPMENT OF PERSONAL EPISTEMOLOGY AMONG UNIVERSITY STUDENTS

Developing students' personal epistemology in higher education is not only a matter of teacher–student interaction. The context of that interaction will also be of importance. For example, Hofer (2004) and Brownlee and Berthelsen (2008) underline how both assessment and instructional practice may affect students' personal epistemology.

Brownlee and colleagues implemented a teaching program designed to involve students in explicit reflection on personal epistemology, using both journals and interviews, and also reflection on research methods and skills (Brownlee & Berthelsen, 2008). This intervention was integrated in the study program for a full semester. The results indicated that students developed more sophisticated personal epistemology. The need to be aware of and reflect on one's personal epistemology is also emphasized by Muis

(2007). She suggests that the development of personal epistemology rests on students experiencing many encounters with conflicting information. The idea of exposing students to contradictory information has also been employed in a couple of studies on the use of refutational texts. Such texts present a widely held assumption about an issue and refute it with an alternative theory using scientific evidence.

In a study on change in preservice teachers' personal epistemology, Gill, Ashton, and Algina (2004) combined the use of augmented activation with the reading of a refutational text. Augmented activation implies that students are asked to focus on salient information in the text that conflict with their own beliefs. Using this procedure, Gill et al. (2004) asked participants to read a text about mathematical teaching and learning while a control group read a standard expository text on the same topic. The results showed that the instructional intervention of augmented activation and refutational text promoted a greater change in students' personal epistemology than did the reading of a traditional text. Likewise, Kienhues, Bromme, and Stahl (2008) found that the use of a refutational text changed participants' personal epistemology. However, the results indicated that the nature of students' initial beliefs seemed to affect the way beliefs changed during the intervention. Only students having beliefs not conforming to the refutational aspects of the text developed those beliefs in the expected direction.

Although there is no strong research base on change in personal epistemology following interventions, the results indicate that students profit from both the processing of conflicting information and from interventions initiating explicit reflection on personal epistemology. Both kinds of interventions are aimed at raising students' awareness of personal epistemology. We also believe university teachers need to raise their awareness of their own personal epistemology and the possible implications for teaching. Whereas recent research on higher education teachers' beliefs mainly has focused on teaching beliefs (Kane et al., 2002), we will argue that the role of those teachers' personal epistemology should receive more attention.

BELIEFS AMONG FACULTY—TEACHING BELIEFS AND PERSONAL EPISTEMOLOGY

Teaching beliefs have been described in several different ways, with many different beliefs possibly underpinning effective teaching (Calderhead, 1996). Here we consider only those teaching beliefs frequently referred to in research in higher education. In their review of 50 studies in the field, Kane et al. (2002) mainly refer to teaching beliefs as beliefs about teaching and students' learning. A common way to conceptualize the results from studies on teachers' beliefs has been to label one group of beliefs as *teaching as transmission of knowledge* and a second group as *teaching as learning facilitation.* Transmission beliefs seem to imply that information is presented and transmitted to students, that is, teaching is seen as the delivering of content with students as more or less passively receiving and storing it in memory. Such beliefs have also been labeled teacher- or content-centered, with student-centered beliefs being at the other end of a continuum. Student-centered, or facilitation beliefs, focus on stimulating students to think about and engage in the subject. Teaching involves designing learning environments where students are able to develop problem solving and critical thinking skills. Of course, teachers often express beliefs including elements of both transmission and facilitation, but will often emphasize one of the belief orientations more than the other. As teachers in higher education seldom engage in any formal study of teaching, it is assumed that their beliefs about teaching and learning may stem from their own experiences as students from primary school through university (Kane et al., 2002). With teaching beliefs probably rooted in countless personal experiences it seems reasonable to describe them as relatively robust, episodic in nature, and more or less implicit (Nespor, 1987; Pajares, 1992).

The difference between transmission beliefs and facilitation beliefs could be exemplified by two cases included in a study by Muis and Sinatra (2008) on personal epistemology among students in different academic environments. The two groups of students attended undergraduate-level mathematics courses at two different universities. At both universities courses were taught by the means of traditional lectures and demonstration of problem sets. In addition, one of the universities offered tutorial sessions, including collaborative problem solving and discussion of problem solutions with a teaching assistant, with this being labeled a "more constructivist approach to learning" (p. 146) by the researchers. Now, looking back at the different teaching beliefs conceptualizations, it seems reasonable to see the lectures as a consequence of transmission beliefs whereas the tutorials are more in line with facilitation beliefs. Muis and Sinatra (2008) also found significant differences in the two student groups' personal epistemologies, with students attending the tutorials reporting a more constructivist view of knowledge, that is, knowledge as tentative, flexible, and constructed by individuals. Muis and Sinatra (2008) did not ascribe the more constructivist course design to teachers' beliefs. However, such a design could be seen as a result of teachers holding student-centered beliefs, and perhaps related to teachers' constructivist personal epistemologies. Such a relationship between teachers' teaching beliefs and personal epistemology is also proposed in a model by Entwistle, Skinner, Entwistle, and Orr (2000) where more dualistic beliefs correspond to teaching beliefs emphasizing transmission and more constructivist beliefs correspond to student-centred teaching beliefs. In our opinion, such a relationship between teaching beliefs and personal epistemology is plausible, considering that teachers have related to academic knowledge in a context of teaching and learning activities throughout their careers as students and teachers. However, results from a couple of studies indicate that teachers do not necessarily hold personal epistemologies that are congruent with teaching beliefs (Chai, Teo, & Lee, 2010) or teaching practice (Olafson & Schraw, 2006). We believe there are reasons to expect that teachers in higher education may hold even less congruent beliefs, as personal epistemologies are probably more strongly related to research than to teaching at this level.

Whereas beliefs about teaching are assumed to be deeply rooted in university teachers' personal experiences as students and teachers (Kane et al., 2002; Nespor, 1987; Pajares, 1992), personal epistemology possibly stems from people's experiences from activities involving knowledge development and knowledge evaluation. Teachers in higher education institutions, at least at universities, will probably associate the development and evaluation of knowledge with research activities. In an interview study including faculty from two research-intensive universities, Elen, Lindblom-Ylänne, and Clement (2007) found that participants' identity as researchers seemed to be stronger than their identity as teachers, and that research activity at the university was perceived as the core characteristic distinguishing it from other educational institutions. Rather than underlining teaching experience, the participants stressed their competence as researchers in describing the quality of teaching and learning at the university. Still, those teachers will also carry with them more or less implicit beliefs about teaching based on personal experiences acquired during a considerable period of time as students. With university teachers holding personal epistemologies that have developed from another field of activity other than teaching beliefs, one could hypothesize that those two beliefs systems may not always be in accordance with each other. To our knowledge, no studies on the possible relationships between teaching activity and teachers' belief in higher education have included both teaching beliefs and personal epistemology. Such studies have mostly included teaching beliefs (Kane et al., 2002), whereas some studies have looked at university teachers' epistemic beliefs without relating them explicitly to teaching activities (e.g., Samarapungavan, Westby, & Bodner, 2006; Schommer-Aikins, 2008).

Donald (1990) interviewed 36 professors from six different fields of study about validation processes in their disciplines. Natural and social science professors referred significantly more than humanities professors referred to empirical evidence as a validation process. Whereas humanities professors referred to the use of peer review as a validation process significantly more often than the two other groups. Regarding validation criteria, the professors in all disciplines most commonly mentioned "consistency", with this implying that a proposition corresponds to a real-world phenomena and is confirmed by agreement across cases and by reliable measurement. At a general level the professors' beliefs about justification seemed to have several common features across disciplines, although there were differences for example regarding how strongly they stressed empirical evidence and the use of peer review. Those differences became more obvious when the participants were exemplifying their beliefs, indicating that university teachers' personal epistemologies are more or less contextualized in their domain of expertise.

In a study on personal epistemology in chemistry, Samarapungavan et al. (2006) illustrated that professors in the field hold quite discipline specific beliefs as they constantly exemplify personal epistemology by referring to their own research. This was also evident when they responded to general questions on science. They also demonstrated that personal epistemology is closely related to their expertise in the field. Whereas the professors expressed a "variety of epistemic norms and pragmatic heuristics" (p. 487) for justifying and evaluating discipline specific knowledge claims, Samarapungavan et al. (2006) noticed that high-school and undergraduate students were seldom able to articulate personal epistemology regarding knowledge claims in chemistry. Likewise, Schommer-Aikins (2008) reported that undergraduates in psychology differed noticeably from experts regarding epistemic beliefs about mathematical knowledge. In this study, participants were asked explicitly about mathematical knowledge related to dimensions of personal epistemology. It was evident that undergraduates differed from the experts regarding the stability, the simplicity, the source, and the justification dimension. Thus, it seems reasonable to assume that discipline specific personal epistemology is closely related to discipline expertise.

These studies underline the importance of personal epistemology in university teachers' views on research and knowledge development within their field of expertise. When we turn to issues regarding teaching and learning, the question is whether those teachers also link personal epistemology to students' learning in the field. In a recent study on university teachers' expectations regarding students' beliefs about knowledge and knowing, Greene (2009) found that the participants expected students' personal epistemology to be related to their grades. Faculty were instructed to read descriptions of four different students and then rank the students according to how well they were likely to do in the teachers' courses. The results showed that the students described as *rationalists*, holding sophisticated beliefs about both the nature of knowledge (tentative, complex) and justification of knowledge claims (multiple forms), also were the students ranked as most likely to do well in the university teachers' courses. The results from this study indicate that faculty clearly sees students' personal epistemology as related to learning and grades. However, this study included no data on possible relationships between faculty's personal epistemology and how they chose to organize teaching activities.

The results from Greene's (2009) study imply that university teachers expect their students to hold, or develop, certain kinds of personal epistemologies related to the discipline they study. At the same time the studies by Donald (1990) and Samarapungavan et al. (2006) demonstrate that teachers' own personal epistemology seem to be deeply embedded in their experiences as researchers. An important question then is: To what extent are university teachers' personal epistemology also mirrored in their teaching practices? A separate study by Elen et al. (2007) seems to confirm that university teachers emphasize their research identity when talking about teaching. However, results from the Kane et al. (2002) review indicate a relationship between university teachers' teaching beliefs and teaching practice. If the expectations university teachers have regarding students' learning and development are related to personal epistemology (Greene, 2009) and their teaching practice is more strongly related to teaching beliefs (Kane et al., 2002), the alignment between teachers' goals and practice might vary according to the degree of agreement between teachers' personal epistemology and their teaching beliefs.

Given that the sources of the two different belief systems are possibly based on two different kinds of experiences, as a researcher (personal epistemology) and as a student/teacher (teaching), we hypothesize that those belief systems could differ regarding the goals and teaching practice in higher education. For example Hofer (2004) observed that two teachers at the same university organized and lectured in introductory chemistry courses in quite different ways, with the two different approaches also conveying different underlying assumptions about knowledge. One teacher underlined the constructive and tentative nature of knowledge in chemistry, whereas the other teacher seemed to emphasize memory of facts and formula. Although the two teachers may have held quite different personal epistemologies about knowledge in the discipline, we find it even more likely that the different approaches were related to differences in teaching beliefs. That is, for at least one of those teachers there was probably a lack of alignment between personal epistemology and teaching beliefs. In light of this example from Hofer (2004) and the assumption that teachers in higher education may have beliefs about teaching and about knowledge stemming from different forms of experiences (teaching and research), we hypothesize that one important aim for faculty development programs should be to encourage teachers to examine their own beliefs about teaching and about knowledge in order to judge the relationship between such beliefs and teaching practice.

FACULTY TRAINING PROGRAMS

In many countries there are no requirements regarding formal pedagogical competence for university teachers. A number of universities do, however, offer some kind of training, with this sometimes being compulsory in order to gain tenure. Such training also should offer opportunities to develop teachers' awareness of the possible role of personal epistemology in students' learning, as well as awareness of how teachers' own beliefs may affect teaching and students' learning. One may then assume that faculty training programs could make a difference regarding teaching practice and students' learning.

In a review of 36 different studies on the possible outcomes of faculty training programs, Stes, Min-Leliveld, Gijbels, and Van Petegem (2010) were unable to conclude definitively that faculty training makes a difference. Training programs vary greatly with regards to scope and content, and the nature of the outcome measures in the reviewed studies also varied, with some measuring development in teachers' beliefs, knowledge, or behavior, and others emphasizing student outcomes. Despite the incompatible nature of the studies reviewed, Stes et al. (2010) found it reasonable to draw a limited number of conclusions.

Firstly they state that faculty training over time increases the possibility of positive outcomes more than one-time events. This also makes sense if teachers are to make beliefs explicit and consider possible consequences for teaching. Although teachers in higher education, being experts, are probably more accustomed to talking and reflecting about questions on knowledge and knowing in their domain than novices, they possibly link such beliefs more to research than to teaching. With teaching beliefs being potentially more implicit and closely linked to teaching practice, time is needed to make those beliefs more explicit and to discuss whether personal epistemology and teaching beliefs correspond to the intentions of the teaching activity. Teaching beliefs change slowly, and there are results from several studies suggesting that faculty training programs should run for at least 4 months in order to affect teachers beliefs (Gibbs & Coffey, 2004; Postareff, Lindblom-Ylänne, & Nevgi, 2008).

Secondly, Stes et al. (2010) concluded that the nature or format of the program did not seem to affect the outcomes to a significant degree, and that both discipline general and discipline specific programs had a seemingly positive impact on the different outcome measures. The content of the different programs was not included in the analyses, probably because there was a great variation in what content designers chose to include in the programs. Given the seemingly discipline-specific nature of teachers' personal epistemology, however, it seems reasonable to organize discipline-specific programs when personal epistemology is included as a topic.

CONCLUSION

We acknowledge that recommendations regarding change of university students' personal epistemology would be based on a meager research base. Even less research exists on how faculty may be trained to address the task of developing students' personal epistemology. Still we believe some tentative recommendations may be offered, as the development of students' personal epistemology seems to be of importance whether one chooses to emphasize how those beliefs may affect processes of learning or the normative aspect of developing such beliefs—or both. Our point of departure has been research demonstrating that students' personal epistemology do matter. We have also been concerned with how university teachers may relate different belief systems to teaching, hypothesizing that teachers' personal epistemology may be more strongly related to research activity than to teaching, whereas teaching beliefs, constructed through years of educational experiences, are probably more strongly related to teaching practice. Following our discussion of those issues, we conclude with a set of tentative recommendations for university teachers and faculty developers:

A. Students' personal epistemology plays an important role in their learning and teachers need to be aware of this. Teachers should not ignore students' beliefs when deciding how to reach their educational goals. This implies that teachers in higher education must make an effort to map out students' personal epistemology early in courses by for example letting them discuss to what degree knowledge in the course is certain/tentative and how researchers know what they know in the specific subject.

B. University teachers should attempt to facilitate the development of students' personal epistemology. A small number of studies indicate that such development could be supported by inviting students to explicitly reflect on their own beliefs and to expose them to contradicting information about central issues in the subject. Research from science instruction also suggests that the development of students' beliefs could be facilitated by offering students opportunities to examine concepts from different perspectives, engaging students in reflective inquiry activities, making students explore stories of the actual activities of scientists, and, finally, challenge students to reflect on the teacher's epistemological objectives (Qian & Alvermann, 2000).

C. As experts, university teachers most likely have well developed personal epistemologies regarding knowledge and knowing in their domains. These beliefs are probably primarily related to their experiences as researchers, whereas teaching beliefs more likely stem from numerous experiences as students and teachers. In order to calibrate those two belief systems, teachers should be encouraged to explicitly reflect on them. Faculty training programs could be an excellent framework for such activity.

D. In order to calibrate teaching beliefs and personal epistemology, teachers should be exposed to cases—possibly from their own teaching practice—where the two belief systems are contradictive regarding how teaching and learning could be organized.

E. Research on faculty training programs indicate that one-time events have little effect, and that such programs should probably run for the duration of one semester in order to offer opportunities for changes in beliefs. In addition to the findings from the review of Stes et al. (2010) regarding the importance of time of faculty programs, several other researchers suggest that beliefs are resistant to change and that time is critical to achieve enduring changes (Eichenbaum & Bodkin, 2000; Kane et al., 2002).

F. Reflection and discussions about personal epistemology and teaching beliefs should be linked to teachers' teaching activity, and as such discipline specific programs may be advantageous. There is some evidence (Pajares, 1992) indicating that when beliefs are closely linked to activity, or even operationalized as activities and experienced by the teachers, those teachers will be more inclined to reflect on and also modify beliefs.

With research-based teaching often highlighted as a cornerstone of higher education, reflections on how knowledge develops should be an important aspect of such teaching. In order to involve students in such processes of reflection, and thereby engaging them in questions related to personal epistemology, instructional methods should reflect criteria and validation processes used to determine the value of knowledge in the discipline and not only the teachers' beliefs about teaching and learning. Therefore, we believe it is important that teachers in higher education are offered opportunities to reflect on the relationship between their teaching beliefs, their personal epistemology, and their teaching practice.

REFERENCES

Abelson, R. P. (1979). Differences between belief and knowledge systems. *Cognitive Science, 3*, 355–366.

Bandura, A. (1997). *Self-efficacy: The exercise of control*. New York: W. H. Freeman.

Barnett, R. (2009). Knowing and becoming in the higher education curriculum. *Studies in Higher Education, 34*, 429–440.

Bråten, I. (2010). Personal epistemology in education: Concepts, issues, and implications. In E. Baker, B. McGaw, & P. Peterson (Eds.), *International encyclopaedia of education* (Vol. 5; pp. 405–422). Oxford: Elsevier.

Bråten, I., & Strømsø, H. I. (2010). Effects of task instruction and personal epistemology on the understanding of multiple texts about climate change. *Discourse Processes, 47*, 1–31.

Bråten, I., & Strømsø, H. I. (2010). When law students read multiple documents about global warming: Examining the role of topic-specific beliefs about the nature of knowledge and knowing. *Instructional Science* 38, 635–657.

Bråten, I., Strømsø, H. I., & Samuelstuen, M. S. (2008). Are sophisticated students always better? The role of topic-specific personal epistemology in the understanding of multiple expository texts. *Contemporary Educational Psychology, 33*, 814–840.

Brownlee, J., & Berthelsen, D. (2008). Developing relational epistemology through relational pedagogy: New ways of thinking about personal epistemology in teacher education. In M. S. Khine (Ed.), *Knowing, knowledge, and beliefs: Epistemological studies across diverse cultures* (pp. 405–422). New York: Springer.

Brownlee, J., Walker, S., Lennox, S., Exley, B., & Pearce, S. (2009). The first year university experience: Using personal epistemology to understand effective learning and teaching in higher education. *Higher Education, 58*, 599–618.

Buehl, M. M., & Alexander, P. A. (2005). Motivation and performance differences in students' domain-specific epistemological belief profiles. *American Educational Research Journal, 42,* 697–726.

Calderhead, J. (1996). Teachers: Beliefs and knowledge. In D. C. Berliner & R. C. Calfee (Eds*.), Handbook of educational psychology* (pp. 709–725). New York: Prentice Hall International.

Chai, C. S., Teo, T., & Lee, C. B. (2010) Modelling the relationships among beliefs about learning, knowledge, and teaching of pre-service teachers in Singapore. *The Asia-Pacific Education Researcher, 19,* 25–42.

Conway, M. A. (2008). Exploring episodic memory. In E. Dere, A. Easton, L. Nadel, & J. P. Huston (Eds.), *Handbook of episodic memory* (pp. 19–30). Oxford: Elsevier.

DeBacker, T. K., Crowson, H. M., Beesley, A. D., Thoma, S. J., & Hestevold, N. L. (2008). The challenge of measuring epistemic beliefs: An analysis of three self-report instruments. *The Journal of Experimental Education, 76,* 281–312.

Donald, J. G. (1990). University professors' views of knowledge and validation processes. *Journal of Educational Psychology, 82,* 242–249.

Eichenbaum, H., & Bodkin, J. A. (2000). Belief and knowledge as distinct forms of memory. In D. L. Schacter & E. Scarry (Eds.), *Memory, brain, and belief* (pp. 176–207). Cambridge, MA: Harvard University Press.

Elen, J., Lindblom-Ylänne, S., & Clement, M. (2007). Faculty development in research-intensive universities: The role of academics' conceptions on the relationship between research and teaching. *International Journal for Academic Development, 12,* 123–139.

Entwistle, N., Skinner, D., Entwistle, D., & Orr, S. (2000). Conceptions and beliefs about "Good teaching": An integration of contrasting research areas. *Higher Education Research & Development, 19,* 5–26.

Gibbs, G., & Coffey, M. (2004). The impact of training of university teachers on their teaching skills, their approach to teaching and the approach to learning of their students. *Active learning in higher education, 5,* 87–100.

Gil, L., Bråten, I., Vidal-Abarca, E., & Strømsø, H. I. (2010). Summary versus argument tasks when working with multiple documents: Which is better for whom? *Contemporary Educational Psychology, 35,* 157–173.

Gill, M. G., Ashton, P. T., & Algina, J. (2004). Changing preservice teachers' epistemological beliefs about teaching and learning in mathematics: An intervention study. *Contemporary Educational Psychology, 29,* 164–185.

Greene, J. A. (2009). Collegiate faculty expectations regarding students' epistemic and ontological cognition and the likelihood of academic success. *Contemporary Educational Psychology, 34,* 230–239.

Greene, J. A., Azevedo, R., & Torney-Purta, J. (2010). Empirical evidence regarding relations among a model of epistemic and ontological cognition, academic performance, and educational level. *Journal of Educational Psychology, 102,* 234–255.

Hagen, Å., Strømsø, H. I., & Bråten, I. (2009). *Epistemic beliefs and external strategy use when learning from multiple documents.* Paper presented at the biennial meeting of the European Association for Research on Learning and Instruction, Amsterdam, The Netherlands.

Hofer, B. K. (2004). Exploring the dimensions of personal epistemology in differing classroom contexts: Students interpretations during the first year of college. *Contemporary Educational Psychology, 29,* 129–163.

Hofer, B. K., & Pintrich, P. R. (1997). The development of epistemological theories: Beliefs about knowledge and knowing and their relation to learning. *Review of Educational Research, 67,* 88–140.

Kane, R., Sandretto, S., & Heath, C. (2002). Telling half the story: A critical review of research on the teaching beliefs and practices of university academics. *Review of Educational Research, 72,* 177–228.

Kienhues, D., Bromme, R., & Stahl, E. (2008). Changing epistemological beliefs: The unexpected impact of a short-term intervention. *British Journal of Educational Psychology, 78,* 545–565.

Muis, K. R. (2007). The role of epistemic beliefs in self-regulated learning. *Educational Psychologist, 42,* 173–190.

Muis, K. R., & Sinatra, G. M. (2008). University cultures and epistemic beliefs: Examining differences between two academic environments. In M. S. Khine (Ed.), *Knowing, knowledge, and beliefs: Epistemological studies across diverse cultures* (pp. 137–150). New York: Springer.

Nespor, J. (1987). The role of beliefs in the practice of teaching. *Journal of Curriculum Studies, 19,* 317–328.

Olafson, L., & Schraw, G. (2006). Teachers' beliefs and practices within and across domains. *International Journal of Educational Research, 45,* 71–84.

Pajares, M. F. (1992). Teachers' beliefs and educational research: Cleaning up a messy construct. *Review of Educational Research, 62,* 307–332.

Postareff, L., Lindblom-Ylänne, S., & Nevgi, A. (2008). A follow-up study of the effect of pedagogical training on teaching in higher education. *Higher Education, 56,* 29–43.

Qian, G., & Alvermann, D. E. (2000). Relationship between epistemological beliefs and conceptual change learning. *Reading & Writing Quarterly, 16,* 59–74.

Samarapungavan, A., Westby, E. L., & Bodner, G. M. (2006). Contextual epistemic development in science: A comparison of chemistry students and research chemists. *Science Education, 90,* 468–495.

Schommer, M. (1990). Effects of beliefs about the nature of knowledge on comprehension. *Journal of Educational Psychology, 82,* 498–504.

Schommer-Aikins, M. (2008). Applying the theory of an epistemological belief system to the investigation of students' and professors' mathematical beliefs. In M. S. Khine (Ed.), *Knowing, knowledge, and beliefs: Epistemological studies across diverse cultures* (pp. 303–323). New York: Springer.

Stes, A., Min-Leliveld, M., Gijbels, D., & Van Petegem, P. (2010). The impact of instructional development in higher education: The state-of-the-art of the research. *Educational Research Review, 5,* 25–49.

Strømsø, H. I., Bråten, I., & Samuelstuen, M. S. (2008). Dimensions of topic-specific epistemological beliefs as predictors of multiple text understanding. *Learning and Instruction, 18,* 513–527.

5 Self-Authorship in Child Care Student Teachers
Is there a Link Between Beliefs and Practice?

Joanne Brownlee, Angela Edwards, Donna Berthelsen, and Gillian Boulton-Lewis

ABSTRACT

Research related to personal epistemology in teacher education indicates that teachers' beliefs about knowing and learning influence their pedagogical practices. In the current study, we interviewed 31 child care students to investigate the relationship between personal epistemology and beliefs about children's learning as they engaged in teaching practices with young children. We drew on self-authorship theory to analyze this data, which considers the evolving capacity of learners to analyze and make informed judgments about knowledge (personal epistemology) in the light of their professional identity (intrapersonal beliefs) and interdependent social relationships (interpersonal beliefs). The majority of students described practical personal epistemologies which involved either modeling, reflection on, or evaluation of practical strategies. These epistemologies have implications for child care teachers' professional identities and their relationships with families, children, and staff in child-care contexts.

BACKGROUND

In Australia, teachers of young children working in early childhood education and care settings, such as child care, are prepared through vocational education courses. These courses are delivered within competency-based learning frameworks, as designated by national training packages for specific professional areas. The focus in child care training is to have students achieve core competencies that have been identified as important professional skills for those who work with young children. For example, a core competency is to develop an understanding of children's interests and developmental needs. A competency-based approach to training is not designed to promote complex learning or critical thinking necessary to be an effective and reflective teacher of young children in child care settings. In order to promote quality learning experiences for children, professional preparation programs need to support students to be critically reflective of their practice. There is evidence to suggest that a focus on developing sophisticated personal epistemologies may be one way in which to promote critical and reflective thinking (Kuhn & Udell, 2001).

Over the last 30 years, the personal epistemology literature has provided different perspectives on how to improve teaching and learning, particularly in higher education contexts. Although there are a number of traditions within this literature, the developmental paradigm has probably been the most significant over this period of time. For example, Perry (1970), Belenky, Clinchy, Goldberger, and Tarule, (1986), Baxter Magolda (1994), and Kuhn and Weinstock (2002) have described changes in personal epistemologies for adults, as they progress through academic contexts.

These developmental traditions hold that individuals may move from simple views of knowledge through to complex evidenced-based ways of knowing and learning. For example, *Absolutist* beliefs are unchanging and unreflective views about the transmissive nature of knowledge. Within this tradition, some individuals realize that it is not possible to know everything and that some things remain unknowable and accept that, at least for the time being, personal opinions count. These can be described as *multiplist* beliefs where knowledge is viewed as a personal construction. Other individuals may develop, over time, *evaluativist* beliefs. Like multiplists, they acknowledge that knowledge is personally constructed. However evaluativist beliefs are characterized by a capacity to be analytical and that evidence must be examined in order to construct personal meaning. From this perspective knowledge is evolving, tentative, and evidenced-based.

Personal epistemology, specifically an informed, evaluativistic stance, is an important goal of professional training for child care. Child care teachers are increasingly required to function in complex professional environments that require an analytic, evidenced-based approach to knowing and learning. However, cognitive complexity alone may not promote effective participation in these complex environments. We argue that it is important to go beyond the cognitive (personal epistemology) to include respectful and supportive interactions with others (families, children, colleagues) in the context of personal beliefs and values about child care. This is the essence of self-authorship.

Self-authorship proposes three dimensions of personal beliefs systems—an epistemological dimension, an interpersonal dimension concerned with beliefs about social relationships, and an intrapersonal dimension that focuses on beliefs about self and identity (Pizzolato & Ozaki, 2007). These three dimensions are interconnected. According to Meszaros (2007), the construct of self-authorship provides a platform on which to build a cultural change about how we view effective thinking and learning in higher education and, we would add, in vocational education, such as professional courses in child care training.

Self-authorship seems to follow a trajectory much like that described in relation to personal epistemology. Individuals evolve from a focus on formulas, to a transitional phase described as being at the "crossroads", through to "self-authorship" as a position of personal understanding (Creamer & Laughlin, 2005). When individuals rely on *formulas* to organize their experiences there is a focus on accepting others' truths (similar to absolutist beliefs). This also means that individuals' identities are externally derived (intrapersonal dimension). Social interactions are influenced by a strong affinity with one's social group, often remaining quite judgmental about cultural differences (interpersonal dimension; King & Baxter Magolda, 2005).

Individuals who become more aware of their own beliefs and values are described as being at the *crossroads*. There is a realization that knowledge is personally constructed. Therefore there is less reliance on experts, which is similar to the epistemological position of multiplism (Creamer & Laughlin, 2005). They are also more likely to explore their own identity (intrapersonal dimension) and interact with different social groups in less judgmental ways. However, they may still remain dependent on relationships with people who are considered similar to themselves (interpersonal dimension; Creamer & Laughlin, 2005; King & Baxter Magolda, 2005).

Finally, when individuals begin to engage in *self-authorship* they construct knowledge by weighing up multiple perspectives. This is similar to *evaluativism*. They are more likely to have a strong, internally-generated sense of self (intrapersonal dimension) and be able to engage with others and be respectful of their perspectives because they are not so threatened by differences (interpersonal dimension; Creamer & Laughlin, 2005). Child care teachers interact not only with a range of children, but also their families, other staff, and the community. The ability to engage in a respectful way with a range of stakeholders is important in quality child care. The extent to which a child care teacher is able to demonstrate such skills can be informed by the theory of self-authorship.

In this study, we investigated the nature of child care students' beliefs about self-authorship and how these beliefs were related to their practices with children in their child care field placement. Specifically our research questions were:

1. How can we characterize self-authorship beliefs in child care student teachers?
2. How is self-authorship related to child care students' beliefs and practices regarding children's learning as a dimension of personal epistemology?

METHOD

Context and Participants

Thirty-one child care students completing a field placement for their vocational course participated in stimulated recall interviews. Digital photographs of their practices with children were used as the stimuli for discussion.

The child care students participating in this study were completing a Diploma of Children's Services at two metropolitan institutes of Technical and Further Education (TAFE). Competency-based training is a key aspect of the Diploma of Children's Services qualification as required by national regulation of vocational education. Examples of the 11 core competencies for the Diploma are: Ensure children's health and safety; care for children; respond to illness, accidents, and emergencies; work within a legal duty of care and ethical framework; support the development of children in the service; and interact effectively with children. The diploma is a nationally endorsed qualification that enables students to be eligible to be employed as group leaders in long day care programs in Australia. A group leader generally is responsible for a group of children in a child care program. Each semester, students in child care courses complete field placements of 1 day per week and in 2-week blocks in child care settings.

The 31 students were completing either their 1st ($n = 13$) or 2nd ($n = 18$) year of study in the Diploma of Children's Services. There were 2 males and 29 females. Ages ranged from 18–25 ($n = 26$) and 25–35 yrs ($n = 5$). A range of cultural backgrounds was evident with students from India, Korea, Japan, China, and Australia represented in the sample. These international students had been in Australia for between 3 months and 5 years. Most students already held either Certificate III in Children's Services ($n = 16$) or had entered the course directly from secondary school ($n = 9$). The remainder held higher qualifications including Diploma ($n = 1$), Degree ($n = 3$), or Masters ($n = 2$) qualifications in other discipline areas.

Interviews and Observations

Students were contacted through their TAFE colleges and 80% of those contacted agreed to participate. The research assistant then made contact with the institutes to organize observation visits at the various sites of students' field placements (child care centers in the community). The research assistant contacted the centers and organized a convenient date for the observation session within which the research assistant took digital photos of the students in their interactions with children. The photos were used as the basis of the subsequent interviews with students which were held immediately after the observation session. Relevant consents were obtained from the center director, the student, and parents of the children in the classroom in which the photos were taken.

Students were observed for one morning during their field placement (for up to 90 minutes). Up to eight photos were taken during each observation session as the student engaged in activities and interactions with children. The research assistant photographed significant routine and non-routine events and regular and routine activities interactions. The research assistant had substantial experience in child care contexts and had been a child care director for 10 years.

Within each center, field notes were made about the center philosophy from the displayed documentation, and the physical and organizational environment. On the basis of the field notes, the centers were categorized as traditional or child-centered environments. This is in line with the distinction proposed by Katz (2001) on *constructivist* (child-centered) and *instructivist* (traditional) program orientations. In a traditional program, each age group might have a specific program that followed an activity-based routine with teacher-initiated and teacher-directed activities that are relatively formal and product-oriented. In child-centered environments, there is greater flexibility with a focus on play-based activities chosen by children and a stronger process orientation that allows children to construct their own meaning from their engagement with peers and materials. In these latter centers, more extended and elaborative teacher interactions with children were observed.

The stimulated recall interviews, using the photos to prompt recall of specific events and interactions, lasted 50 minutes on average. They took place immediately after the photo session in the center in another location from where the observations sessions were held. Interviews were audio taped and later transcribed verbatim. Students were asked to reflect on:

(a) Their beliefs about how children learn (How do you think children learn? Can you think of an experience you have had with a child where you really noticed that he or she had learnt something? How do you know when a child has learnt something?)
(b) The three dimensions of self-authorship theory:
   • Interpersonal (Are there people who have had a significant influence on how you see your role in child care? How have they influenced you?)
   • Epistemological (Why are these people's opinions important to you?)

- Intrapersonal (If these people had different views to you, about what you do in your role as a child care worker how would you handle these different viewpoints? How does what you learn here in your placement centre, as a childcare worker, influence your identity?)

Finally the digital photos were presented to the student as a basis for reflection on interactions with children.

Data Analysis

Analyses focused on the content of the interviews that reflected the self-authorship dimensions, how the student thought children learn, and the level of reflective capacity on responses to the photographs of their practice. The categories were analyzed inductively which allowed themes to emerge from the interviews. Each of these aspects is discussed in turn.

1. Evidence for the dimensions of self-authorship within the interview, was based on the following criteria:
   - *Personal epistemology* were differentiated on the extent to which students saw knowledge about child care practice as constructed and their capacity to analyze this knowledge from different perspectives.
   - *Intrapersonal beliefs* construed as a professional identity were differentiated by the extent to which students held independent views about their professional role that were less reliant on the personal opinions of others.
   - *Interpersonal beliefs* were differentiated on the extent to which students viewed their profession as requiring effective interactions with colleagues, parents and children.
2. Beliefs about children's learning were differentiated on a continuum of learning as observation and modeling to learning through the active construction of meaning.
3. Students' reflections on their practices were differentiated according to the level of critical understanding about how child care is constructed and evident, or not, in their own actions.

Two of the researchers reviewed the interview scripts in separate reading and coded responses. The research team was in agreement on approximately 75% of the initial judgments. Differences in coding were resolved through discussion. The analyses were reviewed and discussed within the research team to arrive at final consensual judgments about the nature of the students' belief[1] systems. This is a form of dialogic reliability (Akerlind, 2005).

FINDINGS

This research explored how self-authorship is evident in the beliefs of child care student teachers about their professional role and how these beliefs related to beliefs about children's learning and students' observed practice and reflective capacity on their practice.

Table 5.1 provides a summary of the findings. There were four main levels of thinking that emerged in this study. They are not described as personal epistemologies but rather as broader patterns of student thinking which are differentiated according to the epistemological dimension. This dimension is considered as the core of 'knowing' that influences other beliefs and knowledge (Schommer-Aikens, 2004). The patterns of thinking are described as *practical implementation, practical reflection, practical evaluativist,* and *complex evaluativist.* The first two columns in the table summarize the dimensions of epistemology, professional identity, and interpersonal relationships that together represent the construct of self-authorship.

The third column summarizes beliefs about children's learning and was derived by examining both the responses to the questions about beliefs about children's learning and the practices that were evident in the digital photos. The fourth column reflects a summary of the context in which the students completed their field placement. These contexts were broadly described as either traditional or child-centered in nature as described above and were based on field notes taken by the researcher.

Practical Implementation Pattern

Fourteen students viewed knowing and knowledge as Practical Implementation. This view of knowledge was a pragmatic view of practice that there was just 'one way to do things'. These students indicated that they simply implemented what they saw happening in their centers by following what others were doing around them.

> Before I start prac [field placement] in every classroom and every centre I try to talk to the director and assistant. I just watch them, how they act, what they do when they interact with the children and when they talk to the children. (Sandra)

There was no evidence of reflection on the practices observed and no discussion about what would happen if the strategy was not effective. These beliefs represented a very practical epistemology that was firmly embedded in 'doing the right thing'. This is similar to "absolutist" beliefs described by a range of researchers including Kuhn and Weinstock (2002) where knowledge is given and not questioned.

Table 5.1 Students' Patterns of Thinking Involving Self-Authorship and Children's Learning

Pattern of epistemic beliefs	Intrapersonal & interpersonal beliefs	Beliefs about children's learning	Child care contexts
Practical implementation (*n* = 14)	Formula followers	Children learn through modeling Children learn through modeling and activities.	Traditional environment (n = 11) Child-centered environment (n = 3)
Practical reflection (*n* = 12)	Mixed beliefs (follows other ideas but some evidence for development of professional child care beliefs)	Children are active learners (by doing, trial and error, problem-solving, exploration) Children are active learners who can learn from constructing meaning in supportive environments	Traditional environment (n = 8) Child-centered environment (n = 4)
Practical evaluativist (*n* = 4)	Sense of professional identity for child care work; engages in decision-making with others	Children are competent and active learners who can construct their own meaning	Traditional (n = 2) Child-centered (n = 2)
Complex evaluativist (*n* = 1)	Strong professional identity and believes in interdependent relationships	Children are competent, active learners who construct their own meaning; need to be respected as learners	Traditional (n = 1)

The students who demonstrated this pattern of thinking tended to follow others' ideas and did not discuss the role played by their own beliefs in this process. For example:

> Group leaders are very important people . . . because they have much more information than me because they had so many stories and experience to play and take care of the children. (Sandra)

This quote suggests a dependence on the knowledge of others (the interpersonal dimensions). The student is aware that the Group Leader has more knowledge. Baxter Magolda (2004c, cited in Creamer & Laughlin, 2005) described *formula following* in the self-authorship construct as a reliance on others.

The modeling described by these students in terms of epistemological, interpersonal, and intrapersonal dimensions was also evident in how they talked about children's learning and how they interacted with children:

> Children learn by watching others. A lot of them just observe and see what other people are doing and then they try that themselves. They like to imitate people. (Stacey)

Whereas these students typically described children's learning as modeling, there were a few variations which included a view that children learn by being active. These students (*n* = 3) still described children's learning as modeling but their ideas were extended to include children learning through activity.

> I went to the centre and they had play dough for the children, so the children could make their shapes, whatever they liked. In China, the staff always model for the children, for example they make something and show the children—see this is what I do. In Australia the staff always let the children do it by themselves because they have their own creativity. That's the difference with Chinese culture. I prefer the Australian way, because I agree that children have their own feelings. (Josie)

This form of planning is the basis of what the students referred to as the emergent curriculum style of planning. These students are starting to develop an understanding of this style of planning and were using it in its most basic form. All of the students with practical implementation thinking patterns who described children's learning as active were completing their field experience in a child-centered early childhood setting (See Table 5.1). It is of interest that students in child-centered environments (n = 3), rather than the more traditional ones (n = 11), were able to describe children's learning as active.

Practical Reflection Pattern

The focus on practical epistemology, which was evident in the previous pattern, was also evident in the pattern called Practical Reflection. The difference between these two patterns related to how students processed practical information. In the previous pattern of practical implementation, students did not reflect on their knowledge. Students who described practical reflection (n = 12) discussed how they implemented observed teaching strategies but they were more likely to reflect on the success of the strategy and make adjustments to their practices as a result of this reflection. Whereas this was a limited level of reflection, students did make decisions about their further actions based on their reflection. For example:

> I would listen to any advice that she gave me (Group leader). If it made sense to me then I would probably take the advice. If it didn't I would probably just stick with my thing and see if it did work and change around bits, learn by trial and error. (Lisa)

This quote suggests a view of knowing that is *multiplist* in nature because knowledge is a personal construction but relatively unexamined (Kuhn & Weinstock, 2002). There is no analysis of other perspectives, just a need to have it make sense.

In terms of the intrapersonal dimension, it is clear in this quote that personal beliefs are important in the process of constructing practical knowledge. This suggests a development of professional beliefs about child care practice. However, whereas they are developing professional beliefs about child care, they are reliant on others to "give" them information to be implemented. Reliance on others for direction indicated that they were less able to function independently in the child care context, although clearly the students in this pattern of thinking are starting to move towards independence (interpersonal dimension). There is also an evolving awareness of other people's values, beliefs, and cultures as evidenced in the following quote:

> Just the way I speak to people and talk to people. With working in childcare I've realized a lot of families are different, have different values and cultural values and all that. Before I did this course and before I even worked in childcare, I didn't really know that families had so different values, but now I do. (Wendy)

The views about diversity evident in this quote are an important characteristic of intrapersonal patterns of thinking. It marks an understanding that families are to be respected, even though our documentation of practice through the digital photos did not provide evidence of this in their practices.

These students' views about children's learning were also mixed. They described a range of beliefs about children's learning and also demonstrated such beliefs in their practice. It is clear that students with patterns of practical reflection understand children's learning as more than modeling, which was the key characteristic of children's learning in the previous pattern of thinking. On the whole, the views about children's learning in the practical reflection pattern could be described as "active". Most students talked about children being independent explorers of their environments. Even if students did talk about the role of modeling in children's learning they did so in addition to considering children as active learners. These views did not appear to be influenced by the nature of their field experience because as evident in Table 5.1, students in both child-centered and more traditional settings held similar beliefs about children's learning.

Practical Evaluativist Pattern

In the previous two patterns, the capacity to engage in reflection distinguished practical implementation from practical reflection. Those who described a practical reflection thinking pattern typically reflected on an action after a strategy was implemented. In the third pattern, students with Practical Evaluativistic beliefs (n = 4) talked about reflecting on and weighing up different strategies from different sources before implementing a strategy and coming to their own informed opinion about the strategy to be implemented. These students were much more reflective about this process than were students in the previous pattern of thinking, particularly in the process of developing an informed approach to child care. For example:

> Well I guess I would think about the reasons why I think that way to start with. I would think about my values and my thoughts and then I would evaluate, I suppose, depending on all the requirements in my head that which ones—why that person thinks that way and then maybe even talk to them about them. I might, depending on what decision I come to, change the way I think or change my opinion on something depending on somebody else's; if they're more informed or they know a bit more than me. (Helen)

This quote shows the extended focus on evaluation of evidence. What is also clear is that the student's opinion could change as a result of this evaluation of evidence. The four students who indicated practical evaluativist were developing a sense of professional identity for child care practice. They described themselves as being part of the decision-making process in their work environments (interdependent relationships), rather than simply following others:

> I always try to take the positive aspects of other people's opinions and try and relate it to my situation. I will think about it and I'll maybe jot

down some notes and maybe different strategies on different ways I can approach whatever situation it may be. In the end I'll usually do it my way and then I will reflect on that, my own personal practice, and gauge from that whether that worked or not and then I will probably ask, say my director, or other people what they feel or how I could have changed it. . . . I think it's really important to have a go at things and to try and just go,—yeah, I'm just going to try. I don't think I would let people just crush my ideas. (Steph)

These quotes show how the student made use of others' ideas. This would suggest a pattern of thinking that is approaching *self-authorship* because she is less dependent on others in the process of constructing knowledge about child care.

These students talked about children as competent learners (*n* = 1). They talked about how children actively constructed meaning (*n* = 2) and learn through problem solving (*n* = 1). The following quote demonstrates both these qualities in the reflection on a photographic stimulus:

They're interested in it to start with. They're interested in cars. They have been for the last two weeks. Important because I think it still explores size and shape and I think the capacity to make a mess. So it's a bit of an education there even though they've no mathematics. They seemed to be very focused on this and I didn't want to invade or become involved. I think this focus could have been shifted to something that they weren't interested in. Whereas if they're doing—that's what they're focused and they're doing I think we leave them to do it. (Helen)

Students in this pattern of thinking did not describe children as learning through modeling as was the case with the previous two patterns. There was a clearer focus on constructivist views of children's learning. Students in both traditional and child-centered environments described children's learning in similar ways.

Complex Evaluativist Pattern

The final pattern of thinking, Complex Evaluativist, shared characteristics with the previous pattern related to evaluation. Only one student demonstrated this pattern of thinking. The student went beyond practical strategies to include theoretical ideas. This pattern is similar to evaluativism described by Kuhn and Weinstock (2002). Commenting on a child's difficult behavior in a photo, she said:

I've seen the behavior management plan because he has been assessed and I could see what we could do and I've seen what other carers have actually done. Also from my opinions I keep going back and making sure that he knows that he is getting recognized. . . . I've learned through TAFE and also through the behavior management plan. . . . So all the opinions are met. . . . So you need to know the theory but you also need to know the practical stuff as well and put it in place. When I see both . . . so that's how, the best way I've learnt. (Jill)

In the next example, the student shows how that she is not dependent on others, demonstrating an interdependence which goes beyond formula following. She has been given freedom to set up the environment and try her own ideas, which has been instrumental in assisting her to develop a strong professional identity.

Last year when I was here we got to change the play, the home corner and they gave me free reign of how to make it. I got to make it up the way I could see kids getting more experience so that was really good. They asked my opinions . . . about how to make a room more stimulating. . . . If I want to do an activity with the kids they are happy for me to go and do that activity with the kids and it's like being given free reign so it's really good. (Jill)

The freedom to experiment and be part of the decision making process at her placement centre has made her feel part of the team. This promoted interdependent thinking and relationships.

In terms of children's learning, Jill believed that children need to be respected and that children need to be able to make choices and engage in thinking. Reflecting on a photograph of her interacting with children in the sandpit:

Yeah, I love the sandpit . . . they learn so much in the sandpit. They share toys, they make things. They use their imagination which is such a vital thing to have them to just use their mind and the kids, they get the chance to do group time together in small little groups. Like, they get to share the toys, they, they just have fun. (Jill)

The field experience setting did not appear to play a role in how this student viewed children's learning. Even though she was in a fairly traditional centre environment, she was still able to articulate and demonstrate a constructivist view about children's learning. This complex evaluativist thinking pattern was related to strong professional identity and interdependence which is reflective of *self-authorship*.

DISCUSSION

The various patterns of thinking described by students in this study demonstrated that practical ways of knowing are common for these childcare students. All students, with the exception of one, talked about ways of knowing that involved either modeling, reflection on, or evaluation of practical strategies. The various ways of knowing were linked to their professional identities and relationships in the childcare contexts, forming a relatively cohesive self-authorship pattern. Practical implementation was linked to *formula following*; practical reflection was linked to both formula following and developing professional beliefs (similar to crossroads), whereas evaluativist (both practical and complex) was related to strong professional identities and interdependence (approaching *self-authorship*). Further, it seemed that these patterns of thinking were related to beliefs about children's learning. As students described increasingly self-authored views, there was a corresponding shift towards thinking about children's learning in terms of a constructivist perspective.

The first main finding of the study was that although there were differences in the nature of practical epistemology, essentially the focus was on "what worked", with the exception of one student with complex evaluativist beliefs. Reflective capacity is a key characteristic of self-authorship (Boes, Baxter Magolda, & Buckley, 2010). Only one student described the need to reflect upon a range of perspectives including theory and practice to arrive at informed opinions which would be expected in an evaluativistic stance (Kuhn & Weinstock, 2002). Reflective capacity is an important characteristic for effective interactions with young children. It was evident that students who reflected on a range of perspectives and arrived at a professional opinion (practical and complex evaluativist) were more able to construct their own beliefs for practice. These students also described more constructivist views about children's learning. Boes at al. (2010) also noted that personal characteristics such as complex making meaning (evident in more evaluativistic beliefs) enabled individuals to be more open to others perspectives. In the current study, the students with practical and complex evaluativist patterns of thinking that enabled them to confidently interact with colleagues and others and conceived of children as learning in more constructivist ways.

The majority of child care students could be described as being at the *crossroads* in terms of self-authorship. They understood that knowledge was personally constructed, although this knowledge was essentially practical in nature. There was less reliance on others to transmit information to them and growing understanding that new information has to fit with their own beliefs. There was a weighing up of evidence which is typical of an evaluativistic stance; however, the evaluation of evidence was limited to practical knowledge and not theory.

This finding contributed to the personal epistemology literature by providing a more nuanced way of understanding evaluativist beliefs. Previous research has described evaluativist as an overall evaluation of a range of perspectives including theory. Our study shows that evaluativist beliefs can also relate to practical forms of knowledge such as teaching strategies (see also Brownlee, Boulton-Lewis, & Berthelsen, 2008), which is a new contribution to the personal epistemology literature.

A second main finding of this study was that many students were clearly moving towards a professional identity in which their personal beliefs mattered (Creamer & Laughlin, 2005; King & Baxter Magolda, 2005). It would appear that this group of students is moving towards *self-author-ship* in the context of their child care profession. Their professional self is more fully developed (intrapersonal dimension) and they are more likely to develop respectful, cohesive relationships with others (interpersonal dimension; Creamer & Laughlin, 2005). When child care students rely on formulas to interact in the child care context, as was the case with students who held practical implementation patterns. This is similar to absolutism (Kuhn & Weinstock, 2002). Such a reliance on others means that professional identities are externally derived (intrapersonal), which in turn makes for dependent relationships (intrapersonal) with others (King & Baxter Magolda, 2005).

Whereas the theory of self-authorship holds promise as a construct for informing professional practice in child care, the context plays an important role in the expression of such beliefs and values. That is, students may only enact self-authorship if the context in which they find themselves is supportive (Pizzolato, 2007). More research is needed to investigate the impact of the context (e.g., the nature of the field placement) on self-authorship.

A third main finding was that field placement contexts were particularly influential for international students. The international students in this study ($n = 8$) were all described as having practical implementation patterns of thinking. In most cases these students had been in Australia for 18 months or less. It was very clear that these students relied on being "told" what to do by their group leaders and did not yet have an independent professional identity and way of thinking.

This is preliminary data, but it may be worthwhile investigating this further with a view to establishing how the nature of the context for field placements can support these international students more effectively. Pizzolato and Ozaki (2007) suggest that higher and further education promote formula followers because they provide too many structures to be followed. This is certainly the case with competency-based child care training. However, it is also not enough to merely expose students to complexity and diversity in their field placement. There needs to be explicit reflection and engagement with complex ideas in practices throughout their vocational training to be affective teachers of young children. Students in teacher education program need to develop greater awareness of the importance of personally constructing meaning about child care practice and this approach to learning and knowledge for practice needs to be actively encouraged by their educators in the vocational context and by their supervisors in their field placements.

NOTES

1. We recognize that the beliefs described in this study were not discrete internal representations and that they may exist in varying degrees of focus depending on the situation experienced. When students were described as holding certain beliefs we recognize that they may hold other views, but

those reported in the study were the ones foregrounded in their responses at this point in time. For this reason, we have used the term "patterns of thinking" rather than "categories" of beliefs.

REFERENCES

Åkerlind, G. (2005). Variation and commonality in phenomenographic research methods. *Higher Education Research and Development, 24*(4), 321–334.

Baxter Magolda, M. B. (1994). Post-college experiences and epistemology. *Review of Higher Education, 18*(1), 25–44.

Belenky, M. F., Clinchy, B. M., Goldberger, N. R., & Tarule, J. M. (1986). *Women's ways of knowing: The development of self, voice and mind.* New York: Basic Books.

Boes, L., Baxter Magolda, M., & Buckley, J. (2010). Foundational assumptions and constructive-developmental theory: Self-authorship narratives. In M. Baxter Magolda, E. Creamer, & P. Meszaros (Eds.), *Development and assessment of self-authorship. Exploring the concept across cultures* (pp. 3–23). Sterling, Virgina: Stylus.

Brownlee, J., Boulton-Lewis, G., & Berthelsen, D. (2008). Epistemological beliefs in child care: Implications for vocational education and course design. *British Journal of Educational Psychology, 78,* 457–471.

Creamer, E., & Laughlin, A. (2005). Self-authorship and women's career decision making. *Journal of College Student Development, 46*(1), 13–27.

Katz, L. G. (2001). Program content and implementation. In *USA Background Report for the OECD Thematic Review* (pp. 73–89). Washington, DC: US Department of Education, Office of Educational Research and Improvement.

King, P., & Baxter Magolda, M. (2005). A developmental model of intercultural maturity. *Journal of College Student Development, 46*(6), 571–592.

Kuhn, D., & Udell, W. (2001). The path to wisdom. *Educational Psychologist, 36*(4), 261–264.

Kuhn, D., & Weinstock, M. (2002). What is epistemological thinking and why does it matter? In B. Hofer & P. Pintrich (Eds.), *Personal epistemology: The psychological beliefs about knowledge and knowing* (pp. 121–144). Mahwah, NJ: Lawrence Erlbaum Associates.

Meszaros, P. (2007). The journey of self-authorship: Why is it necessary? In P. S. Meszaros (Ed.), *Self-authorship: Advancing student's intellectual growth: New directions for teaching and learning* (No. 109, pp. 5–14). San Francisco, CA: Jossey-Bass

Perry, W. G. (1970). *Forms of intellectual and ethical development in the college years.* New York: Holt, Rinehart and Winston.

Pizzolato, J. E. (2007). Assessing self-authorship. In P. S. Meszaros (Ed.), *Self-authorship: Advancing student's intellectual growth: New directions for teaching and learning* (No. 109, pp. 31–42). San Francisco, CA: Jossey-Bass

Pizzolato, J., & Ozaki, C. (2007). Moving toward self-authorship: Investigating outcomes of learning partnerships. *Journal of College Student Development, 48*(2), 196–214.

Schommer-Aikens, M. (2004). Explaining the epistemological belief system: Introducing the embedded systemic model and coordinated research approach. *Educational Psychologist, 39*(1), 19–29.

6 Personal Epistemology in Preservice Teachers
Belief Changes Throughout a Teacher Education Course

Sue Walker, Jo Brownlee, Beryl Exley, Annette Woods, and Chrystal Whiteford

ABSTRACT

There is strong evidence to show that beliefs about knowing and knowledge held by individuals (personal epistemologies) influence preservice teachers' learning strategies and learning outcomes (Muis, 2004). However, we know very little about how preservice teachers' personal epistemologies change as they progress through their teacher education programs. The current study provides the first longitudinal data of changes in personal epistemologies for preservice teachers. This study investigated (a) the relationship between personal epistemologies and beliefs about learning, and (b) changes in personal epistemologies and beliefs about learning for a group of preservice teachers as they progressed through the first 3 years of a 4-year Bachelor of Education. The study reports on two phases of data collection. Preservice teachers completed the Epistemological Beliefs Survey (EBS; Kardash & Wood, 2000) in 2007 when they commenced their course (Phase 1) and then again in 2009 when they were in the 3rd year of their course (Phase 2). On completion of the survey, randomly selected preservice teachers were invited to participate in Phase 1 and Phase 2 follow-up interviews. Both the quantitative and qualitative data indicated that there were changes in preservice teachers' personal epistemologies between course entry and the third year of their course. Specifically, results indicated that most of the preservice teachers demonstrated a change towards more sophisticated personal epistemologies over time. Importantly, these changes may be related to more effective, deeper approaches to learning. Results are discussed in terms of the implications for teaching and teacher education.

INTRODUCTION

Classrooms of the 21st century are complex systems. They support diverse learners from varied contexts and function in a "messy" *bricolage* of policy contexts. This complexity is also evident in the nature of teaching and learning deployed in these classrooms. There is also, in current contexts, a general expectation that teachers will support students to construct, rather than simply receive knowledge. This process of constructing knowledge requires a focus on critical thinking in complex social and real world contexts (see also Elen & Clarebout, 2001; Yang, Chang, & Hsu 2008). Critical thinking, which involves the identification and evaluation of multiple perspectives when making decisions, is a process of knowing—a tool of wisdom (Kuhn & Udell, 2001). Schommer-Aikens, Bird, and Bakken (2010) refer to classrooms that encourage critical thinking as "epistemologically based" in which "the teacher encourages his/her students to look for connections among concepts within the text, with their prior knowledge, and with concepts found in the world beyond themselves" (p. 48).

In dealing with complex problems it is important, therefore, that knowledge processes, not just knowledge products, are focused on in learning settings. Beliefs about knowing and knowledge held by individuals (personal epistemology) are central to development of knowledge processes, such as critical thinking (Kuhn & Udell, 2001). Despite this recognized link between knowledge and personal epistemology, the understanding has yet to make a great impact on teaching and learning in teacher education. In the current study, we are interested in understanding more about preservice teachers' personal epistemologies and how beliefs change as individuals progress through a teacher education program. This is an area of research that has received very little research attention and yet may "provide an important theoretical basis for education as well as teacher training and development" (Bendixen & Feucht, 2010, p. 7).

The meaning of personal epistemology is debated and can be influenced by the approach from which it is studied. Different approaches may refer to personal epistemology as stages, levels, beliefs, reflections, theories, ways of knowing, metaknowing, and resources (Hofer, 2004a, 2004b). A common theme amongst these views is that personal epistemology relates to an individual's thinking about knowing and knowledge (Pintrich, 2002).

Kuhn and her colleagues (see Kuhn, Cheney, & Weinstock, 2000; Kuhn & Weinstock, 2002) described a trajectory of personal epistemology. They described the development of personal epistemology from *absolutist* (knowledge as absolute and transferable), to *multiplist* (knowledge based on personal opinions), to *evaluativist* (knowledge based on judgments of evidence from multiple perspectives; Kuhn & Weinstock, 2002). Of interest here is the role played by critical thinking in each of these levels. Clearly if "reality is directly knowable" (Kuhn et al., 2000, p. 311; the Absolutist) or personally created (the Multiplist), critical thinking is not central. In these early levels there is no need to evaluate multiple perspectives in order to arrive at an evidenced-based outcome. In contrast, we believe that teachers need to engage in critical thinking in order to promote effective teaching and learning in diverse communities of learners.

Personal Epistemology and Preservice Teachers

Personal epistemological beliefs affect learning and influence the extent to which understanding is developed and meaning is made (Hofer, 2002). There is strong evidence to show that preservice teachers' personal epistemologies influence their learning strategies and learning outcomes (Muis, 2004). That is, we know that personal epistemologies filter how preservice teachers experience learning in teacher education courses (Many, Howard, & Hoge, 2002; Muis, 2004; Peng & Fitzgerald, 2006; Yadav & Koehler, 2007) and engage in meaningful approaches to learning (Muis, 2004). These meaningful approaches to learning are described as deep-holistic learning strategies (Ramsden, 2003, in Thompson, Pilgrim, & Oliver, 2005) and reflect qualitative conceptions of learning (Marton, Dall'Alba, & Beaty, 1993). Such strategies focus on building personal meaning and organizing ideas so that links are made to prior knowledge, connecting ideas and evaluating a range of evidence (critical thinking). On the other hand, surface-atomistic strategies focus on the surface-level literal meaning with few interconnections made between topics and theories. Often this results in rote learning (Ramsden, 2003, in Thompson et al., 2005) and may reflect quantitative conceptions of learning (Marton et al., 1993).

A number of studies have shown that sophisticated personal epistemologies are related to meaningful approaches to learning. Bondy et al. (2007) investigated how personal epistemologies were related to preservice teachers' approaches to learning by analyzing data based on interviews with 14 preservice teachers. These researchers also found a relationship between personal epistemology and approaches to learning whereby preservice teachers with sophisticated personal epistemologies (knowledge is uncertain and integrated) were more likely to be open to multiple perspectives and to make connections between ideas. Brownlee, Berthelsen, and Boulton-Lewis (2004) also found similar relationships in a group of early years teachers in Australia. Teachers who described evaluativistic patterns of beliefs also described deeper approaches to learning where connections were made between new and prior knowledge. Some research also suggests that personal epistemologies may be related to levels of critical thinking, a dimension of meaningful approaches to learning. Bråten and Strømsø (2006) showed that 1st-year Norwegian preservice teachers' personal epistemologies about the speed of knowledge acquisition influenced their capacity to engage in critical thinking in the context of evaluating Web-based resources. Muis (2004) described these personal epistemologies as *availing* because their personal epistemologies were supportive or availing of deep approaches to learning.

Collectively, these studies demonstrate that personal epistemologies influence learning in terms of students' beliefs about learning and this is clearly an important body of research for understanding how preservice teachers navigate their teacher education courses and develop a sound body of knowledge and skills for entry into the teaching profession. However, we still know very little about how preservice teachers' personal epistemologies change as they progress through their teacher education programs. Whereas there are no longitudinal studies to date, Bendixen and Corkhill (this volume) investigated personal epistemologies in teachers at various stages of their professional journeys. Using a cross-sectional research design, they examined personal epistemology in beginning and final year preservice teachers, as well as beginning and experienced inservice teachers. Their study showed that beginning preservice teachers tend to have more naïve beliefs regarding the certainty and simplicity of knowledge, but more sophisticated beliefs about the nature of innate intelligence (incremental view of intelligence) when compared to experienced teachers. Brownlee (2003) also investigated changes in preservice teachers' personal epistemologies as they completed a 1-year Graduate Diploma in primary teaching and progressed into their teaching careers. Twenty nine preservice teachers were interviewed at the beginning and end of their teaching course and then 11 teachers were re-interviewed in their 3rd year of teaching. Over the three time phases, 7 teachers described more evaluativist personal epistemologies, 2 remained the same and 2 regressed to more objectivist personal epistemologies. However, the process of changing epistemological beliefs of preservice teachers as they progress through their teacher education course was not addressed in this study. Thus, the current study will provide the first longitudinal data of changes in personal epistemologies for preservice teachers.

THE STUDY

Given the research evidence showing that personal epistemology influences learning, this study investigated (a) the relationship between personal epistemologies and beliefs about learning, and (b) changes in personal epistemologies and beliefs about learning for a group of early childhood and primary preservice teachers as they progressed through the first 3 years of a 4-year Bachelor of Education. The study reports on two phases of data collection that track preservice teachers through their 4-year teacher education program. A final phase of data collection will take place in 2010 as these preservice teachers complete the fourth and final year of the teacher education program. It is anticipated that this final phase of data will provide additional evidence of change in personal epistemologies and beliefs about learning which can be used to inform teacher education programs.

Participants and Context

Preservice teachers in the Bachelor of Education (Early Childhood) undertake a full-time internal degree, which is recognized by the Queensland College of Teachers as meeting the requirements for Queensland teacher registration. The degree prepares preservice teachers to teach in prior-to-school contexts as well as in the first 3 years of school. Practicum is undertaken in Semester 1 and Semester 2 of the 2nd year, Semester 1 of the 3rd year, and Semester 2 of the 4th year. Phase one of the data collection occurred at the beginning of 2007 whereas Phase 2 of the data collection (epistemological belief questionnaires and interviews) occurred at the beginning of Semester 1, 2009. At this point in time, preservice teachers had completed two practicums and were preparing to undertake a third.

Preservice teachers in the Bachelor of Education (Primary) undertake a full-time internal degree that will lead to registration as a teacher in Queensland. The degree prepares preservice teachers to teach school aged-children from the Preparatory Year (aged 5.5 years) through to Year 7 (aged 12.5 years). Practicum is undertaken in Semester 1 of the 2nd year, Semester 2 of the 3rd year, and Semesters 1 and 2 of the 4th year. At the time of Phase 2 data collection, preservice teachers had completed one practicum and were preparing to undertake a second.

The Epistemological Beliefs Survey

Preservice teachers were invited to complete the Epistemological Beliefs Survey (EBS, Kardash & Wood, 2000) in 2007 when they commenced their course (Phase 1) and then again in 2009 when they were in the 3rd year of their course (Phase 2). Phase 1 data collection occurred in the 1st week of the 2007 academic year for all preservice teachers (194 Early Childhood Education students; 136 Primary Education students), whereas Phase 2 data collection occurred in Week 1 of Semester 1, 2009, for the Early Childhood Cohort ($n = 80$) and in Week 1 of Semester 2, 2009, for the Primary Cohort ($n = 131$).

The EBS assesses student beliefs about the structure of knowledge (integration of knowledge), speed of knowledge acquisition (learning is quick or not at all), knowledge construction (learning takes place through a process of constructing personal meaning), characteristics of student success (e.g., views about innate ability), and attainability of truth (the certainty of knowledge). Responses are scored on a 5-point Likert scale (1 = strongly disagree, 5 = strongly agree). Following Kardash and Wood (2000), items were summed for each sub-scale to produce factor scores for Structure ($\alpha = 0.74$), Speed ($\alpha = 0.69$), Knowledge Construction ($\alpha = 0.62$), Success ($\alpha = 0.60$), and Truth ($\alpha = 0.54$). Higher scores on all factors represent more sophisticated beliefs.

Semi-structured Interviews

On completion of the survey, randomly selected preservice teachers were invited to participate in Phase 1 follow-up interviews. Fifteen early childhood and 14 primary preservice teachers participated in the Phase 1 interviews. In Phase 2, 8 early childhood and 5 primary preservice teachers (a total of 13 students) were re-interviewed. Interview responses at Phase 1 and Phase 2 were compared to establish the extent to which changes had taken place in the preservice teachers' personal epistemologies over time. Interviews were conducted by a research assistant who was provided with interview procedure training. The audio-taped interviews were semi-structured, scenario based and ranged from 30 to 60 minutes in length.

The study used scenario-based interviews adapted from the work of Stacey et al. (2005) to encourage reflection and to facilitate clear articulation of personal epistemologies within the context of the preservice teachers' fields of study. Whereas the scenarios were varied to reflect the teaching experiences typically encountered by both early childhood and primary preservice teachers, the questions relating to the scenarios remained similar. Specifically the scenario for both groups of students involved a literacy teaching experience. Students were presented with a situation in which a preservice teacher was confronted with an experienced teacher enacting pedagogy that was not considered to be best practice in literacy teaching.

The interview questions, based on Hofer and Pintrich's (1997) epistemological framework, focused on beliefs about knowing and beliefs about knowledge. Beliefs about knowing, and how experts are used in student's learning, were sought by asking "Do you trust the opinions of experts?" The questions: "Sometimes people talk about there being 'right answers' or 'truth'. What are your views?"; "Do you agree with the idea that there are no right answers?"; and "Do think that anybody's opinion is as good as another's?" were asked to access preservice teachers' beliefs about knowledge. The questions about learning were: "How do you go about learning?"; "How do you know when you have learnt something?"

The interview transcripts were examined using content analysis for "patterns, themes, biases and meanings" (Berg, 2007, p. 304). Well defined categories of personal epistemology have been developed through traditions of research. Thus, a theory-driven approach (deductive approach) was used to categorise the interview responses; Kuhn and Weinstock's (2002) categories were organized into an analytic rubric. Categorizations included: objectivism, subjectivism, and evaluativism. The categories of beliefs about learning were analyzed deductively using Marton et al.'s (1993) qualitative and quantitative conceptions of learning. Although the researchers were guided by a deductive approach, they were aware that variations could appear as categories were applied. These categories and variations are presented in Tables 6.1 and 6.2.

To ensure the consistency of coding, a 'double coding' (Miles & Huberman, 1994) approach was taken. The use of 'double coding' assists in ensuring the rigor of the analyses and the reliability of interpretations from the data (Ming Went et al., 2002). At both Phase 1 and Phase 2, 25% of the transcripts were cross-checked by a second researcher. The second researcher interrogated the category descriptions and the quotes exemplifying each category. Initial agreement was 66% for Phase 1 and 88% for Phase 2. Points of difference mainly occurred when data sets showed evidence of multiple categories and discussion centered on which category best suited. When responses could be categorized in multiple ways, the highest category in evidence was recorded. All points of difference in the coding were discussed and 100% agreement was reached. Agreement was measured by the extent to which the upper level of coding was evident. For example, if one researcher indicated a response provided evidence of complex evaluativism and practical evaluativism and another researcher only

Table 6.1 Categories of Personal Epistemologies and Examples of Participant Responses

Personal epistemology	Example participant responses
Objectivism very limited analysis evident; expert opinions often unquestioned	Me, I think I try what the research says because they have done the research, yeah. (Do you trust the opinions of experts such as your university lecturers and researchers?) Yeah, I think I try almost everything but sometimes I will be oh maybe it's true. Sometimes I can doubt a little bit or I can't really trust everything. Think I just learn from the research yeah and I generally believe all of books they have—they all can help children with their literacy. (Tania)
Subjectivism knowledge based on personal opinions	Everyone has their own opinion and is entitled to it. (Wendy)
Practical evaluativism evaluate and critique a range of observable teaching strategies	Say if someone says the best thing for Daniel is to have the mum, the teacher and Daniel interacting, but then say Daniel might have gone through a tough time with his family during that morning. So you can deal with things differently. Use that information but then use your own knowledge and your own experiences. Maybe build on their knowledge. (Wendy)
Complex evaluativism knowledge evolving and context-dependent; constructed & open to critique; evaluate a range of perspectives including theory	Difference between respecting someone and someone's right to have an opinion and valuing their right to have an opinion versus respecting the opinions that they come out with. Also, I think, opinions are there to be questioned and people should be free to share their opinions in a way that encourages them to share opinions. But also in a way that encourages them to question their opinions. Readings from the experts, but they're all just someone's opinion backed up by case study . . . I just know how many readings that we've done in uni [university] that haven't correlated to each other and that have completely different views on things. So I guess you just want to be well aware of all the stuff out there. (Jordan)

Table 6.2 Categories of Beliefs About Learning and Examples of Participant Responses

Beliefs about learning	Example of participant responses
Quantitative absorb information from an external source; intention of reproducing the information at a later date	I know when I've learnt something if someone is talking about a certain subject or a question and I can answer it confidently without questioning anything in my head and I know that I've learnt it. (Clare)
Application intention of reproducing or applying the information	I think that it's acquiring knowledge about certain things and being able to use it confidently in the right sort of contexts. So gathering together knowledge and being able to speak confidently to someone about it, being able to write something you know. (Clare)
Qualitative—sense making simple level of understanding; make sense of the task or text; no analysis of perspectives for meaning	Going over it, and over it, and over it. And writing it, and putting it into my own words so that I understand if it is something that is totally going over my head and lots of big words. Actually breaking it down and putting into my own words, and giving myself an example of it. Like how that would actually work in practice. (Mia) So I guess I would kind of relate it to things that I know because my memory about children sticks in my head because I've related them to someone or something. (Sam)
Qualitative active role in own learning; analyzing many points of view; collaborate with others	Talk with others. Share our ideas with friends, people in my course and with that you can have kind of an understanding if you don't understand, then having an understanding to begin with and that gives you the opportunity to further research and look at other books and a variety of things [multimodal things] to kind of have another understanding and grasp the whole subject, but yes most importantly how I learn is by sharing and being able to communicate with others and having their ideas and my ideas and having a group understanding. (Wendy)

believed it represented complex evaluativism, then the upper level of complex evaluativism was considered to be the key point of agreement.

RESULTS

Changes in Personal Epistemology

Paired sample t-tests were used to examine changes in preservice teachers' personal epistemologies over time from Phase 1 to Phase 2. Means and standard errors for each of the sub-scales are presented in Table 6.3. Overall results indicated that there were significant differences between Time 1 and Time 2 on the sub-scales of Speed, t (136) = -4.17, p = .000; Structure, t (136) = -2.48, p = .015; and Truth, t (138) = -2.03, p = .044, indicating that preservice teachers evidenced more sophisticated epistemological beliefs on these dimensions in the 3rd year of their course than in the 1st year of their course. Specifically, results indicate that 3rd year preservice teachers were more likely than 1st year preservice teachers to believe that learning might take time, that knowledge is integrated rather than consisting of a series of facts, and that knowledge is uncertain. There were no significant differences between Time 1 and Time 2 on the sub-scales of Knowledge Construction, t (136) = .698, p = .49; or Success, t (138) = -1.06, p = .29, indicating that 3rd year preservice teachers were no more likely than 1st year preservice teachers to view knowledge as personally constructed or to believe that the characteristics of successful students include more than innate ability.

The interview analysis also revealed changes in personal epistemologies from Time 1 to Time 2. Table 6.4 shows that the majority of preservice teachers interviewed (n = 10) evidenced change towards more sophisticated personal epistemologies over time. Of these preservice teachers, 4 described practical evaluativistic beliefs at Time 1 and then complex evaluativistic beliefs at Time 2. The remaining 6 preservice teachers moved

Table 6.3   Means and Standard Errors for the Sub-scales of the EBS

	Time 1 M (SE) (N = 330)	Time 2 M (SE) (N = 211)
Speed	4.01 (.03)	4.16 (.03)***
Structure	2.90 (.04)	3.00 (.05)*
Construction	3.69 (.05)	3.66 (.03)
Success	3.61 (.04)	3.67 (.05)
Truth	3.43 (.06)	3.56 (.06)*

Note: *** indicates $p < .001$, * indicates $p < .05$

Table 6.4 Changes in Personal Epistemologies From Time 1 to Time 2 Interviews

Time 1	Time 2	Frequency
Increased sophistication		
Practical evaluativism	Complex evaluativism	4
Subjectivism	Complex evaluativism	2
Subjectivism	Practical evaluativism	4
TOTAL Increased sophistication		10
No change		
Subjectivism and Objectivism	Subjectivism and Objectivism	2
Practical and Complex evaluativism	Practical and Complex evaluativism	1
TOTAL No change		3

from subjectivist to evaluativistic beliefs (n = 2 complex evaluativism; n = 4 practical evaluativism) at Time 2. Only 3 preservice teachers did not demonstrate any changes, and of these, 1 preservice teacher already held sophisticated beliefs at Time 1, suggesting that further development would not be likely to take place over time due to a ceiling effect. This means that only 2 preservice teachers who were interviewed at Time 2 held naïve personal epistemologies which did not change over time.

Changes in Beliefs about Learning

Changes in beliefs about learning were also evident in the interview analysis. Table 6.5 shows that many preservice teachers (n = 7) demonstrated changes towards qualitative beliefs about learning.

Table 6.5 Changes in Beliefs About Learning Between Time 1 and Time 2 Interviews

Time 1	Time 2	Frequency
Increased sophistication		
Quantitative	Quantitative and application	1
Quantitative	Qualitative	3
Quantitative	Qualitative sense-making	2
Qualitative sense-making	Qualitative	1
TOTAL increased sophistication		7
No change		
Quantitative	Quantitative	1
Qualitative sense-making and application	Qualitative sense-making and application	1
Qualitative	Qualitative	3
TOTAL no change		5

Note: One not codable for changes over time

Table 6.6   Relationships Between Individuals' Personal Epistemologies and Beliefs About Learning

Personal epistemology	Beliefs about learning	Number of students
Subjectivism	Quantitative/application	1
Subjectivism	Quantitative	1
Practical evaluativism	Qualitative sense-making	2
Practical evaluativism	Quantitative/application	1
Complex evaluativism	Qualitative	6
Complex evaluativism	Quantitative/application	1
Complex evaluativism	Qualitative sense-making	1
TOTAL		13

Of these, 1 student moved from a sense making view of learning to a qualitative perspective and 1 student moved from quantitative to application. Five preservice teachers did not change their beliefs over time, although it should be noted that 3 of these preservice teachers already held qualitative beliefs at Time 1.

Relationship Between Personal Epistemologies and Beliefs about Learning

The next aspect of the data analysis involved looking at each individual's interview to investigate if there was a relationship between their personal epistemologies and beliefs about learning. This involved analyzing what each individual had to say about learning and knowing at Time 2 and reporting on this relationship as described in Table 6.6.

The data in Table 6.6 show that a relationship exists between personal epistemology and beliefs about learning which will be discussed. Complex evaluativistic beliefs were associated with qualitative conceptions of learning, practical evaluativistic beliefs were linked with qualitative sense-making, and application and subjectivist beliefs were related to quantitative conceptions.

DISCUSSION

Changes in Personal Epistemologies

Both the quantitative and qualitative data indicated that there were changes in preservice teachers' personal epistemologies between course entry and the 3rd year of their course, thus reflecting a move towards more sophisticated understandings about the nature of knowing and knowledge. With respect to the quantitative survey data, results indicated that 3rd year preservice teachers were more likely than 1st year preservice teachers to believe that learning might take time, that knowledge is integrated rather than consisting of a series of facts, and that knowledge is uncertain. The higher scores on the dimensions of structure, truth, and speed of knowledge acquisition may indicate that as the preservice teachers progress through their degree they perceive knowledge as integrated, truth as not absolute but changing, and that knowledge acquisition takes time compared to when they commenced tertiary study. These findings are supported by previous research which has indicated that educated individuals are more likely to be reflective about multiple perspectives, remain open to new information, and develop a personal, evidence-based opinion (see e.g., Baxter Magolda & Terenzini, 2004; Jehng, Johnson, & Anderson, 1993; Schommer, 1998).

The qualitative data provide a complementary perspective on the changes in personal epistemologies associated with engaging in preservice teacher preparation at the tertiary level. Specifically, the interview data indicated that the majority of preservice teachers demonstrated a change towards more sophisticated personal epistemologies over time, moving from subjectivist/practical evaluativistic beliefs at Time 1 to more complex evaluativistic beliefs at Time 2. Importantly, these changes may be related to more effective, deeper approaches to learning.

Relationships between Personal Epistemology and Learning

The noted changes in personal epistemologies from Time 1 to Time 2 are mirrored in qualitative changes in personal beliefs about learning. The data indicated that more complex evaluativistic beliefs were associated with qualitative conceptions of learning and that there were changes across both these dimensions from 1st to 3rd year of the teacher education course. Thus, as preservice teachers' personal epistemologies became more sophisticated, there appears to be a corresponding change in their beliefs about learning to more qualitative conceptions. Preservice teachers with a more sophisticated personal epistemology viewed learning as qualitative in nature, meaning that they sought multiple perspectives in their quest to make personal meaning. Preservice teachers with subjectivist beliefs view personal learning as reproductive in nature. This is of concern as such beliefs can influence their ability to engage in critical thinking often encouraged in higher education. This area of concern raises questions about the scope of the current teacher education program to shift firmly embedded subjectivist beliefs.

Such findings are in-line with prior research which describes epistemological belief structures as based on a relationship between core and peripheral beliefs (Brownlee, Boulton-Lewis, & Purdie, 2001). Core beliefs about knowing reveal core values that are interconnected with other beliefs, such as peripheral beliefs about learning. The findings of the present study support the notion that a relationship exists between core and peripheral beliefs.

Implications for Teaching and Teacher Education

These findings are of importance when we consider that the core business of teachers relates to learning and knowing. Teachers with more sophisticated personal epistemologies and beliefs about learning are likely to be able to engage in complex problem solving tasks, and argue based on evidence for a "best" solution. This is an important skill for any workplace environment, especially in complex teaching environments. However, whereas sophisticated personal epistemologies may be an important goal for teacher education programs, often preservice teachers who finish their courses and enter the profession still hold relatively naïve personal epistemologies (White, 2000). Wilson (2000) noted that teachers with 4-year degrees or less were more likely than teachers with graduate qualifications to hold objectivist personal epistemologies in teaching. This means that teaching is more teacher-centered and transmissive, with less focus on student engagement in the process of learning. Joram (2007, in Olafson & Schraw, 2010) also showed that preservice teachers and beginning teachers were more likely to hold objectivist personal epistemologies than experienced teachers. Our data do not support these previous findings, with many preservice teachers showing growth in their personal epistemologies by half way through their teacher education course. However, we need to know what happens once teachers enter the beginning years of teaching. These variations in personal epistemology from preservice teachers to beginning teachers would be significant for helping us to understand teachers and teaching.

Teacher education programs need to assist preservice teachers to promote sophisticated personal epistemologies and qualitative conceptions of learning (see for example, DeCorte, Op't Eynde, Depaepe, & Verschaffel, 2010). This draws attention to a need to help preservice teachers to reconstruct personal epistemologies. Such reconstruction may be possible through a focus on explicit reflection on personal epistemologies (Valanides & Angeli, 2005). Although there is evidence that shows the importance of preservice teachers reflecting on personal epistemologies and the nature of critical thinking, there is no clear consensus for how this should occur. However, recent research focusing on interventions may highlight how effective reflections on personal epistemologies can be achieved.

One teaching intervention focused on critical thinking with preservice teachers. Valanides and Angeli (2005) investigated how two types of interventions, the *Infusion* intervention (where preservice teachers discussed an article, prepared outline for a paper on the issue, and reflected on their thinking, listened to a short lecture, and a conversation with the researcher) and the *General* intervention program (preservice teachers listened to lectures and had a discussion of an article for preparation for a paper) were implemented. It was found that preservice teachers involved in the *Infusion* intervention experienced more change in personal epistemologies than those involved in the *General* intervention.

Another way to promote explicit reflection on personal epistemologies involves the use of calibration. In order for teachers to reconstruct their existing personal epistemologies, it may be important for them to calibrate their personal epistemologies with teaching knowledge (Cunningham et al., 2004 in Maggioni & Parkinson, 2008, p. 454). It is suggested that well-calibrated teachers can clearly identify the extent of their existing beliefs and therefore work to obtain knowledge/beliefs in areas where they lack understanding (Cunningham et al., 2004). It is necessary to build understanding of effective calibration training for preservice teachers to promote more effective explicit reflections on personal epistemologies (Maggioni & Parkinson, 2008).

Whereas calibration training may assist teacher educators to increase awareness of general beliefs/knowledge and the extent to which their teaching practice reflect these understandings, personal epistemologies may in turn influence the extent to which teachers are able to engage in calibration (Maggioni & Parkinson, 2008). It is argued by Stahl et al. (2006) that teachers with sophisticated personal epistemologies are more adept at calibrating "their goal setting and planning to the difficulty of the task" (cited in Maggioni & Parkinson, 2008, p. 455). In order for teachers to calibrate their personal epistemologies to those specific to a teaching paradigm, teachers need to be explicitly aware of the beliefs involved (Muis, 2007, cited in Maggioni & Parkinson, 2008). This requires explicit reflection on personal epistemologies in order for teachers to understand their personal epistemologies, to calibrate these to a variety of teaching situations, and thus reconstruct their personal epistemologies.

The current research has shown changes have taken place in beliefs about knowing and learning over the first 2 years of a teacher education course. It would be interesting to determine what factors may have promoted such changes. Whereas time and maturation may certainly play a role in the development of these preservice teachers' personal epistemologies, it could be speculated that the nature of a teacher education program, with a specific emphasis on reflective practice, may also effect significant changes. It is expected that the Time 3 data collection scheduled to take place in late 2010 will shed some light on preservice teachers' perceptions of why changes have taken place and enable a critical reflection of the ways in which our preservice teacher education programs may or may not facilitate such changes to more sophisticated ways of knowing.

REFERENCES

Baxter Magolda, M., & Terenzini, P. (2004). Learning and teaching in the 21st century: Trends and implications for practice. *American College Personnel Association*, http://www.acpa.nche.edu/srsch/magolda_terenzini.html

Bendixen, L. D., & Feucht, F. C. (2010). *Personal epistemology in the classroom: Theory, research, and implications for practice.* Cambridge, MA: Cambridge University Press.

Berg, B. (2007). *Qualitative research methods for the social sciences.* Boston: Pearson.

Bondy, E., Ross, D., Adams, A., Nowak, R., Brownell, M., Hoppey, D., et al. (2007). Personal epistemologies and learning to teach. *Teacher Education and Special Education: The Journal of Teacher Education Division of the Council for Exceptional Children, 30,* 67–82.

Bråten, I., & Strømsø, H. (2006). Epistemological beliefs, interest, and gender as predictors of Internet-based learning activities. *Computers in Human Behaviour, 22,* 1027–1042.

Brownlee, J. M. (2003). Paradigm shifts in preservice teacher education students: A case study of changes in epistemological beliefs for two teacher education students. *Australian Journal of Educational & Developmental Psychology, 1*(3), 1–6.

Brownlee, J., Berthelsen, D., & Boulton-Lewis, G. (2004). Working with toddlers in child care: Personal epistemologies and practice. *European Early Childhood Education Research Journal, 12*(1), 55–70.

Brownlee, J., Boulton-Lewis, G., & Purdie, N. (2001). Core beliefs about knowing and peripheral beliefs about learning: Developing a holistic conceptualisation of epistemological beliefs. *Australian Journal of Educational and Developmental Psychology, 2,* 1–16.

DeCorte, E., Op't Eynde, P., Depaepe, F., & Verschaffel, L. (2010). The reflexive relation between students' mathematics-related beliefs and the mathematics classroom culture. In L. D. Bendixen & F. C. Feucht (Eds.), *Personal epistemology in the classroom: Theory, research, and implications for practice* (pp. 292–327). Cambridge, UK: Cambridge University Press.

Elen, J., & Clarebout, G. (2001). An invasion in the classroom: Influence of an ill-structured innovation on instructional and epistemological beliefs. *Learning Environments Research, 4,* 87–105.

Hofer, B. (2002). Personal epistemology as a psychological and educational construct: An introduction. In B. Hofer & P. Pintrich (Eds.), *Personal epistemology: The psychological beliefs about knowledge and knowing* (pp. 3–14). Mahwah, NJ: Lawrence Erlbaum Associates.

Hofer, B. (2004a). Epistemological understanding as a metacognitive process: Thinking aloud during online searching. *Educational Psychologist, 39*(1), 43–55.

Hofer, B. K. (2004b). Exploring the dimension of personal epistemology in differing classroom contexts: Student interpretations during the first year of college. *Contemporary Educational Psychology, 29,* 129–163.

Hofer, B., & Pintrich, P. R. (1997). The development of epistemological theories: Beliefs about knowledge and knowing and their relation to learning. *Review of Educational Research, 67*(1), 88–144.

Jehng, J. J., Johnson, S. D., & Anderson, R. C. (1993). Schooling and students' epistemological beliefs about learning. *Contemporary Educational Psychology, 18,* 23–25.

Kardash, C. M., & Wood, P. (2000, April). *An individual item factoring of epistemological beliefs as measured by self-reporting surveys.* Paper presented at the American Educational Research Association, New Orleans, Louisiana.

Kuhn, D., Cheney, R., & Weinstock, M. (2000). The development of epistemological understanding. *Cognitive Development, 15*(3), 309–328.

Kuhn, D., & Udell, W. (2001). The path to wisdom. *Educational Psychologist, 36*(4), 261–264.

Kuhn, D., & Weinstock, M. (2002). What is epistemological thinking and why does it matter? In B. Hofer & P. Pintrich (Eds.), *Personal epistemology: The psychological beliefs about knowledge and knowing* (pp. 121–144). Mahwah, NJ: Lawrence Erlbaum Associates.

Maggioni, L., & Parkinson, M. (2008). The role of teacher epistemic cognition, epistemic beliefs, and calibration in instruction. *Educational Psychology Review, 20*(4), 445–461.

Many, J., Howard, F., & Hoge, P. (2002). Epistemology and preservice teacher education: How do beliefs about knowledge affect our students' experiences? *English Education, 34*(4), 302–322.

Marton, F., Dall'Alba, G., & Beatty, E. (1993). Conceptions of learning. *International Journal of Educational Research, 19*, 277–300.

Miles, M. B., & Huberman, A. M. (1994). *Qualitative data analysis* (2nd ed.). Thousand Oaks, CA: Sage Publications.

Ming Went, L., Thomas, M., Jones, H., Orr, N., Moreton, R., Hawe, P., et al. (2002). Promoting physical activity in women: Evaluation of a 2-year community-based intervention in Sydney, Australia. *Health Promotion International, 17*(2), 127–137.

Muis, K. (2004). Personal epistemology and Mathematics: A critical review and synthesis of research. *Review of Educational Research, 74*(3), 317–377.

Olafson, L., & Schraw, G. (2010). Beyond epistemology: assessing teacher.' epistemological and ontological worldviews. In L. Bendixen & F. Feucht (Eds.), *Personal epistemology in the classroom* (pp. 516–551). New York: Cambridge University Press.

Peng, H., & Fitzgerald, G. (2006). Relationships between teacher education students' epistemological beliefs and their learning outcomes in a case-based hypermedia learning environment. *Journal of Technology and Teacher Education, 14*(2), 255–285.

Pintrich, P. (2002). Future challenges and directions for theory. In B. Hofer & P. Pintrich (Eds.), *Personal epistemology: The psychological beliefs about knowledge and knowing* (pp. 389–414). Mahwah, NJ: Lawrence Erlbaum Associates.

Schommer, M. A. (1998). The influence of age and education on epistemological beliefs. *British Journal of Educational Psychology, 68*, 551–562.

Schommer-Aikens, M., Bird, M., & Bakken, L. (2010). Manifestations of an epistemological belief system in preschool to grade twelve classrooms. In L. Bendixen & F. Feucht (Eds.), *Personal epistemology in the Classroom,* (pp. 31–54). New York: Cambridge University Press.

Stacey, P. S., Brownlee, J., Thorpe, K., & Class EAB016. (2005). Measuring and manipulating epistemological beliefs in early childhood pre-service teachers. *International Journal of Pedagogies and Learning, 1*, 6–17.

Thompson, G., Pilgrim, A., & Oliver, K. (2005). Self-assessment and reflective learning for first year university geography students: A simple guide or simply misguided? *Journal of Geography in Higher Education, 29*(3), 403–420.

Valanides, N., & Angeli, C. (2005). Effects of instruction on changes in epistemological beliefs. *Contemporary Educational Psychology, 30*, 314–330.

White, B. (2000). Pre-service teachers' epistemology viewed through the perspectives on problematic classroom situations. *Journal of Education for Teaching, 26*(3), 279–306.

Wilson, B. (2000). The epistemological beliefs of technical college instructors. *Journal of Adult Development, 21*, 179–186.

Yadav, A., & Koehler, M. (2007). The role of epistemological beliefs in preservice teachers' interpretation of video cases of early-grade literacy instruction. *Journal of Technology and Teacher Education, 15*(3), 335–361.

Yang, F., Chang, C., & Hsu, Y. (2008). Teacher views about constructivist instruction and personal epistemology: A national study in Taiwan. *Educational Studies, 34*(5), 527–542.

7 Personal Epistemology Change Due to Experience?

A Cross-Sectional Analysis of Preservice and Practicing Teachers

Lisa D. Bendixen and Alice J. Corkill

ABSTRACT

This chapter describes a study that examined the personal epistemologies of teachers at various stages of professional experience. Using a cross-sectional approach, four groups of teachers were identified: (1) beginning preservice teachers (n = 174); (2) completing preservice teachers (n = 146); (3) new teachers (n = 140); and (4) experienced teachers (n = 37). Statistical analyses using MANOVA found significant differences between groups in the nature of the epistemological beliefs of the teachers. Experienced teachers viewed knowledge as more complex and uncertain compared to teachers with less experience. Experienced teachers also viewed learning ability as more fixed than teachers who had spent less time in classrooms. Based on the findings, recommendations are made regarding teacher education and teacher professional development that includes raising awareness of the importance of teachers' beliefs in relation to practice. This may allow the development of a more nuanced understanding of the impact of teachers' personal epistemologies on student learning.

INTRODUCTION

The central role of teachers' personal epistemologies in learning and instruction has gained significant importance and momentum in recent theory and research. Teachers' beliefs about knowledge and knowing are now considered a major component of the classroom climate (Bendixen & Feucht, 2010). Even with this expanding literature the *development* of teachers' personal epistemologies has received very little empirical attention. Do beliefs such as these change over time based on experiences in teacher education efforts and interactions with students in the classroom? The purpose of this chapter is to describe a study that examined the personal epistemologies of teachers at various experience levels. Clarifying the personal epistemologies of teachers and how they may change over time has considerable implications for classroom practice, student learning, and teacher education programs (Brownlee & Berthelsen, 2008; Feucht & Bendixen, 2010).

Definition of Personal Epistemology

In an effort to integrate various conceptual frameworks in the field, Hofer and Pintrich (2002) define personal epistemology as four identifiable and interrelated dimensions that develop over time. The first two dimensions describe the *nature of knowledge*: (1) the certainty of knowledge is focused on the perceived stability and the strength of supporting evidence, and (2) the simplicity of knowledge describes the relative connectedness of knowledge. The remaining two dimensions relate to the *process of knowing*: (3) the justification of knowledge explains how individuals proceed to evaluate and warrant knowledge claims, and (4) the source of knowledge describes where knowledge resides, internally and/or externally.

One area of research on personal epistemology focuses on its development (e.g., Chandler, Hallett, & Sokol, 2002; King & Kitchener, 1994). Research evidence suggests that personal epistemologies develop and change over time. What isn't clear is how and when these changes take place (Bendixen & Rule, 2004). The course of epistemological development has been described as a predictable developmental sequence of epistemological growth. In early stages, individuals hold simple, dichotomous views of knowledge (i.e., absolutism), reasoning then becomes increasingly more complex and relativistic (i.e., relativism). As personal epistemology further develops, views about knowledge focus more on the evaluation and decision making among differing viewpoints (i.e., evaluativism; Kuhn & Weinstock, 2002). Some in the field have questioned the exact nature of this developmental pattern (e.g., Bendixen & Feucht, 2010, Chandler et al., 2002). Additional research is certainly needed to more fully understand if these patterns of development apply to teachers as well and the ways in which development can be optimized.

Teachers' Personal Epistemology and Its Development

A vital factor in learning and instruction is the role played by teacher's personal epistemologies (Bendixen & Feucht, 2010). Both theoretical models and empirical evidence are mounting in terms of how teachers' beliefs about knowledge and knowing impact the classroom environments they create (e.g., DeCorte, Op't Eynde, Depaepe, & Verschaffel, 2010; Feucht, 2010), their teaching practices (e.g., Daniels & Shumow, 2003; Gill, Ashton, & Algina, 2004), and subsequent student beliefs and achievement (e.g., Muis & Foy, 2010; Rule & Bendixen, 2010). Because of these important influences, understanding how teachers' beliefs may develop over time and the potential impact of teacher education/professional development on teacher belief development is crucial.

Although the direct impact of teacher education has not been a focus of research, there are a few intervention studies that offer insight into how teachers' personal epistemologies can be influenced. Howard, McGee, Scwartz, and Purcell (2000) used constructivist teaching approaches to advance the personal epistemologies of inservice teachers (i.e., beliefs about simple knowledge, quick learning, and certain knowledge) whereas Gill, Ashton, and Algina (2004) used refutational texts to promote constructivist/relativist beliefs towards mathematics education in preservice teachers (see also Brownlee, Purdie, & Boulton-Lewis, 2001; White 2000).

In terms of the impact of teacher education, Patrick and Pintrich (2001) describe how teachers' personal epistemologies could affect these intervention attempts. If teachers hold the belief that knowledge is certain, for example, they may be less amenable to new and/or contradictory ideas in teaching and learning and this position could impede conceptual change. This propensity to reject new ways of thinking about teaching has actually been shown to be a characteristic of more experienced teachers (Richardson & Placier, 2001). In terms of the simplicity of knowledge, the more teachers view knowledge as made up of discrete, unrelated, facts the more likely this might limit, "teacher-education efforts to have teachers think about models and theories of learning, motivation, and instruction in more contextualized ways" (Patrick & Pintrich, 2001, p. 136).

Purpose

At this point it is apparent that more questions than answers exist concerning how teachers' personal epistemologies may develop over time. This chapter attempts to shed light on questions such as these by describing an exploratory study focused understanding change in teachers' personal epistemologies. Using a cross-sectional research approach, we compared groups of teachers at various points in their professional career to see if beliefs about knowledge and knowing were different over time with age, level of education, and level of practical experience as influencing variables. We hypothesized that participants with relatively little instructional responsibility (preservice teachers) would have less complex personal epistemologies (e.g., that knowledge is certain and simple) than those with greater levels of instructional responsibility (practicing teachers) who would have more advanced personal epistemologies (e.g., knowledge is tentative and complex).

METHOD

To examine the development of teachers' personal epistemologies, this study uses a cross-sectional research design in which different groups of participants are studied at the same time.

Participants

There were 491 participants in the study (393 females, 98 males). These students, attending education courses at a large southwestern university, volunteered to participate or participated in a research subject pool to receive course credit. In the overall sample, the ages ranged from 18 to 61 years. The ethnicity of the participants was primarily Caucasian.

Two groups of preservice teachers were identified: (1) *Beginning preservice teachers.* These participants were at the beginning of their teacher preparation program (n = 168). There were 127 females and 41 males. The mean age was of this group was 25.44 years (SD = 7.53). (2) *Completing preservice teachers.* These participants were at the end of their teacher preparation program, having just completed their student teaching placement (n = 146). There were 123 females and 23 males. The mean age was 26.47 years (SD = 7.13).

Two groups of practicing teachers were identified: (1) *New teachers.* These participants had 5 years or less of public school teaching experience (n = 140). There were 113 females and 27 males. The mean age was 31.90 years (SD = 8.08). The mean years of teaching experience was 2.77 years. (2) *Experienced teachers.* These participants had more than 5 years of public school teaching experience (n = 37). There were 30 females and 7 males. The mean age was 37.81 years (SD = 10.08). The mean number of years of teaching experience was 12.10 years.

Materials

The 32-item *Epistemic Beliefs Inventory* (EBI) developed by Schraw, Bendixen, and Dunkle (2002) was used to assess five domain-general dimensions of epistemological beliefs. This inventory is based on Schommer's (1990) proposed five epistemological dimensions which include: (1) simple knowledge (e.g., "Too many theories just complicate things."); (2) certain knowledge (e.g., "What is true today will be true tomorrow."); (3) omniscient authority (e.g., "When someone in authority tells me to do something, I usually do it."); (4) quick learning (e.g., "If you don't learn something quickly, you will never learn it."); and (5) fixed ability (e.g., "Smart people are born that way."). All items were written using a 5-point, Likert-type scale.

In a validation study, Schraw et al. (2002) compared the EBI with Schommer's (1990) *Epistemological Questionnaire* (EQ). The EBI measured all five epistemological dimensions and explained 20% more variance with half the number of items as compared to the EQ. The EBI was also found to have better test–retest reliability than the EQ. Two of the dimensions of the EBI (i.e., quick learning and fixed ability) pertain more to beliefs about learning and ability and not epistemological beliefs specifically but because they are viewed as closely tied to teachers' personal epistemologies (Hofer & Pintrich, 2002) we decided to include them in our analyses.

A brief demographic questionnaire was also administered that asked about years of teaching experience, age, gender, and ethnicity.

Procedure

Participants completed the EBI and the demographics questionnaire in a 10- to 15-minute time period during one of their College of Education courses or as part of a departmental subject pool for course credit. Those individuals in the subject pool participate in research studies within the educational psychology department or write a summary about a research article as part of their course requirement.

RESULTS

EBI Factor Analysis and Reliability

Before addressing the main purpose of our study, the factor structure and internal consistency of the EBI was examined. We expected the factors to be correlated; therefore, a principal component factor analysis with oblique rotation was used. Because prior theoretical work (e.g., Schommer, 1990) and empirical studies (e.g., Schraw, et al., 2002) on the EBI have identified five dimensions of epistemological beliefs, we forced a 5-factor solution. After eliminating additional items that cross loaded on multiple factors in the analysis, 22 items remained. These items clustered on five interpretable factors with eigenvalues greater than 1 that accounted for 38.34% of the total sample variation and had item-to-factor loadings in excess of .30 (see Table 7.1). The 5 factors that emerged were similar to those found by Schraw et al. (2002). The 5 factors and their corresponding reliability indicators, based on Cronbach's alpha, were: (1) fixed ability (alpha = .70); (2) quick learning (alpha = .55); (3) omniscient authority (alpha = .52); (4) certain knowledge (alpha = .45); and (5) simple knowledge (alpha = .36).

Analyses of Group Differences

To examine differences between groups in teachers' personal epistemologies, scores on the 5 factors of the EBI for participants from the four defined teacher groups (i.e., beginning preservice teachers, completing preservice teachers, new teachers, and experienced teachers) were calculated. The scales scores for: Fixed Ability, Quick Learning; Omniscient Authority; Certain Knowledge, and Simple Knowledge constituted the dependent variables.

Initially, we examined the effects of age of the participants as a potential confound. A Multivariate Analysis of Covariance (MANCOVA) indicated that age was not a significant covariate, therefore, a Multivariate Analysis of Variance (MANOVA) was considered appropriate. MANOVA provides an omnibus test to examine group differences when multiple independent and multiple and related dependent variables are included in the analyses so that Type 1 errors are minimized. The means and standard deviations on the scale scores for each of the teacher groups are presented in Table 7.2. In addition to teacher group status, gender was also included as an independent variable in the MANOVA analyses.

Table 7.1 Factor Structure of the Epistemic Beliefs Inventory (EBI)

Factor	Item	Loading
Factor 1: Fixed Ability (Eigenvalue = 4.25)	How well you do in school depends on how smart you are.	.68
	Really smart students don't have to work as hard to do well in school.	.67
	Smart people are born that way.	.64
	Some people will never be smart no matter how hard they work.	.62
	Students who learn things quickly are the most successful.	.51
	Some people just have a knack for learning and others don't.	.47
Factor 2: Quick Learning (Eigenvalue = 2.64)	If you haven't understood a chapter the first time through, going back over it won't help.	.66
	If you don't learn something quickly, you won't ever learn it.	.59
	Working on a problem with no quick solution is a waste of time.	.58
	Things are simpler than most professors would have you believe.	.49
Factor 3: Omniscient Authority (Eigenvalue = 2.06)	The moral rules I live by apply to everyone.	.67
	People should always obey the law.	.56
	Absolute moral truth does *not* exist.*	.55
	When someone in authority tells me what to do, I usually do it.	.55
	Parents should teach their children all there is to know about life.	.44
Factor 4: Certain Knowledge (Eigenvalue = 1.87)	Sometimes there are no right answers to life's big problems.*	.64
	You can study something for years and still not really understand it.*	.64
	I like teachers who present several competing theories and let their students decide which is best.*	.31
	Truth means different things to different people.	.40
Factor 5: Simple Knowledge (Eigenvalue = 1.45)	Instructors should focus on facts instead of theories.	.54
	It bothers me when instructors don't tell students the answers to complicated problems.	.47
	The more you know about a topic, the more there is to know.*	.44

Note. * reversed score.

Table 7.2 Means and Standard Deviations for Teacher Groups and Gender on the 5 Factors of the EBI

Factor	Teacher Group, Gender	Mean	SD
Fixed Ability	Beginning preservice teachers	14.04	3.88
	Completing preservice teachers	13.65	3.78
	New teachers	15.21	3.43
	Experienced teachers	15.71	4.08
	Females	13.89	3.63
	Males	16.24	3.91
Quick Learning	Beginning preservice teachers	7.95	2.30
	Completing preservice teachers	7.98	1.87
	New teachers	7.78	1.75
	Experienced teachers	7.49	1.62
	Females	7.79	1.94
	Males	8.22	2.11
Omniscient Authority	Beginning preservice teachers	16.18	2.79
	Completing preservice teachers	16.15	3.15
	New teachers	15.95	3.01
	Experienced teachers	15.20	3.17
	Females	16.08	2.97
	Males	15.86	3.09
Certain Knowledge	Beginning preservice teachers	8.76	2.30
	Completing preservice teachers	8.90	2.62
	New teachers	8.19	2.14
	Experienced teachers	7.71	1.66
	Females	8.49	2.35
	Males	8.83	2.33
Simple Knowledge	Beginning preservice teachers	8.65	1.88
	Completing preservice teachers	8.82	1.79
	New teachers	8.00	1.73
	Experienced teachers	1.73	1.99
	Females	8.45	1.89
	Males	8.24	1.83

There was a significant main effect for Teacher Group, $F (15, 1347) =$ 2.64, $p < .01$ and Gender, $F (5, 447) = 6.29, p < .001$. There were no significant interactions. Univariate analyses of the significant main effect for Teacher Group yielded significant differences among groups on three dimensions of the EBI. The three dimensions that yielded significant differences were: (1) Fixed Ability, $F (3, 451) = 4.85, p < .01$; (2) Certain Knowledge, $F (3, 451) = 2.81, p < .05$; and (3) Simple Knowledge, $F (3, 451) = 4.29, p < .01$.

Univariate analyses of the significant main effect for Gender yielded significant differences on the Fixed Ability dimension, $F (1, 451) = 26.65, p <.001$) of the EBI. Male teachers had higher scores on the dimension of Fixed Ability (i.e., ability is innate) compared to the female teachers in the sample (see Table 7.2).

Post hoc Tukey comparisons of the significant main effect for the independent variable of teacher group indicated that more experienced teachers viewed ability as fixed or innate as compared to completing preservice teachers (see Table 7.3). New teachers were more likely to view ability as more fixed than both completing preservice and beginning preservice teachers. In addition, experienced teachers viewed knowledge as more uncertain or tentative than the completing preservice teachers. Finally, a trend was found in beliefs about knowledge as simple and factual versus knowledge as complex in that with more experience, teachers viewed knowledge as more complex.

Table 7.3 Tukey Pairwise Comparisons Including Means for Dimensions of the EBI and Significant Mean Differences

EBI Dimension	Teacher group (M), Gender (M)	Mean difference
Fixed Ability	B.P.S. (14.03) versus N.T. (15.21)	1.17*
	C.P.S. (13.65) versus N.T. (15.21)	1.56**
	C.P.S. (13.65) versus E.T. (15.71)	2.07*
	Females (13.89) versus Males (16.24)	2.35***
Certain Knowledge	C.P.S. (8.90) versus E.T. (7.71)	1.19*
Simple Knowledge	B.P.S. (8.65) versus N.T. (8.00)	.65*
	B.P.S. (8.65) versus E.T. (7.23)	1.42***
	C.P.S. (8.82) versus N.T. (8.00)	.82**
	C.P.S. (8.82) versus E.T. (7.23)	1.59***

Note. B.P.S. = Beginning Preservice, C.P.S. = Completing Preservice, N.T. = New Teacher, E.T. = Experienced Teacher.
*$p < .05$. **$p < .01$. ***$p < .001$

DISCUSSION

This chapter examines the personal epistemologies of teachers and provides new information concerning how personal epistemologies may change with teaching experience. These results are exploratory and preliminary and further research is needed to confirm these findings.

Certainty/Uncertainty of Knowledge

We found that preservice teachers completing their student teaching viewed knowledge as more certain than the experienced teachers in our sample. Beliefs about the certainty of knowledge are considered to be a key dimension of personal epistemology (Hofer & Pintrich, 2002; Schommer, 1990). The certainty of knowledge is often conceptualized along a continuum of knowledge ranging from unchanging to constantly evolving. Our results are consistent with Feucht and Bendixen's (2010) interview study that found that the majority of practicing elementary teachers (both in the United States and in Germany) viewed knowledge as uncertain and always changing. They also point out that viewing knowledge as uncertain does not fully complete the picture in terms of what kind or level of personal epistemology is being espoused. For example, an absolutist can be temporarily uncertain about an aspect of knowledge but believe that eventually the truth will be discovered. A multiplist, on the other hand, sees uncertainty as a given and further effort to gain certainty is unnecessary. Finally, an evaluativist acknowledges uncertainty but aims to resolve it, at least temporarily, by committing to knowledge claims within the limits of a particular context (Kuhn & Weinstock, 2002)

Because of this lack of clarity, additional information would be required (beyond the EBI's Likert scale format used in the current study) to get a clearer picture of the experiences teachers' beliefs about the uncertainty of knowledge (Feucht & Bendixen, 2010). More descriptive research methods, such as interviews and/or think-aloud protocols, could provide the opportunity to retrieve more details regarding beliefs about uncertainty, which in turn, allows for more information about the personal epistemologies of participants.

Simplicity/Complexity of Knowledge

There was a trend that more years of teaching experience made it more likely that knowledge was viewed as complex (rather than simple and factual). These results may be due, in part, to teaching experiences occurring over the years that require different interpretations of instructional practice. For instance, practicing teachers may discover first-hand that there is more than one effective approach to teaching science concepts and that this may contradict the "textbook version" of teaching science communicated in traditional education courses. Along these same lines, teaching science (or any content area) could also influence how an instructor views scientific knowledge itself. For example, scientific knowledge may be viewed as comprised of simple facts at first but after several years of "working with" the content and teaching it to others, the complexities of the material may become apparent. Teachers understanding the epistemology of the content areas they teach is an important aspect of effective learning and instruction (Bromme, Kienhues, & Stahl, 2008; Feucht, 2010; Mason, 2010).

A belief that knowledge is simple and certain could coincide with the view that teaching should then be very simple and straight forward as well. For instance, Patrick and Pintrich (2002) reported that preservice teachers felt that teaching should follow a set of sequenced tasks and that learning is more mechanical. It could also be argued that teachers who have taught for a number of years have had a chance to experience success and an increase in self-efficacy and because of this they are now more confident and open to the complexities of the classroom (Hoy & Woolfolk, 1993).

Fixed Ability/Learning as Incremental

An additional finding related to level of teacher experience pertains to beliefs about ability and learning. Experienced teachers viewed learning ability as more fixed and innate than the preservice teachers completing their program. In addition, the beginning preservice teachers and completing preservice teachers viewed learning as more incremental than the new teachers. Therefore, more classroom experience seemed to align with a fixed ability view. On some levels this was an unexpected finding and contradicts previous studies of beginning preservice teachers who were reported as viewing intelligence and ability as fixed (e.g., Dweck & Bempechat, 1983; Patrick & Pintrich, 2002) and that they believe that learning is highly dependent on motivation (i.e., if students try hard enough, everyone can succeed) lack critical knowledge about their students including individual differences (Blumefeld, Hicks, & Krajcik, 1996).

On the other hand, these findings may coincide with findings that report that practicing teachers are much more aware of student differences (Phelan & McLaughlin, 1995). In summarizing their research, Jordan, Schwartz, and McGhie-Richmond (2009) state that the more teachers view their crucial role and responsibility in student knowledge that is built incrementally (including students with special needs) the more effective their teaching practices will be (i.e., constructivist teaching).

The multi-dimensional and complex nature of teachers' personal epistemologies was quite evident in the current study and this is consistent with other theory and research (e.g., Jordan et al., 2009). How these various beliefs work together (or not) is an interesting question for future research. For example, experienced teachers may have held some advanced epistemological beliefs (knowledge is uncertain and complex) and more naïve views as well (ability is fixed). Are some beliefs more dominant in a teachers' epistemic profile than others? Would a strong belief about ability "cancel out" others views of knowledge and would this show up more in a teacher's actual practice?

Teacher Education

Awareness and the metacognitive processes of teachers' personal episte-mologies is a key. We see that teacher education could also play an impor-tant role in raising teachers' awareness and cohesiveness in their personal epistemology and, in turn, aid them in understanding how their beliefs may impact their instruction. Currently, there is encouraging evidence to support the idea that interventions can impact beliefs. For example, some experimental studies indicate that teachers writing reflective diaries and participating in more constructivist tasks can advance their beliefs towards more evaluativist views (e.g., Gill et al., 2004). In addition, more advanced graduate training has also been linked to more evaluativist beliefs in teach-ers (Schraw & Olafson, 2002). Longitudinal studies could also be done to investigate how the influence of teacher training may change beliefs over time as actual in-class teaching experience increases.

There is unsettling evidence to suggest that teacher education pro-grams have little or no impact on preservice teachers' general beliefs (e.g., Brookhart & Freeman, 1992). This may be due, in part, to a lack of focus in terms of the specific goals of teacher education. With the field of per-sonal epistemology research in mind, making the educational agenda of teacher training more explicit (e.g., the advancement of teachers' personal epistemologies) could make teacher education efforts more successful. For instance, training teachers to have more of an evaluativistic view of learn-ing and instruction should be a specific goal of teacher education (Bendixen & Feucht, 2010). How this plays out in actual teacher education curricula and practice needs to be clarified for all involved.

Whereas the results of this study are exploratory, the findings are consis-tent with the growing body of research literature that stresses the important links between constructivist views of teaching and more advanced notions of personal epistemology (i.e., viewing knowledge as complex and uncer-tain; Howard et al., 2000; Muis & Foy, 2010).

Recommendations

In this section, we highlight and support a number of suggestions that stem from the current study and from the literature on teachers' personal epis-temologies. Brownlee and Berthelsen (2008), for instance, propose a more social constructivist view of teachers' beliefs about knowledge and knowing that includes teacher education focusing on both explicit and implicit con-sideration of personal epistemologies as a vehicle for critical and reflective thinking about practice. Training to include teachers becoming more aware of their own personal epistemologies (e.g., Mason, 2010) is a must and this needs to be done systematically "as they move their beliefs from tacit to explicit and from transitional to well-developed and enacted" (Fives & Buehl, 2010, p. 508; see also Gill et al., 2004).

We also suggest more exposure to constructivist teaching practices and ontology training (Howard et al., 2000; Muis & Foy, 2010). Preservice training may be the ideal time for this as teachers' beliefs may still be forming (Schommer-Aikins, Bird, & Bakken, 2010). Finally, Jordan et al.'s (2009) suggestion for teacher training refers back to the current study's findings related to teachers' beliefs about learning:

> What may be needed in both teacher education and in-service preparation is to challenge teachers' beliefs about ability and disability as immune to learning, and their resulting beliefs about their roles and responsibilities, as well as their epistemological beliefs about the nature of knowing, knowledge and the process of acquiring knowledge. (p. 540)

In essence, the more we can solidify and communicate what role personal epistemology should play in teacher education and student learning the more this can become a reality.

REFERENCES

Bendixen, L. D., & Feucht, F. C. (2010). *Personal epistemology in the classroom: Theory, research, and implications for practice.* Cambridge, UK: Cambridge University Press.

Bendixen, L. D., & Rule, D. C. (2004). An integrative approach to personal epistemology: A guiding model. *Educational Psychologist, 39,* 69–80.

Blumefeld, P. C., Hicks, L., & Krajcik, J. S. (1996). Teaching educational psychology through instructional planning. *Educational Psychologist, 31,* 51–61.

Bromme, R., Kienhues, D., & Stahl, E. (2008). Knowledge and epistemological beliefs: An intimate but complicated relationship. In M. S. Khine (Ed.), *Knowing, knowledge and beliefs* (pp. 423–441). New York: Springer.

Brookhart, S. M., & Freeman, D. J. (1992). Characteristics of entering teacher candidates. *Review of Educational Research, 62,* 37–60.

Brownlee, J., & Berthelsen, D. (2008). Developing relational epistemology through

relational pedagogy: New ways of thinking about personal epistemology in teacher education. In M. S. Khine (Ed.), *Knowing, knowledge and beliefs* (pp. 405–422). New York: Springer.

Brownlee, J., Purdie, N., & Boulton-Lewis, G. (2001). Changing epistemological beliefs in pre-service teaching education students. *Teaching in Higher Education, 6,* 247–268.

Chandler, M. J., Hallett, D., & Sokol, B. W. (2002). Competing claims about competing knowledge claims. In B. K. Hofer & P.R. Pintrich (Eds.), *Personal epistemology: The psychology of beliefs about knowledge and knowing* (pp. 145–168). Mahwah, NJ: Lawrence Erlbaum Associates.

Daniels, D. H., & Shumow, L. (2003). Child development and classroom teaching: A review of the literature and implications for educating teachers. *Applied Developmental Psychology, 23*, 495–526.

DeCorte, E., Op't Eynde, P., Depaepe, F., & Verschaffel, L. (2010). The reflexive relation between students' mathematics-related beliefs and the mathematics classroom culture. In L. D. Bendixen & F. C. Feucht (Eds.), *Personal epistemology in the classroom: Theory, research, and implications for practice* (pp. 292–327). Cambridge, UK: Cambridge University Press.

Dweck, C., & Bempechat, J. (1983). Children's theories of intelligence: Consequences for learning. In S. Paris & G. Olson (Eds.), *Learning and motivation in the classroom* (pp. 239–256). New York: Wiley.

Feucht, F. C. (2010). Epistemic climate in elementary classrooms. In L. D. Bendixen & F. C. Feucht (Eds.), *Personal epistemology in the classroom: Theory, research, and implications for practice* (pp. 55–93). Cambridge, UK: Cambridge University Press.

Feucht, F. C., & Bendixen, L. D. (2010). Exploring similarities and differences in personal epistemologies of US and German elementary school teachers. *Cognition and Instruction, 28*(1), 39–69.

Gill, M. G., Ashton, P. T., & Algina, J. (2004). Changing preservice teachers' epistemological beliefs about teaching and learning in mathematics: An intervention study. *Contemporary Educational Psychology, 29*, 164–185.

Hofer, B. K., & Pintrich, P. R. (2002). *Personal epistemology: The psychology of beliefs about knowledge and knowing*. Mahwah, NJ: Lawrence Erlbaum Associates.

Howard, B.C., McGee, S., Schwartz, N., & Purcell, S. (2000). The experience of constructivism: Transforming teacher epistemology. *Journal of Research on Computing in Education, 32*(4), 455–465.

Hoy, W. K., & Woolfolk, A. E. (1993). Teachers' sense of self-efficacy and the organizational health of schools. *Elementary School Journal, 93*, 355–372.

Jordan, A., Schwartz, E., & McGhie-Richmond, D. (2009). Preparing teachers for inclusive classrooms. *Teaching and Teacher Education, 25*, 535–542.

King, P. M., & Kitchener, K. S. (1994). *Developing reflective judgment*. San Francisco: Jossey-Bass.

Kuhn, D., & Weinstock, M. (2002). What is epistemological thinking and why does it matter? In B. K. Hofer & P. R. Pintrich (Eds.), *Personal epistemology: The psychology of beliefs about knowledge and knowing* (pp. 121–144). Mahwah, NJ: Lawrence Erlbaum Associates.

Mason, L. (2010). Beliefs about knowledge and revision of knowledge: On the importance of epistemic beliefs for intentional conceptual change in elementary and middle school students. In L. D. Bendixen & F. C. Feucht (Eds.), *Personal epistemology in the classroom: Theory, research, and implications for practice* (pp. 258–291). Cambridge, UK: Cambridge University Press.

Muis, K. R., & Foy, M. J. (2010). The effects of teachers' beliefs on elementary students' beliefs, motivation, and achievement in mathematics. In L. D. Bendixen & F. C. Feucht (Eds.), *Personal epistemology in the classroom: Theory, research, and implications for practice* (pp. 435–469). Cambridge, UK: Cambridge University Press.

Patrick, H., & Pintrich, P. R. (2001). Conceptual change in teachers' intuitive conceptions of learning, motivation, and instructions: The role of motivational and epistemological beliefs. In B. Torf & R. Sternberg (Eds.), *Understanding and teaching the intuitive mind* (pp. 117–143). Mahwah, NJ: Lawrence Erlbaum Associates.

Phelan, A. M., & McLaughlin, H. J. (1995). Educational discourses, the nature of the child, and the practice of new teachers. *Journal of Teacher Education, 46*, 165–174.

Richardson, V., & Placier, P. (2001). Teacher change. In V. Richardson (Ed.), *Handbook of research on teaching* (pp. 905–947). Washington, DC: American Educational Research Association.

Rule, D. C., & Bendixen, L. D. (2010). The integrative model of personal epistemology development: Theoretical underpinnings and implications for education. In L. D. Bendixen & F. C. Feucht (Eds.), *Personal epistemology in the classroom: Theory, research, and implications for practice* (pp. 94–123). Cambridge, UK: Cambridge University Press.

Schommer, M. (1990). Effects of beliefs about the nature of knowledge on comprehension. *Journal of Educational Psychology, 82,* 498–504.

Schommer-Aikins, M., Bird, M., & Bakken, M. (2010). Manifestations of an epistemological belief system in preschool to grade twelve classrooms. In L. D. Bendixen & F. C. Feucht (Eds.), *Personal epistemology in the classroom: Theory, research, and implications for practice* (pp. 31–54). Cambridge, UK: Cambridge University Press.

Schraw, G., Bendixen, L. D., & Dunkle, M. E. (2002). Development and validation of the Epistemic Belief Inventory (EBI). In B. K. Hofer & P. R. Pintrich (Eds.), *Personal epistemology: The psychology of beliefs about knowledge and knowing* (pp. 261–275). Mahwah, NJ: Lawrence Erlbaum Associates.

Schraw, G., & Olafson, L. (2002). Teachers' epistemological worldviews and educational practices. *Issues in Education, 8(2),* 99–148.

White, B. C. (2000). Pre-service teachers' epistemology viewed through perspectives on problematic classroom situations. *Journal of Education for Teaching, 26,* 279–305.

8 One Preservice Teacher's Developing Personal Epistemology about Teaching and the Explicit Connection of Those Beliefs to Future Practice

Helenrose Fives

ABSTRACT

This case study provides an examination of one preservice teacher's (Hope) evolving personal epistemology during the first semester of a two-semester field-based alternative certification program in relation to her planned teaching activities. Findings indicate that Hope's personal epistemology about the nature of her content area and the field of teaching served as both a filter for interpreting new information and as a guide for unit and lesson planning. Further, it seems that inconsistencies among Hope's espoused beliefs and intended practices may be related to both her developing personal epistemology and the organization of the program. Implications for practice based on these findings include the need for teacher educators to (1) explore students' beliefs, and (2) recognize personal epistemology as a developing rather than static belief system.

BACKGROUND

Researchers have begun to closely examine the role of teachers' personal epistemologies in relation to teaching practice and the process of learning to teach (e.g., Brownlee, 2004; Olafson & Schraw, 2010). Personal epistemology refers to the domain-specific or general multidimensional beliefs that individuals hold about the nature of knowledge (e.g., Buehl & Alexander, 2001). Dimensions of these beliefs refer to the source (where does knowledge come from?); stability (does knowledge change?); structure (is knowledge isolated and simple or integrated and complex?); and justification of knowledge (what "counts" as knowledge; e.g., Buehl, Alexander, & Murphy, 2002; Hofer & Pintrich, 1997).

Growing interest in teachers' personal epistemologies has led to a variety of avenues for investigation (see Yadav, Herron, & Samarapungavan, this volume). For instance, Olafson and Schraw (2010) have argued that teachers' worldviews or ontologies (which may include some epistemic perspectives) are more fruitful areas for explication of teaching practices than personal epistemologies alone. Muis and Foy (2010) focused on teachers' domain-specific personal epistemologies and found that teachers' beliefs about mathematics as integrated, negatively predicted students' beliefs about mathematics as simple and positively predicted student achievement. My colleague, M. Buehl, and I have framed teachers' knowledge as a domain and have attempted to understand the nature of beliefs teachers hold about knowledge of teaching (Fives & Buehl, 2010). These are just a few of the varied perspectives that have been used to examine teachers' personal epistemologies and each has informed the field in meaningful ways. However, what remains unclear is how beliefs about knowledge emerge during the process of learning to teach, which belief dimensions become most salient, and what role, if any, do they play in facilitating or hindering the construction of meaning about teaching practices?

One Context for Learning to Teach

Schools in high need areas (typically urban and rural schools) face additional challenges in recruiting and retaining teachers. In communities where poverty levels are high and student achievement levels are critically low, teacher turnover and retention are of constant concern (Ingersoll, 2001). Thus, in the United States the trend to employ Alternative Certification (AC) programs designed to recruit and prepare new teachers has increased dramatically within the last two decades (NCEI, 2005). These programs tend to emphasize the need for domain expertise and attract many future teachers to secondary school settings.

The existing domain expertise of these future teachers is often assumed in AC programs, a prerequisite for admission is typically a degree in a major content area (e.g., mathematics, science, literature, etc.). These programs are designed to provide future secondary teachers the "education" content needed for successful teaching. This provides an interesting backdrop for the examination of preservice teachers' personal epistemologies as they intersect across their academic domains of "expertise" and the domain of pedagogy.

PRESENT INVESTIGATION

A descriptive case study methodology (Yin, 1993) informed by the strategies of naturalistic inquiry (Lincoln & Guba, 1985) was used to investigate one preservice teacher's evolving personal epistemology regarding the nature of teaching in an interdisciplinary AC program. It also examined how this preservice teacher sought to make meaning among her beliefs, the course material, and her future practice. Specifically, the study addressed the following research questions:

1. How does this preservice teacher's knowledge of and beliefs about teaching change during one semester of intensive field-based course work?
2. What learning experiences or events seemed most salient in exposing and challenging this preservice teacher's personal epistemology?
3. How did this preservice teacher's personal epistemology influence her ability to learn and apply her philosophy of teaching to proposed pedagogical activities?

Participant and Setting

Hope was a 23-year-old White woman who had recently graduated with honors in English from a large southwestern university. Following graduation she applied and was accepted to ProjectREAL (Recruiting Educators through Alternative Licensure), an interdisciplinary Alternative Certification cohort program funded by the US Department of Education's *Transition to Teaching* grant program that would enable her to become certified to teach English.

ProjectREAL allowed students to complete their course work and student teaching in one academic year. In addition to a content area bachelor's degree teacher candidates were required to complete five education courses (i.e., educational psychology, reading in the content areas, teaching for diversity, curriculum, and teaching methods) to become eligible for certification in the state. The program was situated in two Professional Development High Schools identified as high need. Students spent 2 days a week at each high school. All university courses were taught onsite at the two schools and students were given ample opportunity to observe course content in practice through their daily classroom observations. For a detailed explanation of the program and course work see Myers, McMillan, Price, Anderson, and Fives (2007).

Data Sources

The case is bounded by the single semester during which Hope participated in the coursework portion of her teacher preparation program and the written documents developed by Hope as part of that coursework. These written documents provided multiple data sources for analysis in this study and included a weekly informal journal, four in-class prospectus papers, and Hope's final portfolio. The portfolio included a statement of teaching philosophy, a philosophy Maxim-Artifact Matrix, and supporting artifacts that demonstrated how she planned to put her philosophy into practice (e.g., scope and sequence, unit plan, lesson plans). The Maxim-Artifact Matrix required students to explicate the core ideas of their philosophy— their maxims, and map out how artifacts (e.g., sample lesson plans, assessments) reflected these maxims in practice. Included in this matrix was a brief (1–2 sentences) explanation of how each artifact reflected each maxim. Thus, through the compilation of the portfolio this preservice teacher was able to make explicit her beliefs about teaching, learning, assessment, and motivation and to offer specific examples of how those beliefs influenced her future practice.

Data Analysis

Data were analyzed through a multi-step process reminiscent of Strauss and Corbin's (1998) content analysis. First, I engaged in an initial reading of all the data looking for initial identification of meaningful categories, insights into the research questions, and potential codes. Through this process I gathered reflective notes on the data and possible interpretations. Second, I coded each meaningful "chunk" of data using terms reflective of the content. Data chunks could be as long as a page of text or as short as a sentence, these chunks were reflective of meaningful constructs related to Hope's personal epistemology. Some codes used included "knowledge claim," "structure," and "expansion/deepening." During the coding process I noticed shifts in Hope's statements over time and made reflective notes. This led to the third step in this data analysis where I specifically looked for emergent themes that spanned both the chunks of coded data and the timeline of the study. Fourth, I examined the emergent themes in light of the research questions to identify data relevant to the goals of this study. I used active formal memoing throughout this these steps to maintain a record of my insights and interpretations (Birks, Chapman, & Francis, 2008).

Establishing Trustworthiness

Lincoln and Guba (1985) identified criteria to establish trustworthiness of qualitative research. These criteria include issues of credibility, transferability, and dependability. Credibility refers to the degree to which the findings presented are reflective of the data and is assured in this investigation through a number of techniques: Prolonged engagement, multiple data sources, think descriptions, and comparisons to previous work. Transferability of these findings must be determined by the reader who is deeply aware of his/her context of practice. In this respect I am responsible for providing a thick description of the data and the experience such that the reader can make informed decisions regarding the transferability of these findings. Dependability refers to the degree to which consistent systematized methods were employed during data analysis. The description of my data analysis offered above indicates the dependability of this work.

In interpretive research it is important to identify the researcher's perspective and beliefs as these beliefs influence the credibility of data analysis. I approached these data from a constructivist perspective wherein I recognize that multiple interpretations exist for any phenomenon and that my own interpretations are influenced by my beliefs about the nature of knowledge and teaching (Creswell & Miller, 2000). Further, I approached the data with specific research questions in mind and with the goal of understanding if and how Hope's personal epistemology was evidenced in these data. In analyzing these data my full knowledge of the personal epistemology field was employed. It is important to note that the findings discussed in this chapter reflect my interpretation of Hope's beliefs and experiences and that these interpretations may not be how Hope or others would describe the same data (Simon & Tzur, 1999).

FINDINGS AND DISCUSSION

The analysis of these data led to four emergent themes. The first describes how Hope's beliefs were deepened over the course of the semester and provides the reader with a profile of Hope's philosophy of education. The second describes how specific learning experiences led Hope to meaningful revelations about teaching and how these revelations seem to expose some aspects of Hope's personal epistemology. The third describes how Hope's beliefs about the nature of knowledge may have served as filters for her interpretations of learning experiences and guides for her planning activities. The final theme suggests that some of the inconsistencies between Hope's espoused beliefs and practice might be best understood in terms of competing epistemological perspectives.

Changes in Depth of Understanding

The nature of belief change needs to be considered beyond the development of alternative perspectives (e.g., for or against constructivism) to include more fine-grained analysis of belief evolution that includes the deepening of existing beliefs. This is particularly relevant to the study of personal epistemology development in teachers. Current developmental models of personal epistemology focus on stage-like shifts from more naïve to sophisticated beliefs (e.g., Bendixen & Rule, 2004; Brownlee, 2004) which provide a big-picture perspective on change. What these models typically miss is an explication of *how* small additive shifts in personal epistemologies are shaped and built upon existing belief structures. Findings provided here emphasize Hope's tendency to develop greater depth in her understanding of the material rather than to actually change her beliefs from one perspective to another. As is seen in the literature on conceptual change massive restructuring of knowledge is rare (Chinn & Brewer, 1993). The same was found with this preservice teacher. Rather than completely restructuring her beliefs about how students learn or the role of assessment she instead refined those beliefs by sanding away misconceptions and adding meaningful supports through explicit experiences.

In the 2nd week of the semester, students read a chapter that reviewed six philosophies of education, perennialism, progressivism, essentialism, existentialism, reconstructivism, and behaviorism (Parkay & Hardcastle, 1990). In class students worked cooperatively with this material to apply the perspective of each theory to a series of school level dilemmas. The following class session students were given 15 minutes to write a philosophy prospectus paper in class. They were asked to "Create a statement of philosophy of education that addresses these questions: What is your educational philosophy, how has it been informed by our reading and class discussion? How will these beliefs influence your teaching?" This assignment was revisited at the end of the semester when students were required to integrate the content across the five certification courses into a personal prospectus on education.

A close examination of Hope's written responses to these tasks illustrates how her thinking and espoused beliefs about the nature and purpose of education became more refined and deepened rather than changed in their core tenets. The conclusion of her initial essay demonstrated that she embraced parts of the six philosophies and borrowed from each some key idea that she felt reflected her personal beliefs.

> It looks like, at this point, I am primarily an essentialist who agrees with the idea of critical thinking in perennialism and the need to decide one's own purpose such as existentialists think. I also believe that modifying behavior is important, such as behaviorists think, and I do believe it's important to go along with reconstructivists in incorporating the community into the classroom. However, I am primarily an essentialist. (Paragraph 6, Philosophy Prospectus Paper, 1/26)

It is important to note Hope's interpretation of essentialism at this time. In the same paper she stated "I agree quite a bit with essentialism—I do believe that schooling should be practical and applicable to life, and that the core skills should be reading, writing, and speaking."

Although Hope borrowed across several philosophies, she had some core ideas that were uniquely hers: Critical thinking and connecting school to life. This initial essay revealed both core beliefs in Hope's perspective as well as a limitation in her understanding of the breadth of the philosophies and the fuzzy boundaries between them. Thus, she seemed to believe that knowledge of teaching philosophies was well-structured and included discrete independent claims that could be accepted or rejected and shaped into her own amalgamation of ideas (see previous quote).

At the end of the semester Hope discussed her philosophy of education more concisely and drew heavily from Vygotsky's socio-cultural theory and reconstructivism to describe her beliefs. These ideas were illustrated in Hope's Maxim-Artifact Matrix. For example, she emphasized the importance of critical thinking in her third and fifth maxims and connected critical thinking to both how it should be taught (via teacher modeling) and the importance of her content area (English) as a conduit for learners to use and experience this type of engagement.

Hope also maintained her perspective on the nature of the curriculum. In her first philosophy paper she stated "I probably disagree with progressivism the most. I do not think curriculum should start with the child. I believe curriculum should start with the subject matter and then be made relevant to each child's life if possible" (Paragraph 2, Philosophy Prospectus Paper, 1/26). At the end of the semester Hope placed a great deal of emphasis on connecting what is learned in school to real life experiences. In maxim four Hope articulated the belief that "instruction should begin with materials that are relevant to and reflective of the students' cultures." Whereas Hope later emphasized connecting content to the child she did not give up the central role of her content to the pure interests of the learner. Instead, she solidified her beliefs and reached a compromise. At the end of the semester she stated that education should be "augmented by authentic life experiences" and that there are a "myriad of ways to make these grand ideas relevant to the daily lives of my students" (Philosophy of Education, p. 8). Thus, we can see that whereas Hope may have narrowed her theoretical base and refined her language she did not give up the core ideas evident in her initial paper that included the importance of critical thinking and connecting school to life. Rather, these beliefs were in many ways deepened over the course of the semester.

Dooley (2008), in a case study of 8 AC beginning literacy teachers, reported that change occurred for some teachers in relation to some topics, and that when conceptual change occurred it led to a "broadening of ideas" (p. 67). Dooley (2008) argued that her participants developed more expansive and inclusive perspectives about the nature of literacy (e.g., what counts as literacy) and multiculturalism (e.g., culture is more than race). Further, she drew from Alexander's (1998) theoretical contribution of *microtransformations* to conceptual change to better explain the ongoing process experienced by the beginning teachers in the study. Microtransformations were posited as mini conceptual changes that occur over time that eventually build into a larger shift in understanding (Alexander, 1998). In the present study, Hope's deepening personal epistemology may be explained by this same phenomenon. Hope's perspective on education shifted and was refined over the course of the semester in a series of microtransformations. Moreover, it may be that these shifts occurred somewhat independently across belief dimensions, which might explain some of the inconsistencies among her espoused beliefs and intended practice.

Revelations in Learning to Teach Expose Underlying Personal Epistemology

It was evident from Hope's weekly journal reflections that the most salient learning experiences occurred during her classroom observations and that these revelations seemed to be filtered through the lens of her implicit personal epistemology about pedagogy. Here I describe one example evidenced from the data. This example is based on her dual observation sites and hints at Hope's underlying belief in, or preference for, structure in learning experiences that may be reflective of a belief in knowledge as well-structured. This example also demonstrates the beginnings of Hope's tension between more traditional teaching practices typified by well-structured lessons, content, and teacher-direction, and the more constructivist approaches advocated in her courses that emphasized student-centered instruction, authentic experiences, and collaboration.

Multidimensional models of personal epistemology (e.g., Schommer, 1990; Buehl et al., 2002) espouse that one dimension of knowledge beliefs reflects beliefs about the structure of knowledge. In this dimension, beliefs range from the perspective that knowledge can be described as well-structured with clear organizing systems and little ambiguity or ill-structured reflecting more organic and interrelated ideas that can be conceptualized in a variety of ways (Buehl et al., 2002; Schommer, 1990).

During the construction of the ProjectREAL program one of the goals in the curriculum design was to utilize the Professional Development School (PDS) model and expand the students' experiences to two sites (Myers et al., 2007). The high schools selected were both recognized as "high need" based on student socio-economic status. The first school, *Traditional High*, was an established PDS with the university. The second school, *New High,* became a PDS through this program. Despite the identification of both schools as high need there were several differences between the two contexts. Traditional High was the oldest high school in the city, it boasted an international baccalaureate program, and had a strong principal and administrative staff. New High was a relatively newer school in the district, it offered magnet courses in law and medicine, and had suffered the loss of a much loved principal who was replaced by a succession of principals and administrators that led to a sense of inconsistency and confusion.

Hope spent two mornings a week in each school in specific English classes. Her reflections revealed a comparison of the classroom experiences across the two schools and an attempt to understand the underlying processes that led to or stifled learning. At the end of the 3rd week of observations/classes Hope wrote:

> It's remarkable how different the two schools are. At Traditional High, the classes are highly structured and perhaps not as "best practices" based as you might want, but the teachers seem happier and more in control of their environments. Both my teachers at New High have a wartorn look about them. Although it seems that their classes are more "best practice" based, my teachers appear to be exhausted and beat down, and the students don't seem to be retaining as much information. . . . Perhaps there's not anymore motivation at Traditional High than at New High,

but maybe since there is more order, there is at least the possibility of
a higher level interaction. At New High there is no order . . . and even
those that wanted to learn are being stifled. (Journal, 2/21)

This entry exposes some of the tension Hope seemed to experience throughout the semester as she attempted to manage her existing beliefs about teaching, based on prior experiences and the classroom observations, with the
content she was presented in the AC courses. The AC courses emphasized
a constructivist perspective of knowledge, learning, and teaching. Moreover, in the methods course associated with the program the students were
expressly taught *Best Practice Principles* (e.g., education should be: student
centered, authentic, collaborative; Zemelman, Daniels, & Hyde, 1998) and
were required to incorporate them into their final lesson plans and portfolio.
As noted in the previous section, Hope had, early in the semester, articulated
a belief that education should be curriculum-focused not student-centered
and that structure was imperative to learning (a claim that repeats through
the data both in reference to her own learning and her expectations for teaching). The opportunity to observe at two schools and spend large chunks of
time (at least 1.5 hours a day) in these classrooms provided Hope an opportunity to look for the types of teaching advocated in her courses and compare
those practices with real classroom experiences.

This journal entry also seems to reveal a microtransformation that by
the end of the semester became a meaningful shift. Here, Hope described
a tension between the two approaches (order and best practices) with the
highly ordered "Traditional High" seeming to be superior, because students
there were, at least, learning. At the end of the semester Hope emphasized
in her final portfolio a need for order and structure in her classes while
still incorporating several best practice or constructivist principles. For
example, in her Maxim-Artifact Matrix she indicated that she will start
each class session with a "Daily Oral Lesson" (DOL). Her explanation for
this choice was "When each class starts with a DOL, challenging material
is encountered both individually and collaboratively, and a consistent, daily
routine is established" (Maxim-Artifact Matrix, No. 4). Thus, by the end
of the semester she seemed to blend a core component of her beliefs about
teaching and learning (need for structure) with the constructivist principals
espoused in her coursework. Moreover, she did this without having a "per-
fect" model of such practices from which to draw.

Another example that provided evidence of an underlying personal epistemology that viewed knowledge as well-structured is revealed in the lesson materials and learning objectives articulated in her unit and lesson
plans. Here it seems that her understanding of content knowledge was particularly well-structured and somewhat impervious to integration across
or within domains. For instance, she provided a detailed plan for a unit
on Arthurian Legends and offered an example of a "concept web" to illustrate the content in the unit. Hope attempted to use a concept mapping

technique which should have allowed for her to illustrate the interconnectedness of the content in the unit (e.g., Novak, 1990); however her "web" was actually a linear outline of the content that circled around the page in a unidirectional path that could easily have followed a traditional outline format. There were no explicit links across topics within this web or to other bodies of knowledge (within the domain of English literature or to other fields of study).

Personal epistemology is understood to include multidimensional beliefs reflective of the source, structure, certainty, and justification of knowledge (Hofer & Pintrich, 1997). In the analysis of Hope's data issues surrounding the structure of knowledge were readily apparent and emerged as a meaningful theme. However, the other dimensions of personal epistemology did not emerge from the data, nor was there substantial evidence of them in the data when I reviewed for these dimensions specifically. The lack of evidence regarding these dimensions may be due to the limited nature of these data. The journals, papers, and portfolio documents did not expressly ask or evoke issues related to where knowledge comes from, how certain it is, or how it is justified. Alternatively, it may be that, for Hope, beliefs about the structure of knowledge were most frequently accessed and questioned during the semester and therefore became evident across her writings.

Personal Epistemology as Filter and Guide

Theorists in the field of teachers' beliefs have posited that beliefs can serve as either (or both) filters or guides (see: Pajares, 1992; Fives & Buehl, under review). Fives and Buehl (under review) offered a theoretical premise for how teachers' beliefs might serve as mechanisms for filtering new interpretations and guidance for intended action. When beliefs function as a filter they influence how individuals understand and attend to new information and life experiences (e.g., Feiman-Nemser, 2001; Nisbett & Ross, 1980). When beliefs function as a guide, beliefs are thought to influence teachers' outward actions, their decision making, self-regulation and intended practices. In our work we theorized that "beliefs about the structure of teaching knowledge" as simple or complex might serve as filters for interpreting experiences and therefore "may affect how and to what extent new information is elaborated on and connected to prior knowledge" (Fives & Buehl, 2010, p. 476). These same beliefs may also guide practice by providing an impetus for teachers to engage in particular teaching and learning behaviors. An examination of the data gathered from Hope gives some examples of these mechanisms at work.

The evidence here suggests that Hope's beliefs about "structure" reflected an underlying epistemic premise and that this belief served as both filter and guide during this semester. This filter-guide role of beliefs can be observed in how Hope came to understand the notion of "student-centered" instructional activities which she repeatedly advocated in her final portfolio project. Recall that in her first prospectus paper Hope wrote "I do not think the curriculum should start with the child" (Paragraph 2, Philosophy Prospectus, 1/24). She suggested that the curriculum should be made relevant to the learner, "if possible." This emphasis on a well-structured domain of knowledge which exists beyond the individual was prevalent in Hope's beliefs at the beginning of the semester. This belief was then used to filter new information as she was exposed to ideas from the course work, specifically, the conception of "student-centered" instruction.

The methods course in the AC program emphasized the works of Fried (2005) and Zemelman and colleagues (1998). These authors advocated the use of student-centered instruction and defined it as (1) classroom activities wherein "knowledge and meaning have not been predetermined by teacher or textbook, but instead will emerge from their [the students'] *own* efforts, guided and structured by their teacher" (Fried, 2005; p. 5); and (2) starting investigations into the content from the students' questions—which should take precedence over the content matter itself (Zemelman et al., 1998).

In contrast, Hope's lesson and unit plans depicted activities that require a great deal of student *involvement* (e.g., discussion, jigsaw cooperative lessons, team jeopardy games) which she refered to as "student-centered." Thus, it seems that she associated the conception of "student-centered" to mean student involvement and collaboration during learning activities. In this way her beliefs about well-structured knowledge for students to learn could remain intact and in agreement with the "best practice" of student-centered instruction. Her beliefs seem to have filtered her interpretation of the content into a perspective that was coherent within her personal epistemology.

This filtering role was also evident in the types of teacher behaviors she attended to during her classroom observations. For instance, the journal excerpt comparing the two school sites (discussed previously) suggests that her own beliefs about well-structured knowledge may have influenced the elements of instruction that she observed. In this entry, she focused on the structure of the lesson and issues of management, rather than the content investigated, motivational approaches, or the potential ability for students to learn in less structured experiences.

Her beliefs about the nature of knowledge also seemed to guide her instructional decision making and planning activities. As described above, her unit plan "knowledge web" demonstrated a hierarchical, unidirectional conception of knowledge about Arthurian Legends. This may have been the result of her underlying belief in knowledge as well-structured and this belief may have been guiding her instructional practice.

Personal Epistemology in Development: Differences in Espoused Beliefs and Future Teaching Activities

It seems that the underlying issue that might explain the lack of agreement between Hope's espoused beliefs about knowledge and her proposed teaching activities may be the existence of competing epistemologies, either within Hope herself or between Hope and the course requirements. Specifically, Hope's portfolio statement and explanations of her teaching activities claim to employ what are essentially constructivist teaching principles. However, a close study of the actual unit/lesson objectives and planned activities reveal traditional teaching practices that are teacher-driven and content focused. For instance, Hope's learning objectives reflected a static nature of knowledge and emphasized lower levels of cognition as characterized by Bloom's taxonomy (e.g., knowing, understanding, application; Anderson, Krathwohl, & Bloom, 2001). It seems that there may be some epistemological premises to reaching higher levels of Bloom's taxonomy. Specifically, for learners to engage in synthesis and evaluation their needs to be some recognition that the students *can* be a source of knowledge construction and that the field of study is well-integrated such that students can make meaningful and unique connections. Although, Hope claimed to emphasize these learning goals, her actual lessons and objectives did not permit this. The reason for this tension may be this underlying belief about the domain as well-structured and comprised of discrete items of information that must be transferred to students and then practiced. Additionally, it may be that the espoused constructivist stance reflected what she felt were the "correct" responses for these assignments.

There seems to be a tension between Hope's understanding of the nature of constructivist teaching practices and her own beliefs about the nature of teaching. Specifically, she does not fully accept the epistemological stance that is inherent in constructivism and as a result the teaching techniques associated with this stance are re-configured to fit within her existing belief system (recall the treatment of "student-centered" described previously). Chinn and Brewer (1993) might refer to this response as a *reinterpretation* of the data to fit within her existing schema. Thus, in Hope's case the application of constructivist principles of practice become diluted and particular strategies were misidentified in her description of her work.

CONCLUSIONS

What does Hope's Story Tell us about Teacher Education?

Hope reminds teacher educators of the importance of existing beliefs. It seems clear that teacher educators and programs need to address the epistemological perspectives of *both* their students and the theories advocated. In this case, Hope remained steadfast in some of her beliefs. Her course work, observational, and classroom experiences served to deepen her existing beliefs and perspectives. Teacher educators should be on the lookout for instances when educational theory or practice is re-interpreted by future teachers to fit within an unchanged belief system.

Teacher educators need to recognize that at any point in time a teacher's personal epistemology may include beliefs that are *unexamined* (implicit) or *under development*. In the beginning of the semester Hope's personal epistemology regarding the nature of knowledge seemed largely unexamined. Throughout the semester as she interacted with the course material, and worked in real classrooms, it seemed that her personal epistemology was becoming explicit and that she was developing an integrated understanding of teaching practice within her belief system. Thus, the lack of cohesion evident across her work might best be considered a byproduct of initial learning experiences that teacher educators should prepare for in order to better facilitate the systematic development of these beliefs.

Hope's beliefs about teaching and the knowledge of her domain are best recognized as *under development* and as such inconsistencies can be expected as seemingly distinct bodies of content information are studied and integrated into her schema. Simon and Tzur (1999) described a similar shift in the beliefs of the preservice mathematics teachers' they worked with to develop constructivist teaching practices. Simon and Tzur (1999) found that when preparing teachers in constructivist methods the teachers first seemed to develop *perception-based* understanding of mathematics pedagogy, focusing on the need to perceive mathematics with real life examples and moving away from a traditional didactic understanding of teaching. However, these beliefs were not fully *conception-based* understandings that would reflect a deep understanding of constructivist philosophy and the ability to recognize the learner's needs. Brownlee's (2004) work has explicated four levels of personal epistemology that reveal preservice teachers beliefs about truth and the structure of knowledge. These levels reflect beliefs that move from a stance of absolute truth reception to a mixture of received and constructed truth, to reasoned truth construction. Each of these studies and the data presented here emphasize the importance of developmental shifts, large or small, that undergird personal epistemologies.

A focus for teacher education should be to consider whether or not these beliefs continue to develop into a coherent and consistent system that can guide teaching practice once new teachers enter the field. How can we prepare new teachers to sustain their own reflection on these beliefs in the face of the daily challenges of classroom life and not allow more modern practices to atrophy?

REFERENCES

Alexander, P. (1998). Positioning conceptual change within a model of domain literacy. In B. Guzzetti & C. Hynd (Eds.), *Perspectives on conceptual change: Multiple ways to understand knowing and learning in a complex world* (pp. 55–76). Mahwah, NJ: Lawrence Erlbaum Associates.

Anderson, L. W., Krathwohl, D. R., & Bloom, B. S. (2001). *A taxonomy for learning, teaching, and assessing: A revision of Bloom's taxonomy of educational objectives.* New York: Longman.

Bendixen, L. D., & Rule, D. C. (2004). An integrative approach to personal epistemology: A guiding model. *Educational Psychologist, 39,* 69–80.

Birks, M., Chapman, Y., & Francis, K. (2008). Memoing in qualitative research: Probing data and processes. *Journal of Research in Nursing, 13,* 68–75.

Brownlee, J. (2004). Teacher education students' epistemological beliefs: Developing a relational model of teaching. *Research in Education, 72,* 1–17.

Buehl, M. M., & Alexander, P. A. (2001). Beliefs about academic knowledge. *Educational Psychological Review, 13,* 385–418 (special issue).

Buehl, M. M., Alexander, P. A., & Murphy, P. K. (2002). Beliefs about schooled knowledge: Domain specific or domain general? *Contemporary Educational Psychology, 27,* 417–449.

Chinn, C. A., & Brewer, W. F. (1993). The role of anomalous data in knowledge acquisition: A theoretical framework and implications for science education. *Review of Educational Research, 61,* 1–49.

Creswell, J. W., & Miller, D. L. (2000). Determining validity in qualitative inquiry. *Theory Into Practice, 39,* 124–130.

Dooley, C. M. (2008). Multicultural literacy teacher education: Seeking micro-transformations. *Literacy Research and Instruction, 47,* 55–75.

Feiman-Namser, S. (2001). From preparation to practice: Designing a continuum to strengthen and sustain teaching. *Teacher College Record, 103,* 1013–1055.

Fives, H., & Buehl, M. (under review). Spring cleaning for the "messy" construct of teachers' beliefs: What are they? Which have been examined? What can they tell us? *APA Educational Psychology Handbook.*

Fives, H., & Buehl, M. M. (2010). Teachers' articulation of pedagogical knowledge beliefs: Conceptualizing a belief framework. In L. D. Bendixen & F. C. Haerle (Eds.), *Personal epistemology in the classroom: Theory, research, and implications for practice* (pp. 470–515). New York: Cambridge University Press.

Fried, R. L. (2005). *The game of school: Why we all play it, how it hurts kids, and what it will take to change it.* San Francisco, CA: Jossey-Bass.

Hofer, B. K., & Pintrich, P. R. (1997). The development of epistemological theories: Beliefs about knowledge and knowing and their relations to learning. *Review of Educational Research, 67,* 88–140.

Ingersoll, R. (2001). Teacher turnover and teacher shortages: An organizational analysis. *American Educational Research Journal, 38*(3), 499–534.

Lincoln, Y. S., & Guba, E. G. (1985). *Naturalistic inquiry.* Beverly Hills, CA: Sage Publishing.

Muis, K. R., & Foy, M. J. (2010). The effects of teachers' beliefs on elementary students' beliefs, motivation, and achievement in mathematics. In L. D. Bendixen & F. C. Haerle (Eds.), *Personal epistemology in the classroom: Theory, research, and implications for practice* (pp. 435–469). New York: Cambridge University Press.

Myers, S., McMillan, S., Price, P., Anderson, C., & Fives, H. (2007). Partnering with secondary schools to prepare highly qualified teachers: Alternative certification through a professional development school model. *Journal of the National Association for Alternative Certification, 2,* 18–28.

National Center for Educational Information (2005). Alternate routes to teacher certification: An Overview. Retrieved June 10, 2005 from http://www.ncei.com/alt-teacer-cert.htm

Nisbett, R. E., & Ross, L. D. (1980). *Human inference: Strategies and shortcomings of social judgment.* Englewood Cliffs, NJ: Prentice-Hall.

Novak, J. D. (1990). Concept mapping: A useful tool for science education. *Journal of Research in Science Teaching, 27*(10), 937–949.

Olafson, L., & Schraw, G. (2010). Beyond epistemology: Assessing teachers' epistemological and ontological worldviews. In L. D. Bendixen & F. C. Haerle (Eds.), *Personal epistemology in the classroom: Theory, research, and implications for practice* (pp. 516–551). New York: Cambridge University Press.

Pajares, M. F. (1992). Teacher's beliefs and educational research: Cleaning up a messy construct. *Review of Educational Research, 62,* 307–322.

Parkay, F. W., & Hardcastle, B. (1990). *Becoming a teacher: Accepting the challenge of a profession.* Needham Heights, MA: Allyn and Bacon.

Schommer, M. (1990). Effects of beliefs about the nature of knowledge on comprehension. *Journal of Educational Psychology, 82,* 498–504.

Simon, M. A., & Tzur, R. (1999). Explicating the teacher's perspective from the researchers' perspectives: Generating accounts of mathematics teachers' practice. *Journal for Research in Mathematics Education, 30*(3), 252–264.

Strauss, A., & Corbin, J. (1998). *Basics of qualitative research: Techniques and procedures for developing grounded theory* (2nd ed.). Thousand Oaks, CA: Sage Publications, Inc.

Yin, R. (1993). *Applications of case study research.* Beverly Hills, CA: Sage.

Zemelman, S., Daniels, H., & Hyde, A. (1998). *Best practice: New standards for teaching and learning in America's schools* (2nd ed.). Portsmouth, NH: Heinemann.

9 Personal Epistemologies and Pedagogy in Higher Education
Did We Really Mean to Say that to our Students?

Rose M. Marra and Betsy Palmer

ABSTRACT

In this chapter we explore the importance of the relationships between tertiary faculty pedagogical choices and students' personal epistemologies. We argue that university-level faculty need to be cognizant of not only the importance of the content of their instruction but also of how their pedagogical choices may be impacting and interacting with the personal epistemologies of the students in their classrooms. We review literature related to the impact of tertiary faculty pedagogical practices on students' personal epistemologies, how such beliefs may mediate other learning outcomes, and illustrate these ideas via two studies from the authors on how student personal epistemologies are impacted by faculty pedagogical choices in different academic domains. Implications are discussed—with a particular emphasis on tertiary faculty who prepare future teachers—for how this knowledge of the relationship between faculty's pedagogical choices and student epistemologies may guide tertiary institution faculty members' choices.

INTRODUCTION

Scholars have defined personal epistemology as the theories and beliefs that individuals hold about knowledge and knowing (Hofer & Pintrich, 1997). Beginning with William Perry's (1970) study of the development of the cognitive structures of university students, theorists and researchers of personal epistemology have alluded to the role that epistemology plays in the students' learning experiences. First studied as a desired outcome of educational experiences, more recently, scholars have also theorized and researched how the epistemological stances of students may influence students' approaches to learning and their perceptions of instructional activities (see Hofer, 2001).

Underlying these studies is an assumption that different pedagogical experiences can influence (and be influenced by) students' personal epistemologies (Hofer, 2001). As the architects of the learning experience in tertiary classrooms, university-level faculty need to be cognizant of not only the importance of the content of their instruction but also of how their pedagogical choices may be impacting and interacting with the personal epistemologies of the students in their classrooms.

It is this relationship between tertiary faculty pedagogical choices and students' personal epistemologies that we explore in this chapter. Questions that we explore include: What are the implications for how tertiary faculty teaches for students' personal epistemologies? How do students' existing personal epistemologies interact with the pedagogies they experience in their classes? And, similarly, does faculty inadvertently teach in ways that are a mismatch with students' epistemologies?

We begin this chapter with a brief review of literature related to the impact of tertiary faculty pedagogical practices on students' personal epistemologies and also how such beliefs may mediate other learning outcomes. We then describe two studies regarding how student personal epistemologies are impacted by faculty pedagogical choices in different academic domains. We conclude with a discussion of how this knowledge of the relationship between faculty's pedagogical choices and student epistemologies in different domains may guide tertiary institution faculty members' individual choices with a particular emphasis on tertiary faculty who prepare future teachers.

A variety of studies over the past 40 years have examined the intersection of university students' personal epistemologies and their experiences with teaching and learning. Hofer (2001) suggests that student epistemology may be related to learning and instruction in three separate ways. First, developing complex personal epistemologies may be seen as a desirable outcome of educational activities. Second, personal epistemologies may mediate students' abilities to achieve other academic outcomes (content, test scores). Third, students may use their personal epistemologies as one of many resources accessed in the process of context specific learning activities.

Initially, we focus our review of the literature on studies that describe instructional activities that both *intentionally* and *unintentionally* impact students' personal epistemologies. Next, we examine the ways students' personal epistemologies intersect with their learning and their approaches to instructional activities. Our review examines research at the tertiary level across a broad array of disciplinary contexts; however, because of the impact of university-level teacher preparation programs, we also address tertiary-level initiatives focused on preservice teachers at the university level.

PERSONAL EPISTEMOLOGY AS TERTIARY-LEVEL EDUCATIONAL OUTCOME

A number of research studies indicate that intentionally structured pedagogical activities can have a positive effect on university students' personal epistemologies. Early studies in the 1970s examined instructional interventions designed to advanced students along the Perry scheme of Intellectual Development. Both Knefelkamp (1974) and Widick and Simpson (1978) compared an experimental course to a control group and found that the intentional inclusion of instruction designed to enhance students' development on the Perry model produced positive results. Similarly, students in a course designed to encourage first-year students to move from dualist positions to a more relativistic stage on the Perry scheme showed substantially greater gains in intellectual development than those in the control group (Stephenson & Hunt, 1977). More recently, in an information systems course which utilized a variety of active-learning, student-centered instructional activities, Tolhurst (2007) found that students scored significantly higher from pretest to posttest on two of four scales on Hofer's domain-specific beliefs questionnaire and on 5 of 13 sub-scales on Schommer's Epistemological Beliefs Questionnaire.

Studies at the university-level conducted with preservice teachers show similar results. Hill (2000) found that preservice teachers who participated in an experimental course designed to enhance intellectual development showed significantly higher levels of personal epistemologies as measured by the Measure of Intellectual Development (MID) than those in the control group. In another study, students in an intentionally designed year-long educational psychology course which incorporated weekly reflections on their own epistemology showed significant gains in personal epistemologies in comparison to a control group who did not participate in the reflective journaling activity (Brownlee, Purdie, & Boulton-Lewis, 2001). Additionally, in a discipline-specific study, Gill, Ashton, and Algina (2004) found that an intervention designed to challenge preservice teachers' beliefs about mathematical knowledge produced greater change in implicit personal epistemologies (as measured by teaching scenarios designed to elicit their understanding of the nature of math teaching and learning) for the experimental than the control group. Taken together, these studies show that designing instruction that challenges less developed personal epistemologies (e.g., problems that have multiple "correct" answers, or confronting students with conflicting data sources) in a supported way, can in fact impact students' epistemologies.

Students' personal epistemologies may also be influenced by learning environments that are not intentionally structured to change personal epistemologies. Marra, Palmer, and Litzinger (2000) report a statistically significant impact on Perry ratings for engineering students who completed a project-focused, active-learning first-year design course. The authors concluded that the challenges inherent in a team-based, open-ended design project may provide the type of intellectual environment that stimulates students' natural progression towards more complex thinking. In a similar study of two mathematics classrooms, Hofer (1999) also found that students in a more active, collaborative classroom expressed more sophisticated personal epistemologies than those in a more traditional calculus class.

PERSONAL EPISTEMOLOGY AS MEDIATOR
TO OTHER EDUCATIONAL OUTCOMES

A larger body of research addresses how students' existing personal epistemologies may mediate their experiences in educational contexts and produce differential learning outcomes on a variety of measures. In the United States, more sophisticated personal epistemologies have been linked to higher course grades and overall grade point averages (Hofer, 2000; Kardash & Howell, 2000; Schommer, 1990). However, Zhang and Watkins (2001) found that more complex epistemology predicted achievement for a US sample but not for a sample of students from Hong Kong. More complex epistemologies have also been related to improved text comprehension (Kardash & Scholes, 1996; Kardash & Howell, 2000; Schommer, Crouse, & Rhodes, 1992; Schraw, Bendixon, & Dunkle, 2002; Mason & Boscolo, 2004), and problem-solving abilities (Nussbaum, Sinatra, & Poliquin, 2008; Wineburg, 1991). Specifically regarding problem solving, Schraw, Dunkle, and Bendixen (1995) found that students' self-reported personal epistemologies influenced their performance on ill-structured problem-solving tasks but not well-structured tasks. The researchers concluded that students' strong belief in the certainty of knowledge prevents a thorough analysis of alternative solutions, whereas beliefs in omniscient authority may limit the set of viable solutions considered to those suggested by experts.

A number of studies have linked students' personal epistemologies to their approaches to learning. Students who express a dualistic epistemology are more likely to describe a passive approach to learning than students with a more evaluativist epistemology (Lonka & Lindbloom-Ylanne, 1996). Similarly, students with less sophisticated epistemological views report using less effective study strategies (Schommer et al., 1992)—meaning, for instance, they used their time less effectively and were not effective at selecting main ideas from reading. Other researchers found that students with less sophisticated epistemological views also use less productive motivational strategies as they self-regulate their learning (Paulsen & Feldman, 1999). Muis (2007) theorized, based upon an extensive review of literature, that students' personal epistemologies and self-regulated learning processes may have a reciprocal relationship—influencing each other in different contexts and at different times.

Lastly, several researchers have described how students used epistemological resources (Hammer & Elby, 2002) or personal epistemological theories (Hofer, 2001) in particular learning contexts. For both of these theorists, personal epistemologies are seen less as unitary cognitive structures, but rather as smaller cognitive units. These are termed "resources" by Hammer and Elby (2002, p.176) which individuals can access as they make sense of a particular situation; thus the use of the term *epistemological resources*. A number of studies have described how individual students

(Hammer, 1994; Lising & Elby, 2005) or groups of students (Scherr & Hammer, 2009) make use of epistemological resources as they solve problems in physics.

In the next section of this chapter, we examine two studies from the authors that specifically address how faculty pedagogical choices may interact with students' personal epistemologies. We then summarize the implications of all of these studies on the pedagogical choices of tertiary faculty generally, and teacher education faculty in particular.

FACULTY PEDAGOGICAL CHOICES
AND PERSONAL EPISTEMOLOGIES

In order for faculty to be able to address personal epistemologies in their instruction, they need to understand how their pedagogical choices may be impacting students' personal epistemologies—intentionally and perhaps unintentionally. We now describe two studies from the authors that address how student personal epistemologies are impacted by faculty pedagogical choices. The first study, described briefly, shows how *individual* student personal epistemologies may vary greatly from one academic knowledge domain (e.g., the sciences, versus social sciences) to another, and the second study showed how faculty pedagogies may be interacting with students' personal epistemologies. Both studies provide evidence of inconsistencies in student epistemologies—one in different knowledge domains and the other between faculty pedagogies and student personal epistemologies. We will discuss how knowledge of the interaction between course instructional strategies implemented by faculty and student epistemologies can provide useful data for faculty and form the basis for strategies that could enhance tertiary faculty's ability to impact student epistemologies.

Our research for both studies on domain-specific epistemologies grew out of a larger study of the personal epistemologies of science and engineering university students (Marra et al., 2000) where the authors noted that a number of students discussing the nature of knowledge, would make a distinction between knowledge in sciences versus knowledge in contrasting domains such as the humanities or social sciences. Therefore in the first study we were examining whether this observation held true for the entire data set. Through systematic investigation using interview data from a total of 90 third- and fourth-year university students, we developed an emergent theory regarding distinct personal epistemologies in different knowledge domains grounded in data from student interviews (Palmer & Marra, 2004).

In our analysis, we found patterns of personal epistemologies that expressed a simple *dualistic* epistemology, a *multiplistic* epistemology and a more complex, *evaluativist* epistemology for two knowledge domains: Sciences and Humanities/Social Sciences. Figure 9.1 and Figure 9.2 present

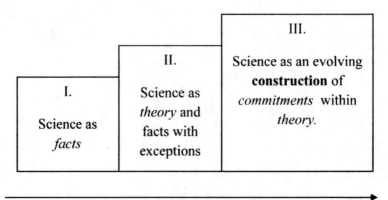

Figure 9.1   Personal epistemologies in science.

a summary of these domain-specific personal epistemologies with the least sophisticated beliefs (e.g., dualistic for that domain) labeled as Roman numeral I and the most complex as Roman numeral III (e.g., evaluativist). These findings in and of themselves are not surprising, as they complement existing research which show similar epistemological trajectories (e.g., King & Kitchener, 1994; Kuhn, 1999; Perry, 1970). What makes this study distinctive, however, is the number of students (approximately 78%) who expressed views of the nature of knowledge and knowing that are inconsistent across the two knowledge domains. Table 9.1 shows the relative epistemological categorizations for individuals.

Table 9.1 is divided into three main sections arranged from top to bottom. The top section (Science Beliefs > Social Science (SS)/Humanities Beliefs) includes the frequencies for students who evidenced personal epistemologies in science that were more advanced than their SS beliefs. The

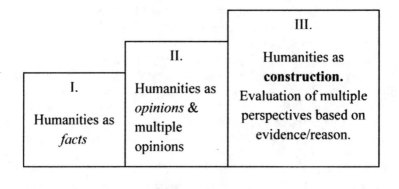

Figure 9.2   Personal epistemologies in the social sciences/humanities.

middle section is for those where their personal epistemologies in science were the same as SS beliefs and the third section is a summary of students whose personal epistemologies in SS beliefs were more advanced than their science beliefs. In each of the three sections, each row shows a combination of a science and social science epistemological belief position, then the frequency of students who evidenced that combination. For example, in the top section, there are 2 students who evidenced a Science belief II-III (fairly advanced) in combination with SS belief of I (not very advanced). Overall, the majority of the students (59% shown in the bottom section) evidenced

Table 9.1 Science/Social Science—Humanities Relative Beliefs Categorization and Frequencies

Science	SS/Humanities	N	%
Science Beliefs > SS/Humanities Beliefs			
II-III	I	2	2.44%
II-III	II	10	12.20%
II	I	1	1.22%
II	I-II	1	1.22%
III	II-III	1	1.22%
Subtotal		15	18.29%
Science Beliefs = SS/Humanities Beliefs			
I	I	1	1.22%
I-II	I-II	2	2.44%
II	II	10	12.20%
II-III	II-III	3	3.66%
III	III	2	2.44%
Subtotal		18	21.95%
Science Beliefs < SS/Humanities Beliefs			
I	I-II	1	1.22%
I	II	22	26.83%
I	II-III	6	7.32%
I-II	II	17	20.73%
I-II	II-III	1	1.22%
II	II-III	1	1.22%
II-III	III	1	1.22%
Subtotal		49	59.76%
TOTAL		82	100.00%

a more advanced set of personal epistemologies in humanities/social sciences (soft domains), whereas only 18% of the students evidenced more sophisticated (i.e., multiplistic or evaluativist) beliefs in sciences (Marra & Palmer, 2008).

Our second study arose from further examination of these data that revealed another result. Not only were individual students' epistemologies varying across domains, they were also not necessarily in alignment with the pedagogical experiences they were encountering in their classes. In other words—the traditional teacher-centered pedagogical activities that faculty chose for these students were frequently not geared to actually helping to advance student personal epistemologies. In this study we examined students' descriptions of the *pedagogical activities* they experience in science courses and the *relationship* between those perceptions and students' personal epistemologies in the sciences. Our analysis used verbatim transcripts of interviews with 30 junior and senior college students whose majors were primarily concentrated in liberal arts domain. We had already coded these students for their personal epistemologies in science (see Figure 9.1); we then coded the interviews for statements that addressed how students perceived teaching in their science courses—we called this science pedagogical perceptions. We then analyzed how these constructs aligned to determine how the pedagogies students were experiencing were related to the personal epistemologies in science.

We agreed upon the following emergent codes to describe the pedagogical activities that were salient to the students in their science classes (not necessarily all of their science classroom experiences, but the ones that stood out for them and represented their "lived experience" of science classes).

- Traditional: Teacher-centered pedagogical approaches such as lecture, student memorization of facts, or labs that follow strict procedures to produce a pre-determined result.
- Non-traditional: Student-centered instruction or activities that include student input such as class discussions and working in groups. This code also included comments on science lectures or laboratory experiences if they were "discovery based".
- Mixed: Science pedagogy using both traditional and non-traditional methods.
- Not ratable: Did not provide sufficient statements about science pedagogies.

Table 9.2 presents the intersection of students' perceptions of science pedagogy and personal epistemologies. The majority of the students expressed beliefs about the nature of scientific knowledge that was primarily dualistic in nature (Science Beliefs I and I-II). Ten of the students were coded as Science Belief I and an additional 11 students showed slightly more sophisticated beliefs at Science I-II. Three students were rated at Science Belief II; 5 students were rated at Science II-III, and 1 student was rated with Science Belief III.

Table 9.2 Perceptions of Science Pedagogy Relative to Personal Epistemologies in Science

Personal epistemologies in science (total)	Perceptions of Science Pedagogy			
	Traditional	*Mixed*	*Non-traditional*	*Not ratable*
I (10)	7			3
I-II (11)	8*	1		2
II (3)	2*	1		
II-III (5)	1*	2	2	
III (1)	1*			
Total (30)	19	4	2	5

* = disconnect between perceived pedagogy and epistemology

For science pedagogical perceptions we found that 19 of the 30 students (63%) reported perceptions of science course instruction to predominantly use traditional lecture-based approaches. The following student describes the traditional lecture setting in university-level science classrooms where a student's role is generally limited to passively listening and taking notes:

> For starters, science courses are generally held in very large symposium style lecture halls and . . . you don't expect to contribute much to learning. . . . That is why they have these recitations. So you can get together with your T.A. But even with your T.A. you are not expected to say well, no, what are your theories on erosion. You don't ask this. You are told how erosion works. You are told how the solar system works. You are told how geology works.

Only 2 students described non-traditional pedagogical experiences in science and 4 students described their experiences as a mixture of traditional and non-traditional pedagogical approaches.

The intersection of pedagogy and personal epistemologies provides faculty with interesting insights on how what we do as faculty interacts with and potentially builds upon or detracts from students' personal epistemologies. For the students with a dualistic perception of science knowledge (Science Belief I), traditional pedagogies offered no contradiction with their expectations of how science should be taught. From our data, it is impossible to know whether these students have expressed these perceptions of science pedagogy because it fits their personal epistemologies or if they have been exposed to non-traditional pedagogies that present a more complex view of science knowledge and they are unwilling or unable to adopt that more sophisticated view of science epistemology.

Another group of students also reported science pedagogy in alignment with their personal epistemologies—however these students exhibited more sophisticated personal epistemologies (beliefs I-II and above). These 6 students (4 in the "mixed" column and 2 in "non-traditional") reported non-traditional pedagogical approaches to science (mixed and non-traditional) and also described a more sophisticated epistemological view of science knowledge. The following student's comments provide strong evidence of what she experiences in science courses and describe science knowledge as evolving and pedagogical approaches that represent scientific knowledge as subject to proof:

> In science they present the evidence to back things up whereas in a humanities course they tend to say 'Well, this person thought this . . . thought that.' In science, the ideas they present they could be, well, back in this time they thought this and then they discovered this is the way it is.

Twelve students (over 1/3 of our sample), however, reported signs that their personal epistemologies about the nature of scientific knowledge were at odds with how science was presented to them in the classroom (see cells marked with asterisks in Table 9.2). These students described their experience of science teaching as less sophisticated than their own understanding of knowledge in the science domain. For example, this senior who was preparing for a medical career is clearly not convinced that the instructor knows the complete truth, even though science knowledge is presented that way in class: "You see professors who know or believe that they know exactly what they are talking about and there is no room for a discussion because this is the way it is, in the sciences."

The clearest example of this disconnect between student and instructional epistemologies was for a student rated at the highest level of science epistemology, Science Belief III, whose perception of science teaching was clearly traditional. The student succinctly comments on his experience in college level science classrooms and expresses his own awareness of the disconnection between his sophisticated science epistemology and his experiences of science teaching.

> They [science instructors] seem to think of themselves as pretty high and mighty and so everything they teach, they teach as absolute truth. In reality, it is based on what we know right now.

This illustrates how a student with sophisticated personal epistemology in the sciences may come to dismiss a faculty member's lesson content when the epistemological messages of the instruction are clearly misaligned with the student's personal epistemologies.

To summarize this second study, our results show that students as a group evidence a range of both personal epistemologies in the sciences *and* describe pedagogical experiences in the science that vary and range from traditional teacher-centered experiences to non-traditional ones where students are actively involved in learning. When we examine the intersection between *individual* students' personal epistemologies and their science pedagogical experiences we showed that a large portion of our sample experienced a disconnect between these factors. The importance of this disconnect is that students with advanced epistemological science beliefs who perceive traditional science pedagogies that communicate less sophisticated epistemologies may come to dismiss a faculty member's lesson content when there exists this misalignment.

DISCUSSION

Implications for Tertiary Faculty and Tertiary Teacher Education Faculty

In this chapter we have addressed how students' personal epistemologies can impact their learning, how faculty's pedagogical choices can impact students' personal epistemologies and how those beliefs may not be consistent across knowledge domains. The authors' studies revealed how there may be inconsistencies between faculty's pedagogical choices and students' personal epistemologies. We conclude with a discussion of the relevance of the findings from our studies taken together with prior literature on how this knowledge of the relationship between faculty pedagogical choices and student epistemologies may guide tertiary institution faculty members' individual pedagogical choices with an emphasis on those preparing pre-service teachers.

Our first study provided evidence of how *individual* student personal epistemologies can vary from one knowledge domain to another; we examined this in the context of the social science and science domains and found that only about 21% of the sample showed "equal" epistemologies in both domains and that the majority of students evidenced more sophisticated beliefs in the humanities. We hypothesize that students may more easily make the leap from dualistic to multiplistic epistemology in the social sciences and humanities because tertiary faculty in these domains often focus on how theories can explain social phenomenon. Supporting this hypothesis, results from Jehng, Johnson, and Anderson (1993) and Paulsen and Feldman (1999) both found that students in the soft fields (which are arguably would include the social sciences and the humanities) make the leap to an understanding of knowledge as non-static more readily than do students in "hard" science fields.

Class discussions and debates, writing essays, hearing an instructor's view that differs from or expands on what the text says, and assessment systems (e.g., writing research papers) are all pedagogical activities commonly used by tertiary faculty in the social science domain and all have the possibility of encouraging independent thinking that may lead students to believe that these disciplines are composed of many opinions (Perry, 1970). From this quotation about a humanities instructor, we see students' epistemological development can be encouraged by thoughtful instructional approaches.

> The study of two opposing views and how they interact with each other. And she [the instructor] had her own opinion. And she said the first day . . . 'this is my opinion. I'm telling you right now just so you know'.

The second study showed evidence of the potential mismatch between faculty's instructional activities and the personal epistemologies students bring into classrooms. Although not always the case, we believe it is important for faculty to realize that students may be coming into their courses with quite sophisticated beliefs about the nature of knowledge. We would hope that this news would be refreshing to the higher education community and additionally that such awareness can be cause for faculty to reconsider the types of instructional activities they choose and deliver. Further, faculty should be aware, if indeed students do hold these more sophisticated beliefs, that they may very well be experiencing the "disconnect" between their own beliefs and the implied epistemological stances of the pedagogies they are experiencing.

Certainly we *want* students to experience some types of "disconnects" in college classrooms. For instance a student who entered a science classroom holding a belief in creationism may experience a disconnect when he encounters evidence of the theory of evolution. This type of disconnect can lead to intellectual development. However, the disconnect the students in our sample experienced—a disconnect between the actual nature of knowledge and the pedagogies they experienced—we argue is more fundamental and may suppress intellectual development.

Essentially, we argue that faculty should strongly consider the epistemological implications of their pedagogical choices. We support this stance with evidence from several sources. First, from our study that shows the potential mismatch between faculty pedagogical activities and student personal epistemologies. This evidence, combined with the literature that shows that faculty choices can impact student epistemological development, *and* that students' epistemological stances can mediate other learning outcomes and their approaches to study, should provide strong evidence for the need to be aware of the epistemological implications of faculty pedagogical choices.

Although an understanding of the relationship between students' epistemologies and how faculty teach is important for all faculty, we believe it is particularly crucial for faculty who instruct preservice teachers to be cognizant of the epistemological implications of instructional practices. What faculty model to our future teachers impacts not only students' personal epistemologies, but the students of these future teachers.

For all tertiary faculty, the literature provides a consistent message regarding instructional activities and student epistemological development. Activities, such as open-ended design problems, that are student-centered and that require students to resolve, in a supported environment, multiple and potentially conflicting sources of knowledge can positively impact epistemological development (e.g., Stephenson & Hunt, 1977; Valanides & Angeli, 2005).

We suggest, however, that teacher education faculty may wish to not only consider these practices, but also incorporate more direct tactics to both raise awareness of these future teachers' concepts of their *own* views on the nature of knowledge, but also on the epistemological implications of classroom pedagogical practices. Several methods might be used to accomplish these outcomes.

First, simplified implementation of a measure of personal epistemologies with preservice teachers can make what may be an abstract concept more understandable and more easily applied. The Epistemological Beliefs Inventory (Schraw et al., 2002) uses a Likert scale where respondents indicate their level of agreement with statements about knowing and the nature of knowledge such as *Absolute moral truth does not exist*, or *Truth means different things to different people*. Even when these instruments are not marked as intended to produce a numerical summary score, simply completing the instrument and using it as a basis for discussion and to illustrate the different facets of personal epistemologies could prove a valuable way to address this construct with preservice teachers.

This tactic draws support from work from several theorists (Kitchener, 1983; Kuhn, 1999) who have suggested that personal epistemologies are a part of a larger system of metacognitive activities that affect learning. In addition to more general portions of typical teacher education programs designed to help preservice teachers understand the cognitive processing of their future students, we need to incorporate material and activities—such as the one just described—that facilitates their understanding of personal epistemology and how it interacts with other cognitive processes in a complex system of learning. Understanding how and why particular instructional methods are accepted or resisted by students at the metacognitive level will help these future teachers to become more effective educators. We argue that operationalizing personal epistemology to preservice teachers can help achieve that goal.

Raising awareness of personal epistemology, however, may not be sufficient to help future teachers actively consider epistemology in their instructional designs. As our own research shows even when a faculty member has expertise in her content area and presumably an advanced understanding of the nature of knowledge in that field (Palmer & Marra, 2009), she may still communicate a relatively unsophisticated epistemological belief through pedagogical activities. The "reflective practice" framework from Schon (1983) posits the importance of professionals considering and revising approaches to complex problems (such as teaching) via reflection on practice. Actively involving preservice teachers in progressive pedagogical activities coupled with reflection may impact preservice teachers' pedagogical choices. There is precedent for this type of activity. Prior work from Brownlee et al. (2001) showed that weekly reflections by preservice teachers on their personal epistemologies resulted in epistemological growth.

Extending this idea of promoting meaningful reflection on the epistemological implications of pedagogies, current technologies could be employed to support this activity. Specifically we posit that collaborative reflections supported by current technologies such as a Wiki or even a simple threaded discussion forum, when paired with individual reflection, might produce better results than individual reflections alone. Studies have shown that discussion with peers promotes comparison of multiple perspectives (Prestridge, 2010; Sutherland, Howard, & Markauskaite, 2010) which of course is an important component of developing personal epistemologies. A study currently being conducted (Cho, 2010) will examine how supporting collaborative reflections in a Wiki-based environment amongst preservice teachers engaged in field experiences over and above individual reflections will impact subjects' reflection quality, personal epistemologies, and teaching plans. We anticipate that results from such studies can further inform the teacher education community on promising practices to promote preservice teachers' awareness of and implementation of personal epistemologies in their instructional choices.

And to conclude our discussion more broadly—again addressing the idea that faculty awareness of their own epistemologies and their students' epistemologies and then how to consider this knowledge in the choice of pedagogical strategies—we point to several studies that have examined how to change faculty beliefs. For instance, Dahlgren, Castensson, and Dahlgren (1998) conducted research on how the use of problem-based learning environments influenced how tertiary instructors view themselves as teachers. They found that the experience did help some faculty view themselves in less of a directive (teacher-centered) role and more of a role where one supports student learning. Lastly, Major and Palmer (2006) examined the impact of the use of problem-based learning on tertiary instructors' beliefs about teaching and learning finding that faculty not only changed their views of their roles as instructors, but also their beliefs about the nature of knowledge in their disciplines and the importance of pedagogical choices to learning outcomes.

SUMMARY

This chapter has addressed how faculty at the tertiary level through their pedagogical choices can influence student personal epistemologies, and in some cases (as our second study showed), perhaps inadvertently communicate epistemological beliefs that we as an educational community do not ultimately wish to promote. We argue that this "mismatch" between the epistemological implications of pedagogical choices and students' personal epistemologies may impede student development.

Although personal epistemologies are developed throughout a learner's lifetime, the time many learners spend in tertiary institutions can be influential. This is particularly true for those studying to be teachers. The tertiary years are where these future teachers actively engage in learning to create and design instructional methods to support desired learning outcomes for their students.

Through a review of pertinent literature as well as summarizing the authors' studies, we hope to both raise awareness for tertiary faculty of the existence of these mismatches between pedagogical choices and personal epistemology and suggest how faculty—teacher education faculty in particular—might address these issues.

We do recognize that even if faculty are aware of the impact of these pedagogies that there are barriers to implementing the kinds of instructional activities that have been shown to positively impact personal epistemologies and that may help preservice teachers make choices with their future students that promote epistemological growth. But as this entire volume communicates, we argue that the importance of carefully considering how we educate our future teachers has far-reaching consequences and is thus worth significant investments.

REFERENCES

Brownlee, J., Purdie, N., & Boulton-Lewis, G. (2001). Changing epistemological beliefs in preservice teacher education students. *Teaching in Higher Education, 6(2)*, 247–268.

Cho, Y. (2010). *Wiki-based collaborative reflection on field experiences for elementary preservice teachers* (Unpublished doctoral dissertation proposal). University of Missouri.

Dahlgren, M., Castensson, R., & Dahlgren, L. (1998). PBL from the teacher's perspective. *Higher Education, 36(4)*, 437–447.

Gill, M., Ashton, P., & Algina, J. (2004). Changing preservice teachers' epistemological beliefs about teaching and learning in mathematics: An intervention study. *Contemporary Educational Psychology, 29(2)*, 164–185.

Hammer, D. (1994). Epistemological beliefs in introductory physics. *Cognition and Instruction, 12(2)*, 151–183.

Hammer, D., & Elby, A. (2002). On the form of a personal epistemology. In B. K. Hofer & P. R. Pintrich (Eds.), *Personal epistemology: The psychology of beliefs about knowledge and knowing* (pp. 169–190). Mahwah, NJ: Lawrence Erlbaum Associates.

Hill, L. (2000). What does it take to change minds? Intellectual development of pre-service teachers. *Journal of Teacher Education, 51(1)*, 50.

Hofer, B. K. (1999). Instructional context in the college mathematics classroom: Epistemological beliefs and student motivation. *Journal of Staff, Program, and Organizational Development, 16(2)*, 73–82.

Hofer, B. K. (2000). Dimensionality and disciplinary differences in personal episte-mology. *Contemporary Educational Psychology, 25*(4), 378–405.

Hofer, B. K. (2001). Personal epistemology research: Implications for learning and teaching. *Journal of Educational Psychology Review, 13*(4), 353–383.

Hofer, B. K., & Pintrich, P. R. (1997). The development of epistemological theories: Beliefs about knowledge and knowing and their relation to learning. *Review of Educational Research, 67*(1), 88–140.

Jehng, J.-C. J., Johnson, S. D., & Anderson, R. C. (1993). Schooling and students' epistemological beliefs about learning. *Contemporary Educational Psychology, 18*, 23–25.

Kardash, C. M., & Howell, K. L. (2000). Effects of epistemological beliefs and topic-specific beliefs on undergraduates cognitive and strategic processing of dual-positional text. *Journal of Educational Psychology, 92*, 524–535.

Kardash, C. M., & Scholes, R. J. (1996). Effects of preexisting beliefs, epistemo-logical beliefs, and need for cognition on interpretation of controversial issues. *Journal of Educational Psychology, 88*(2), 260–271.

King, P. M., & Kitchener, K. S. (1994). *Developing reflective judgment.* San Fran-cisco, CA: Jossey-Bass.

Kitchener, K. S. (1983). Cognition, metacognition, and epistemic cognition. *Human Development, 26*, 222–232.

Knefelkamp, L. (1974). *Developmental instruction: Fostering intellectual and per-sonal growth in college students* (Unpublished doctoral dissertation). University of Minnesota, Minneapolis-St. Paul.

Kuhn, D. (1999). Metacognitive development. In L. Balter & C. S. Tamis-LeMonda (Eds.), *Child psychology: A handbook of contemporary issues* (pp. 258–286). Philadelphia: Psychology Press.

Lising, L., & Elby, A. (2005). The impact of epistemology on learning: A case study from introductory physics. *American Journal of Physics, 73*(4), 372–382.

Lonka, K., & Lindbloom-Ylanne, S. (1996). Epistemologies, conceptions of learn-ing and study practices in medicine and psychology. *Higher Education, 31*(1), 5–24.

Major, C., & Palmer, B. (2006). Reshaping teaching and learning: The transfor-mation of faculty pedagogical content knowledge. *Higher Education, 51*(4), 619–647.

Marra, R. M., Palmer, B., & Litzinger, T. (2000). The effects of a first-year engi-neering design course on student intellectual development as measured by the Perry scheme. *Journal of Engineering Education, 89*(1), 39–45.

Marra, R., & Palmer, B. (2008). Epistemologies of the sciences, humanities and social sciences: liberal arts students' perception. *Journal of General Education, 57*(2), 100–118.

Mason, L., & Boscolo, P. (2004). Role of epistemological understanding and inter-est in interpreting a controversy and in topic-specific belief change. *Contempo-rary Educational Psychology, 29*, 103–128.

Muis, K. R. (2007). The role of epistemic beliefs in self-regulated learning. *Educa-tional Psychologist, 42*(3), 173–190.

Nussbaum, E. M., Sinatra, G. M., & Poliquin, A. (2008). Role of epistemic beliefs and scientific argumentation in science learning. *International Journal of Sci-ence Education, 30*(15), 1977–1999.

Palmer, B., & Marra, R. (2009). *Students' views of college science: Are instruction and epistemology consistent or conflicting?* Paper presented at the annual meet-ing of AERA, San Diego, April 13–17.

Palmer, B., & Marra, R. M. (2004). College student epistemological perspectives across knowledge domains: A proposed grounded theory. *Higher Education, 47*(3), 311–335.

Paulsen, M. B., & Feldman, K. A. (1999). Student motivation and epistemological beliefs. *New Directions for Teaching and Learning, 78,* 17–25.

Perry, W. G. (1970). *Intellectual and ethical development in the college years: A scheme.* New York: Holt, Rinehart & Winston.

Prestridge, S. (2010). ICT professional development for teachers in online forums: Analysing the role of discussion. *Teaching and Teacher Education, 26,* 252–258.

Scherr, R. E., & Hammer, D. (2009). Student behavior and epistemological framing: Examples from collaborative active-learning activities in physics. *Cognition and Instruction, 27*(2), 147–174.

Schommer, M. (1990). Effects of beliefs about the nature of knowledge on comprehension. *Journal of Educational Psychology, 82,* 498–504.

Schommer, M., Crouse, A., & Rhodes, N. (1992). Epistemological beliefs and mathematical text comprehension: Believing it is simple does not make it so. *Journal of Educational Psychology, 84*(4), 435–443.

Schön, D. (1983). *The reflective practitioner: How professionals think in action.* New York: Basic Books.

Schraw, G., Bendixon, L. D., & Dunkle, M. E. (2002). Development and validation of the Epistemic Belief Inventory (EBI). In B. K. Hofer (Ed.), *Personal epistemology: The psychology of beliefs about knowledge and knowing* (pp. 261–275). Mahwah, NJ: Lawrence Erlbaum Associates.

Schraw, G., Dunkle, M. E., & Bendixen, L. D. (1995). Cognitive processes in well-defined and ill-defined problem solving. *Applied Cognitive Psychology, 9,* 523–538.

Stephenson, B., & Hunt, C. (1977). Intellectual and ethical development: A dualistic curriculum intervention for college students. *Counseling Psychologist, 6,* 39–42.

Sutherland, L., Howard, S., & Markauskaite, L. (2010). Professional identity creation: Examining the development of beginning preservice teachers' understanding of their work as teachers. *Teaching and Teacher Education, 26,* 455–465.

Tolhurst, D. (2007). The influence of learning environments on students' epistemological beliefs and learning outcomes. *Teaching in Higher Education, 12*(2), 219–233.

Valanides, N., & Angeli, C. M. (2005). Effects of instruction on changes in epistemological beliefs. *Contemporary Educational Psychology, 30*(2), 314–330.

Widick, C., & Simpson, D. (1978). Developmental concepts in college instruction. In C. Parker (Ed.), *Encouraging development in college students.* Minneapolis: University of Minnesota Press.

Wineburg, S. S. (1991). Historical problem-solving: A study of the cognitive processes used in the evaluation of documentary evidence and pictorial evidence. *Journal of Educational Psychology, 83*(1), 73–87.

Zhang, L. F., & Watkins, D. (2001). Cognitive development and student approaches to learning: An investigation of Perry's theory with Chinese and U. S. university students. *Higher Education, 41,* 239–261.

Part II

Inservice Teachers
and Teaching

10 Fostering Critical Awareness of Teachers' Epistemological and Ontological Beliefs

Gregory Schraw, Lori Olafson,
and Michelle VanderVeldt

ABSTRACT

We examined epistemological and ontological beliefs using pre–posttest surveys, essays, and end-of-semester interviews on a sample of 16 graduate students enrolled in an education class at a large university in the western United States. We made two predictions. The first was that the majority of students would hold consistent beliefs across the 15-week semester. The second was that participation in action research would promote reflection and critical awareness of personal beliefs and how those beliefs are related to teaching practice. Results indicated that approximately 63% of participants had consistent beliefs. Another 30% experienced minor changes, whereas only one experienced substantial change. As expected, participation and reflection positively affected all students by enhancing awareness and development of beliefs. We describe four ways that participatory action promoted greater understanding of course information and personal beliefs. We concluded that whereas beliefs do not change during a 15-week course, educational experiences nevertheless helped teachers develop explicit awareness of their beliefs and use this awareness to make informed curricular and pedagogical choices in their classrooms. We summarized these findings in a 4-stage sequence that links action research to greater awareness and changes in teachers' intended classroom practice.

INTRODUCTION

This study examines teachers' epistemological and ontological beliefs and how action research may be used to promote critical reflection on their beliefs and the relationship between beliefs and practices. Several previous studies have examined changes in epistemological and ontological beliefs across time (Brownlee, 2004; Marra, 2005; Olafson, Schraw, & Vander-Veldt, in press; Trumbull, Scarano, & Bonney, 2006); however, none of these studies examined how formal education experiences are related to belief change among teachers or whether changing world views is linked to activities embedded within their ongoing educational experience.

Defining Epistemological and Ontological Beliefs

Epistemology is the study of beliefs about the origin and acquisition of knowledge (Hofer, 2004). In the present study, we use the generic term *epistemological beliefs* to refer to a teacher's collective beliefs about the nature and acquisition of knowledge. We use the term synonymously with terms such as *epistemological world view* (Schraw & Olafson, 2002), *personal epistemology* (Chan & Elliott, 2004; Hofer, 2001), and *epistemological stances* (Johnston, Woodside-Jiron, & Day, 2001) that refer to a set of beliefs or a personal theory about knowledge and knowledge justification. Similarly, we use the term *ontological beliefs* to refer to a teacher's collective beliefs about the nature of reality and being (Guba & Lincoln, 2000; Merricks, 2007; Mertens, 2005; Ponterotto, 2005). Like epistemology, ontological beliefs may be tacit or explicit, and are presumed to change due to knowledge and instructional activities (e.g., personal reflection journals) that promote critical awareness of beliefs (Bendixen & Rule, 2004; Brownlee, Purdie, & Boulton-Lewis, 2001; Schraw & Olafson, 2002). We assume that epistemological and ontological beliefs work in tandem to determine an individual's collective world view about learning and instruction (Schraw & Olafson, 2008; Olafson et al., in press).

Previous Research

Most prior research has focused on the structure and development of college students' epistemological beliefs (Baxter Magolda, 2002; Hofer, 2004; Kuhn, Cheney, & Weinstock, 2000; Perry, 1970; Schommer-Aikins, 2002). However, recent research also has investigated teachers' epistemological and ontological beliefs (Brownlee & Berthelsen, 2006). These studies argued that teachers' epistemological and ontological beliefs influence teaching practices in two ways (Brownlee, 2003; Chan & Elliott, 2004; Haney & McArthur, 2001; Ozgun-Koca & Sen, 2006; Trumbull et al., 2006). One is that teachers with more sophisticated world views tend to endorse student-centered instructional practices that emphasize critical reasoning (Lidar, Lundqvist, & Ostman, 2005). A second is that teachers' beliefs affect students' epistemological development and learning (Johnston et al., 2001; Lidar et al., 2005; Louca, Elby, Hammer, & Kagey, 2004; Marra, 2005).

The development of teachers' epistemological beliefs has been of interest as well. Brownlee (2004) and Brownlee, Purdie, and Boulton-Lewis (2001) reported that preservice teachers in a program that emphasized relational pedagogy experienced more growth in sophisticated epistemological beliefs as compared with preservice teachers in a tutorial group. Marra (2005) reported similar findings in a study of how constructivist instruction affected the development of graduate student teachers at a university by helping them adopt constructivist beliefs that emphasized the role of student interactions. In general, a number of researchers have proposed that belief change may be due to a variety of ongoing educational experiences such as exposure and integration of new information, classroom discussion, essays, or presentations that require individuals to describe and justify their beliefs, personal and group reflection on course content or beliefs, and course-related activities such as action research (Baxter Magolda, 2002; Bendixen & Rule, 2004; Brownlee & Berthelsen, 2006; Gill, Ashton, & Algina, 2004; Joram, 2007; Marra, 2005).

Nevertheless, discrepancies between teachers' espoused beliefs and their enacted beliefs are common (Wilcox-Herzog, 2002). Several studies reported that although preservice teachers reported a preference for constructivist beliefs, they found it difficult to put these beliefs into practice (Haney & McArther, 2001; Ozgun-Koca & Sen, 2006). This pattern has also been observed with practicing teachers. Olafson and Schraw (2006) and White (2000) reported that teachers claimed to use student-centered teacher and assessment practices even when classroom observation and interviews suggested the use of teacher-centered activities characterized by direct instruction and limited independent or small-group student work.

The Current Study

The current research examined whether teachers' epistemological and ontological beliefs changed during a 15-week graduate class and what role participatory action research played in change. Based on previous work (Olafson & Schraw, 2006; Olafson et al., in press) we expected most students to maintain consistent beliefs across the semester based on pre- and posttest measures, even though some students were expected to change. One reason for consistency of beliefs in the present case is that most participants are practicing teachers with well-established beliefs about curriculum, pedagogy, and the nature of schooling (Olafson et al., in press). A second reason is that participants were currently enrolled in a graduate degree program at a major university, suggesting they are engaged and reflective with regard to their beliefs and practices, and based on research, more likely to have sophisticated beliefs (Baxter Magolda, 2002; Bendixen & Rule, 2004; Olafson et al., in press). In addition, we predicted that participation in an action research project would heighten individuals' awareness of their beliefs and lead to beneficial reflection regarding the relationship between beliefs and teaching practices. Based on previous research, there is reason to believe that even experienced teachers have not had the opportunity to articulate their personal epistemological and ontological beliefs, discuss or reflect on these beliefs in a group setting, or consider situations in which their beliefs may change (Johnston et al., 2001; Marra, 2005: White, 2000; Wilcox-Herzog, 2002). Our own research also suggests that conducting and reflecting upon classroom-based action research provides a catalyst for reflective practice and greater self-awareness of beliefs (Olafson et al., in press).

METHOD

Participants and Context

Participants in this mixed-methods study were enrolled in a graduate class called *The Study of Teaching* at a large university in southern California where they were pursuing a Master's of Education degree. The class met for 2 ½ hours for 15 weeks. Sixteen female graduate students participated voluntarily in the study, whose age ranged from 20 to 41 with between 1 and 9 years of teaching experience.

The primary course objective was for students to examine images of teaching in relation to the literature and their own practices in a critical manner. The progression of major assignments allowed students to bond through their history of teaching, through sharing different perspectives about teaching and other teachers, and by comparing and justifying teaching practices in their own classrooms.

The class began with the Metaphor assignment in which they discussed and explained the connection of their metaphor(s) to the act of teaching and what it means to be a teacher. The purpose of this assignment was to offer an opportunity for students to reflect on their personal notions of the role of a teacher through the use of metaphor. This was followed by the Timeline assignment in which students focused on their journey of becoming a teacher. The purpose of this assignment was to examine patterns that shaped their identities as teachers and how these experiences continued to inform and transform teaching.

Students also conducted a semester-long action research project to examine an aspect of their teaching. Participants identified a research question based on course objectives, collected data from within their own classrooms, and submitted a 10-page written report at the end of the semester. They also were asked specifically to consider their epistemological and ontological beliefs, and to investigate and reflect on their own teaching practices in relationship to their beliefs.

Materials

Three instruments were used to assess beliefs at the beginning and end of the course, including the Four Quadrant Scale, the Teacher Belief Vignettes, and essays. At the end of the course students were also interviewed to investigate changes in beliefs.

Four Quadrant Scale

The Four Quadrant Scale partitions epistemological and ontological beliefs along two separate dimensions, which yield four separate quadrants, including a realist-realist, realist-relativist, relativist-realist, and relativist-relativist quadrant. Individuals read a brief summary of each quadrant (see

Appendix 1), and selected a point in the four-quadrant array that best corresponded to their personal epistemological and ontological beliefs about teaching. The point selected can be scored in terms of its epistemological coordinate on a 100-millimeter scale, its ontological coordinate on an equivalent 100-millimeter scale, and the quadrant (1–4) it is placed in. A detailed explanation of the development, scoring, and validation of this approach is provided in Schraw and Olafson (2008).

Teacher Belief Vignettes

The Teacher Belief Vignettes consist of three vignettes that portray realist, contextualist, and relativist views of teaching. Participants rated the degree to which they agreed with one of three views of teaching described in a short vignette (Schraw & Olafson, 2002). The realist world view assumes that there is an objective body of knowledge that is best acquired through experts via transmission and reconstruction. The contextualist world view assumes that learners construct shared understanding in collaborative contexts in which teachers serve as facilitators. The relativist world view assumes that each learner constructs a unique knowledge base that is different but equal to that of other learners.

Essays

After completing the Four Quadrant Scale and Teacher Vignettes, participants were asked to write a one-page essay that justified their epistemological and ontological beliefs, as well as why they placed themselves in one of the four quadrants rather than the remaining quadrants.

Interviews

We conducted individual, semi-structured interviews with each participant with three prompts at the end of the semester to examine how and why their beliefs might have changed over the semester. The first prompt asked participants if their course experiences affected their development as teachers. The second asked them to reflect more specifically on course experiences and how they impacted their learning and development. The third asked if their thinking about epistemology and knowing changed during the course, and if so, what triggered this change.

RESULTS

Quantitative Findings

Means and standard deviations for all pre- and posttest scores are shown in Table 10.1. Dependent *t*-tests for the epistemology and ontology coordinates

Table 10.1   Means and Standard Deviations for Pre- and Posttest Variables

	Pretest		Posttest	
	M	SD	M	SD
Age	26.79	4.72		
Years teaching	2.71	2.41		
Quadrant	2.06	1.55	1.81	1.36
Epistemology Coordinate	58.32	23.59	60.55	26.29
Ontology Coordinate	88.28	10.42	78.98	16.40
Realist Vignette	2.50	.89	2.70	1.06
Contextualist Vignette	4.50	.91	4.00	1.09
Relativist Vignette	3.06	.85	3.38	1.25

showed no significant differences between the pre- and posttest. We also examined quadrant placement across time. Ten of 16 participants remained in the same cell at pretest and posttest. Three switched from cell 4 to 1, two switched from cell 1 to 4, and one switched form cell 1 to 3. The frequency of changes was not statistically significant, and in addition, all but one of the changes occurred between adjacent cells (e.g., cell 4 to cell 1). Specifically, those who moved from cell 4 to cell 1 changed from epistemological realism to a more relativistic view, whereas those who moved from cell 1 to cell 4 changed from epistemological relativism to a more realist view.

We also conducted a 2 (time: pretest, posttest) x 2 (type of belief: epistemological, ontological) repeated measures analysis of variance (ANOVA) to compare pre- and posttest means for the epistemological and ontological coordinate scores. The only test to reach significance was for the type of beliefs variable, $F (1, 15) = 31.23, p < .001$. This difference was due to significantly higher (i.e., relativist) scores for the ontological versus epistemological coordinate score. In addition, we conducted a 2 (time: pretest, posttest) x 3 (type of vignette: realist, contextualist, relativist) repeated measures analysis of variance (ANOVA) to compare pre- and posttest means for the teacher vignette scores. The only test to reach significance was the type of vignette variable, $F (2, 30) = 21.83, p < .001$. This difference was due to significantly higher scores for the contextualist scores compared to the realist and relativist scores. Relativist and realist means did not differ from each other.

Collectively, the results showed that on average beliefs do not change significantly over the course of the 15-week semester, even though some individuals do change. About half of those who changed became more relativistic, whereas the other half became more realistic. Similarly, none of the other pre- and posttest scores changed significantly over time, suggesting that beliefs are stable and that a one-semester course does not significantly change the strength of self-reported beliefs. However, it may be the case that the course activities increase awareness of beliefs and encourage students to consider in more detail the relationship between beliefs and classroom practices. We discuss these effects in the qualitative section below. In addition, the quantitative analyses also showed that teachers are significantly more relativistic on the ontology compared to the epistemology scale, and reported a significantly stronger commitment to the contextualist position than the realist and relativist positions. Teachers may adopt a more realist epistemological stance due a belief that a core body of knowledge exists that must be imparted to students (see Theme 1 below). However, the statistically significant effect for the contextualist vignette suggests that teachers believe that students learn best when they construct shared understanding in collaborative contexts in which teachers serve as facilitators along with other students (Cole, 1996; Rogoff, 1990).

Qualitative Findings

The transcribed interviews and essays were imported as primary documents into Atlas.ti to investigate teacher's perception of how their epistemological beliefs change over time. Atlas.ti is a software program that facilitates many of the activities involved in qualitative data analysis and interpretation, but does not automate these processes (Muhr, 2004). During open coding, an initial list of codes was developed as we began the analysis of the interviews and essays. This initial list was refined as we analyzed each data source. The final coding scheme consisted of 44 codes that were grouped together in a higher order of classification to form the resulting three themes.

Theme 1: Absence of Meaningful Change

As noted in the quantitative results, participants did not experience significant belief change as measured by the Four Quadrant Scale and the EBI. Seven participants changed their quadrant placement, and three of these participants became more realist. In their essays they indicated a continuing belief in the importance of core knowledge. Additionally, they described a tension between core knowledge and student construction of knowledge which was also noted by participants who remained realist. For example, Nancy remained in quadrant 4 throughout the course. She noted in her post essay, "In regards to my epistemological beliefs, I feel that there are specific skills that all students should master, but I don't think an emphasis should be on memorization. At the same time, I also think that learning should be relevant to students' lives." We expected the graduate students to become more contextualist, yet those participants who stayed or moved to quadrant 4 (epistemological realists) appeared to indicate in their interview responses that epistemologically, they were not completely realist in their beliefs.

Additionally, 4 participants became more relativist epistemologically by moving from quadrant 4 to quadrant 1. However, similar to the participants who became more realist, these participants also expressed some epistemological tension between core knowledge and student constructed knowledge. In her post essay, Kimberly wrote: "I am a firm believer that instruction should be student centered and driven by student interests. I also think that there are certain things all students should know, adding, multiplication, sentence structure, and the like."

For the few participants who changed their quadrant placements, the nature of this change was primarily epistemological in nature. Upon further examination of their written justifications and interviews, however, it became clear that these participants had not experienced any substantial change that fundamentally changed their world view. Nevertheless, even in the absence of meaningful change, all participants expressed developing a greater awareness of their beliefs, which is addressed in detail below.

Theme 2: The Development of Greater Awareness

During the interviews, participants were asked directly if their beliefs had changed as a result of participating in *The Study of Teaching* course. None of the participants indicated that they had experienced a fundamental belief change, yet all participants spoke of developing a greater explicit awareness of their beliefs. Kimberly described the impact of the course on her beliefs by saying, "And my awareness of my own beliefs as a teacher definitely increased. It made me think a lot." Some participants talked about how their existing beliefs were reinforced. Sarah, for example, noted that her previous beliefs were solidified, "And so I've always believed these things but then when I like read and did the work about that it just solidified." Other participants described how their existing beliefs had been tacit, and that the format of the course allowed them opportunities to articulate their beliefs. Sherry said, "I was able to kind of bring those beliefs to the surface by actually trying to look at them," and Kristin described a similar experience, "I think I knew that in the back of my mind but I wasn't aware of it until this class." Clearly, *The Study of Teaching* led to an increased awareness of beliefs then, and the ability to more clearly articulate these beliefs. In the next theme described, we look at the experiences that promoted this awareness.

Theme 3: Action Research Promotes Greater Awareness of Beliefs

The course experience that seemed to have the greatest impact on the participants' developing awareness of their beliefs was the action research project. All participants spoke at length about their projects and the extent to which action research promoted greater awareness, which was summarized by one participant stating, "If you know where you stand, then you see that in what you do." These projects promoted awareness of beliefs in four ways. First, it provided an opportunity to implement a new practice in the classroom. When participants were deciding on their topic, they were encouraged to choose an area of their practice that was not a strength, so that the results of their project could lead to improved practice. Laura said, "She gave us opportunities to go, you know, try things in the classroom that I might not have done without the class," and another participant said "it helped me jump into an area that I was unsure of."

Second, the action research project provided a forum where participants were able to examine the relationship between their own beliefs and practices in a particular context. Gina, for example, observed another teacher integrating technology in a first grade classroom:

> by the end I realized wow, you know, maybe, that's what I strive to do but at the same time then I was thinking wait, I probably am not exactly there, I'm probably more, like not more this way but more maybe kind of in the middle of relativist and realist. So at the end I realized that maybe I'm not quite there yet but I would love to be like that. But really I wasn't as far along as I thought I would be because I realized that, you know, there, I mean obviously I have a lot to learn but there are so many things out there that I could be doing or, you know, even if I can't, even with the things that, the resources that I have.

As a part of their final paper, participants were asked to consider their epistemological and ontological beliefs in relation to their action research projects. In the following interview excerpt, Sherry described how she used the 4-quadrant scale to think about her beliefs and practices:

> The four quadrant scale that we had to do made me think a lot. And we used it in the paper and so it definitely made me think about what am I. And so it made me particularly aware of the fact that I might say I'm this quadrant, but I need to make sure that I'm putting that into practice in my actual teaching and it helped me to reflect on ways that I could do that especially when I was observing the teachers for evidence of their epistemological and ontological beliefs. Before I was an epistemological realist, and I still think there's definitely some things the students still need to know but I realize that it's a continuum. It definitely helped me realize that it's more important for me to cater to my students than it is to all have them have the same answers on the paper.

Third, the action research project promoted awareness of beliefs when participants connected theory to practice. The hands-on nature of the project, said Kristin, was the difference between "really doing the research rather than just reading an article." Sherry expressed a similar idea when describing how the action research project had an impact on her beliefs: "It was the difference between the theoretical and the practical and me actually doing something versus me just thinking about it."

Finally, the action research project required systematic reflection on the process and on participants' beliefs. As noted previously, participants provided a discussion of the results of their research and connections to their epistemological and ontological beliefs. Candice noted that one of the possible outcomes of this kind of systematic reflection can be improved practice:

> We're always encouraged to um reflect on things that we did and I just think that any time you kind of step back and look at what you're doing and what you believe in it only makes you better, it makes you grow. And when you look at back at things that maybe didn't work or that you don't like then you can change.

DISCUSSION

Our research examined whether teachers' epistemological and ontological world views changed during a 15-week graduate class and what role participatory action research played in change and greater awareness of world views. We found that most participants did not experience a substantial change in world views, and of those who experienced change, their change was a matter of degree rather than of kind. This finding is consistent with previous research that did not report significant short-term change among inservice teachers (Olafson et al., in press). In contrast, several studies have reported change in beliefs among preservice teachers using different instructional formats. Generally, change in beliefs has occurred when classes focused on constructivist instruction that emphasized the role of student cooperative discussion and reflection on personal beliefs (Brownlee, 2004; Gill et al., 2004; Marra, 2005). One difference between these two types of studies is that inservice teachers may have greater explicit awareness of their beliefs and how beliefs are related to their classroom practice, thereby limiting the degree of observed change over a one-semester time frame.

As expected, participants reported increased awareness of their beliefs due to the research activity, classroom discussion, and the action research project in particular. We described previously under Theme 3 four ways that action research promoted greater awareness, including opportunities to try new activities in a real-life context, a forum to examine beliefs, connecting theory to practice, and promoting reflection on beliefs and how beliefs are related to practice. Each of these four reasons was consistent with our finding that participants rated the contextualist-oriented classroom vignette as significantly higher than the realist or relativist classroom orientations.

These findings suggested a tentative 4-stage development-of-awareness sequence shown in Figure 10.1 that participants experienced during the semester. Stage 1 consisted of course content and activities that promoted discussion, reflection, and selection of an action research project in Stage 2 that was aligned to course objectives and activities. These critical reflective experiences promoted greater awareness of beliefs and teaching practices in Stage 3, which lead to transforming theory into practice and understanding the relationship between beliefs and classroom practices in Stage 4. Figure 10.1 shows a schematic diagram of this sequence with 4 stages that include course content and activities (Stage 1), participatory and reflective experiences (Stage 2), increased awareness of beliefs and the relationship between beliefs and practices (Stage 3), and change in teaching behaviors related to greater awareness as suggested by the interviews (Stage 4). This sequence is similar in nature to other change and developmental models described in the literature (Baxter Magolda, 2002; Bendixen, 2002; Bendixen & Rule, 2004; Brownlee, 2004; Brownlee et al., 2001). However, we emphasize that additional research is needed to replicate and verify the sequence proposed in Figure 10.1 and isolate the effects attributable specifically to participation in the action research project.

Based on the present findings, we suggest that the most critical stage in the sequence is the participation and reflective practice stage, which includes peer-based discussion, personal reflection, and reflection on action that occurs during the action research project. These activities are consistent with social-constructivist activities described widely in the developmental literature that promote a reasoned change in action due to greater awareness of one's beliefs, skills, and knowledge (Baxter Magolda, 2002; Cole,

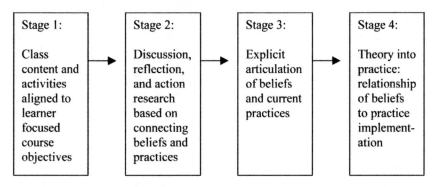

Figure 10.1 The development-of-awareness sequence observed in our research.

1996; Glassman, 2001; Hung, 1999; McCaslin & Hickey, 2001; Rogoff, 1990; Schon, 1983).

Given our results, we highlight two key findings that have important implications for understanding teachers' beliefs and how beliefs are related to classroom practice.

The first is that a teacher's classroom practices may change even when the teacher's beliefs do not change. Based on our findings, activities that promote greater awareness of beliefs through reflection may be sufficient to invoke change in the classroom, although this conclusion would need to be investigated in greater detail. The second finding is that meaningful activity that is situated within a legitimate classroom context serves as a catalyst for discussion, reflection, and experimentation with new classroom behaviors (O'Donnell, 2006; Rogoff, 1990; Wertsch, 2008).

Implications for Teacher Training

Our findings have two implications for teacher training. The first is to help teachers become more aware of their beliefs and world views. Indeed, the development of greater explicit awareness of beliefs and world views by participants in our study can be attributed, in part, to participation in a learning environment that focused explicitly on identifying epistemological and ontological world views and on examining the relationship between world views and teaching practices. Within this learning environment, reflection played a central role as participants investigated their teaching personae and their views of learners (ontological aspects of teaching), their beliefs about curriculum and how knowledge is acquired (epistemological aspects of teaching), and their actual teaching practices.

A second implication is to include activities that promote reflection and discussion. Activity-based reflection helps individuals clarify their beliefs, revise beliefs as necessary, and make explicit connections between theory and practice. Indeed, a number of theories suggest that activity and reflection on activity promote greater explicit awareness of beliefs which lead to changed behavior (Bendixen & Rule, 2004; Schon, 1983). Consistent with this claim, Brownlee and Berthelsen (2006) concluded that it is important for teachers to reflect on their epistemological beliefs to be able to develop a personally constructed knowledge base. Reflection also allows teachers to confront their ontological beliefs, or "why they think as they do about themselves as teachers" (Kincheloe, 2003, p. 47).

REFERENCES

Baxter Magolda, M. B. (2002). Epistemological reflection: The evolution of epistemological assumptions from age 18 to 30. In B. Hofer & P. R. Pintrich (Eds.), *Personal epistemology: The psychology of beliefs about knowledge and knowing* (pp. 89–102). Mahwah, NJ: Lawrence Erlbaum Associates.

Bendixen, L. D. (2002). A process model of epistemic belief change. In B. K. Hofer & P. R. Pintrich (Eds.), *Personal epistemology: The psychology of beliefs about knowledge and knowing* (pp. 191–208). Mahwah, NJ: Lawrence Erlbaum Associates.

Bendixen, L. D., & Rule, D. C. (2004). An integrative approach to personal epistemology: A guiding model. *Educational Psychologist, 39,* 69–80.

Brownlee, J., (2003). Changes in primary school teachers' beliefs about knowing: A longitudinal study. *Asia-Pacific Journal of Teacher Education, 31*(1), 87–98.

Brownlee, J. (2004). Teacher education students' epistemological beliefs. *Research in Education, 72,* 1–17.

Brownlee, J., & Berthelsen, D. (2006) Personal epistemology and relational pedagogy in early childhood teacher education programs. *Early Years, 26,* 17–29.

Brownlee, J., Purdie, N., & Boulton-Lewis, G. (2001). Changing epistemological beliefs in pre-service teaching education students. *Teaching in Higher Education, 6,* 247–268.

Chan, K. W., & Elliott, R. G. (2004). Relational analysis of personal epistemology and conceptions about teaching and learning. *Teaching and Teacher Education, 20,* 817–831.

Cole, M. (1996). *Cultural psychology: A once and future discipline.* Cambridge, MA: Harvard University Press.

Gill, M. G., Ashton, P. T, & Algina, J. (2004). Changing preservice teachers' epistemological beliefs about teaching and learning in mathematics: An intervention study. *Contemporary Educational Psychology, 29,* 164–185.

Glassman, M. (2001). Dewey and Vygotsky: Society, experience, and inquiry in educational practice. *Educational Researcher, 30,* 3–14.

Guba, E. G., & Lincoln, Y. S. (2000). Paradigmatic controversies, contradictions, and emerging confluences. In N. K. Denzin & Y. S. Lincoln (Eds.), *Handbook of qualitative research* (2nd ed.; pp. 163–188). Thousand Oaks, CA: Sage Publications.

Haney, J., & McArthur, J. (2001). Four case studies of prospective science teachers' beliefs concerning constructivist practices. *Science Education, 86,* 783–802.

Hofer, B. (2001). Personal epistemology research: Implications for learning and teaching. *Educational Psychology Review, 13,* 353–384.

Hofer, B. (2004). Exploring the dimensions of personal epistemology in differing classroom contexts: Student interpretations during the first year of college *Contemporary Educational Psychology, 29,* 129–163.

Hung, D. W. L. (1999). Activity, apprenticeship, and epistemological appropriation: Implications from the writing of Michael Polanyi. *Educational Psychologist, 34,* 193–205.

Johnston, P., Woodside-Jiron, H., & Day, J. (2001). Teaching and learning literate epistemologies. *Journal of Educational Psychology, 93*(1), 223–233.

Joram, E. (2007). Clashing epistemologies: Aspiring teachers', practicing teachers', and professors' beliefs and knowledge and research in education. *Teaching and Teacher Education, 23,* 123–135.

Kincheloe, J. (2003). Critical ontology: Visions of selfhood and curriculum. *Journal of Curriculum Theorizing, 19*(1), 47–64.

Kuhn, D., Cheney, R., & Weinstock, M. (2000). The developmental of epistemological understanding. *Cognitive Development, 15,* 309–328.

Lidar, M., Lundqvist, E., & Ostman, L. (2005). Teaching and learning in the science classroom: The interplay between teachers' epistemological moves and students' practical epistemologies. *Science Education, 90,* 148–163.

Louca, L., Elby, A., Hammer, D., & Kagey, T. (2004). Epistemological resources: Applying a new epistemological framework to science instruction. *Educational Psychologist, 39*(1), 57–68.

Marra, R. (2005). Teacher beliefs: The impact of the design of constructivist learning environments on instructor epistemologies. *Learning Environments Research, 8,* 135–155.

McCaslin, M., & Hickey, D. T. (2001). Educational psychology, social constructivism, and educational practice: A case of emergent identity. *Educational Psychologist, 36,* 133–141.

Merricks, T. (2007) *Truth and ontology.* Oxford, England: Oxford University Press.

Mertens, D. M. (2005). *Research and evaluation in education and psychology: Integrating diversity with quantitative, qualitative, and mixed methods (2nd edition).* Thousand Oaks, CA: Sage Publications.

Muhr, T. (2004). *ATLAS.ti v5.0 User's guide and reference, 2nd edition.* Berlin: Scientific Software Development.

O'Donnell, A. (2006). The role of peer and group learning. In P. A. Alexander & P. H. Winne (Eds.), *Handbook of Educational Psychology* (2nd ed.; pp. 781–802). Mahwah, NJ: Lawrence Erlbaum Associates.

Olafson, L. J., & Schraw, G. (2006). Teachers' beliefs and practices within and across domains. *International Journal of Educational Research, 45,* 71–84.

Olafson, L. J., Schraw, G., & VanderVeldt, M. (in press). Consistency and development of teachers' epistemological and ontological world views. *Learning Environments Research.*

Ozgun-Koca, S., & Sen, A. (2006). The beliefs and perceptions of pre-service teachers enrolled in a subject-area dominant teacher education program about "effective education." *Teaching and Teacher Education, 22,* 946–960.

Perry, W. G., Jr. (1970). *Forms of intellectual and ethical development in the college years.* New York: Academic Press.

Ponterotto, J. G. (2005). Qualitative research in counseling psychology: A primer on research paradigms and philosophy of science. *Journal of Counseling Psychology, 52,* 126–136.

Rogoff, B. (1990). *Apprenticeship in thinking: Cognitive development in social context.* New York: Oxford University Press.

Schommer-Aikins, M. (2002). An evolving theoretical framework for an epistemological belief system. In B. K. Hofer & P. R. Pintrich (Eds.), *Personal epistemology: The psychology of beliefs about knowledge and knowing* (pp. 103–118). Mahwah, NJ: Lawrence Erlbaum Associates.

Schon, D. A. (1983). *The reflective practitioner.* New York: Basic Books.

Schraw, G., & Olafson, L. (2002). Teachers' epistemological world views and educational practices. *Issues in Education, 8,* 99–148.

Schraw, G., & Olafson, L. (2008). Assessing teachers' epistemological and ontological worldviews. In M. Khine (Ed.), *Knowing, knowledge, and beliefs: Epistemological studies across diverse cultures* (pp. 25–44). New York: Springer.

Trumbull, D., Scarano, G., & Bonney, R. (2006). Relations among two teachers' practices and beliefs, conceptualizations of the nature of science, and their implementation of student independent inquiry projects. *International Journal of Science Education, 28*(14), 1717–1750.

Wertsch, J. V. (2008). From social interaction to higher psychological processes: A clarification and application of Vygotsky's theory. *Human Development, 51,* 66–79.

White, B. C. (2000). Pre-service teachers' epistemology viewed through perspectives on problematic classroom situations. *Journal of Education for Teaching, 26,* 279–305.

Wilcox-Herzog, A. (2002). Is there a link between teachers' beliefs and behaviors? *Early Education and Development, 13,* 79–106.

APPENDIX 1

Instructions to Participants

We want you to rate and explain your epistemological and ontological world views. Please read the following description of terms used in this study. Then indicate with an "X" where you would place yourself in the four quadrants shown on the Rating Sheet. To make your X, find the point where your ratings intersect on the epistemology dimension and the ontology dimensions.

Please note that the descriptions provided below represent endpoints on each of the scales. Your own beliefs may lie anywhere between these two endpoints. You may use any part of the four quadrant area.

After you make your rating, please describe in as much detail as possible on the Explanation Sheet your reasoning for your self-rating.

Epistemology

Epistemology is the study of what can be counted as knowledge, where knowledge is located, and how knowledge increases. The personal epistemology of teachers is characterized by a set of beliefs about learning and the acquisition of knowledge that drives classroom instruction.

Epistemological Realist

An epistemological realist would believe that there is an objective body of knowledge that must be acquired. From a teacher's perspective, this position would hold that curriculum is fixed and permanent and focuses on fact-based subject matter. An epistemological realist might believe the following:

There are certain things that students simply need to know.
I am teaching information that requires memorization and mastery.
There are specific basic skills that need to be mastered.

Epistemological Relativist

An epistemological relativist would describe curriculum as changing and student-centered. Problem-based or inquiry curricula are examples at the other end of the continuum from a perspective of a one size fits all curriculum. One of the central features of curriculum from this position is the notion that curriculum is not fixed and permanent. An epistemological relativist might agree with the following statements:

The things we teach need to change along with the world.

The content of the curriculum should be responsive to the needs of the community.

It is useful for students to engage in tasks in which there is no indisputably correct answer.

Students design their own problems to solve.

Ontology

Ontology is the study of beliefs about the nature of reality. The personal ontology of teachers is characterized by a set of beliefs regarding whether students share a common reality and what a classroom reality should look like.

Ontological Realist

A teacher who is an ontological realist assumes one underlying reality that is the same for everyone. Instructionally, this means that all children should receive the same type of instruction at the same time regardless of their individual circumstances and context. An ontological realist would agree with the following:

Student assignments should always be done individually.

It's more practical to give the whole class the same assignment.

The teacher must decide on what activities are to be done.

Ontological Relativist

An ontological relativist assumes that different people have different realities. From an instructional perspective, teachers are seen as collaborators, co-participants, and facilitators of learning who work to meet the individual needs of students. Instructional practices are less teacher-directed, such as:

Students need to be involved in actively learning through discussions, projects, and presentations.

Students work together in small groups to complete an assignment as a team.

11 Teachers' Personal Epistemologies as Predictors of Support for their Students' Autonomy

Michael Weinstock and Guy Roth

ABSTRACT

Much of the research on teachers' personal epistemologies concerns their learning. Surprisingly little research has looked at how personal epistemologies are related to teachers' teaching and other aspects of their interactions with students. In this chapter we investigate teachers' personal epistemologies and the extent to which they predict autonomy-supporting behaviors. Such behaviors have been found to predict positive educational outcomes. Six hundred students in 21 Grade 7 and 8 classrooms were administered surveys regarding two aspects of autonomy support: The extent to which their teachers tried to take their perspective and provided them with rationales for prosocial behavior. At the same time, their teachers' personal epistemologies were assessed. Students of teachers scored as having advanced personal epistemologies reported that their teachers were more likely to take their perspective. We conclude that teacher education in personal epistemology and autonomy-supportive practices should have positive effects both for the teachers and their students.

INTRODUCTION

Personal epistemology has been conceptualized as an individual's perspective on the characteristics of knowledge and the nature of knowing (Hofer & Pintrich, 1997). Since its roots in Perry's (1970) research on college student development, most research on people's epistemologies has been concerned with the relationship between one's epistemology and how one operates in the learning environment (e.g., Bråten & Strømsø, 2005, 2006; Hofer, 2004; Nussbaum, Sinatra, & Poliquin, 2008; Schommer, 1993). As the central role of teachers is to facilitate their students' acquisition of and inquiries into knowledge in the learning environment, teachers' theories of knowledge and knowing processes may well play a role in the classroom environment and affect students' attitudes towards learning. But most research on teachers' epistemologies has focused on teachers and student teachers as learners (e.g., Brownlee, 2001; Brownlee,

Walker, Lennox, Exley, & Pearce, 2009) consistent with the general thrust of much other research on epistemology. Surprisingly little research has looked at how teachers' epistemologies might influence how they teach or relate to student outcomes.

Hofer (2000) proposed that people have theories about four essential dimensions of knowledge and knowing: The certainty, simplicity, source, and justification of knowledge. From this perspective on personal epistemology, people's theories in each dimension are found along a spectrum from a naïve, objectivist view of knowledge, to a sophisticated, relativist view of knowledge. For instance, those who tend to view knowledge as objective would hold that knowledge can be certain, that it is simple, that the source of knowledge is in external reality or authority, and that knowledge needs no justification because it is self-evident. In contrast, those viewing knowledge as relative would not think that something could be known with absolute certainty, would regard knowledge as admitting multiple perspectives and would be complex, would hold that the source of knowledge is individual or social construction, and would recognize that knowledge must be justified to attain the status of knowledge. Whereas some researchers hold that people have qualitatively different understandings of knowledge rather than having theories of knowledge that lie along a spectrum from naïve to sophisticated, and, further, that there are qualitatively different types of relativism (see Hofer & Pintrich, 1997; King & Kitchener, 1994; Weinstock & Cronin, 2003), there is general agreement that the key distinction is between primarily objectivist and relativist understandings (Chandler, Boyes, & Ball, 1990; Kuhn, Cheney, & Weinstock, 2000; Kuhn & Weinstock, 2002).

Whether teachers tend towards objectivist or relativist views of knowledge may influence their interactions with students in the knowledge-centered environment of school. Although it might be expected that personal epistemology would come to play explicitly in pedagogical practice, the few studies that exist have generally shown that teachers' professed personal epistemologies bear little relationship to their teaching (Olafson & Schraw, 2006). For instance, those expressing relativist epistemologies that value individual construction of knowledge may well still employ traditional teaching practices in which learning is relatively passive. There have also been few studies that have investigated relationships between teachers' and students' personal epistemologies, although Bell and Linn (2002) report that teachers with naïve epistemologies are less likely to instruct to promote higher levels of epistemological understanding.

This certainly does not rule out the possibility that teachers' personal epistemologies influences other aspects of their interactions with students. But, there has been little, if any, research on how teachers' personal epistemologies might impact a range of issues important in education such as achievement, motivation, reasoning, or learning. The study reported in this chapter investigates a proposed relationship between teachers' personal epistemologies and their support of children's autonomy, which is important in students' autonomous motivation to learn. Support for autonomy is a more specific and implicit teaching behavior than might be found in a particular pedagogy, and it might appear in relationships between teachers and students outside of formal teaching. Moreover, a child who perceives support for autonomy should have greater autonomous motivation (Deci & Ryan, 2000), which, in itself, is an important educational goal and a basis for effective classroom engagement (Assor, Kaplan, & Roth, 2002; Jang, 2008; Reeve & Halusic, 2009; Roth, Assor, Kanat-Maymon, & Kaplan, 2007; Roth, Assor, Niemiec, Ryan, & Deci, 2009). Autonomous thinking—that is, being active in constructing knowledge rather than passively acquiring externally given knowledge—and the motivation to engage may also be essential to advanced epistemological development (Kuhn & Park, 2005; Kuhn & Weinstock, 2002).

Support for Autonomy

According to Self-Determination Theory (SDT; Deci & Ryan, 2000), the fulfillment of three essential needs—for autonomy, for relatedness, and for competence—is the basis of autonomous motivation. The need for autonomy refers to the striving to feel that one's major goals and acts emanate from one's true self and are experienced as self-chosen rather than being a product of external or internal (intra-psychic) coercion. Consistent with this definition, teacher behaviors that promote a child's feeling that she or he does things out of understanding of, and identifying with, their value are defined as autonomy-supportive acts (Assor & Kaplan, 2001; Assor et al., 2002; Deci & Ryan, 2008; Grolnick, 2003; Grolnick, Ryan, & Deci, 1991; Reeve, 2006; Ryan & Deci, 2000). In contrast, teacher behaviors that have a child feeling pressured to make particular choices and doing things to meet someone else's expectations are not autonomy-supportive. Research on parenting and teaching has shown that autonomy-supportive behaviors of parents and teachers indeed promote optimal academic functioning in children (Assor et al., 2002; Reeve, Bolt, & Cai, 1999; Roth, 2008; Roth et al., 2009; Vansteenkiste, Simons, Lens, Soenens, & Matos, 2005).

SDT-based research has differentiated among several components of autonomy support in the socialization context: (a) taking the child's perspective, (b) providing choice, (c) demonstrating the relevance of the subjects being learned to the students' goals and interests, and (d) allowing criticism and encouraging independent thinking (Assor et al., 2002; Grolnick, Deci, & Ryan, 1997; Reeve, 2006; Roth et al., 2009; Williams & Deci, 1996). Relationships have been found between teachers' support for autonomy in these ways and various pupil outcomes. For instance, Assor et al. (2002) found that elementary school children's perceptions of their teacher's fostering of relevance positively predicted their reports of behavioral and cognitive engagement in schoolwork, whereas their perceptions of the teacher's suppression of criticism negatively predicted their engagement. With rater assessments that included these aspects of autonomy support, Reeve, Jang,

Carrell, Jeon, and Barch (2004) found that their ratings of teachers' autonomy-supporting behaviors predicted ratings of students' engagement across time and groups. Research with adolescents and students found that among those expressing high levels of autonomy support, teachers' provision of structure predicted self-regulated learning (Sierens, Vansteenkiste, Goossens, Soenens, & Dochy, 2009), and that autonomy-supportive contexts predicted depth of processing, test performance, and persistence on learning tasks (Vansteenkiste, Simons, Lens, Sheldon, & Deci, 2004). Students' reports of teachers' support for autonomy also was found to be correlated with grade point average (Soenens & Vansteenkiste, 2005).

Perceived teachers' support for autonomy has also predicted broader educational outcomes such as the development of moral judgment (Weinstock, Assor, & Broide, 2009), resistance to conformity (Assor, 1999), persistence in school versus dropping out (Vallerand, Fortier, & Guay, 1997), and exploration, commitment, and intention in career planning (Soenens & Vansteenkiste, 2005).

THE PRESENT STUDY

The study proceeds from the premise that autonomy is related to more advanced, relativistic personal epistemologies. People with a naïve epistemology will believe that knowledge is external to the knower. Thus, both teacher and learner will believe that gaining knowledge is a passive process. In contrast, people with advanced personal epistemologies will believe that knowledge has a subjective element and, thus, requires active construction. Teachers less inclined to believe in absolute, objective perspectives should be more likely to accept the possible legitimacy of the students' autonomous perspectives, and thus support their autonomy by taking the student's perspective, providing choices, allowing criticism, and encouraging independent thinking.

We expect that teachers who hold sophisticated, relativist epistemological theories—that the knower plays an active role in constructing knowledge, that knowing is a process of critically evaluating claims and choosing the best justified explanation among alternatives, that knowledge may not be certain, objective, and simple—will be perceived by their students as autonomy-supporting. A previous study (Roth et al., 2007) found that teachers' autonomous motivation to teach was related with students' perceptions of receiving autonomy support from their teachers. The study concluded that teachers who taught out of interest and made their own teaching choices were perceived by students as autonomy-supporting. Students who perceived their teachers as being autonomy-supporting in turn indicated higher levels of autonomous motivation to learn. Similarly, we are investigating the relationship between teachers' personal epistemologies and students' perceptions of teacher autonomy support to gain more understanding of the characteristics of autonomy-supporting teachers in light of good evidence that such support benefits students academically and promotes their autonomous thinking and learning.

The teacher's autonomy-supporting behaviors that we expect would be predicted by their personal epistemology are taking the child's perspective and providing children with rationales for prosocial behaviors. It shc uld be noted that neither of these behaviors need be directly related to academic knowledge acquisition. But each would occur as part of the teacher's general role as a classroom educator. We have specific reasons to think that these particular behaviors would reflect a teacher's personal epistemology. Taking the child's perspective would likely reflect a basic, relativist epistemological understanding that there can be more than one legitimate perspective and that the source of one's truth comes from individual construction and not solely from outside authority, such as that of the teacher. Providing a rationale for prosocial behavior would likely reflect the relativist epistemological understanding of the importance of justifying one's position. See Hofer (2000), Hofer and Pintrich (1997), and Kuhn and Weinstock (2002) for descriptions of a range of epistemological understandings.

METHOD

Participants and Procedures

The sample consisted of 600 Israeli junior high school students (50% females) in Grades 7 and 8 from 21 classes in four schools serving students from lower-middle to middle-class socioeconomic backgrounds. Mean age was 13.2 years (SD = .51).

Adolescents reported on their perceptions of teachers as providing autonomy support and teachers reported on their personal epistemologies. Research assistants with special permission to work with students administered the questionnaires in the last quarter of the school year to students in their classrooms while teachers were not present. In the same period, assessments of teachers' personal epistemologies were collected at the beginning of a school staff meeting by a trained research assistant. Parental consent for the adolescents' reports was obtained according to the Israeli Ministry of Education guidelines.

Instruments

Teachers' Personal Epistemologies

The teachers completed Hofer's (2000) personal epistemology questionnaire. In this questionnaire, participants were instructed to rate their level of agreement with statements while considering a specific academic discipline. With our sample of 21 teachers, we instructed them to consider the discipline of history because history appears to be particularly well suited to invoke epistemic thinking (Donnelly, 1999; Weinstock, 2009). The instrument theoretically tests for four dimensions of epistemology: Certainty, source, simplicity, and justification of knowledge. However, because of the small number of teachers, we could not perform an adequate factor analysis. For the statistical analysis, we used the items from the certainty and source of knowledge because out of Hofer's proposed dimensions, these held together the best (Hofer, 2000) and because there was a good fit conceptually with the construct of autonomy-supported teaching. Autonomy-supportive teachers should be less likely to insist that what they are teaching represents certain truth and that authorities—such as teachers—are the source of knowledge. Moreover, an analysis of all the items showed that these items had greatest coherence. They, in fact, loaded on the same scale in an exploratory principal components analysis. Examples of items from the instrument in these dimensions include: "In this subject, most work has only one right answer," and "If you read something in a textbook for this subject, you can be sure it's true." There was high internal reliability among the 14 items we used from these combined sub-scales, with Cronbach's alpha being .92.

Autonomy-Supportive Teaching

The students completed an instrument that assessed their perceptions of their teacher's support of autonomy (Assor et al., 2002; Roth et al., 2007). The instrument asked students to rate the degree to which a teacher displays behavior that should support their autonomy. In this study, the autonomy-supporting teaching behaviors assessed were the teacher's taking of the student's perspective and the provision of rationale for prosocial behavior. These behaviors should support the choice of the student to act in a certain way out of her or his valuing of the action, and not out of imposition.

The sub-scale assessing the extent to which the homeroom teachers make an effort to take the adolescents' perspectives consists of 9 items. Examples of these items are: "The teacher discusses with us things that bother us in class" and "The teacher encourages us to say what we would like to change in class." Cronbach's alpha for this sub-scale was .88. The other sub-scale, provision of rationale for prosocial behavior, consisted of 6 items, such as: "The teacher explains to us why it is important to be considerate to one another;" and "The teacher explains to us how much a lack of consideration hurts and offends." This sub-scale was reliable with Cronbach's alpha of .83.

RESULTS

To test the relationship between teachers' personal epistemologies and students' perceptions of autonomy support we conducted the analysis using Hierarchical Linear Modeling (HLM; Raudenbush & Bryk, 2002) because the students are nested within 21 classes and the teachers' personal epistemologies vary at the class level. HLM is an effective analytical tool to address issues of nested data. It is a robust analytical method that is increasingly employed in educational research. Educational data are often collected in schools and classrooms. There is a lack of independence among individuals in classrooms and therefore a reduction in variability. Because of pre-existing similarities (i.e., students within a cluster such as a classroom are more similar than students who would be randomly selected), the shared instructional environment means that variability across classrooms is more likely to be greater than variability within classrooms. The Intraclass Correlation (ICC) is a measure of relatedness or dependence of clustered data. First we will present descriptive statistics including correlations among the research's variables separately for students' level and class's level, and then the HLM results will be presented.

Table 11.1 describes the distribution of the scores in teachers' personal epistemologies and students' reports of their teachers taking students' perspectives and providing rationales for prosocial behavior. Higher scores in personal epistemology represent higher agreement with naïve, absolutist belief statements. Higher scores in the two reports of teacher support for autonomy sub-scales represent greater support for students' autonomy; therefore, we expected negative correlations. Pearson's correlations showed similar results (see Table 11.2) at both the class and students level. The comparison of scores aggregated within each classroom showed that each teacher's personal epistemology was negatively correlated with the extent the teacher takes the students' perspectives. This means that the more naïve the personal epistemology, the lower the ratings for teachers taking students' perspectives. Personal epistemology was not related to the provision of a rationale for prosocial behavior. A similar pattern was seen at the students' level, which was the aggregation of all scores without regard to

Table 11.1 Means and Standard Deviations of Scores of Autonomy Support and Personal Epistemology Scores

| | *Level of analysis* | |
Variables	Student level	Classroom level
Teachers' autonomy-supportive behaviors[a]		
Provision of rationale	3.44 (1.04)	3.46 (.33)
Taking students' perspective	3.59 (.94)	3.60 (.34)
Personal epistemology[b]	2.53 (.69)	2.57 (.71)

Note. Student level = total mean score; Classroom level = mean of scores calculated by class.
[a] In a range of 1–5, higher scores represent report of greater display of autonomy-supportive behavior.
[b] In a range of 1–5, higher scores represent a more naïve personal epistemology.

Table 11.2   Correlations Among the Autonomy-Support Variables and Personal
Epistemology

Variables	1	2	3
Teachers' autonomy-supportive behaviors			
1. Provision of rationale	-	.76**	-.17
2. Taking students' perspective	.72**	-	-.41*
3. Personal epistemology	-.05	-.21**	-

Note. The values above the diagonal are the between-class correlations, and the values under
the diagonal are the within-class correlations.
* $p < .05$
** $p < .01$

classroom. It is important to note that the two sub-scales of autonomy-
supportive teaching (i.e., provision of rationale and taking the child perspective) are highly correlated. This finding is in line with past research
that recommended separating the two despite the shared variance because
they have somewhat different correlates, thus the separate analysis is more
informative (Assor et al., 2002).

To test whether teachers' personal epistemologies could account for differences in the students' reports of teachers' autonomy support, we computed a fully unconditional HLM analysis, analogous to an analysis of
variance (ANOVA), with the students' perceptions of the extent to which
teachers took the students' perspectives as the dependent variables, and
with classroom as the grouping variable. This analysis enabled computation
of the Intraclass Correlation Coefficients (ICC), which allowed an estima-
tion of the within-class homogeneity of aggregated group-level constructs.
Values of 5% or above can be regarded as support for a variable's adequate
group level properties, warranting aggregation (e.g., Gavin & Hofmann,
2002). Results indicated that the current ICC is 7%.

In the next stage, taking the student's perspective was predicted by
teachers' personal epistemologies as a class level predictor. In line with the
hypothesis, the relationship was found to be negative and significant ($\gamma =
-.18$, $p < .05$), meaning that those with more naive personal epistemologies
were less likely to be seen by their students as being autonomy-supportive in
this way. The predictor explains 17% of the autonomy support variance in
the class level. Teachers' personal epistemologies did not predict their students' perceptions of them as providing rationales for prosocial behavior.

DISCUSSION

The results support the hypothesis of a relationship between teachers' personal epistemologies and an aspect of their teaching behavior, their support

of students' autonomy. Importantly, the results indicate that some autonomy-supporting behaviors perceived by students are related to personal epistemology whereas others might not be. In this study, we assessed the teacher's taking of the child's perspective and the provision of rationales for prosocial behavior as two autonomy-supporting behaviors. Only the students' reports of the teachers taking their perspective were found to be related to the teacher's personal epistemology. Other SDT research has found that correlated autonomy-supporting behaviors might individually predict outcomes. Weinstock et al. (2009) found that students' sense of their teachers encouraging criticism, but not choice, predicted moral development. Assor et al. (2002) found that provision of rationales positively predicted school engagement whereas suppression of criticism negatively predicted engagement. In the current study, we found that students' perceptions of a particular one of their teacher's autonomy-supporting behaviors has an antecedent in personal epistemology. A belief that there might be multiple perspectives on knowledge might better afford a teacher to try to understand and take the child's perspective. In turn, the child sees this as supportive of his or her autonomy. That the provision of rationale for prosocial behavior was not related with personal epistemology also makes sense. Teachers with either naïve or advanced personal epistemologies might provide a rationale, with the former stressing the acquisition of correct behavior as an important goal and the latter stressing the importance of the child's construction of an understanding.

The findings suggest that it would be worthwhile to test in further detail the relationship between personal epistemology and other autonomy-supporting behaviors. For instance, the provision of choices might be characteristic of teachers who believe that there are no single, objective answers, and, in particular, that a teacher is not an absolute, objective authority who would obviate the choices of students. Teachers who encourage criticism might also believe that knowledge claims are open to criticism and need to be justified in the face of possible alternative viewpoints. With each of these behaviors, the teacher's willingness to cede authority and allow the students to think autonomously would appear to require that a teacher believes that knowledge is not black-and-white and determined by objective authorities.

As this is not a causal study, we cannot conclude that a teacher's personal epistemology is responsible for his or her support of autonomy. But the findings suggest intriguing follow-up experimental studies that are particularly relevant to teacher education. One would be to investigate whether explicitly focusing on epistemology in educating teachers would, in turn, produce more autonomy-supporting behavior. Apart from testing the hypothesis that teachers' epistemologies do affect aspects of their teaching, such research would provide impetus to the little-explored effort to develop instructional interventions with the aim of fostering epistemological change (among the few examples of instructional approaches with the specific aim of influencing personal epistemology are Brownlee & Berthelsen, 2008; Kienhues, Bromme, & Stahl, 2008; Valanides & Angeli, 2005).

Future research might not only include more autonomy-supporting behaviors, but a better differentiation between epistemological dimensions. It is possible that some behaviors are specifically related to some dimensions. One clear limitation of the study presented here is the small number of teachers. This did not allow for finer differentiation of the epistemological dimensions. It also limits the generalizability of the findings, although the significant results are fairly straightforward and very strong. Despite this, the study does allow for a case that teachers' personal epistemologies are related to their interactions with students as manifest in their autonomy-supporting behaviors. In doing so, the study has brought together two research traditions, both of which place value in the learner's autonomy.

The results also point to a way to look at the value of a teacher's epistemological position for pedagogy. There might be more apparently obvious relationships to investigate. For instance, it might appear to make sense to test for a relationship between teachers' personal epistemologies and the personal epistemologies of their students. There are notably few examples of this (Brownlee & Berthelsen, 2008; Johnston, Woodside-Jiron, & Day, 2001), and none that we know of that test this relationship with reference to the construct of personal epistemology that is the basis of the Hofer instrument (Hofer, 2000). However, given the proposed long and difficult course of epistemological development (Chandler et al., 1990; King & Kitchener, 1994; Kuhn & Weinstock, 2002) it is not expected that something as indirect as a teacher being a model of an epistemology would have much impact on students' epistemologies. However, whether contextual factors might affect students' personal epistemologies is a little-explored area. Such factors might account for inconsistencies in the description of epistemological development and the difficulty of pinning particular ages to particular epistemological levels (Chandler, Hallett, & Sokol, 2002). Perhaps having teachers who have different epistemologies than one another to a degree influences the student's epistemology in particular school years and classes. However, it would seem that more targeted pedagogy would be required to have any large effect on students' epistemologies. Moreover, a teacher with a naïve personal epistemology would not be likely to model or directly teach to promote more advanced epistemologies.

Another apparently likely avenue of research would be whether teachers' professed personal epistemologies are manifest in manners of teaching consistent with such beliefs. Studies regarding a relationship between teachers' professed epistemologies and its relationship to their teaching have returned mixed results with some indicating a relationship, (Kang, 2008; Yang, Chang, & Hsu, 2008) at least in how they conceive of if not in the practice of instruction. However, as mentioned in the introduction, other studies have found that teachers are not necessarily consistent in this regard (Kang, 2008; Oflason & Schraw, 2006; Schraw &

Olafson, 2002). In any event, we really do not know why there is not a more clearly consistent relationship. Consistent with the findings of this study, the hints of a relationship between teaching practices and personal epistemology might reflect that whereas teachers may not adapt every aspect of their pedagogy to their personal epistemologies, they might be more autonomy-supportive in their teaching. Contextual and institutional demands might well constrain teachers' practices in a way that obscures the appearance of their personal epistemologies in classroom pedagogy (Kang, 2008; White, 2000). Perhaps a focus on how teachers handle knowledge in the classroom in ways to directly influence students' epistemologies, although a reasonable and desired outcome of a teacher's personal epistemology, is too narrow. There are many ways that teachers' epistemologies might appear in their interactions with and have an impact on their students without directly influencing the students' epistemologies. A possible future step to the study described in this chapter could be to investigate whether the teacher's support of students' autonomy in turn influences the students' epistemological development.

An implication of our findings is that a teacher's personal epistemology might be related to ways a teacher interacts with students outside of the formal, pedagogical relationship. Such interactions might, in turn, have some effect on how students approach learning and engage with the learning environment. We have focused on one, the relationship between the teacher's personal epistemology and his or her support for the student's autonomy. Given the positive education outcomes of a student's perceived autonomy support (Assor et al., 2002; Reeve et al., 2004; Roth et al., 2009; Sierens et al., 2009; Soenens & Vansteenkiste, 2005; Vansteenkiste et al., 2004), a teacher's personal epistemology would appear to have at least an indirect important role in education. These findings suggest that attempts both to raise teachers' epistemological understandings and, perhaps even more, teach them how to be autonomy-supportive, would be important in teacher education.

Our assumption in this study is that a teacher's personal epistemology is fairly stable over time, whereas a teacher's teaching behaviors, such as support for autonomy, are more malleable. However, as this is a correlational study that does not establish a causal, directional relationship between the constructs, it might be worthwhile to consider a bidirectional relationship in further research. A teacher who truly learns what autonomy-supportive teaching is, which would include valuing the students' autonomy, might then develop the epistemological understandings that there may be legitimate multiple perspectives and that knowledge is constructed through autonomous thinking and not just handed down from external sources, such as teachers.

If the process were bidirectional, then a teacher's learning to be autonomy-supportive would promote epistemological development, which would in turn provide a solid basis for the continuation and the consistent application of autonomy-supportive teaching. Although we can only specu-late about this bidirectional relationship, there is good reason to suspect that providing an explicit focus on the meaning of people holding alterna-tive perspectives might promote epistemological development. Having to make sense of alternative perspectives in academically and socially diverse environments (Perry, 1970; Weinstock & Zviling-Beiser, 2009) and in focused knowledge tasks (Kienhues et al., 2008) appears to be a factor in epistemological change. Perhaps educating teachers to seriously consider that children have unique perspectives and to find ways to take their stu-dents' perspectives might be the sort of focused activity that would bring shifts in personal epistemology. As personal epistemology has been shown to have value for all students' learning, preservice teachers would benefit both as students and as teachers from learning autonomy-supportive teach-ing behaviors. Given that researchers on personal epistemology have paid surprisingly little attention to designing methods to foster epistemologi-cal development, the possibility that learning autonomy-supportive teach-ing behaviors—which are valuable on their own—could be a purposeful method of promoting the epistemological development of preservice teach-ers would be worthwhile to explore.

REFERENCES

Assor, A. (1999). Value accessibility and teachers' ability to encourage independent and critical thought in students. *Social Psychology of Education, 2,* 315–338.

Assor, A., & Kaplan, H. (2001). Mapping the domain of autonomy support: Five important ways to enhance or undermine students' experience of autonomy in learning. In A. Efklides, J. Kuhl, & R. M. Sorrentino (Eds.), *Trends and prospects in motivation research* (pp. 101–120). Boston: Kluwer Academic Publishers.

Assor, A., Kaplan, H., & Roth, G. (2002). Choice is good, but relevance is excel-lent: Autonomy-enhancing and suppressing teacher behaviours in predicting student's engagement in school work. *British Journal of Educational Psychol-ogy, 72,* 261–278.

Bell, P., & Linn, M. C. (2002). Beliefs about science: How does science instruction contribute? In B. Hofer & P. Pintrich, *Personal epistemology: The psychology of beliefs about knowledge and knowing* (pp. 321–346). Mahwah, NJ: Law-rence Erlbaum Associates.

Bråten, I., & Strømsø, H. I. (2005). The relations between epistemological beliefs, implicit theories of intelligent and self regulated learning among Norwe-gian postsecondary students. *British Journal of Educational Psychology, 75,* 539–565.

Bråten, I., & Strømsø, H. I. (2006). Predicting achievement goals in two different academic contexts: A longitudinal study. *Scandinavian Journal of Educational Research, 50,* 127–148.

Brownlee, J. (2001). Knowing and learning in teacher education: A theoretical framework of core and peripheral epistemological beliefs. *Asia Pacific Journal of Teacher Education & Development, 4,* 167–190.

Brownlee, J., & Berthelsen, D. (2008). Developing relational epistemology through relational pedagogy: New ways of thinking about personal epistemology in teacher education. In M. S. Khine (Ed.), *Knowing, knowledge and beliefs: Epistemological studies across diverse cultures* (pp. 405–422). Netherlands: Springer.

Brownlee, J., Walker, S., Lennox, S., Exley, B., & Pearce, S. (2009). The first year university experience: Using personal epistemology to understand effective learning and teaching in higher education. *Higher Education: The International Journal of Higher Education and Educational Planning, 58*, 599–618.

Chandler, M., Boyes, M., & Ball, L. (1990). Relativism and stations of epistemic doubt. *Journal of Experimental Child Psychology, 50*, 370–395.

Chandler, M. J., Hallett, D., & Sokol, B. W. (2002). Competing claims about competing knowledge claims. B. K. Hofer & P. R. Pintrich (Eds.), *Personal epistemology: The psychology of beliefs about knowledge and knowing* (pp. 145–168). Mahwah, NJ: Lawrence Erlbaum Associates.

Deci, E. L., & Ryan, R. M. (2000). The 'what' and 'why' of goal pursuits: Human needs and the self-determination of behavior. *Psychological Inquiry, 11*, 227–268.

Deci, E. L., & Ryan, R. M. (2008). Facilitating optimal motivation and psychological well-being across life's domains. *Canadian Psychology, 49*, 14–23.

Donnelly, J. (1999). Interpreting differences: the educational aims of teachers of science and history, and their implications. *Journal of Curriculum Studie·, 31*, 17–41.

Gavin, M., & Hofmann, D. A. (2002). Using hierarchical linear modeling t investigate the moderating influence of leadership climate. *Leadership Quarterly, 13*, 15–33.

Grolnick, W. S. (2003). *The psychology of parental control: How well-meant parenting backfires.* Mahwah, NJ: Lawrence Erlbaum Associates.

Grolnick, W. S., Deci, E. L., & Ryan, R. M. (1997). Internalization within the family: The self-determination theory perspective. In J. E. Grusec & L. Kuczynski (Eds.), *Parenting and children's internalization of values: A handbook of contemporary theory* (pp. 135–161). New York: Wiley.

Grolnick, W. S., Ryan, R. M., & Deci, E. L. (1991). The inner resources for school performance: Motivational mediators of children's perceptions of their parents. *Journal of Educational Psychology, 83*, 508–517.

Hofer, B. K. (2000). Dimensionality and disciplinary differences in personal epistemology. *Contemporary Educational Psychology, 25*, 378–405.

Hofer, B. K. (2004). Epistemological understanding as a meta-cognitive process: Thinking aloud during online searching. *Educational Psychologist, 39*, 43–55.

Hofer, B. K., & Pintrich, P. R. (1997). The development of epistemological theories: Beliefs about knowledge and knowing and their relation to learning. *Review of Educational Research, 67*, 88–140.

Jang, H. (2008). Supporting students' motivation, engagement, and learning during an uninteresting activity. *Journal of Educational Psychology, 100*, 798–811.

Johnston, P., Woodside-Jiron, H., & Day, J. (2001). Teaching and learning literate epistemologies. *Journal of Educational Psychology, 93*(1), 223–233.

Kang, N.-H. (2008). Learning to teach science: Personal epistemologies, teaching goals, and practices of teaching. *Teaching and Teacher Education, 24*, 478–498.

Kienhues, D., Bromme, R., & Stahl, E. (2008). Changing epistemological beliefs: The unexpected impact of a short-term intervention. *British Journal of Educational Psychology, 78*, 545–565.

King, P. M., & Kitchener, K. S. (1994). *Developing reflective judgment: Understanding and promoting intellectual growth and critical thinking in adolescents and adults.* San Francisco: Jossey-Bass.

Kuhn, D., Cheney, R., & Weinstock, M. (2000). The development of epistemological understanding. *Cognitive Development, 15*, 309–328.

Kuhn, D., & Park, S.-H. (2005). Epistemological understanding and the development of intellectual values. *International Journal of Educational Research, 43*, 111–124.

Kuhn, D., & Weinstock, M. (2002). What is epistemological thinking and why does it matter? In B. K. Hofer & P. R. Pintrich (Eds.), *Personal epistemology: The psychology of beliefs about knowledge and knowing* (pp. 121–144). Mahwah, NJ: Lawrence Erlbaum Associates.

Nussbaum, E. M., Sinatra, G. M., & Poliquin, A. (2008). Role of epistemic beliefs and scientific argumentation in science learning. *International Journal of Science Education, 30*, 1977–1999.

Olafson, L., & Schraw, G. (2006). Teachers' beliefs and practices within and across domains. *International Journal of Educational Research, 45*, 71–84.

Perry, W. (1970). *Forms of intellectual and ethical development in the college years.* New York: Holt.

Raudenbush, S. W., & Bryk, A. S. (2002). *Hierarchical linear models: Applications and data analysis methods* (2nd ed.). Newbury Park, CA: Sage.

Reeve, J. (2006). Teachers as facilitators: What autonomy-supportive teachers do and why their students benefit. *Elementary School Journal, 106*, 225–236.

Reeve, J., Bolt, E., & Cai, Y. (1999). Autonomy-supportive teachers: How they teach and motivate students. *Journal of Educational Psychology, 91*, 537–548.

Reeve, J., & Halusic, M. (2009). How K 12 teachers can put self-determination theory principles into practice. *Theory and Research in Education, 7*, 145–154.

Reeve, J., Jang, H., Carrell, D., Jeon, S., & Barch, J. (2004). Enhancing students' engagement by increasing teachers' autonomy support. *Motivation and Emotion, 28*, 147–169.

Roth, G. (2008). Perceived parental conditional regard and autonomy support as predictors of young adults' self- versus other-oriented prosocial tendencies. *Journal of Personality, 76*, 513–534.

Roth, G., Assor, A., Kanat-Maymon, Y., & Kaplan, H. (2007). Autonomous motivation for teaching: How self-determined teaching may lead to self-determined learning. *Journal of Educational Psychology, 99*, 761–774.

Roth, G., Assor, A., Niemiec, C. P., Ryan, R. M., & Deci, E. L. (2009). The negative emotional and behavioral consequences of parental conditional regard: Comparing positive conditional regard, negative conditional regard, and autonomy support as parenting practices. *Developmental Psychology, 45*, 1119–1142.

Ryan, R. M., & Deci, E. L. (2000). Self-determination theory and the facilitation of intrinsic motivation, social development, and well-being. *American Psychologist, 55*, 68–78.

Schommer, M. (1993). Epistemological development and academic performance among secondary students. *Journal of Educational Psychology, 85*, 406–411.

Schraw, G., & Olafson, L. (2002). Teacher's epistemological worldviews and educational practices. *Issues in Education, 8*, 99–148.

Sierens, E., Vansteenkiste, M., Goossens, L., Soenens, B., & Dochy, R. (2009). The synergistic relationship of perceived autonomy support and structure in the prediction of self-regulated learning. *British Journal of Educational Psychology, 79*, 57–68.

Soenens, B., & Vansteenkiste, M. (2005). Antecedents and outcomes of self-determination in three life domains: The role of parents' and teachers' autonomy support. *Journal of Youth and Adolescence, 34*, 589–604.

Vallerand, R. J., Fortier, M. S., & Guay, F. (1997). Self-determination and persistence in a real-life setting: Toward a motivational model of high-school dropout. *Journal of Personality and Social Psychology, 72*, 1161–1176.

Vansteenkiste, M., Simons, J., Lens, W., Sheldon, K. M., & Deci, E. L. (2004). Motivating learning, performance, and persistence: The synergistic role of intrinsic goals and autonomy-support. *Journal of Personality and Social Psychology, 87,* 246–260.

Vansteenkiste, M., Simons, J., Lens, W., Soenens, B., & Matos, L. (2005). Examining the motivational impact of intrinsic versus extrinsic goal framing and autonomy-supportive versus internally controlling communication style on early adolescents' academic achievement. *Child Development, 2,* 483–501.

Valanides, N., & Angeli, C. (2005). Effects of instruction on changes in epistemological beliefs. *Contemporary Educational Psychology, 30,* 314–330.

Weinstock, M. (2009). Like an expert: Representing the problem, epistemic requirements, and competence in an everyday reasoning task. *Learning and Individual Differences, 19,* 423–434.

Weinstock, M., Assor, A., & Broide, G. (2009). Schools as promoters of moral judgment: The essential role of teachers' encouragement of critical thinking. *Social Psychology of Education, 12,* 137–151.

Weinstock, M., & Cronin, M. A. (2003). The everyday production of knowledge: Individual differences in epistemological understanding and juror-reasoning skill. *Applied Cognitive Psychology, 17,* 161–181.

Weinstock, M., & Zviling-Beiser, H. (2009). Separating academic and social experience as potential factors in epistemological development. *Learning and Instruction, 19,* 287–298.

White, B. C. (2000). Pre-service teachers' epistemology viewed through perspectives on problematic classroom situations. *Journal of Education for Teaching, 26,* 279–306.

Williams, G. C., & Deci, E. L. (1996). Internalization of biopsychosocial values by medical students: A test of self-determination theory. *Journal of Personality and Social Psychology, 70,* 767–779.

Yang, F.-Y., Chang, C.-Y., & Hsu, Y.-S. (2008). Teacher views about constructivist instruction and personal epistemology: A national study in Taiwan. *Educational Studies, 34,* 527–542.

12 If There is No One Right Answer?
The Epistemological Implications of Classroom Interactions

Iris Tabak and Michael Weinstock

ABSTRACT

In a typical classroom interaction, the teacher asks questions, students answer, and the teacher—knowing the answer—evaluates the responses. This structure might cultivate a view of knowledge as objective, uncontested, and immutable. In response to criticisms of such models, teachers increasingly encourage students' self-expression, communicating the validity of multiple solutions and perspectives. Stressing that there is "no one right answer," might be important in countering absolutist and encouraging relativist understandings of knowledge. Cultivating more qualified and critical perspectives that seek to use criteria to judge an answer's quality and identify better answers from among a set of "right answers" may be more difficult to achieve, and might explain the prevalence of multiplist and paucity of evaluativist positions among youth. We suggest that teacher training that emphasizes pedagogy apart from subject-matter learning might contribute to practices that encourage individual expression without providing the domain-specific tools or values of evaluating knowledge claims.

> "Do you know what a niche is? No? If, um, you are a student that is very successful, that has figured out a way to understand what a teacher wants to um study for tests, you have found a niche. . . ." (Ms. Quill, West High School, Biology Class: February 17, 1998)

INTRODUCTION

Classroom subject-matter discourse, like the one quoted above, is multilayered. The analogy used in the quote above not only explains the meaning of an ecological niche, but depicts knowledge as a rare commodity passed as a tariff from students to teachers. This can lead to viewing knowledge acquisition as a means for gaining rewards rather than an end. These multiple layers of meaning in day-to-day interactions shape our roles, norms, and values through a process of language socialization (Schieffelin & Ochs,

1986). We suggest that personal epistemologies, views about the nature of knowledge, are shaped, in part, by such classroom language socialization processes, which we refer to as epistemic socialization (Tabak & Weinstock, 2008).

In this chapter, we discuss how different types of classroom interactions might foster different epistemological positions. At this point, in the absence of definitive research that shows an association between such interactions and personal epistemologies, we base our conjectures on a theoretical analysis of the affinity between the characteristics of personal epistemological positions and of classroom interactions. We propose that cultivating an understanding of these processes be incorporated into the teacher education curriculum.

WHAT ARE PERSONAL EPISTEMOLOGICAL POSITIONS?

The model we draw on (Kuhn & Weinstock, 2002) specifies three personal epistemological positions that include understandings of the certainty, source, and simplicity of knowledge, and of how knowledge is justified. An absolutist position views knowledge as an objective self-evident reflection of reality that authorities have been able to glean. Knowledge comes from gathering and reporting facts, and from separating correct from incorrect information. A multiplist position views knowledge as an idiosyncratic subjective construction. Evidence is secondary, because it can be interpreted in different ways to construct different, but equally franchised, explanations. An evaluativist position also views knowledge as constructed, but not as radically subjective. Rather, it takes a qualified subjectivity stance that recognizes that knowledge claims can be judged and evaluated, based in part, on the methods used and strength of the evidence in support of these claims.

Kuhn and Weinstock's (2002) "justification framework" differs from some others in its focus on qualitative differences between the positions, especially between the relativist positions of *multiplism* and *evaluativism*, rather than regarding personal epistemology as more or less objectivist/subjectivist across a continuous spectrum (c.f., Schommer, 1990). Additional differences include a focus on the process of epistemic reasoning with less emphasis on beliefs (c.f., Schraw, Bendixen, & Dunkle, 2002), looking for how multifaceted epistemological understandings are reflected in argument or responses to discrepant knowledge claims. In contrast to commonly used Likert-scale belief surveys, the justification framework assessments present competing knowledge claims to invoke the participant's "theory-in-action" (Kuhn & Weinstock, 2002) about the nature and source of discrepancies in knowledge. Kuhn and Weinstock (Kuhn & Park, 2005; Kuhn & Weinstock, 2002; Tabak & Weinstock, 2008; Weinstock, 2009) also have proposed that values play a significant role in cultivating personal epistemology. For instance, cultures or contexts that value or give preference to authority as a source of knowledge might engender less multiplist or more absolutist thinking (Karabenick & Moosa, 2005; Weinstock, 2009).

SCHOOLING AND PERSONAL EPISTEMOLOGICAL DEVELOPMENT

Young children, adolescents, and adults tend to reflect different personal epistemological positions. Although there are no hard stages in the Piagetian sense, children tend towards absolutism and adolescents towards multiplism. In late adolescence, there appears to be a shift away from multiplism and towards evaluativism (Kuhn, Cheney, & Weinstock, 2000; Weinstock, Neuman, & Glassner, 2006), although substantial numbers remain multiplist. The turn from absolutism towards multiplism seems a more necessary and simpler developmental transition, with a further transition towards evaluativism as less necessary and requiring more specific experience and intention (Chandler, Boyes, & Ball, 1990; Kuhn & Weinstock, 2002). According to some accounts, true evaluativism is only seen with great frequency among those with graduate levels of education (e.g., King & Kitchener, 1994).

Views about knowledge influence how students approach the task of knowledge construction and learning in school contexts. Studies have found relationships between personal epistemology and outcomes such as academic achievement (Cano, 2005), learning strategies (Bråten & Strømsø, 2005), motivation (Kizilgunes, Tekkaya, & Sungur, 2009), written argument (Mason & Scirica, 2006), conceptual understanding (Nussbaum, Sinatra, & Poliquin, 2008), and knowledge integration (Songer & Linn, 1991). Evaluativist positions in particular are associated with stronger academic performance.

Although epistemological development in general proceeds with age, there do not appear to be necessary associations between particular ages and particular epistemological levels (Kuhn & Weinstock, 2002). It seems that informal and formal learning experience (Perry, 1970; Weinstock & Zviling-Beiser, 2009), disciplinary experience (Tabak, Weinstock, & Zviling-Beiser, 2010; Tabak & Weinstock, 2005), and specific epistemological intervention (Kienhues, Bromme, & Stahl, 2008) may play roles in the rate of development and ultimate attainment of different personal epistemologies. Although, much more research is needed on which particular educational activities promote epistemological development. Moreover, with the exception of isolated research endeavors (e.g., Khishfe & Abd-El-Khalick, 2002; Kienhues et al., 2008), the nature of knowledge is seldom an explicit part of the curriculum (Kuhn & Park, 2005). Thus, gaining a better understanding of how classroom interactions communicate and cultivate personal epistemologies can have productive implications for teacher education and curricular design.

LANGUAGE SOCIALIZATION

Socialization is the process through which people become competent participants of their community. Through routine interactions people gradually take on the norms and patterns of behavior that their community values. This process is highly mediated by language (Garrett & Baquedano-Lopez, 2002; Schieffelin & Ochs, 1986). These very subtle processes are often brought to light through cross-cultural studies. Juxtaposing cultural routines can highlight regularities within each community, disparities between communities, and the emergent persona reflected within each pattern of interaction.

For example, such comparisons can reveal how different societies cultivate different notions of taste and individuality. Ochs, Pontecorvo, and Fasulo (1996) recorded family dinners of middle-class Caucasian American and Italian families. The Italian families' talk emphasized food as pleasure, and catered to individual tastes through the varied, customized, selections that were made available at mealtime. The American families did not present such customized options, nor did they emphasize the pleasurable aspects of food. In cases where different options were available, they were usually demarcations between adult and child preferences. For the Italian families preparing a favored dish was a way to show affection, and this in turn created the expectation for recognition and appreciation. Italian children depended on the adults for fulfilling tastes and happiness, and the adults depended on the children's gratitude for their self-esteem. Thus, the different meal-time talk and practices not only cultivated different approaches to food and taste, but also fostered different ways of conceiving of individuality as interdependent in the Italian families or as autonomous in the American families.

In the same vein, in classrooms, the type of claims that are presented, by whom, and the ways in which they are or are not justified, attune learners to ways of conceiving of knowledge. These interactions do not necessarily occur in the context of "learning about knowledge," in fact such contexts rarely occur. Rather, as teachers and students discuss the meaning of mathematical functions, the precursors to the French revolution, or the workings of the respiratory system, they are also constructing a view of what types of knowledge are valued, and how knowledge is produced and sanctioned. In what follows we consider the epistemological socialization consequences of different types of classroom interactions.

CLASSROOM INTERACTIONS AND EPISTEMIC SOCIALIZATION

The ways in which classroom interactions can imbue particular personal epistemologies stem from material as well as discursive resources. Just as the availability of multiple, customized, food choices was inseparable from the type of pleasurable talk about food in cultivating the Italian versus American orientation to food and individuality, so learning materials are part and parcel of the classroom's role in shaping personal epistemology (e.g., Tabak & Baumgartner, 2004). We present examples of classroom interactions and the associated materials and participant structures, and suggest how they may give rise to the three epistemological positions introduced above.

The Epistemological Consequences of Traditional Recitation Classes

Instruction that is based on recitation tends to depict knowledge as transmitted from authority figures without much attention to alternatives, justifications, or processes of adjudication, thus, as we describe below, it is likely to foster absolutist positions. Traditionally, recitation classes rely on textbooks and the teacher as sources of knowledge, they do not engage in analysis and synthesis of multiple sources of information to construct evidence-based explanations, and the primary mode of interaction is the *Initiation–Response–Evaluation* (IRE; Cazden & Beck, 2003) sequence.

In IRE exchanges, a teacher asks students a "test question" (Nystrand, 1997), where the speaker knows the answer but asks the question in order to assess the audience's knowledge; students are then expected to answer this question; and the teacher follows with an evaluation of the students' response. Students are socialized to this communicative pattern early in their schooling. In fact, students whose out of school experiences do not align well with this form of talk have a more difficult time fitting in with the intellectual activity of the class (e.g., Heath, 1983).

The norms associated with this pattern do not allow for questioning interpretations and challenging knowledge claims. It would be unusual and mostly unacceptable for a student to reply to a teacher's query with a query of their own (Wertsch, 1998). This narrow space of acceptable responses positions the teacher as the authority over knowledge, and students as having minimal agency in the production of knowledge. The teacher's evaluation in the third turn suggests that knowledge can be either right or wrong, leaving little room for considerations of subjectivity and relativism.

Even processes typically associated with complex views of knowledge, such as debates, are obscured in typical recitation classrooms. Debates usually consist of raising alternatives and considering the quality of competing explanations in light of evidence. Yet, based on an in-depth analysis of 60 high school science classes taught by 20 different teachers, Lemke (1990) found that rather than turning to warrants and backings, teacher–student debates were characterized by teachers invoking abstract scientific principles. These principles were often unfamiliar to the students, and were left unexplicated. In the absence of acquiescence, teachers closed the debate by exerting their classroom authority.

The reliance on teachers and textbooks as sources of knowledge in recitation classes makes the process of knowledge construction invisible to students, and obviate the need for justified evidence. In this constellation, backings for claims refer to undisputed authoritative principles to which only the teacher has access. This further projects an image of knowledge as simple, certain, and stemming from authority.

Beyond the "One Right Answer"

Consider in contrast, a situation where teachers and students try to explain phenomena by observing and analyzing primary data. In this case, both teachers and students can appeal to interpretations of the data to back their claims. For example, in a high school biology class where students were investigating animal survival in a simulated ecosystem (Tabak & Reiser, 2008), a student and a teacher were looking at some observation notes of animal behavior (field notes). They were trying to understand why some birds were dying while others were able to survive, and engaged in a very different form of student–teacher debate than the one depicted above.

In the excerpt below (Tabak & Baumgartner, 2004), we see that the teacher is focused on the eating behavior of the bird, and infers that something about the bird's beak does not allow it to eat. The student, however, attends to a segment in the field notes that specifies that, by the time the bird arrived at the location, the other birds had already finished eating, and he therefore conjectures that the bird was slow which might be related to its leg size.

In this exchange, the student seems to have equal footing with the teacher and justifies his claim in reference to primary data, rather than couching his claim as a question, and acquiescing to a teacher's explanatory response. Such interactions can problematize and complicate views of knowledge and evidence for the students. They exemplify that "facts do

3	A	Student	By the time he got there.
	B		They had already finished eating [*describing what is written in the field notes that appear on the screen*]
	C		So he
	D		Was either too slow or
4		Teacher	Ooo or his beak wasn't strong enough
5	A	Student	No, it's not his beak
	B		By the time he got
	C		The shells was already broken
	D		So he was too slow
6		Teacher	Maybe
7		Student	Maybe it's his leg size

(City High School, 1998, Galapagos Finches, Session No. 4, Group 3)

not speak for themselves," because both teacher and student are observing the same information, but attend to different aspects of the information in relation to a particular question, and reach different interpretations and conclusions. In this exchange, evidence and persuasion carry more weight than institutional authority in reconciling debates.

In inquiry learning environments, such as the one depicted in the example above, students investigate their own or teacher-assigned questions. Typically, students are expected to deliver a report or explanation that is backed by evidence. These final products are often also presented to the whole class as a culminating activity. Teacher feedback tends to focus on the coherence and detail of the explanation and on the strength of the evidence (e.g., Crawford, 2000; Kelly, 2007a; Van Zee, Iwasyk, Kurose, Simpson, & Wild, 2001). This type of support can be found in the learning materials as well as in teacher feedback, especially in learning technologies where specific spaces and prompts are provided for causal connectors and evidence (De Jong, 2006; Sandoval, 2004).

Consider for example the ways that the teacher from the example above engages groups in the refinement of their intermediate and final explanations. As the students report on their findings the teacher prompts them to be more explicit about the chain of causality on which they report, on the evidentiary basis for their claims, and on presenting these claims and warrants in a way that would be comprehensible to a naïve audience (Tabak & Reiser, 1999).

The excerpt below is taken from a whole-class discussion that concluded the investigation activity which had taken place over about 7, 45-minute class periods. Each group of students reported orally on the final explanation they constructed in response to the question of why the birds were dying and what enabled the surviving birds to survive. We present a segment from one of the briefer presentation sequences:

Although this dialogue is characterized by back and forth turns between the teacher and students, it does not conform to the IRE structure, because the follow-up teacher turn does not evaluate the students' response against a normative response. Instead, the teacher asks for clarification, prompts the students to continue their account in a causal way, or queries about supporting evidence. Thus, the hidden messages about objective knowledge stemming from authority that characterize the IRE are not present in these types of interaction.

The task context within which this discussion is set also suggests the possibility of multiple accounts, because all the students observe the same corpus of data and inductively arrive at somewhat different explanations for the same situation. This suggestion is then reinforced by the teacher's willingness to accept multiple explanations, provided they are substantiated. In Line 19, for example, the teacher explicitly tells the students that they do not have to agree, and she notes the different accounts that she has

1.	Ms. Patrick	And that pressure selected what? This is where I'm not sure I understand. It selected what?
2.	Students	[students call out responses, but it is hard to distinguish statements]
3.	Ms. Patrick	The beak? It selected which beak?
4.	Hanna	The longer.
5.	Ms. Patrick	The longer beak. Now, I really get fuzzy—why?
6.	Dan	Because the only food around was harder to reach
7.	Ms. Patrick	. . . because the only food that was left during the dry season was hard
8.	Dan	And was hard to break open
9.	Ms. Patrick	And was hard to break open. OK. And . . . finish the story . . .
10.	Dan	And
11.	Ms. Patrick	So the
12.	Dan	the weaker ones . . .
13.	Ms. Patrick	So the weaker ones, the weaker finches could what?
14.	Roy	The females and the younger ones the fledglings had a harder time . . .
15.	Sam	Cracking
16.	Evie	Consumption went down
17.	Ms. Patrick	How did you know that their food consumption went down?
18.	Evie	Said so in the field notes
19.	Ms. Patrick	All right, it said so in the field notes? Ok, I just wondered what your evidence was. Ok. Did you all agree? You don't have to agree. You told me some things about mating, you had evidence about their mating habits. Someone said something about, Sam I think it was you, that maybe the beak length allowed them to reach, was that you? [student responds "yeah"] Reach food that was higher? Did you have evidence to support that?
20.	Sam	Yeah.
21.	Ms. Patrick	What did it say?
22.	Sam	I don't know it's not here.
23.	Ms. Patrick	What do you remember?
24.	Evie	We had kind of like
25.	Sam	Them reaching for the food, something about reaching for the food
26.	Ms. Patrick	OK, so you got a sense that the food was higher up.

(City High School, 1998, Galapagos Finches, culminating, whole-class) heard so far as legitimate candidate explanations. Her main emphasis is on induction from data and support for claims (Lines 17–21).

These types of inquiry learning environments, in which students explore data in order to articulate and defend explanations, create settings where interpretation, construction, and evidence are salient. Thus, these environments, in contrast to traditional recitation environments, can drive a movement away from absolutist conceptions.

Between Knowledge-Centered Ideas and Student-Centered Practices

Some form of inquiry-based learning can be found in more and more classrooms around the world, as exhibited by mention of this type of pedagogy in national curriculum standards for most subjects in different countries (e.g., National Center for History in the Schools, 2010; NRC, 2000; Qualifications and Curriculum Authority, 2010). For example, a study on inquiry in Israel found that most classes in most of the 90 schools sampled included activities where students used source materials in order to investigate a question or topic (Gordon, Levin-Rozalis, Kainan, & Bar-On, 2003).

Repeated experiences with inquiry, of generating evidence-based explanations that are recognized, respected, and legitimized by the teacher, can support an appreciation for the constructed nature of knowledge, and for the importance of evidence in this process. Yet, most studies surveying adolescents' personal epistemological positions report that youths hold predominantly multiplist positions. If inquiry-based learning is conducive to evaluativist positions, and inquiry is becoming wide-spread, why do multiplist positions prevail?

One reason why evaluativist positions may be rare despite increasing exposure to inquiry experiences may be related to the ways in which inquiry-based learning is enacted. This seems especially pertinent in light of converging evidence, as reviewed above, on the role of education rather than strictly age-related stage-like development in cultivating personal epistemology. Some have argued that merely engaging in inquiry is not sufficient, and that explicit reflective instruction focused on epistemological ideas is necessary (Khishfe & Abd-El-Khalick, 2002).

We suggest an additional explanation: That inquiry-based instruction tends to focus on individual construction, and neglects processes of comparison, evaluation, and adjudication among competing accounts. This achieves a movement away from absolutist positions to multiplist positions, but leaves learners with a sense that all accounts are equally valid. Although giving credence to evidence, adolescent learners may posit that any account that is backed by evidence is as equally valid as any other. Thus, the disparity between this position and an evaluativist position is the notion that knowledge claims can be judged and that some can be preferred over others.

In the example above, each group's explanation concerning differential bird survival was carefully scrutinized and critiqued to determine the source of the claims being made, thus challenging multiplist conceptions that knowledge merely reflects idiosyncratic, subjective, opinions. Yet, this evaluation was limited to examining the local coherence of each explanation within itself and in relation to the available data, but no attention was given to comparing among the different student explanations. Did one group's explanation account for more of the data? Did one explanation offer a simpler explanation? Such a step seems crucial to us for fostering evaluativist positions. This focus on individual explanations seems common (Gordon et al., 2003), and is especially true in inquiry contexts in which each student or group of students examine a different topic or question.

The focus on individual explanations is also built into some of the material supports for inquiry. There are spaces and prompts for elaborating individual explanations and for supporting claims with evidence, but rarely are there dedicated material supports for selecting or constructing a preferred explanation out of the pool of class explanations. Inquiry environments that include argumentation activities involve more attention to competing explanations, because they require learners to explicitly address competing claims (Nussbaum et al., 2008). But, even in argumentation contexts learners tend to focus on defending their own position, as opposed to identifying a preferred communal explanation. Moreover, typical classroom contexts usually do not motivate a need to persuade (Berland & Reiser, 2009).

What might be the source of this focus on individual constructions? In part, it may be related to teachers associating inquiry learning with child-centered activities that are aimed at giving children an opportunity for self-expression and for constructing their own knowledge, rather than viewing inquiry as exemplifying the ways that knowledge is produced and justified in professional communities. So, inquiry is viewed as a way to motivate students, to have them be active, to express themselves, and to gain experience in finding and critiquing information (Gordon et al., 2003).

Teachers maintain a variety of views about the essence and goals of inquiry-based learning, and an emphasis on process, engagement, and personal development seems to overshadow issues of disciplinary practices and epistemological commitments (Gordon et al., 2003; Lotter, Harwood, & Bonner, 2007; Patrick & Pintrich, 2001; Windschitl, 2002). These views affect the way they frame activities, and the choices that they make in allocating time, priorities, and attention (Pajares, 1992; Richardson, 1996). For example, in an interview, Ms. Patrick, the teacher from our example classroom dialogue, had stated that: "I make it very clear, very often that there is no right answer to this problem and that the important thing is not the right answer but the best answer determined by the most convincing evidence. . . . Most importantly, I want them to get away from the idea of a right answer and begin to question and think critically." Thus, although she had the goal of evaluating and selecting the best answer, the goals of moving away from "the right answer" and becoming critical thinkers outweighed this goal, and might explain the emphases that we saw in her enactment.

We posit that an emphasis on multiple, alternative, individual constructions that is not accompanied by processes of comparison and evaluation is helpful in moving from absolutist to multiplist views, but falls short of cultivating evaluativist views. This emphasis appears to be prevalent in the material and discursive processes of extant enactments of inquiry-based pedagogy, especially in science. Yet, as we illustrate below, it is possible to highlight the constructed nature of knowledge, provide individual students with the opportunity to examine data and articulate their own explanations, while also engaging in critical comparison and judgment of these explanations. We suggest that such classroom interactions may be more successful in cultivating evaluativist positions.

Setting Adjudication Processes as Communal Classroom Goals.

Lampert's (1990) work in elementary mathematics classrooms is one example of the ways in which individual construction and adjudication can be effectively balanced. Setting the goal of constructing classroom-level shared and preferred explanations seems to be the central relevant strategy for paving a path towards evaluativism.

For example, in one activity, the class raised hypotheses about how to figure out the last digit in a power (e.g., 5^4) without multiplying. Students grappled with this problem and then presented their suggestions in a whole class discussion. However, unlike Ms. Patrick's class in the examples above, this discussion was framed as the class as a whole trying to arrive at the best way to figure this out, rather than as a presentation and critique of the culmination of individual work. Criteria for preferring one suggestion over another included the degree of generalizability of the proposed method.

Preferring one student's explanation over another's can raise concerns about social comparison and individual students' well being. However, over time, the teacher had established social norms in the class (Lampert, Rittenhouse, & Crumbaugh, 1996) to safeguard against such unfortunate side effects. For example, they set up a practice that disagreements needed to be phrased as "I want to question so-and-so's hypothesis," and that a reason needed to be given for this questioning so that it came across as a logical refutation rather than a judgment. This alternative framing, where individual work is respectfully scrutinized as part of a process of working towards a preferred solution may prove more conducive to fostering evaluativist positions.

CONCLUSION: IMPLICATIONS FOR TEACHER EDUCATION

We have pointed to a possible relationship between teacher classroom enactments and barriers to evaluativist reasoning. We alluded to four main issues: (1) The absence of epistemology as an explicit instructional goal; (2) recognizing that there are nuanced positions beyond "the one right answer"; (3) conflating numerous pedagogical goals and neglecting the role that inquiry might play in disciplinary and epistemic socialization; and (4) recognizing the implicit epistemic messages that different types of interaction can send. What types of goals and activities might we consider in preservice teacher education in order to cultivate teaching practices that are more conducive to evaluativism?

Teacher education programs have been criticized for their lack of integration and for separating subject-matter from pedagogy (e.g., Darling-Hammond, 2006). This segregation may also stand in the way of epistemological learning goals. It might explain why inquiry pedagogy is more strongly associated with affective and general goals than with discipline-specific goals. An integrated approach, where preservice teachers learn subject-matter and pedagogy through exposure to student learning materials, is essential for promoting a deeper understanding of the underlying rationale of different types of curricula and activities (e.g., Ball, Sleep, Boerst, & Bass, 2009).

Yet, integration is not enough. Instruction in higher education can foster different epistemological perspectives (Tabak et al., 2010). Therefore, this integration should also include an explicit and reflective focus on the nature of knowledge (e.g., Brownlee & Berthelsen, 2008), emphasizing the distinction between multiplist and evaluativist positions, and how they may influence the different ways in which learners may attend to evidence, critique, and persuasion. Hopefully, such an integration and emphasis on epistemological goals will heighten teachers' awareness of the role that inquiry-based learning can play in shaping a view of knowledge as constructed but subject to evaluation.

Preservice teachers are apt to face some serious challenges in comparing and evaluating student-generated explanations, and in encouraging selection and adjudication. Such processes seem in conflict with the strong child-centered pedagogy messages with which preservice teachers are inundated. Preservice teachers may worry that these processes entail social comparison and a movement towards perpetuating the notion of "one right answer." Indeed, we are not suggesting that learners' esteem and well-being be discarded. Rather, we suggest, as evidenced by examples such as Lampert's classroom, that teachers can create supportive and safe environments where competing accounts can be judged dispassionately. Although, we realize that we still have much to learn about how to achieve this well (Kelly, 2007b).

So, in addition to equipping preservice teachers with a repertoire of methods for establishing trust and safety, teacher preparation programs would have to work on countering the reservations that teachers might have in adopting these practices. A related goal is to help preservice teachers develop a long-term perspective of the curriculum and of their teaching, as well as of how instruction can encompass a range of complementary activities. This perspective can help preservice and novice teachers to feel more comfortable devoting time to establishing classroom norms, and to putting some learning goals at bay while focusing on others, without worrying about compromising their curricular charge.

REFERENCES

Ball, D. L., Sleep, L., Boerst, T. A., & Bass, H. (2009). Combining the development of practice and the practice of development in teacher education. *The Elementary School Journal, 109*(5), 458–474.

Berland, L. K., & Reiser, B. J. (2009). Making sense of argumentation and explanation. *Science Education, 93*, 26–55.

Bråten, I., & Strømsø, H. I. (2005). The relations between epistemological beliefs, implicit theories of intelligence and self regulated learning among Norwegian postsecondary students. *British Journal of Educational Psychology, 75*, 539–565.

Brownlee, J., & Berthelsen, D. (2008). Developing relational epistemology through relational pedagogy: New ways of thinking about personal epistemology in teacher education. In M. S. Khine (Ed.), *Knowing, knowledge and beliefs: Epistemological studies across diverse cultures* (pp. 405–422). Berlin: Springer.

Cano, F. (2005). Epistemological beliefs and approaches to learning: Their change through secondary school and their influence on academic performance. *British Journal of Educational Psychology, 75*, 203–221.

Cazden, C. B., & Beck, S. W. (2003). Classroom Discourse. In A. C. Graesser, M. A. Gernsbacher, & S. R. Goldman (Eds.), *Handbook of discourse processes* (pp. 165–197). Mahwah, NJ: Lawrence Erlbaum Associates.

Chandler, M., Boyes, M., & Ball, L. (1990). Relativism and stations of epistemic doubt. *Journal of Experimental Child Psychology, 50*, 370–395.

Crawford, B. A. (2000). Embracing the essence of inquiry: New roles for science teachers. *Journal of Research in Science Teaching, 37*(9), 916–937.

Darling-Hammond, L. (2006). Constructing 21st-century teacher education. *Journal of Teacher Education, 57*(3), 300–314.

de Jong, T. (2006). Technological advances in inquiry learning. *Science, 312*, 532–533.

Garrett, P. B., & Baquedano-Lopez, P. (2002). Language socialization: Reproduction and continuity, transformation and change. *Annual Review of Anthropology, 31*, 339.

Gordon, D., Levin-Rozalis, M., Kainan, A., & Bar-On, N. (2003). *Research projects in the schools: Summative evaluation report*: The Center for Educational Enhancement, Ben Gurion University of the Negev.

Heath, S. B. (1983). *Ways with words*. Cambridge: Cambridge University Press.

Karabenick, S. A., & Moosa, S. (2005). Culture and personal epistemology: US and Middle Eastern students' beliefs about scientific knowledge and knowing. *Social Psychology of Education, 8*, 375–393.

Kelly, G. (2007a). Discourse in science classrooms. In S. K. Abell & N. G. Lederman (Eds.), *Handbook of research on science education* (pp. 443–469). Mahwah, NJ: Lawrence Erlbaum Associates.

Kelly, G. (2007b). Inquiry, activity, and epistemic practice. In R. Duschl & R. Grandy (Eds.), *Establishing a consensus agenda for K–12 science inquiry*. Rotterdam, Netherlands: Sense.

Khishfe, R., & Abd-El-Khalick, F. (2002). Influence of explicit and reflective versus implicit inquiry-oriented instruction in sixth graders' views of nature of science. *Journal of Research in Science Teaching, 39*(7), 551–578.

Kienhues, D., Bromme, R., & Stahl, E. (2008). Changing epistemological beliefs: The unexpected impact of a short-term intervention. *British Journal of Educational Psychology, 78*, 545–565.

King, P. M., & Kitchener, K. S. (1994). *Developing reflective judgment: Understanding and promoting intellectual growth and critical thinking in adolescents and adults*. San Francisco: Jossey-Bass.

Kizilgunes, B., Tekkaya, C., & Sungur, S. (2009). Modeling the relations among students' epistemological beliefs, motivation, learning approach and achievement. *The Journal of Educational Research, 102*, 243–256.

Kuhn, D., Cheney, R., & Weinstock, M. (2000). The development of epistemological understanding. *Cognitive Development, 15*, 309–328.

Kuhn, D., & Park, S. (2005). Epistemological understanding and intellectual values. *International Journal of Educational Research, 43*, 111–124.

Kuhn, D., & Weinstock, M. (2002). What is epistemological thinking and why does it matter? In B. K. Hofer & P. R. Pintrich (Eds.), *Personal epistemology: The psychology of beliefs about knowledge and knowing* (pp. 121–144). Mahwah, NJ: Lawrence Erlbaum Associates.

Lampert, M. (1990). When the problem is not the question and the solution is not the answer: Mathematical knowing and teaching. *American Educational Research Journal, 27*, 29–63.

Lampert, M., Rittenhouse, P., & Crumbaugh, C. (1996). Agreeing to disagree: Developing sociable mathematical discourse. In David R. Olson & Nancy Torrance (Eds.), *The handbook of education and human development: New models of learning, teaching and schooling* (pp. 732–764). Malden, MA: Blackwell Publishers, Inc.

Lemke, J. L. (1990). *Talking science: Language, learning, and values.* Norwood, NJ: Ablex.

Lotter, C., Harwood, W. S., & Bonner, J. J. (2007). The influence of core teaching conceptions on teachers' use of inquiry teaching practices. *Journal of Research in Science Teaching, 44*(9), 1318–1347.

Mason, L., & Scirica, F. (2006). Prediction of students' argumentation skills about controversial topics by epistemological understanding. *Learning & Instruction, 16*, 492–509.

National Center for History in the Schools. (2010). History Standards. http://nchs.ucla.edu/

NRC. (2000). *Inquiry and the national science education standards: A guide for teaching and learning.* Washington, DC: National Academy Press.

Nussbaum, E. M., Sinatra, G. M., & Poliquin, A. (2008). Role of epistemic beliefs and scientific argumentation in science learning. *International Journal of Science Education, 30*, 1977–1999.

Nystrand, M. (1997). *Opening dialogue: Understanding the dynamics of language and learning in the English classroom.* New York: Teachers College Press.

Ochs, E., Pontecorvo, C., & Fasulo, A. (1996). Socializing taste. *Ethnos, 61*(I–2), 7–46.

Pajares, M. F. (1992). Teachers' beliefs and educational research: Cleaning up a messy construct. *Review of Educational Research, 62*(3), 307–332.

Patrick, H., & Pintrich, P. R. (2001). Conceptual change in teachers' intuitive conceptions of learning, motivation, and instruction: The role of motivational and epistemological beliefs. In B. Torff & R. J. Sternberg (Eds.), *Understanding and teaching the intuitive mind: Student and teacher learning* (pp. 117–143). Mahwah, NJ: Lawrence Erlbaum Associates.

Perry, W. (1970). *Forms of intellectual and ethical development in the college years.* New York: Holt.

Qualifications and Curriculum Authority. (2010). National Curriculum. http://curriculum.qcda.gov.uk/index.aspx

Richardson, V. (1996). The role of attitudes and beliefs in learning to teach. In J. Sikula (Ed.), *Handbook of research on teacher education* (pp. 102–119). New York: Macmillan.

Sandoval, W. A. (2004). Explanation-driven inquiry: Integrating conceptual and epistemic scaffolds for scientific inquiry. *Science Education, 88*, 345–372.

Schieffelin, B. B., & Ochs, E. (1986). Language Socialization. *Annual Review of Anthropology, 15*, 163–191.

Schommer, M. (1990). Effects of beliefs about the nature of knowledge on comprehension. *Journal of Educational Psychology, 82*, 498–504.

Schraw, G., Bendixen, L. D., & Dunkle, M. E. (2002). Development and validation of the Epistemic Beliefs Inventory (EBI). In B. K. Hofer & P. R. Pintrich (Eds.), *Personal epistemology: The psychology of beliefs about knowledge and knowing* (pp. 261–275). Mahwah, NJ: Lawrence Erlbaum Associates.

Songer, N. B., & Linn, M. C. (1991). How do students' views of science influence knowledge integration? *Journal of Research in Science Teaching, 28*, 761–784.

Tabak, I., & Baumgartner, E. (2004). The teacher as partner: Exploring participant structures, symmetry and identity work in scaffolding. *Cognition and Instruction, 22*(4), 393–429.

Tabak, I., & Reiser, B. (2008). Software-realized inquiry support for cultivating a disciplinary stance. *Pragmatics & Cognition, 16*(2), 307–355.

Tabak, I., & Reiser, B. J. (1999, April). *Steering the course of dialogue in inquiry-based science classrooms*. Paper presented at the Annual Meeting of the American Educational Research Association, Montreal, Canada.

Tabak, I., & Weinstock, M. (2008). A sociocultural exploration of epistemological beliefs. In M. S. Khine (Ed.), *Knowing, knowledge, and beliefs: Epistemological studies across diverse cultures* (pp. 177–195). Amsterdam: Springer.

Tabak, I., & Weinstock, M. P. (2005). Knowledge is knowledge is knowledge? The relationship between personal and scientific epistemologies. *Canadian Journal for Science, Mathematics and Technology Education, 5*(3), 307–328.

Tabak, I., Weinstock, M., & Zviling-Beiser, H. (2010). Discipline-specific socialization: A comparative study. In K. Gomez, L. Lyons, & J. Radinsky (Eds.), *Proceedings of the ninth International Conference of the Learning Sciences* (pp. 842–848). Chicago, IL: International Society of the Learning Sciences.

van Zee, E. H., Iwasyk, M., Kurose, A., Simpson, D., & Wild, J. (2001). Student and teacher questioning during conversations about science. *Journal of Research in Science Teaching, 38*(2), 159–190.

Weinstock, M. (2009). Like an expert: Representing the problem, epistemic requirements, and competence in an everyday reasoning task. *Learning and Individual Differences, 19*, 423–434.

Weinstock, M., Neuman, Y., & Glassner, A. (2006). Identification of informal reasoning fallacies as a function of epistemological level, grade level, and cognitive ability. *Journal of Educational Psychology, 98*, 327–341.

Weinstock, M., & Zviling-Beiser, H. (2009). Separating academic and social experience as potential factors in epistemological development. *Learning & Instruction, 19*, 287–298.

Wertsch, J. V. (1998). *Mind as action*. New York: Oxford University Press.

Windschitl, M. (2002). Framing constructivism in practice as the negotiation of dilemmas: An analysis of the conceptual, pedagogical, cultural, and political challenges facing teachers. *Review of Educational Research, 72*(2), 131–175.

13 Personal Epistemology and Ill-Defined Problem Solving in Solo and Dyadic Contexts

Nicos Valanides and Charoula Angeli

ABSRACT

The chapter reports on the results of a mixed-methods study that was undertaken to examine how teachers with different personal epistemologies reasoned about a controversial ill-defined issue individually and with others in dyads. The results of the study showed that teachers used more cognitive statements to support their point of view when they thought alone and more cultural and emotional statements when they thought with others in dyads. Thus, based on the results, controversial ill-defined problem solving within a social context may trigger more emotional activity for an individual than when he or she thinks alone. It is recommended that future studies examine the relationship between epistemic beliefs and reasoning in a contextualized way by assuming an integrative approach so that emotions, epistemological beliefs, and cognition are considered systematically.

INTRODUCTION

Research on personal epistemology has not addressed closely the relationship between context and personal epistemology. Herein, we consider socio-cultural aspects of the context by examining how teachers with different personal epistemologies think about an ill-defined problem alone, and then with another person in a dyad. The results did not reveal a pattern between personal epistemology and ill-defined problem solving in either solo or dyadic contexts. It is speculated that the emotional and cultural nature of the problem affected teachers' problem-solving approaches. It is recommended that future quantitative studies investigate the relationship between personal epistemology and thinking in a contextualized way by assuming an integrative approach so that emotions, culture, personal epistemology, and cognition are considered systemically.

In previous work (Valanides & Angeli, 2008), we investigated the relationship between context and teachers' personal epistemologies by using a correlational approach to research. Specifically, we examined the relationship between teachers' personal epistemologies and their thinking about an ill-defined issue in solo and dyadic problem-solving contexts. The results provided preliminary evidence which indicated that thinking individually was associated with different personal epistemologies rather than thinking collaboratively in dyads. These results also supported previous research that found benefits for collaborative learning in a variety of settings (Dillenbourg, 1999). Whereas our previous work mostly involved quantitative approaches to examining the relationship between personal epistemology and solo and dyadic problem-solving contexts, in this chapter we employed a mixed-method approach in order to better understand how teachers with naïve or sophisticated personal epistemologies think about an ill-defined controversial problem individually or collaboratively in dyads.

In a comprehensive review of the literature, Hofer and Pintrich (1997) stated that there are several approaches for studying personal epistemology. Researchers such as Perry (1970), Baxter Magolda (1992), Belenky, Clinchy, Goldberger, and Tarule (1986), and King and Kitchener (1994) have studied personal epistemology in terms of stage models. In particular, King and Kitchener proposed a 7-stage model to assess two aspects of personal epistemology, namely, view of knowledge and justification of beliefs. Drawing from Perry (1970) and Dewey's (1933) work on reflective thinking, King and Kitchener developed the reflective judgment model to describe how individuals reason about ill-structured problems. Schommer (1998, 1990) suggested a different conceptualization of epistemological development and proposed that personal epistemology would be better conceptualized as a system of more-or-less independent beliefs that do not necessarily develop at the same rate and time. In particular, Schommer (1994, 1998) proposed a taxonomy of five dimensions of epistemological beliefs and constructed a questionnaire with 63 Likert-type items to measure them.

Empirical studies have identified connections between personal epistemology and critical thinking (Brabeck, 1984; King & Kitchener, 1994; Kitchener & King, 1981; Kuhn, 1991). Research evidence indicates that individuals with more sophisticated personal epistemologies engage in more critical thinking (King & Kitchener, 1994; Kuhn, 1991; Perry, 1970). Schraw (2001) argues that critical thinking can be used to effect changes in personal epistemology; that is, "schools should strive to change epistemological beliefs through discussion and modeling, while simultaneously helping students acquire critical thinking skills" (p. 462). Other researchers (e.g., Hofer, 2001; Southerland, Sinatra, & Matthews, 2001) have also argued that personal epistemologies can change when students work collaboratively, and when they are given opportunities to reflect on their thinking and evaluate their beliefs.

Previous research also indicated that personal epistemology is related to problem solving. Sinatra, Southerland, McConaughy, and Demastes (2003) reported research findings that underscore the significance of personal epistemology in the learning of potentially controversial topics. Similarly, research by Bendixen, Dunkle, and Schraw (1994) showed that students who view ability as fixed may be less inclined to pursue challenging intellectual experiences and so may be less inclined to use advanced reasoning skills when thinking about an ill-defined issue. Research by Schraw, Dunkle, and Bendixen (1995) also found that well-structured and ill-structured problems engaged different personal epistemologies. For example, individuals who viewed knowledge from a relativistic perspective adopted multiple strategies to analyze contradiction and ambiguity on ill-structured problems. Research also showed that personal epistemology affects the quality of written arguments about an ill-defined problem (Bendixen, Schraw, & Dunkle, 1998; Bendixen & Schraw, 2001; Schommer & Dunnell, 1997). Schommer and Dunnell (1997) found that the more students believed that the ability to learn is fixed at birth, that learning is quick or not-at-all, and that knowledge is unchanging, the more likely they produced overly simplistic solutions to problems. In essence, this research indicates that learners' personal epistemologies affect their problem-solving strategies and problem-solving performances.

In this chapter, we employed Schommer's (1998) questionnaire to measure preservice teachers' personal epistemologies and then we adopted a mixed-methods approach to understand how teachers with naïve or more sophisticated beliefs thought about a controversial ill-defined problem individually and then collaboratively in dyads. The reason for using Schommer's questionnaire was primarily based on its wide use in different cultural settings. In Schommer's studies, both exploratory and confirmatory factor analyses, using the 12 subsets of items as input variables, have produced a consistent 4-factor structure, rather than the 5-factor structure predicted. We are however aware that research by Chan (2000) showed that in different cultural contexts, items on Schommer's questionnaire did not load into the same factors reported in her studies. In this study, because of the small sample size, we could not conduct any exploratory or confirmatory factor analyses, thus we used the mean scores on the 12 sub-scales of personal epistemology, namely, Seek single answers, Avoid integration, Avoid ambiguity, Knowledge is certain, Depend on authority, Don't criticize authority, Ability to learn is innate, Can't learn how to learn, Success is unrelated to hard work, Learn the first time, Learning is quick, and Concentrated effort is a waste of time. We used all 12 sub-scales because according to Schommer's theoretical conceptualization, personal epistemology is a system of beliefs as measured by these sub-scales on the questionnaire. Nespor (1987) stated that preservice teachers' personal epistemologies are often not addressed within teacher education programs. In fact, the emphasis of teacher education courses is often on information dissemination and content coverage (Griffith & Benson, 1991; Wood & Bennett, 2000). There is however a need to promote personal epistemology in teacher education, because there is preliminary evidence, which shows that some personal epistemologies influence instructional practice (Pajares, 1992; Wood &

Bennett, 2000; Brownlee, 2001; Kang & Wallace, 2005; Tsai, 2000; Yang, Chang, & Hsu, 2008; Muis, 2004; Fitzgerald & Cunningham, 2002). In particular, research by Kang and Wallace demonstrated that teachers' personal epistemologies were related to their teaching goals and subsequently teachers' teaching goals oriented their thinking about teaching and instructional actions.

METHOD

Participants

Twenty elementary school full-time practicing teachers volunteered to participate in the study. These teachers were pursuing a masters' degree in educational sciences. Of the 20 students, 8 were males and 12 females. The average age of the participants was 25.32 years, and their average teaching experience was 8.5 years.

Instruments

Epistemological Beliefs Questionnaire

The epistemological beliefs questionnaire developed by Schommer (1990, 1994) was administered to assess students' personal epistemologies. The questionnaire consists of 63 Likert-type items rated from 1 (strongly disagree) to 5 (strongly agree). The 63 items represent 12 dimensions of epistemological beliefs, namely, Seek single answers, Avoid integration, Avoid ambiguity, Knowledge is certain, Don't criticize authority, Depend on authority, Can't learn how to learn, Success is unrelated to hard work, Ability to learn is innate, Learning is quick, Learn first time, and Concentrated effort is a waste of time. According to Schommer (1990), it is possible for students to be naïve in some beliefs and more sophisticated in others. In Schommer's (1990) studies exploratory and confirmatory factor analyses, using the 12 dimensions as input variables, have produced a consistent 4-factor structure such as: (1) Ability to learn is innate (Innate Ability), (2) Knowledge is discrete and unambiguous (Simple Knowledge), (3) Learning is quick or not at all (Quick Learning), and (4) Knowledge is certain (Certain Knowledge).

Research Procedures

Data were collected in two research sessions. The first research session lasted 80 minutes. During the first 20 minutes, the participants completed Schommer's (1990) questionnaire. Then, they were given 20 minutes to read some materials about the history of Cyprus and the issue of the reunification of Cyprus on the basis of the Annan plan. Specifically, it was explained to them that Cyprus is an artificially divided island with a population of Greek-Cypriots (majority) and Turkish-Cypriots (minority) which was spread throughout the island before the divisive Turkish warfare in 1974. It was also mentioned that the two communities, i.e., Greek-Cypriots and Turkish-Cypriots, live apart, despite many diplomatic efforts to achieve reunification. The latest development has been a United Nations plan named the Annan plan aspiring to reunite the island into a single government with two component states of equal political status.

Subsequently, for the next 40 minutes, students had to work individually in order to write their position on the reunification of Cyprus using a computer tool that was developed specifically for the purposes of this study. Particularly, the instructions stated:

> *In the space below, please discuss your position on the issue of the reunification of Cyprus on the basis of the Annan Plan by bringing in any and all information to make your position convincing. Develop the best analysis of the issue you can, and try to understand and resolve differences in points of view.*

Participants' positions were saved in log files that were later downloaded for analysis purposes. Written instructions asked the participants to analyze the issue broadly from different perspectives, and support their position with reason and evidence. The reading materials were available to the participants throughout the session.

Seven days later, the second research session took place. During this session, which lasted 40 minutes, students were randomly assigned to dyads. Students in each dyad were given the same instructions as in the first session with the only difference that they were instructed to discuss the same issue (i.e., the reunification of Cyprus on the basis of the Annan Plan) using a synchronous text-based computer-supported collaborative environment that was specifically designed and developed for the purposes of this study. The transcript from each dyad was saved into a log file that was downloaded later for analysis. Individual students in each dyad were anonymous and were placed in two different rooms to eliminate physical contact between them. As in the first research session, students could also use the reading materials any time they needed them.

Data Analysis

Log files for individual thinking were downloaded and analyzed by two raters independently. Each rater used Inspiration, a computer software, to diagram the flow of reasoning as reported in each log file. A scheme with scoring rules was provided to the two raters. Specifically, the scoring scheme included criteria essential to good quality thinking such as the extent to which there was a point of view that was clearly supported, explanations, opposing arguments, and discussion of a different point of view and reasons for supporting it. Each rater followed this inductive approach to create different categorizations of the quality of thinking and to classify each log file in one of these categories. Inter-rater reliability was computed using the percentage of agreement between the two raters in terms of classifying a log file in the same category and was found to be 86%. The raters and researchers also discussed observed disagreements and easily resolved the existing differences.

Regarding dyadic thinking, the transcripts from the collaborative sessions were also downloaded and analyzed by the two raters using Inspiration. This analysis focused on the individual contributions to the dialogue and the exchanges between the two partners including the number of disagreements between them. Inter-rater reliability was computed and was found to be 90%.

In order to investigate the differences between solo and dyadic thinking, the transcripts were analyzed using a coding scheme that was developed through a grounded theory approach (Strauss & Corbin, 1990). The first version of the coding scheme was inductively constructed by two researchers and it was then given to an independent rater for confirmation. The independent rater and the researchers then discussed all discrepancies and an improved version of the coding scheme was prepared. The two other independent raters analyzed all solo and dyadic transcripts and a Pearson r between the two ratings was calculated and found to be 0.81, which was regarded satisfactory considering the complexity of the data.

RESULTS

Based on participants' epistemological beliefs scores, participants were found to be naïve in some dimensions of Schommer's (1994) questionnaire and more sophisticated in some others. Total scores ranged from 126 to 170. The median of the distribution was 148 and those participants who scored 148 or below were classified as "Low Epistemological Beliefs" and those who scored above 148 were classified as "High Epistemological Beliefs." Teachers were assigned to 10 dyads based on self-reported beliefs, 7 of which were High/Low dyads, 2 were Low/Low dyads, and 1 was High/High.

Individual thinking

Four categories of thinking, described as Type A, B, C, and D thinking, emerged from the qualitative analysis of the individual log files. *Type A Thinking* reflects low-level thinking with a failure to think about the problem systematically. Instead, several points of view are expressed in a disconnected way without any consistent flow of logic. Of the 20 teachers, 3 of them fell into this category, namely, C114-C5A, C94-C5A, and C109-C5A. C114-C5A scored high on the epistemological beliefs questionnaire and the others low.

Type B Thinking reflects reasoning within a stated point of view supported by a number of reasons. The flow of logic is well-organized and systematic. There is breadth in thinking but not depth, as the arguments presented are not elaborated adequately. Also, the thinking appears to be monological. *Monological thinking* is thinking that rarely considers major alternative points of view, or rarely responds to objections framed by opposing views (Paul, 1995). The majority of teachers fell into this category (i.e., teachers C105-C5A, C101-C5A, C111-C5A, C102-C5A, C112-C5A, C106-C5A, C113-C5A, C107-C5A, C108-C5A, C93-C5A, C104-C5A, and C110-C5A). Of these teachers, 6 scored high on the epistemological beliefs questionnaire and 6 low.

Type C Thinking shows depth and breadth in thinking. In particular, teachers analyzed their point of view in detail by presenting several arguments to support it. However, as was the case with Type B thinking, Type C thinking is also monological in nature because different points of view or opposing arguments are not examined. Three teachers exhibited thinking in this category (C98-C5A, C100-C5A, and C97-C5A). C100-C5A scored high on the epistemological beliefs questionnaire, and the others low.

Type D Thinking shows multilogical thinking or critical thinking. Multilogical thinking is the opposite of monological thinking (i.e., thinking that considers opposite points of view) and examines both supporting and opposing arguments for each view considered (Paul, 1995). Only 2 teachers fell into this category, namely, C96-C5A and C103-C5A. C96-C5A scored high on the epistemological beliefs questionnaire and C103-C5A very low.

The results showed that there were teachers (i.e., C103-C5A, C97-C5A, C98-C5A) who performed poorly on the epistemological beliefs questionnaire but well on the problem-solving task. Also there were teachers (i.e., C114-C5A, C110-C5A, and C105-C5A) who performed well on the epistemological beliefs questionnaire but poorly on the problem-solving task. In essence, the results did not show consistent patterns between epistemological beliefs scores and quality of thinking.

Dyadic thinking

The analyses of the transcripts from the collaborative sessions are shown in Table 13.1. For each participant, Table 13.1 provides information regarding the epistemic score (High or Low), evaluation of the individual performance (i.e., Type A Thinking, etc.), number of messages posted by the individual, number of times the individual interacted with the other person in the dyad by replying to him/her, number of times the individual disagreed with the other person in the dyad, and lastly a calculated number which constituted the inter-subjectivity index. The inter-subjectivity index for each dyad,

Table 13.1 Dyadic Thinking

Dyad	Member ID	Epistemic Score	Solo Thinking	# of contributions	# of interactions	# of disagreements	Inter-subjectivity = Total # of interactions/ Total # of postings
1	C105-C5A	H	Type B	56	17	6	0.40
	C111-C5A	L	Type B	30	17	6	
2	C100-C5A	H	Type C	17	8	1	0.33
	C112-C5A	L	Type B	38	10	3	
3	C106-C5A	H	Type B	26	6	2	0.28
	C113-C5A	H	Type B	35	11	2	
4	C98-C5A	L	Type C	21	6	2	0.32
	C107-C5A	L	Type B	16	6	1	
5	C97-C5A	L	Type C	30	7	4	0.35
	C109-C5A	L	Type A	19	10	0	
6	C104-C5A	H	Type B	42	11	0	0.28
	C108-C5A	L	Type B	38	11	0	
7	C110-C5A	H	Type B	24	9	6	0.45
	C93-C5A	L	Type B	27	14	9	
8	C114-C5A	H	Type A	14	11	0	0.58
	C103-C5A	L	Type D	22	10	2	
9	C96-C5A	H	Type D	30	11	1	0.24
	C101-C5A	L	Type B	56	10	2	
10	C102-C5A	H	Type B	32	12	0	0.30
	C94-C5A	L	Type A	57	15	2	

shown in the last column of Table 13.1, was calculated by dividing the total number of interactions between the partners with the total number of postings from both partners. For example, the calculated inter-subjectivity index for Dyad 8 was found to be .58 (21 / (14 + 22) = 21 / 36). The calculated value shows the degree of interaction between the two members of the dyad. For example, C114-C5A contributed a total of 14 messages, 11 of which were replies to C103-C5A. C103-C5A posted a number of 22 messages, 10 of which were replies to C114-C5A. Thus, Dyad 8 compared to the rest of the dyads had a high degree of interaction (i.e., a high inter-subjectivity index) because the 2 members highly considered each other in the communication process. It is interesting to point out that as shown in Table 13.1, the dyads with the largest number of messages posted by both partners, that is, Dyads 3, 6, 9, and 10, had the lowest inter-subjectivity index signifying that group members did not manage to interact with their partners effectively; instead, each member posted his/her messages without considering the postings of the other person. On the other hand, Dyad 8 had the smallest number of messages posted but the largest inter-subjectivity index showing the effective interaction between the members of the dyad. The results showed that there were teachers, that is, C103-C5A, C93-C5A, C111-C5A, and C97-C5A, with low epistemological beliefs scores who performed well on the collaborative task in terms of intersubjectivity. Also the following teacher dyads, C106-C5A, C113-C5A, C104-C5A, C96-C5A, and C102-C5A, with high scores on the epistemological beliefs questionnaire, performed poorly on the collaborative task.

Based on the results, personal epistemology did not seem to be related to individuals' contribution and performance on the collaborative problem-solving context. Furthermore, an individual's solo performance on the ill-defined problem did not seem to be related with individual's performance on the collaborative problem-solving task. A good example of this is Dyad 8. Specifically, the 2 members of Dyad 8 were C114-C5A who scored very high on the epistemological beliefs questionnaire but had the poorest solo performance on the task, and C103-C5A who scored extremely low on the epistemological beliefs test but had the highest solo task performance. Together, C114-C5A and C103-C5A managed to achieve the highest inter-subjectivity index. The results imply that contextual factors might affect individuals' performances on an ill-defined problem-solving task more so than their epistemological beliefs scores.

Differences Between Solo and Dyadic Transcripts

The analysis of the solo and dyadic transcripts identified 19 different elements of thinking, and these are shown along with their descriptions in Table 13.2.

The 19 elements can be categorized into cognitive, cultural, and emotional elements. Cognitive elements are directly related to reasoning, cultural elements are related to one's culture or cultural identity, and emotional

Table 13.2 Elements of Thinking

Elements	Code	Description
Information from reading materials	Inf (M)	Information present in the reading materials provided to learners.
Cultural Identity	Cid	Knowledge that is directly or indirectly related to, and could only be known from, the learner's culture, as defined by his or her cultural identity.
Emotion	E	Knowledge, experience, event, or activity that is either directly or indirectly emotionally charged.
Information from personal experience	PE	Knowledge, experience, activity, or event that is derived from the individual's personal experience.
Information from other sources	OS	Knowledge, experience, activity, or event that is not directly or personally related on and was not present in the materials provided. This information has no influence on cultural identity.
Inference	Inference	Knowledge in the form of "if x, then y," based upon one or more units either of information contained in the materials or knowledge from the learner/s.
Value judgment not supported by evidence	VJ	An evaluative statement that is clearly judgmental but is not justifiable by any form of knowledge.
Value judgment supported by evidence in the form of information given in the reading materials	VJ(M)	An evaluative statement that is clearly judgmental but also supported by evidence provided in the reading materials.
Value judgment supported by evidence in the form of cultural identity	VJ(CId)	An evaluative statement that is clearly judgmental but is also supported by evidence derived from cultural identity.
Value judgment supported by evidence in the form of an emotion	VJ(E)	An evaluative statement that is clearly judgmental but is also supported by evidence grounded on one's emotions.
Value judgment supported by evidence in the form of personal experience	VJ(PE)	An evaluative statement that is clearly judgmental but is also supported by evidence provided from personal experiences.
Value judgment supported by evidence in the form of information from other sources	VJ(OS)	An evaluative statement that is clearly judgmental but is also supported by evidence provided in information given by other sources.
Question to elicit information	Q(I)	Information questions are objective and have a specific factual answer.
Evaluative Question	Q(E)	Evaluative questions are subjective and are like a judgment call.
Hypothetical Question	Q(H)	A question of what could/would happen.
Clarifying Question	Q(Cl)	A question that asks for clarification.
Social Acknowledgment	SA	All statements or questions that are social greetings or responses.
Personal Data	PD	Personal data.
Clarification	Clarification	Whatever the learner clarified for the other learner.

Table 13.3 Descriptive Statistics for the Elements of Thinking in Solo and Dyadic Problem-Solving Contexts

	Solo			Dyadic		
Element Code	Frequency	Mean	SD	Frequency	Mean	SD
Inf(M)	20	1.11	1.88	14	.78	1.48
Cid	1	.06	.24	0	.00	.00
E	2	.11	.32	6	.33	.69
PE	0	.00	.00	2	.11	.32
OS	4	.22	.55	12	.67	1.24
Inference	9	.50	.79	27	1.50	1.50
VJ	115	6.39	6.84	218	12.11	6.00
VJ(M)	84	4.67	2.52	30	1.67	1.57
VJ(CId)	8	.44	.62	12	.67	.84
VJ(E)	0	.00	.00	8	.44	.71
VJ(PE)	1	.06	.24	1	.06	.24
VJ(OS)	40	2.22	2.10	58	3.22	2.26
Q(I)	0	.00	.00	66	3.67	2.33
Q(E)	6	.33	.97	43	2.39	2.40
Q(H)	3	.17	.51	1	.06	.24
Q(Cl)	0	.00	.00	7	.39	.70
SA	1	.06	.24	75	4.17	2.80
PD	1	.06	.24	7	.39	.80
Clarification	0	.00	.00	6	.33	.77
TE	295	16.39	9.92	595	33.06	13.16

elements are primarily related to the learners' feelings. As shown in Table 13.3, the average number of elements when teachers thought about the problem alone was 16.39 (*SD* = 9.92), but when teachers were put into dyads and were asked to think about the problem with another teacher the average number of elements per teacher increased dramatically to 33.06 (*SD* = 13.16). Also solo thinking was more likely to include value judgments not supported by evidence (*Mean* = 6.39, *SD* = 6.84), value judgments supported by evidence in the form of information given in the reading materials (*Mean* = 4.67, *SD* = 2.52), value judgments supported by evidence in the form of information from other sources (*Mean* = 2.22, *SD* = 2.10), information from reading materials (*Mean* = 1.11, *SD* = 1.88), inferences (*Mean* = .50, *SD* = .79), and value judgments supported by evidence in the form of cultural identity (*Mean* = .44, *SD* = .62).

Similarly, the elements of an individual's thinking when he or she thought about the problem in a group setting was more likely to include value judgments not supported by evidence (*Mean* = 12.11, *SD* = 6.00), social acknowledgment (*Mean* = 4.17, *SD* = 2.80), questions asking for information (*Mean* = 3.67, *SD* = 2.33), value judgments supported by evidence in the form of information from other sources (*Mean* = 3.22, *SD* = 2.26), evaluative questions (*Mean* = 2.39, *SD* = 2.40), value judgments supported by evidence in the form of information given in the reading materials (*Mean* = 1.67, *SD* = 1.57), inferences (*Mean* = 1.50, *SD* = 1.50), information from reading materials (*Mean* = .78, *SD* = 1.48), value judgments supported by evidence in the form of cultural identity (*Mean* = .67, *SD* = .84), and value judgments supported by evidence in the form of an emotion (*Mean* = .44, *SD* = .71).

Repeated measures analyses of variance were subsequently conducted to detect any significant differences between the number of elements of teachers' reasoning when thinking alone and in a dyad. According to the analyses, significant within-subject effects were found for cognitive and emotional elements; that is, Inference ($F = 5.23$, $p < .05$), Value judgments not supported by evidence ($F = 25.32$, $p < .01$), Value judgments supported by evidence in the form of information given in the reading materials ($F = 12.79$, $p < .01$), Value judgments supported by evidence in the form of an emotion ($F = 8.00$, $p < .05$), Evaluative questions ($F = 13.83$, $p < .01$), Social acknowledgment ($F = 119.04$, $p < .01$), and Clarification ($F = 9.00$, $p < .05$). The analyses did not reveal any significant between-subject effects.

DISCUSSION

The chapter reports on the results of a mixed-methods study that sought to better understand how teachers with different personal epistemologies reasoned about an ill-defined issue individually and with others in dyads. According to the results of this study there was not a systematic connection between personal epistemology and ill-defined problem solving in either solo or dyadic contexts. For example, there were teachers who scored very low on the epistemological beliefs questionnaire but achieved high individual performance on the ill-defined problem, and teachers who scored very high on the epistemological beliefs test and achieved low individual problem-solving performance. Similarly, teachers with low epistemological beliefs scores achieved high group performance, and teachers with high epistemological beliefs scores achieved low group performance. There were also instances where teachers with high epistemological beliefs scores achieved high individual problem-solving performance but very low group problem-solving performance. Thus, according to the results of this study, it seems that ill-defined problem solving entails some unique characteristics that influence one's reasoning about the problem.

A qualitative analysis of the transcripts showed that whereas teachers used more cognitive statements (i.e., inferences) to support their point of view when they thought alone, they used more cultural and emotional statements to support their reasoning in their respective dyads. Thus, the results indicate that problem solving within a social context may trigger more emotional activity for an individual than when he or she thinks alone. Furthermore, in this study, the ill-defined problem that was given to the participants was also highly emotional and culturally-based. Based on the results, it seems that the relationship between personal epistemology and problem solving can be better understood if it is conducted in a way, so that the intricacies of the specific context are considered carefully.

Implications for Teacher Education

It is thus our belief, that teacher education programs should engage teachers in *guided* ill-defined problem solving. For example, appropriate pedagogy in teacher education programs would include asking students to constantly draw distinctions not in the abstract but concretely, allowing them to doubt things as well as to engage in debates, and making them aware of the fact that there are multiple ways of carving up the same domain. Also, disagreements should be encouraged, while at the same time learners must learn to control and manage their emotions, or at least learn to be aware of their emotions, and recognize how these affect their thinking about an issue. In essence, we favor learning in environments where the focus is not solely on the cognitive dimension. Thus, we suggest that the study of epistemological development should not be conducted in a decontextualized way ignoring for the most part the subjective experiences of the learner. The inability to include and consider the role of subjective experiences in human thinking has led some researchers to characterize this omission as thinking without the thinker (Labouvie-Vief, 1990). In effect, the failure to consider subjective experiences obscures the way culture and emotions operate on cognition. Thus, we advocate a departure from *cold cognition* towards more integrative approaches in understanding the contextual and dynamic nature of intellectual functioning and epistemological development (Labouvie-Vief, 1990; Neisser, 1963; Norman, 1980; Pintrich, Marx, & Boyle, 1993; Sinatra, 2005; Tomkins, 1963).

REFERENCES

Baxter Magolda, M. B. (1992). *Knowing and reasoning in college: Gender related patterns in students' intellectual development.* San Francisco, CA: Jossey-Bass.
Belenky, M. F., Clinchy, B. M., Goldberger, N. R., & Tarule, J. M. (1986). *Women's ways of knowing: The development of self, voice and mind.* New York: Basic Books.

Bendixen, L. D., Dunkle, M. E., & Schraw, G. (1994). Epistemological beliefs and reflective judgment. *Psychological Reports, 75,* 1595–1600.

Bendixen, L. D., Schraw, G., & Dunkle, M. E. (1998). Epistemic beliefs and moral reasoning. *Journal of Psychology, 13,* 187–200.

Bendixen, L. D., & Schraw, G. (2001). Why do epistemological beliefs affect ill-defined problem solving? Paper presented at the meeting of the American Educational Research Association, Seattle, Washington.

Brabeck, M. (1984). The relationship between critical thinking skills and the development of reflective judgment. *Journal of Applied Developmental Psychology, 4,* 23–34.

Brownlee, J. (2001). Knowing and learning in teacher education: A theoretical framework of core and peripheral epistemological beliefs. *Asia Pacific Journal of Teacher Education & Development, 4*(1), 167–190.

Chan, K. (2000). *Teacher education students' epistemological beliefs—a cultural perspective on learning and teaching.* Paper presented at the meeting of the Association for Active Educational Researchers, Sydney, Australia.

Dewey, J. (1933). *How we think.* Lexington, MA: Heath.

Dillenbourg, P. (1999). What do you mean by collaborative learning? In P. Dillenbourg (Ed.), *Collaborative-learning: Cognitive and computational approaches* (pp.1–19). Oxford: Elsevier.

Fitzgerald, J., & Cunningham, J. W. (2002). Balance in teaching reading: An instructional approach based on a particular epistemological outlook. *Reading and Writing Quarterly, 18*(4), 353–364.

Griffith, B. E., & Benson, G. D. (1991, April). *Novice teachers' ways of knowing.* Paper presented at the Annual Meeting of the American Educational Research Association, Chicago IL.

Hofer, B. K. (2001). Personal epistemology research: Implications for learning and teaching. *Educational Psychology Review, 13*(4), 353–383.

Hofer, B. K., & Pintrich, P. R. (1997). The development of epistemological theories: Beliefs about knowledge and knowing and their relation to learning. *Review of Educational Research, 67*(1), 88–140.

Kang, N., & Wallace, C. S. (2005). Secondary science teachers' use of laboratory activities: Linking epistemological beliefs, goals, and practices. *Science Education, 89,* 140–165.

King, P. M., & Kitchener, K. S. (1994). *Developing reflective judgment: Understanding and promoting intellectual growth and critical thinking in adolescents and adults.* San Francisco, CA: Jossey-Bass Publishers.

Kitchener, K. S., & King, P. M. (1981). Reflective judgment: Concepts of justification and their relationship to age and education. *Journal of Applied Developmental Psychology, 2,* 89–116.

Kuhn, D. (1991). *The skills of argument.* Cambridge, London: Cambridge University Press.

Labouvie-Vief, G. (1990). Wisdom as integrated thoughts: Historical and developmental perspectives. In R. J. Sternberg (Ed.), *Wisdom: Its nature, origins, and development* (pp. 52–83). Cambridge, London: Cambridge University Press.

Muis, K. R. (2004). Personal epistemology and mathematics: A critical review and synthesis of research. *Review of Educational Research, 74*(3), 317–377.

Neisser, U. (1963). The imitation of man by machine. *Science, 139,* 193–197.

Nespor, J. K. (1987). The role of beliefs in the practice of teaching. *Journal of Curriculum Studies, 19*(4), 317–328.

Norman, D. A. (1980). Twelve issues for cognitive science. *Cognitive Science, 4,* 1–32.

Pajares, F. (1992). Teachers' beliefs and educational research: Cleaning up a messy construct. *Review of Educational Research, 62,* 307–332.

Paul, R. (1995). *Critical thinking: How to prepare students for a rapidly changing world*. Santa Rosa, CA: Foundation for Critical Thinking.

Perry, W. G. (1970). *Forms of intellectual and ethical development in the college years: A scheme*. New York: Holt, Rinehart, and Winston.

Pintrich, P. R., Marx, R. W., & Boyle, R. A. (1993). Beyond cold conceptual change: The role of motivational beliefs and classroom contextual factors in the process of conceptual change. *Review of Educational Research, 63*, 167–199.

Schommer, M. (1990). Effects of beliefs about the nature of knowledge on comprehension. *Journal of Educational Psychology, 82*, 498–504.

Schommer, M. (1994). Synthesizing epistemological belief research: Tentative understandings and provocative confusions. *Educational Psychology Review, 6*, 293–320.

Schommer, M. (1998). The influence of age and education on epistemological beliefs. *British Journal of Educational Psychology, 68*, 551–562.

Schommer, M., & Dunnell, P. A. (1997, March). Epistemological beliefs of gifted high school students. *Roeper Review*, 153–156.

Schraw, G. (2001). Current themes and future directions in epistemological research: A commentary. *Educational Psychology Review, 13*(4), 451–464.

Schraw, G., Dunkle, M. E., & Bendixen, L. D. (1995). Cognitive processes in well-defined and ill-defined problem solving. *Applied Cognitive Psychology, 9*, 523–538.

Sinatra, G. M. (2005). The "warming trend" in conceptual change research: The legacy of Paul R. Pintrich. *Educational Psychologist, 40*(2), 107–115.

Sinatra, G. M., Southerland, S. A., McConaughy, F., & Demastes, J. W. (2003). Intentions and beliefs in students' understanding and acceptance of biological evolution. *Journal of Research in Science Teaching, 40*(5), 510–528.

Southerland, S. A., Sinatra, G. M., & Matthews, M. R. (2001). Belief, knowledge, and science education. *Educational Psychology Review, 13*(4), 325–351.

Strauss, A. L., & Corbin, J. (1990). *Basics of qualitative research: Grounded theory procedures and techniques*. Newbury Park, CA: Sage.

Tomkins, S. S. (1963). Simulation of personality: The interrelationships between affect, memory, thinking, perception, and action. In S. S. Tomkins & S. Messick (Eds.), *Computer simulation of personality: Frontier of psychological theory* (pp. 3–57). New York: Wiley.

Tsai, C. (2000). The effects of STS-oriented instruction on female tenth graders' cognitive structure outcomes and the role of student scientific epistemological beliefs. *International Journal of Science Education, 22*(10), 1099–1115.

Valanides, N., & Angeli, C. (2008). An exploratory study about the role of epistemological beliefs and dispositions on learners' thinking about an ill-defined issue in solo and duo problem-solving contexts. In M. S. Khine (Ed.), *Knowing, knowledge and beliefs: Epistemological studies across diverse cultures* (pp. 210–231). The Netherlands: Springer.

Wood, E., & Bennett, N. (2000). Changing theories, changing practice: Exploring early childhood teachers' professional learning. *Teaching and Teacher Education, 16*(5–6), 635–647.

Yang, F.-Y., Chang, C.-Y., & Hsu, Y.-S. (2008). Teacher views about constructivist instruction and personal epistemology: A national study in Taiwan. *Educational Studies, 34*(5), 527–542.

14 Teachers' Epistemological Beliefs and Practices with Students with Disabilities and At-Risk in Inclusive Classrooms
Implications For Teacher Development

Eileen Schwartz and Anne Jordan

ABSTRACT

Teachers' epistemological beliefs are thought to be related, and perhaps influential, in the instructional practices that teachers select. This research study, drawing on the work of Schwartz (2009), explores the personal epistemological beliefs of 12 elementary teachers in inclusive classrooms. A qualitative analysis of teachers' epistemological beliefs is presented from narrative interviews with teachers about their beliefs about their roles and responsibilities in working with students with disabilities. Findings are linked to teachers' observed classroom practices, both with their class as a whole and with individual students with disabilities and at risk of underachieving. The diversity of the teachers' beliefs and the clustering of the beliefs into distinct patterns suggest a link between teachers' epistemological beliefs about ways of knowing, the nature of teaching, learning, knowing and knowledge, their beliefs about ability and disability, and their actions and decisions while teaching in inclusive classrooms. Implications are drawn for teacher educators and those charged with influencing teacher beliefs and practices in inclusive classrooms.

INTRODUCTION

This chapter considers teachers' beliefs about learning, knowing, knowledge, and ability/disability and how these belief dimensions relate to the instructional practices of teachers in inclusive classrooms. We explore whether such beliefs relate to how teachers teach, and whether these beliefs impact on the quality of teachers' instructional interactions with their students, both with and without disabilities. Whereas there is debate about what sets of beliefs constitute personal epistemological beliefs (Schommer, 1994; Hofer & Pintrich, 1997), for the purposes of this chapter, we include as part of teachers' epistemological beliefs their beliefs about the nature of learning, of knowing, and of knowledge.

Teachers vary in their tacit beliefs about ability to learn in terms of seeing learning as either a fixed entity that is unlikely to change or as fluid and able to be built upon incrementally by instruction. Teachers' beliefs about *disability* also seem to differ along a continuum. At one end of the continuum, disability can be viewed as permanent, internal, and pathological. At the other end of the continuum, disability can be viewed as a barrier to learning created by the demands of a mainstream society geared to the abled (Jordan & Stanovich, 2004; Stanovich & Jordan, 1998). Differences in beliefs about ability and disability appear to be correlated with differences in how teachers work with their students, both with and without identified disabilities (Jordan, Glenn, & McGhie-Richmond, 2010; Jordan & Stanovich, 2003)

The Development of the Teachers' Epistemological Beliefs Framework (TEBF)

Teachers' epistemological beliefs are defined as personal theories about the nature of knowledge, how one knows, and how knowledge is acquired. A major focus of this chapter relates to the development of an epistemological analysis framework described as the Teachers' Epistemological Beliefs Framework (TEBF), to ascertain how beliefs about disability and about knowing, knowledge, and learning are aligned with teachers' observed practices (Schwartz, 2009). The development and nature of the TEBF is explained in this section. As well as drawing on the theoretical work of Schommer (1990, 1994) it also drew on Belenky, Clinchy, Goldberger, and

Table 14.1 Teachers' Epistemological Beliefs Framework (TEBF)

	Epistemological beliefs	
Ways of knowing	1A Connected: Empathic, caring, teacher puts self in student's/other's shoes	1B Separate: Detached, standards, expectations, neutral perspective
Nature of teaching and learning	2A Teacher is locus of responsibility: How student learns 2A1 In groups with each other 2A2 Gradual in limitless time frame	2B Teacher is not locus of responsibility: Why student can't learn 2B1 Individual/one-on-one 2B2 Quick in limited time frame
Nature of knowing: Finding out about students	3A Teacher is not sole source of knowing: Source and justification of knowledge is integration of views of others through discussions with other teachers, parents, experts	3B Teacher is sole source of knowing: Source and justification of knowledge is self as authority or others as experts
Nature of knowledge	4A Uncertain, interrelated, to be understood	4B Certain, factual, to be memorized and recalled

Tarule (1986). Table 14.1 contains the components of the TEBF with the definitions that were used for coding. The definitions describe teachers' expressed beliefs using criteria that have been adapted, extended, and redefined from the personal epistemological beliefs literature.

Belenky et al. (1986) identified two categories in the epistemological dimension of *procedural knowledge. Connected knowing* is an empathic and caring approach to knowing involving adopting the perspective of the other's way of thinking and *separate knowing* which is a more detached or impersonal way of knowing involving a neutral perspective. When connected knowing and separate knowing are integrated an individual is thought to know through the category of *constructed knowledge.* These categories of connected and separate knowing are represented in the TEBF in the dimension of "ways of knowing" in Table 14.1 (1A and 1B). The theoretical definitions for connected ways of knowing were adapted, extended, and redefined for the TEBF to take account of the teaching context. Therefore, the definitions developed for connected ways of knowing in the TEBF included the words: Empathic, caring, teacher puts self in the student's/other's shoes (1A) and for separate ways of knowing: Detached, standards, expectations, and neutral perspective (1B).

The TEBF also drew on Schommer's research and theorization about epistemological beliefs. Schommer (1990) developed an Epistemological Beliefs Questionnaire (EBQ) that tapped five areas of beliefs about the nature of learning, knowing, and knowledge. With regard to the *nature of learning*, these elements are distinguished by the speed of knowledge acquisition which can range from quick to gradual. In the TEBF (Table 14.1) these elements are represented by teachers' beliefs about the nature of teaching and learning as a gradual process in limitless time frames and as a quick all-or-none process in limited time frames (2A2 and 2B2). With regard to beliefs about *the nature of knowing*, the elements in the TEBF include the teacher's explanation of how he/she seeks to know his/her students, either through discussion with others, (3A) and/or through self as authority (3B).

Finally, beliefs about *the nature of knowledge* are described in the TEBF as relating to Schommer's description of the stability and structure of knowledge. Stability of knowledge ranges from simple, certain, and absolute to uncertain, tentative, and evolving. The structure of knowledge may be understood as a range from simple unambiguous facts to highly interrelated concepts. These beliefs are represented in the TEBF as teachers' beliefs about knowledge as uncertain, interrelated, to be understood and as certain, factual, to be memorized and recalled (4A and 4B).

Schommer (1994) suggested that individuals can simultaneously hold both naïve and sophisticated beliefs about the nature of learning, knowing, and knowledge. Individuals can also have epistemological beliefs that are characterized by "frequency distributions rather than dichotomies or continuums" (Schommer-Aikins, 2002, p. 106). In this characterization, one could imagine a mature or sophisticated learner who believes that a small percentage of knowledge is certain/absolute whereas a substantial percentage of knowledge is uncertain/evolving.

Teachers' Beliefs about the Nature of Ability and Disability

The TEBF has been constructed to reflect not only epistemological beliefs, but the beliefs teachers hold about the nature of ability and disability. Jordan et al. (2010) interviewed teachers about their beliefs about disability using the *Pathognomonic-Interventionist* (P-I) interview. From analyses of this interview data, the nature of the beliefs of the teachers about disability can be inferred. At one end of the continuum, teachers with *Interventionist (Int)* beliefs see disability as partly resulting from barriers to accessing learning caused by an environment that favors the able. These teachers see themselves as responsible for removing barriers to learning. In contrast, at the other end of the continuum, teachers with *Pathognomonic (Path)* beliefs assume that disability is an internal, structural, and enduring pathological condition of the students themselves, readily recognized and labeled by a medical identification. Because it is assumed the disability cannot be helped, teachers with *Path* beliefs see themselves as having little responsibility for fostering student learning. For instance, teachers who express *Path* beliefs prefer that students with disabilities be withdrawn from the classroom for instruction that is geared to their disability, whereas teachers who have *Int* beliefs prefer that resources be delivered in the classroom to assist them to "get through to" their students (Jordan & Stanovich, 2003).

The *Path-Int* construct about *disability* has many of the characteristics ascribed by Dweck (2000) to teachers' beliefs about ability. According to Dweck, personal epistemological beliefs about ability lie along a continuum, at one end of which are "entity beliefs" that assume that ability is an internal, stable, fixed trait, unlikely to be changed by environmental influences such as teaching. At the other end, "incremental beliefs" hold that ability is malleable and developed through environmentally-mediated learning.

The distinctions made by Jordan et al. (2010) about teachers' beliefs about disability (*Pathognomonic-Inter*ventionist) were included as a dimension in the TEBF. They were coded as beliefs about the Nature of Teaching and Learning (2A and 2B); in terms of whether or not the teachers saw themselves as responsible for learning outcomes in explaining why one or more of their students had not succeeded.

Teacher Beliefs Linked to Teaching Practices

There appears to be a relationship between teacher beliefs about disability and ability, and between such beliefs and differences in teachers' instructional interactions with students (Jordan and Stanovich, 2003). Jordan and Stanovich provided evidence that differences in teacher beliefs about the fixed or fluid nature of disability are related to differences in their instructional practices. In more recent research they observed 34 teachers as they taught in their inclusive elementary classrooms, using the Classroom Observation Scale (COS) and the Teacher–Student Interaction Scale (TSIS), described below (Jordan et al., 2010). An intriguing finding was that style of teaching, coded as the extent and depth of teacher–student interaction on the academic content of the lesson, correlated with teachers' *Path-Int* beliefs about the students with disabilities. Teachers with Interventionist *(Int)* beliefs worked at higher levels of instructional interaction and engagement with all their students as well as with those with disabilities than did teachers with *Path* beliefs who assumed that disability is internal and fixed. This provided evidence of a relationship between teacher beliefs about disability and ability, and between such beliefs and differences in teachers' instructional interactions with students.

The current study explores the relationship between teacher beliefs about disability and ability, and the instructional interactions of 12 elementary teachers in inclusive classrooms. It also investigates how teachers' beliefs about learning, knowing, and knowledge relate to their beliefs about ability/disability and to their interactions with students.

METHOD

Context and Participants for the Research

The research reported in this chapter was conducted across a 2-year period from the fall of 2003 to the spring of 2005 in two public schools and one private school that had policies for including students with disabilities in the general education classroom. The elementary schools were located in a large metropolitan area in Ontario, Canada.

Twelve teachers were selected from a larger sample of 34 teachers because they represented the range of high to low levels of instructional interactions with their classes as a whole, and with 2 students with special education needs. The 34 teachers were a part of the larger study, the Supporting Effective Teachers project (Stanovich & Jordan, 1998). The teachers taught in inclusive classrooms from Grades 1 to 8 and had between 1 and 19 years of teaching experience.

Instruments

Pathognomonic/Interventionist Semi-Structured Interview Protocol (Path-Int)

This interview protocol was developed from interview data from the 34 teachers who participated in the SET project. Detail on the interview protocol is provided in Jordan, Schwartz, and McGhie-Richmond (2009), Jordan et al. (2010), and Jordan and Stanovich (2003). In the interview, the teacher was asked to identify two students who were underachieving or designated as exceptional and to describe in chronological sequence the events that had taken place over the preceding year as he or she taught those students, the decisions that the teacher had made, his or her rationale for making them, and what the teacher had hoped would result. The individual interviews usually took between 45 and 60 minutes and were tape recorded. Schwartz (2009) qualitatively analyzed these interview transcripts using the TEBF to code the teachers' epistemological beliefs about learning, knowledge, and knowing and to seek any connections between such epistemological beliefs and *Path-Int* beliefs about disability and teacher responsibility for student learning.

Classroom Observation Scale (COS)

The COS developed by McGhie-Richmond, Underwood, and Jordan (2007) codes 32 effective teaching practices on 3-point scales (consistent, inconsistent, and not observed). The items measure classroom management (8 items), time management (8 items), and lesson presentation (16 items). Jordan et al. (2010) reported that inter-rater agreement between two independent raters for the COS was 94%.

Teacher–Student Interaction Scale (TSIS)

In addition to the 32 items of the COS, observers rated the extent and type of dialogical instructional interactions used by the teacher on the TSIS, rated for the class as a whole and one rating each for the 2 students with special needs. The TSIS has a 7-point scale that ranges from "teacher had no interaction" with the class or with the observed students, through "teacher 'transmits' knowledge" with no recourse for the class or student to respond, to "teacher co-constructs meaning" in dialogical interaction with members of the class or with each of the students with special needs. Thus, the TSIS represents a scale of dialogical interaction from none to a high level of academic engagement of students with the teacher about the topic of the lesson. The two scales of interaction with the students with special needs are also a proxy that measures the extent of inclusion of those students in the class.

Procedure

The observations took place during a half day when teachers were teaching core lessons (literacy, math, and science) and when the students with special needs were present in the class. Prior to the observation session, teachers were given a list of their students and asked to rate them using 5-point scales on three variables: Academic achievement relative to the class as a whole; extent to which instructional accommodations were needed; and acceptability of behavior. On the day of the observation session, observers used this teacher rating to select 2 students—1 with significant instructional accommodations requiring an Individual Education Plan (IEP) and whose achievement was significantly below the class average; and another who was "at-risk of academic failure" whose achievement was moderately below the class average in achievement and/or behavior and required instructional accommodations. Two observers coded the teachers' interactions with these 2 children based on the 32-item Classroom Observation Scale (COS) and the Teacher Student Interaction Scale (TSIS). The teachers were not aware that 2 students were being specifically observed.

Focus Teachers for the Research Reported in this Chapter

The 12 teachers who were the focus of the analyses reported in this chapter were selected from the larger group of 34 teachers participating in the study. They represented four groups determined by a median split of their scores on the two observational measures—the COS (instructional effectiveness with the class as a whole) and the TSIS (extent and depth of their instructional interactions with the class and the 2 students identified as having a disability or at risk of academic failure). The resulting groups consisted of 5 teachers with high COS and TSIS scores (HH); 2 teachers with high COS scores and low TSIS scores (HL); 1 teacher with a low COS and high TSIS score (LH); and 4 teachers with low COS and low TSIS scores (LL).

Analysis of the P-I Interview Transcripts

The transcripts of the *Path-Int* interview for the 12 teachers were iteratively analyzed using NVivo2 (2002) to identify the nature of the teachers' beliefs about learning, knowing, knowledge, and ability/disability. After several successive examinations of the transcripts, a larger group of codes was collapsed into four main categories of epistemological beliefs that continually reappeared. It was evident that most teacher statements could be coded in at least one or more of these categories of beliefs.

The areas of beliefs were represented dichotomously within the TEBF framework. The theme for the beliefs on the left side of Table 14.1 (1A–4A) involves the social construction of knowing, teaching, and learning incorporating an experiential and "connected" approach to knowing and learning for both teacher and student. The theme for the beliefs on the right side of Table 14.1 (1B–4B) involves individual and "separate" approaches in knowing and learning for both teacher and student.

The transcripts of the teacher interviews were analyzed and the beliefs were coded from the teachers' statements using the following four categories of beliefs:

Table 14.2 Exemplars of Quotations from the Teachers P/I Interviews Coded into Epistemological Belief Categories

Epistemological beliefs

Ways of knowing:
Connected 1A
In response to how targeted student was functioning in the class the teacher responded: "[he] . . . uses a grip, [but he] hates it 'cause it feels uncomfortable & awkward."

Nature of teaching and learning:
Teacher is locus of responsibility 2A
Teacher removes barriers to learning stating that, "So just reduced amount of (hand) writing. They can always type. I always say for good copy, cursive, pen or type and that's for everybody, so kids you know that want to type can type too, so it sort of works out."

Nature of teaching and learning: In peer groupings:
2A1
"I often get them within their own group to help each other . . . just the one-on-one . . . so either myself or her (EA) would work more effective, sometimes the way I explain things may not make sense, but if someone their own age explains it, it will make so much more sense to them, so I try to do that a lot."

Ways of knowing:
Separate 1B
Teacher commented that, "I also have very high expectations of my students. I expect them all to do the best that they can. I am very consistent in checking homework, if I am going to the trouble to give you homework you need to go to the trouble to do it."

Nature of teaching and learning:
Teacher is not locus of responsibility 2B
Teachers' statements that "She is always going to be that low C student. I don't see her getting any higher" "that's the whole nature/ nurture thing . . . it's certainly not being helped by either of their home lives . . . it's biological, it has to be, that's my thinking . . . it's ability, but then that in itself has festered, into other contributing factors."

Nature of teaching and learning: One-on-one: 2B1
Teacher statements that student is able to progress by "basically just the one-on-one . . . so either myself or her (EA) would work with him one-on-one . . . he really doesn't need a lot . . . at first when he's learning the concepts, that's all he needs."

(continued)

Table 14.2 (continued)

Epistemological beliefs	
Speed of learning: Limitless time frame: 2A2 Teachers' statements that "We take one step at a time, whatever she lacks in then it is time to go over and over and over it again." Another teacher states that "it doesn't matter if they (students with difficulties) take a little longer 'cause they don't stick out."	Speed of learning: Limited time frame: 2B2 Teachers' statements that "I have a system in place where if they have two things that are late in a week, they miss our activity time on Friday afternoon, and they've really quite come to enjoy that time. But I'm very consistent there."
Nature of knowing: Teacher is not sole source of knowing/authority: 3A When learning about and getting to know their students, teacher states that, "We reviewed that with the principal, program support . . . I take it to the previous teacher and ask her questions as well . . . see how it went and suggestions . . . for a little bit of advice, to see what worked . . . I like to form my own opinions, kids change . . . wait and see how it's going on my own."	Nature of knowing: Teacher is sole source of knowing/authority: 3B Teacher statements that "I suppose if I had asked for it (material she could have tried with student) then they (special education resource teachers) might have but there were no suggestions because I think most of us know that it has a lot more to do with just getting him to do anything."
Nature of knowledge: Knowledge is uncertain, inter-related, and to be understood: 4A Teacher statements that "once she can read that she will do better at the carpet when I'm going over explanations when we're reading a poem. Or doing science, she can read her sentences, look and understand the dictionary, it *connects* it all."	Nature of knowledge: Knowledge is certain, factual, to be memorized and recalled: 4B Teacher statements that "word problems are difficult even for "my" kids . . . but it's just that . . . they (all students including ones with learning difficulties) count the pieces of information that you need . . . then plug that into the operational formulae which you've read."

1. Ways of knowing (connected and/or separate, see Table 14.1, 1A and 1B);
2. The nature of teaching and learning (teacher as the locus and/or not the locus of responsibility, see Table 14.1, 2A and 2B), including beliefs about learning in groups and/or in one on one interactions (see Table 14.1, 2A1 and 2B1), and beliefs in gradual learning and/or quick learning in a limitless/limited time frame (see Table 14.1, 2A2 and 2B2);
3. Beliefs about the nature of knowing either through discussion with others (see Table 14.1, 3A) and/or through self as authority (see Table 14.1, 3B);
4. Teachers' beliefs about the nature of knowledge as uncertain, inter-related, to be understood (see Table 14.1, 4A) and as certain, factual, to be memorized and recalled (see Table 14.1, 4B).

Three raters, independently applying the definitional criteria to a subset of 10 of the 12 transcripts, were able to agree to an average level of 82% with a range of 78% to 92%. Table 14.2 illustrates the analysis using the TEBF with examples of teachers' statements.

Following the coding, the patterns of teachers' epistemological beliefs were reviewed in relation to their memberships in the groups, HH, HL, LH, and LL. Thus patterns of beliefs were examined in relation to teaching effectiveness with the class as a whole and to teachers' instructional interactions with their exceptional and at-risk students.

FINDINGS

Five teachers, the HH group, were observed to be effective with their class as a whole (high COS score) and with their students with special needs (high TSIS score). Two teachers had high COS scores and low TSIS scores (HL); 1 teacher had a low COS and high TSIS score (LH); and 4 teachers had low COS and low TSIS scores (LL). The teachers' beliefs clustered into patterns associated with their High and Low groupings for observed teaching effectiveness and interaction style with their students with special needs.

Pattern 1: "Effective inclusive teachers"

In Pattern 1 the 5 highly effective teachers (HH) were the only teachers to state their belief that learning is a gradual process. They provided limitless time frames for all their students to learn. The five HH teachers favored both connected and separate ways of knowing their students, held beliefs that the nature of teaching and learning is optimal in co-operative groupings, and considered themselves to be primarily responsible for their students' learning (*Int* beliefs). They also believed that knowledge is acquired gradually over time. These 5 HH teachers had empathy for their students and 'put themselves in the students' shoes' in order to understand their students' difficulties.

Their positive attitude towards inclusion was linked to a belief that learning takes time and effort and requires both empathic and detached approaches towards their students. They also expressed a wish to have their students achieve high standards of behavior and academic success. During observation of their teaching they demonstrated high instructional effectiveness and high levels of dialogical interaction with all their students. One must ask whether their pattern of epistemological beliefs gives rise to or develops from the skill which these teachers demonstrate in their instructional practices.

Pattern 2: "Ineffective teachers"

Four teachers, the LL group, had low COS and low TSIS Scores. They were less effective in time and classroom management and lesson presentation and did not interact dialogically with their students with special needs. Three of these 4 teachers believed that the nature of knowledge is certain, factual, and to be memorized and recalled. Their beliefs contrasted to the 5 effective HH teachers with connected beliefs in knowledge as uncertain, inter-related, and meaningful.

These 3 LL teachers were distinguishable from the 4th member of their group by their belief in the nature of knowledge as certain. They asserted that knowledge is certain and factual and did not at any point propose that knowledge may at times be complex and uncertain. From the observations and their own descriptions, their teaching practices were characterized by extensive use of work sheet exercises that required students to apply operational formula, such as using cloze procedures and filling in the blanks, suggesting that their instructional objectives were to have students focus on "correct" answers.

The 3 LL teachers emphasized student performance in their classroom. One teacher rewarded student performance with marks for correct answers, another teacher rewarded speed for completion of work. The 3rd member of the LL group complained that the student who is LD "just needs to get more done", indicative of the view held by the group that ability and disability are internal characteristics of students, and that the students themselves are responsible for overcoming obstacles to learning.

Like the 4 teachers in the LL group, there were also 3 other teachers (2 HL and 1 LH) who also stated that although they were sometimes responsible for their students, other people should be responsible for learning outcomes, especially for their students with special needs. They believed that the students had problems learning because they did not work hard enough or their families did not support them. This contrasts with the HH teachers who stated that they were primarily responsible for the learning of all their students.

DISCUSSION

Teachers' Epistemological Beliefs and Teaching Practices

The findings of the analyses reported in this chapter suggest a link between teachers' epistemological assumptions and beliefs, their beliefs about ability and disability and the effectiveness of their teaching practices, both with the class as a whole and with individual students with disabilities and at-risk. Five HH teachers were rated on the COS and TSIS as highly effective with their classes as a whole and with their students with disabilities and learning difficulties. The group subscribed to ways of knowing as both connected and separate, demonstrating empathy for their students' learning while maintaining high expectations and external standards for performance. They believed the nature of knowledge to be often uncertain and complex. These beliefs are in line with the findings of Clinchy (2002) who states that connected and separate ways of knowing can co-exist in the same individual and that such people use both to support critical thinking and to enhance learning. Among college students, high scores in both separate and connected knowing predicted beliefs in gradual learning. In turn, beliefs in gradual learning seemed to influence reading comprehension and classroom performance (Schommer & Easter, 2006). Silverman (2007) in a study with 71 preservice teachers found a high correlation between epistemological beliefs and attitudes towards inclusion. Those participants who believed in "gradual, effortful learning and improvable learning ability" also endorsed "positive attitudes toward the benefits of inclusion for all students" (p. 47).

An emphasis on certain knowledge that excludes any belief in knowledge as sometimes uncertain, relative, and contextually-bound may also be an important indicator of teachers' instructional styles and preferences. The pattern of the 3 LL group members, who held that knowledge is factual and certain, is consistent with Stipek, Givvin, Salmon, and MacGyvers' (2001) view that mathematics teachers have a fairly coherent set of beliefs which predict their instructional practices. They found that those teachers who emphasized student performance rather than understanding believe that mathematics is a set of operations and procedures that need to be learned (knowledge as certain and factual), and that acquisition of knowledge can be controlled by the use of extrinsic rewards. Stipek et al. also indicate that teachers with an entity theory of ability also emphasized student performance outcomes over acquiring concepts. Schwartz's (2009) finding however, that teacher beliefs about certain knowledge affects their emphasis on performance rather than on understanding in the classroom, must be regarded as preliminary and in need of further study. Larger samples of teachers and longitudinal analysis are needed to develop an understanding of the complex interrelationships between epistemological beliefs and teaching decisions and instructional practices.

Differences in beliefs about knowledge, how it is acquired, and the nature of ability and disability seem to predict how much attention teachers pay to students who are struggling and the quantity and style of instructional interactions they select during instruction (Stanovich & Jordan, 1998). In addition, their choice of evaluation and motivational techniques may be related to differences in beliefs (Jordan et al., 2010).

The TEBF as a Potential Tool for Understanding Teacher Development

Studies by Elby, Lau, and Hammer (2007) view epistemological beliefs as an individual's collection of epistemological resources. Individuals call upon finely grained cognitive resources whose activation depends sensitively on context. These resources can be organized into different coherent "beliefs" in different settings, forming a "generative tool box" which can be contextually applied (p. 42). Elby et al. suggest that development of epistemologies should be a matter of helping individuals "reframe their practices in ways that consistently activate productive epistemological resources they already possess, rather than changing their epistemological beliefs from scratch" (p. 1).

The TEBF offers a potential investigative tool that could illuminate the teachers' epistemological beliefs and beliefs about ability and disability, and that could be used to assist them to reframe their practices. The Pathognomonic-Interventionist interview technique asks teachers to recount their decisions and actions with their struggling students, and to explain the rationale for their choices. Such a tool might allow researchers and teacher educators to discern patterns of beliefs that underlie more and less effective teaching styles.

One dimension of the TEBF represent beliefs in connected ways of knowing, gradual learning, teacher as responsible for learning outcomes, and for working co-operatively with others, drawing on multiple sources of authority, and understanding knowledge as uncertain, interrelated, and understood. The other dimensions in the TEBF feature separate or neutral ways of knowing, students as responsible for learning outcomes, working one on one, teacher as source of authority, and a belief in learning as quick, and knowledge as certain and factual. These two dimensions should not however be interpreted as representing sophisticated and positive connotations versus naïve and negative connotations, because teacher beliefs need to be interpreted in light of the "situated nature of the construct" (Hofer, 2001, p. 362). Muis (2004) also contends that it is not possible to confer a positive or negative value on a belief because epistemological viewpoints are bound by context. The categories of teachers' epistemological beliefs, whether situated in either dimension of the framework, may determine how well a teacher engages his/her students. The TEBF is offered as an initial tool to be used to examine teacher beliefs in the instructional context and in light of teachers' instructional objectives.

Possibilities for Changing Teachers' Epistemological Beliefs and Practices

Clearly in some contexts certain beliefs are beneficial to student engagement and achievement, whereas in others they are not. One example is the negative connotations of the *path* beliefs of teachers who see certain disabilities as internal, fixed, and students with disabilities as unable to benefit from instruction. Such beliefs are associated with denying access to the inclusive classroom (Jordan et al. 2010). Yet, Pajares (1992) commented how difficult it is to change teachers' assumptions and beliefs. As an example of the resistance of teachers to changing beliefs, White (2007) examined the beliefs and practices of 5 teachers over 5 years, to see how they changed over time and as a result of teaching experiences. All teachers worked in a school system that emphasized inclusion and provided considerable resources and professional development to ensure its success. White found that the thinking of teachers over the intervening time period was largely predicted by the beliefs with which they entered the study. Three teachers with *Pathognomonic* beliefs had changed little over the course of the study. They continued to favor withdrawal programs for struggling students, to differentiate instruction by sending work home, and to blame the students for lack of progress. One novice teacher entered the study expressing *Interventionist* beliefs but with a great deal of uncertainty about practice, yet 5 years later had mastered techniques to differentiate instruction to accommodate a broad range of students in her classroom.

How can teachers be assisted to change beliefs? A prerequisite for change is to assist teachers to make their tacit epistemological beliefs explicit. Howard, McGee, Schwartz, and Purcell (2000) suggest that this occurs when teachers have opportunities for reflection, informal discussion concerning implicit teaching beliefs, and are challenged to examine beliefs through feedback. Other researchers (Bendixen, 2002; Bendixen & Rule, 2004; Brownlee, Purdie, & Boulton-Lewis, 2001; Guskey, 2002; Howard, McGee, Schwartz, & Purcell, 2000; Stuart & Thurlow, 2000) propose that teachers' epistemological beliefs can become more sophisticated through reflection, and that beliefs may change when teachers have positive experiences in their classroom. Giangreco, Dennis, Cloninger, Edelman, and Schattman (1993) document the transformation of beliefs about inclusion of teachers working with students with physical disabilities, noting that the 2 of 19 teachers who strongly resisted change reported previous negative teaching experiences with students with disabilities.

The findings of this research and other studies in the SET project affirm that teacher beliefs are interconnected in ways that may explain teachers' decision-making processes and practices. Raising the awareness of teachers to the underpinnings of their beliefs about knowledge and learning allows them to see how this may be affecting their teaching practices with their students (Brownlee et al., 2001). As Stipek et al. (2001) note, "It is clear that beliefs and practices are linked, and emphasis in teacher professional development on either one without considering the other is likely to fail" (p. 225).

If indeed beliefs are as central to practice as Pajares (1992), Kagan (1992), and others suggest, then the development of effective teaching practices in diverse and inclusive classrooms may hinge on teachers' epistemological assumptions and beliefs about teaching and learning. Repairing ineffective teaching practices may also rely in part on changing their epistemological assumptions and beliefs in order to align them with their inclusive practices. Our research suggests that doing so not only benefits their students with disabilities, but *all* their students.

ACKNOWLEDGMENT

This research was supported by a standard research grant from the Social Sciences and Humanities Research Council of Canada.

REFERENCES

Belenky, M., Clinchy, B., Goldberger, N., & Tarule, J. (1986). *Women's ways of knowing: The development of self, voice and mind.* New York: Basic Books.

Bendixen, L. (2002). A process model of epistemic belief change. In B. Hofer & P. Pintrich (Eds.), *Personal epistemology: The psychology of beliefs about knowledge and knowing* (pp. 191–207). Mahwah, NJ: Lawrence Erlbaum Associates.

Bendixen, L., & Rule, D. (2004). An integrative approach to personal epistemology: A guiding model. *Educational Psychologist, 39*(1), 69–80.

Brownlee, J., Purdie, N., & Boulton-Lewis, G. (2001). Changing epistemological beliefs in pre-service teacher education students. *Teaching in Higher Education, 6*(2), 247–268.

Clinchy, B. (2002). Revisiting women's ways of knowing. In B. Hofer & P. Pintrich (Eds.), *Personal epistemology: The psychology of beliefs about knowledge and knowing* (pp. 63–89). Mahwah, NJ: Lawrence Erlbaum Associates.

Dweck, C. (2000). *Self-theories: Their role in motivation, personality, and development.* Philadelphia: Taylor & Francis Group.

Elby, A., Lau, M., & Hammer, D. (2007, April). *Accounting for variability in a teacher's epistemology.* Paper presented at the American Educational Research Association Conference, Chicago.

Giangreco, M. F., Dennis, R., Cloninger, C., Edelman, S., & Schattman, R. (1993). I've counted Jon: Transformational experiences of teachers educating students with disabilities. *Exceptional Children, 59*(4), 359–372.

Guskey, T. (2002). Professional development and teacher change. *Teachers and Teaching: Theory and Practice, 8*(3/4), 381–391.

Hofer, B. (2001). Personal epistemological research implications for learning and teaching. *Educational Psychology Review, 13*(4), 353–383.

Hofer, B., & Pintrich, P. (1997). The development of epistemological theories: Beliefs about knowledge and knowing and their relation to learning. *Review of Educational Research, 67*(1), 88–140.

Howard, B. C., McGee, S., Schwartz, N., & Purcell, S. (2000). The experience of constructivism: Transforming teacher epistemology. *Journal of Research on Computing in Education, 32*(4), 455–465.

Jordan, A., Glenn, C., & McGhie-Richmond, D. (2010). The Supporting Effective Teaching (SET) project: The relationship of inclusive teaching practices to teachers' beliefs about disability and ability, and about their roles as teachers. *Teaching and Teacher Education, 26*(2), 259–266.

Jordan, A., Schwartz, E., & McGhie-Richmond, D. (2009). Preparing teachers for inclusive classrooms. *Teaching and Teacher Education, 25,* 535–542.

Jordan, A., & Stanovich, P. (2003). Teachers' personal epistemological beliefs about students with disabilities as indicators of effective teaching practices. *Journal of Research in Special Educational Needs, 3*(1), 1–14.

Jordan, A., & Stanovich, P. (2004). The beliefs and practices of Canadian teachers about including students with special education needs in their regular elementary classrooms. *Exceptionality Education Canada, 14*(2 & 3), 25–46.

Kagan, D. (1992). Implications of research on teacher belief. *Educational Psychologist, 27*(1), 65–90.

McGhie-Richmond, D., Underwood, K., & Jordan, A. (2007). Developing effective instructional strategies for teaching in inclusive classrooms. *Exceptionality Education Canada, 17*(1 & 2), 27–52.

Muis, K. R. (2004). Personal epistemology and mathematics: A critical review and synthesis of research. *Review of Educational Research, 74*(3), 317–377.

NVivo2. (2002). *New generation sotftware for qualitative data analysis.* Victoria, Australia: QSR International Pty Ltd.

Pajares, F. (1992). Teachers' beliefs and educational research: Cleaning up a messy construct. *Review of Educational Research, 62*(3), 307–332.

Schommer, M. (1990). Effects of beliefs about the nature of knowledge on comprehension. *Journal of Educational Psychology, 82*(3), 498–504.

Schommer, M. (1994). An emerging conceptualization of epistemological beliefs and their role in learning. In R. Garner & P. Alexander (Eds.), *Beliefs about text and instruction with text* (pp. 25–40). Hillsdale, NJ: Lawrence Erlbaum Associates.

Schommer, M., & Easter, M. (2006). Ways of knowing and epistemological beliefs: Combined effect on academic performance. *Educational Psychology, 26*(3), 411–423.

Schommer-Aikins, M. (2002). An evolving theoretical framework for an epistemological belief system. In B. Hofer & P. Pintrich (Eds.), *Personal epistemology: The psychology of beliefs about knowledge and knowing* (pp. 103–118). Mahwah, NJ: Lawrence Erlbaum Associates.

Schwartz, E. (2009). Elementary classroom teachers' epistemological beliefs and their practices with students with disabilities and at-risk. Unpublished Ed.D. Thesis, University of Toronto.

Silverman, J. (2007). Epistemological beliefs and attitudes toward inclusion in pre-service teachers. *Teacher Education and Special Education, 30*(1), 42–51.

Stanovich, P., & Jordan, A. (1998). Canadian teachers' and principals' beliefs about inclusive education as predictors of effective teaching in heterogeneous classrooms. *Elementary School Journal, 98*(3), 221–238.

Stipek, D., Givvin, K., Salmon, J., & MacGyvers, V. (2001). Teachers' beliefs and practices related to mathematics instruction. *Teaching and Teacher Education, 17,* 213–226.

Stuart, C., & Thurlow, D. (2000). Making it their own: Preservice teachers' experiences, beliefs, and classroom practices. *Journal of Teacher Education, 51*(2), 113–121.

White, R. (2007). Characteristics of classroom teachers which contribute to their professional growth in implementing inclusive practices. Unpublished M.A. Thesis, University of Toronto.

15 The Epistemic Underpinnings of Mrs. M's Reading Lesson on Drawing Conclusions

A Classroom-Based Research Study

Florian C. Feucht

ABSTRACT

This study explored the epistemic underpinnings of a reading lesson on drawing conclusions taught by a 4th-grade teacher. It targeted the epistemic beliefs of the teacher, the epistemic underpinnings of her reading instruction, and the educational materials used. Different qualitative methods and data sources were triangulated using a dimensional and developmental coding scheme (12-Cell Matrix) to identify epistemic patterns in the data. The study revealed that the epistemic beliefs of the teacher differed in part from the epistemic underpinnings of her instruction and the educational materials used. That is, the teacher's espoused epistemic beliefs about reading did not match her enacted epistemic beliefs about teaching reading. Her instruction on what sources to use when drawing conclusions seemed to contradict each other and resulted in mixed epistemic messages. Speculations are drawn on the potential relationships among the teacher's epistemic beliefs, the epistemic underpinnings of instruction, and educational materials used.

INTRODUCTION

Over the last 40 years, a rapidly increasing body of research has focused over the last 40 years on the exploration of individual beliefs about the nature of knowledge and processes of knowing (i.e., epistemic beliefs or personal epistemology). At first, the field of personal epistemology was interested in epistemic beliefs of college-aged and working-class populations (Belenky, Clinchy, Goldberger, & Tarule, 1986; Perry, 1970), but gradually the focus turned to younger learners in PreK–12 education (Burr & Hofer, 2002; Schommer, 1993). This shift might have been partially due to research indicating that personal epistemology can play an important role in student learning and achievement, such as cognitive and strategic processing (e.g., Kardash & Howell, 2000), self-regulated learning (e.g., Muis, 2008), conceptual change learning (e.g., Mason, 2003), and so forth.

With the turn to classroom learning and instruction, teachers' epistemic beliefs became the object of empirical and conceptual work over the last 10 years (e.g., Patrick & Pintrich, 2001; Brownlee, 2001).

However, very few conceptual frameworks (e.g., Feucht, 2010; Hofer, 2001) and empirical research studies (e.g., Louca, Elby, Hammer, & Kagey, 2004; Johnston, Woodside-Jiron, & Day, 2001) have investigated epistemic aspects and dynamics of instruction and learning. For example, what role do teachers' personal epistemologies play in the process of selecting their instruction and of the educational materials, such as textbooks and curricula? What are the epistemic underpinnings of their instruction (e.g., students receive or construct knowledge) and educational materials (e.g., textbook as knowledge authority) they choose—consciously or unconsciously—when they introduce a new topic, rehearse skills, or assess their students' achievement? In other words, how is the nature of knowledge presented in a classroom lesson while learning and instruction are in progress?

The chapter will explore the epistemic climate of a reading lesson on drawing conclusions taught by Mrs. M., a 4th-grade teacher. I provide a definition and framework of personal epistemology and briefly review the construct of epistemic climate and the literature regarding epistemic aspects of teaching reading. I then describe the study's methods and results, based on a portfolio of qualitative methods that was used to investigate Mrs. M's epistemic beliefs about reading and teaching of reading (i.e., drawing conclusions) and the epistemic underpinnings of her instruction and educational materials used during and after teaching about drawing conclusions. The chapter will close with a discussion of the results and implications for teacher training and development.

Defining Personal Epistemology

The field of personal epistemology is dedicated to researching individuals' beliefs about the nature of knowledge and processes of knowing (Hofer, 2001) and the role of these beliefs in learning, teaching, critical thinking, and intellectual-ethical development across different school subjects, academic domains, and everyday life (Bendixen & Feucht, 2010; Hofer & Pintrich, 2002; Khine, 2008). A variety of different frameworks have defined personal epistemology as a developmental trajectory (e.g., Kuhn, 1999), dimensional beliefs or theories (Hofer & Pintrich, 1997; Schommer, 1993), or epistemological resources (Hammer & Elby, 2002).

The framework drawn on in this chapter combines Hofer's dimensional (2001) and Kuhn's developmental frameworks (1999) and was developed by Bendixen et al. (Bendixen & Haerle, 2005; Feucht & Bendixen, 2008). In this study it forms an interlaced matrix or coding scheme to describe and analyze epistemic climates, respectively.

Hofer (2001) defined personal epistemology as subjective theories, which encompass four identifiable, interrelated dimensions that develop in reasonable, predictable directions. The first two dimensions concern the nature of knowledge in terms of: the certainty of knowledge (i.e., the stability of knowledge and the strength of the supporting evidence) and the simplicity of knowledge (i.e., the relative connectedness of knowledge). The third and fourth dimensions describe the process of knowing and pertain to: the justification of knowledge (i.e., the procedures to evaluate and warrant knowledge claims) and the source of knowledge (i.e., where knowledge resides; internally and/or externally). In contrast, Kuhn (e.g., 1999) focused on a developmental trajectory to define personal epistemology along four qualitatively different levels of epistemic thinking, with the last three levels described here as they are integrated in the chapter's framework. An *absolutist* views knowledge as more objective and simple and uses 'right versus wrong' as a criterion to determine truth. A *multiplist* understands knowledge as more subjective and relativistic, with everybody having the right to his/her own opinion. Finally, an *evaluativist* integrates both subjective and objective views of knowledge and evaluates complexity and uncertainty in relation to its context.

The personal epistemology framework used in this chapter draws on two main theories. It builds on the work of Hofer (2001) and Kuhn (1999). Hofer's dimensional framework provides a developmental perspective on personal epistemology (i.e., development occurs in reasonable, predictable directions) without defining specific levels of epistemic development, whereas Kuhn's developmental framework is based on a single epistemological dimension (i.e., objective/subjective views of knowledge). The 12-Cell matrix framework used in this chapter provides a more nuanced perspective of personal epistemology in the classroom by integrating Hofer and Kuhn's frameworks (see Table 15.1). The four epistemic dimensions describing the stability, structure, source, and justification of knowledge and knowing, and the three developmental levels of epistemic thinking described as absolutism, multiplism, and evaluativism are aligned to form a matrix of 12 cells. By drawing on the dimensional and developmental frameworks, the 12-Cell Matrix enables a teacher's personal epistemology to be described as an epistemic pattern. Aspects of an individual's personal epistemology can be assigned to different cells of the matrix based on their developmental and dimensional nature and then charted across the 12 cells (see Table 15.2). Table 15.1 depicts the 12-Cell Matrix with its four dimensions and three developmental levels, and describes the nature of the 12 overlapping points. The 12-Cell Matrix is an exploratory and untested coding scheme that may lead to an interpretation that could differ if an alternative coding scheme were to be used.

The working definition of personal epistemology for this chapter is in accordance with the integrated framework and the 12-Cell Matrix. Personal epistemology reflects the subjective theories that developed along Kuhn's (1999) identified developmental progression and encompass Hofer's (2001) four epistemic dimensions. The term personal epistemology is used interchangeably with epistemic beliefs, as these are the terms most commonly used in the field.

Table 15.1   12-Cell Matrix

Dimensions	Developmental levels		
	Absolutism Knowledge and knowing as absolute facts	**Multiplism** Knowledge and knowing as multiple opinions	**Evaluativism** Knowledge and knowing as evaluated judgments
Stability of Knowledge Knowledge as a certain and/or changing product: Not changing versus changing Certain versus uncertain Across versus within context(s)	Certain and not changing across contexts (because right facts do not change and are universal, unless new knowledge is discovered)	Uncertain and changing across contexts (because opinions are not evaluated against objective criteria)	Relatively certain within context, uncertain across contexts, and subject to change (because judgments are constantly re-evaluated within their context)
Structure of Knowledge Knowledge as structured product: Not connected versus connected	Not connected with other facts	Possibly connected with other opinions (i.e., influenced by persuasion)	Connected with other judgments
Source of Knowing Knowing as a process of accessing different sources of knowledge: External versus internal Objective versus subjective Passively versus actively used	Passively perceived and/or received through external and objective sources (e.g., observation of external world; listen to authority and experts)	Actively formed based on internal and subjective sources (e.g., taste; wishes, and experiences)	Actively formed based on an integration of internal and subjective sources (e.g., observation of external world; listen to authority and experts) and external and objective sources (e.g., taste; wishes, and experiences)
Justification of Knowing Knowing as a process of evaluating knowledge: Evaluated versus not evaluated based on criteria	Evaluated based on absolute truth (criteria): Facts can be either right or wrong	Not evaluated on the basis of objective criteria: Every opinion has the right to be right	Evaluated based on the strength of argument (criteria): One judgment might be better than another judgment

Epistemic Climate and the Epistemology of Teaching Reading

There has been limited research which has investigated the epistemic aspects and dynamics of instruction and learning, in particular the role of teachers' personal epistemologies in the process of selecting their instruction and educational materials. Feucht's (2010) conceptualization of the Educational Model for Personal Epistemology (EMPE) depicted in Figure 15.1 describes different epistemic aspects or components of classroom education in action and assumes a reciprocal relationship among them. The components include the teacher's epistemic beliefs, the underpinnings of the instruction used (i.e., epistemic instruction) and educational materials (i.e., epistemic knowledge representations), such as curricula and textbooks, and the learners' epistemic beliefs. The model is an operationalization of what constitutes the epistemic climate of a classroom or other kinds of learning environments; that is, the nature of knowledge and knowing emerges from the epistemic components and reciprocal relationships presented in the model. Each of the aspects of the EMPE Model is now described in more detail.

Teacher's Epistemic Beliefs

In Figure 15.1 teachers' personal epistemologies are represented as teacher's epistemic beliefs. A variety of studies have focused on investigating the nature of teachers' personal epistemology. Brownlee (2001), Olafson &

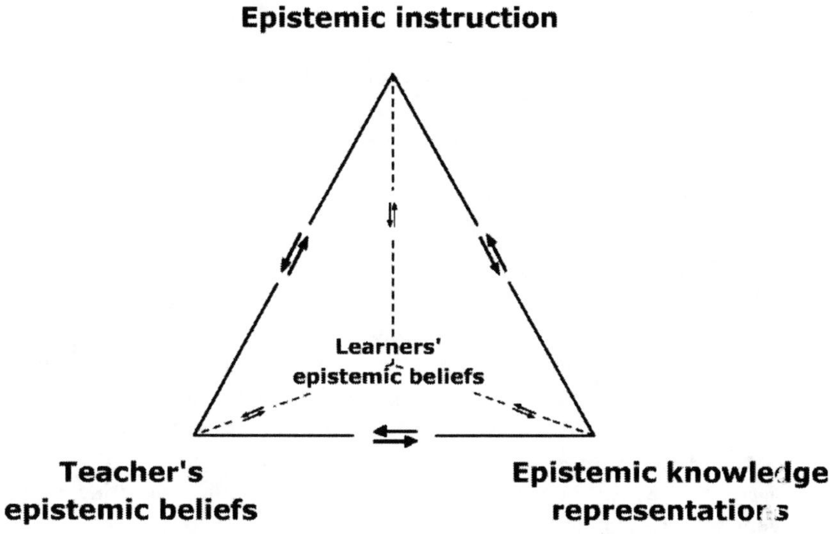

Epistemic instruction

Learners' epistemic beliefs

Teacher's epistemic beliefs

Epistemic knowledge representations

Figure 15.1 The Educational Model for Personal Epistemology (EMPE).

Schraw (2010), and White (2000) found that teachers' personal epistemologies can range between absolutism, multiplism, and evaluativism and identified transitions between these levels. Fives and Buehl (2010) researched the articulation of epistemic beliefs about teaching knowledge and reported that teachers hold different beliefs about the categorization of domains and sources of knowledge within the field of teaching knowledge. Feucht and Bendixen (2010), based on a cross-cultural study, hypothesized that differences in teacher training might influence the awareness of teachers about epistemic components (see Figure 15.1) and their ability to recognize links between their personal epistemologies and teaching approaches. Brownlee, Purdie, and Boulton-Lewis (2001), among other intervention studies, were able to demonstrate that teachers' epistemic beliefs can be accelerated towards more sophisticated levels of epistemic development. These studies show that teachers hold a range of personal epistemologies. We also know that teachers' personal epistemologies may influence their epistemic instruction, which is now described.

Epistemic Instruction

According to Schraw and Olafson (2002), teachers select and use instruction based on their personal epistemology. Johnston and colleagues (2001) illustrated how the epistemic instruction of two English teachers differed according to their absolutistic and multiplistic beliefs, respectively. White (2000) was able to group preservice teachers in five categories based on the epistemic underpinnings of their classroom teaching approaches. Tsai (2002) also found that the personal epistemology and epistemic instruction of science teachers align overtime with increasing teaching experiences. A teacher's personal epistemology not only influences epistemic instruction, but can also determine how educational materials are used (Johnston et al., 2001; Olafson & Schraw, 2010).

Epistemic Knowledge Representations

In Figure 15.1, epistemic knowledge representations refer to resources such as curriculum, textbooks, and other learning resources such as worksheets. Johnston and colleagues (2001) and Olafson and Schraw (2010) found that teachers with different personal epistemologies use and value educational resources differently in their lessons. For example, in a study by Johnston et al., the English teacher who used absolutistic instruction made permanent use of textbooks and worksheets as they represented authoritative knowledge representations, whereas the teacher who employed multiplistic instruction considered students' prior knowledge and their independent knowledge construction as a more important knowledge source. Schraw and Olafson's (2002) theorization indicates that curricula are differently perceived and implemented by teachers depending on their epistemic beliefs. That is, teachers with more absolutistic beliefs, for example, may accept and rely on the mandated curricula, whereas teachers with more multiplistic beliefs may stray from this authority and seek additional sources to complement their teaching and lesson planning. This hypothesis is in line with Benson's (1989) research, who found that teachers who recognize curricula as a governmental prescription presumably follow the stated learning outcomes more strictly than others.

Learners' Epistemic Beliefs

Emerging from these empirical studies and conceptual frameworks is the need to look at how learners' epistemic beliefs are influenced by teachers' epistemic beliefs, epistemic instruction, and epistemic knowledge representations. The vast majority of studies have isolated aspects and processes of epistemic climate in their research and, therein, provided only partial insights into what constitutes epistemic climate. Few studies exist that explore and research the epistemic climate research more holistically. Johnston et al.'s (2001) study, as previously reviewed, sporadically shadowed two English teachers over several months and on the basis of interviews and classroom discourse analyses argued that teachers' epistemic beliefs influences their choices of epistemic instruction and educational materials and the epistemic beliefs of their students. Similarly, Louca et al. (2004) and Rosenberg, Hammer, and Phelan (2006) illustrated in two lesson-based studies how physics teachers made use of epistemic instruction and knowledge representations to simulate their student's personal epistemology and directed them towards more appropriate ways of perceiving the nature of physics.

There has been no research that has investigated the epistemic beliefs of reading teachers and the epistemic climate they create when teaching reading. The purpose of this study, therefore, was to research the epistemic beliefs of a reading teacher as they were enacted during, and reported after, a reading lesson along with the epistemic instruction and knowledge representations used and observed during this lesson. Four research questions were posed: (1) What are the personal epistemologies of a reading teacher? (2) What are the epistemic underpinnings of the instruction used in the reading lesson (i.e., epistemic instruction)? (3) What are the epistemic underpinnings of the educational materials used during the reading lesson (i.e., epistemic knowledge representations)? (4) What are the relationships among the teacher's epistemic beliefs, epistemic instruction, and epistemic knowledge representations? EMPE was used as a research framework to inform the research design and methodology of the study. Whereas the chapter does not report on students' epistemic beliefs, it acknowledges that the epistemic climate described in this study would ultimately influence students' personal epistemologies.

METHOD

A portfolio of qualitative methods was employed to investigate the personal epistemology of a US elementary school teacher called Mrs. M, as well as her use of epistemic instruction and knowledge representations, and the potential reciprocal relations among them. The data collection was focused on a 40-minute reading lesson on drawing conclusions and included a teacher interview, a document review, and the classroom observation.

Participant

The elementary reading teacher, Mrs. M, was a 40-year-old woman, with 3 years teaching experience and a specialization in English and social studies at the elementary school level. She taught reading classes at the 4th-grade level at a public elementary school in a rural, Mid-western area of the United States. Her class included 22 students with a Caucasian, medium socioeconomic background.

Observation, Documents, and Interviews

The reading lesson of the teacher was observed and recorded with two video cameras. A detailed observation transcript was generated that included all classroom communication, teacher–student behaviors, and use of educational materials (Flick, 2002). All documents used during the observed lesson were collected and used as additional primary data sources (Flick, 2002), such as worksheets, textbooks, curricula, and writing on the blackboard.

The teacher was interviewed for 90 minutes. A set of 15 semi-structured interview questions targeted her personal epistemologies about reading (e.g., What does knowledge mean in reading? How do you know that what you know in reading is true?) and about teaching reading (e.g., What instruction do you use typically in reading? How important is the reading curriculum for your teaching?). Probes were used to ensure that the teacher answered the main questions at a sufficient level of breadth, depth, clarity, and that her answers were focused on the observed lesson.

Data Analysis

Qualitative content analysis was used to analyze the data in three systematic steps of summarizing, explicating, and structuring (Flick, 2002). The first step of *summarizing* permitted the reduction of the data into a manageable corpus that reflected the essential content of the original data. Each of the different data sources (i.e., observations, documents, and interviews) was summarized separately. The second step of *explicating* attempted to explain, clarify, and further reduce the data by cutting and sorting them into

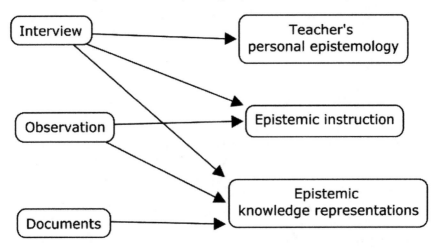

Figure 15.2   Data and method triangulation.

meaningful categories. The 12-Cell Matrix was used as a deductive coding scheme in this process (Table 15.1). The third step of *structuring* allowed the data to be compared, contrasted, and triangulated (see Figure 15.2). This involved the integration of the different data sources to identify epistemic patterns according to the 12-Cell Matrix (Table 15.2) and to search for underlying themes of the epistemic climate (Figure 15.3). Written and graphical summaries of these analyses are provided in the results section.

RESULTS

The results section entails (a) a brief introduction to the reading lesson Mrs. M taught; (b) a description of her personal epistemology, epistemic instruction, and epistemic knowledge representations (i.e., research questions 1–3); and (c) a theme-based data integration of the components to draw a more holistic picture of the potential, reciprocal influences between them (i.e., Research Question 4).

Mrs. M's 4th-Grade Reading Lesson on Drawing Conclusion

During the 4th-grade reading lesson, students were introduced to the skill of drawing conclusions with the help of context clues, prior knowledge, and personal experiences. That is, students learned to identify context clues, such as the characteristics and events of a story, and to use them to support a more general statement about a story being read. Mrs. M applied different instructional approaches (i.e., questioning, explaining, demonstrating, and group discussions) and made use of various educational materials (i.e., a chapter on drawing conclusions in the reading text book and the reading curriculum).

Mrs. M's Epistemic Beliefs

In her interview, Mrs. M expressed absolutistic beliefs as well as evaluativistic beliefs about drawing conclusions in reading. Reflecting absolutist beliefs, Mrs. M believed that knowledge about how to reach conclusions and how to teach reaching conclusions is objectively gained, proven by scientific research, and "did not change since we have books." Reading about drawing conclusions in a textbook meant that readers did not need to conduct the underlying scientific research themselves. She also held evaluativistic beliefs. Mrs. M believed that the process of drawing conclusions entailed making judgments and generalizations based on personal experiences, imagination, and prior knowledge, as well as on experiments and research. For example, she stated that:

> You read the information, and then it gets more complex when you need to infer what you just read. You start with factual questions, and finish with inference questions. (. . .) When you draw conclusions, you use your prior knowledge and your experiences.

Furthermore, she believed that knowledge would become connected by drawing conclusions in the form of generalizing existing information and accessing new knowledge. She explained that knowledge about drawing conclusions was researched by scientists and published by educators in textbook format. The epistemic pattern of Mrs. M's personal epistemology is charted on the 12-Cell Matrix in Table 15.2.

Epistemic Instruction of Mrs. M

Mrs. M's responses on teaching reading and drawing conclusions appeared to be dominated by an absolutistic understanding of reading knowledge, with fewer multiplistic traits. Mrs. M taught content and skill knowledge as true and stable (i.e., absolutism). For example, the process of drawing and justifying conclusions was explained several times as a step-by-step recipe of applying different defined rules, or students were questioned to ensure that they understood the content knowledge about fiction and non-fiction. The purpose of drawing and justifying conclusions was to better understand and evaluate the knowledge in the text. Most of the time, students were asked explicitly asked to draw conclusions based on context clues provided in the text (i.e., external and objective sources) to determine a correct understanding of the text (i.e., objective and certain sources). In two instances, however, Mrs. M asked her students to share their personal experiences and prior knowledge (i.e., subjective and internal) to better understand the stories they read or to explain new vocabulary (i.e., multiplism). See Table 15.2 for the epistemic pattern of the epistemic instruction.

Epistemic Knowledge Representations of Mrs. M

The textbook chapter and curriculum, respectively, described the skills and strategies for reading and drawing conclusions as certain and stable. These skills and strategies were presented as clean-cut rules, which—if acquired and executed step-by-step—would allow success in reading and the drawing of conclusions at the end of 4th grade. The purpose of some skills and strategies was described as facilitating the evaluation of knowledge in reading with the focus on identifying its correct meaning (e.g., using context clues and conducting text interpretation). Both knowledge representations emphasized that external and objective sources should be accessed to support this process (i.e., context clues, dictionaries, and encyclopedia). The textbook chapter did not mention prior knowledge and personal experiences as contributing factors in the process of drawing conclusions. Furthermore, it entailed three tasks that asked the learner to draw conclusions to support statements taken from stories provided in the same section. The focus was to make use of context clues to verify the truth of the proposed statements (e.g., the story is right or wrong). Overall, the skills and strategies put forward in both epistemic knowledge representations were mainly absolutistic in nature. See Table 15.2 for the epistemic pattern of the three components revolving around Mrs. M's reading lesson on drawing conclusions.

Table 15.2 Epistemic Pattern of 3 Components in Mrs. M's Reading Lesson on Drawing Conclusions

Dimension	Teacher Personal Epistemology Development			Epistemic Instruction Development			Epistemic Knowledge Representations Development		
	A	M	E	A	M	E	A	M	E
Stability	X			X			X		
Structure			X				X		
Source	X		X	X	X		X		
Justification			X	X	X		X		

Legend: A = Absolutism; M = Multiplism; E = Evaluatism

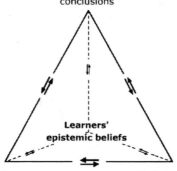

Theme-Based Data Integration: Epistemic Mixed Messages

A conflict between Mrs. M's epistemic beliefs and epistemic knowledge representations seemed to influence her epistemic instruction and the epistemic climate of her classroom (see Figure 15.3). The reading curriculum and book chapter clearly described the purpose of drawing conclusions and its application as certain and unchanging (i.e., absolutistic). The product of this process was a conclusion based on context clues and evaluated along absolute truth criteria (i.e., absolutistic). Similarly, Mrs. M believed that the process of drawing conclusions is based on formal and fixed concepts and rules (i.e., absolutistic). However, she also believed that conclusions should not only be drawn and evaluated on the basis of objective context clues, but also account for own prior knowledge and personal experiences (i.e., evaluativistic).

Interestingly, this evaluativistic notion of drawing conclusions was not identifiable in her epistemic instruction. She promoted an absolutistic and multiple understandings of drawing conclusions that contradicted each other. Sometimes she stressed the need to rely solely on external and objective context clues, and at other times within the same lesson, she switched to examples that emphasized the need to rely on prior knowledge and personal experiences. By switching between objective and external versus subjective and internal knowledge sources to draw and evaluate conclusions, Mrs. M sent mixed epistemic messages to her students.

Epistemic instruction:
Teaching instruction have absolutistic &
multiplistic underpinnings of drawing
conclusions

Learners'
epistemic beliefs

Mrs. M's	**Epistemic knowledge**
epistemic beliefs:	**representations:**
Teacher has absolutistic & evaluativistic	Curriculum, textbook, and worksheets
beliefs about drawing conclusions	have an absolutistic underpinning of
	drawing conclusions

Figure 15.3   Mrs. M's epistemic beliefs, instruction, and knowledge representations about drawing conclusions.

The following excerpt of the observation transcript illustrates how Mrs. M switched from evidence/context clues embedded in the text (i.e., external and objective) to personal experiences and prior knowledge of her students (i.e., internal and subjective) to draw conclusions. Here, the class just finished reading a story excerpt in the textbook about "Hank, The Cow Dog" and, then, quickly rehashed the textbook's rules for drawing context clues. That is, context clues should be based on the text or objective sources, such as encyclopedia, and should be consulted when in doubt. Next the class moved on to the textbooks' worksheet to rehearse the process of drawing conclusions.

Mrs. M: Okay, page 141[of the worksheet]. Amy please read the instructions to me please.

Student A: "When you make decisions about characters or events, you are drawing conclusions."

Mrs. M: (. . .) What's another word for drawing conclusions, you're making an. . . .

Student B: Inference.

Mrs. M: An inference, very good. First thing it says, in the first column, look in the first column, it says "Evidence". In the next column it says "Conclusion". So when it says evidence, you have to go back into the story and find some evidence to support your details (. . .). Okay. The example here gives us the evidence, "Hank [the dog detective] doesn't consider the milk cow a suspect [of killing the chicken]." What can you draw as a conclusion?

Student C: It only eats trees.

Mrs. M: It only eats the trees. The porcupine only eats the trees. The cow only eats the grass. Would a cow have a reason to kill a chicken?

Student D: No.

Student E: Unless it bites it on the tail.

Up to this section in the transcript, Mrs. M followed the absolutistic notion of the textbook and worksheet by reinforcing the need to "go back into the story and find evidence to support your details" when drawing conclusions. Suddenly, she appeals to her students' prior knowledge about animals to draw the conclusion that the cow was not the murderer of the chicken.

Mrs. M: Yeah, but would it really? Think about it. With your prior knowledge have you ever . . . , you've been to a farm. You've all been to a farm at one time or another or the zoo or whatever. Does a cow have a reason to really kill a chicken?

Students: No.

Mrs. M: No. So the answer is going to be the cow has no reason to kill the chicken. Do you get the idea of how to do this worksheet?
Student E: Mm hm.

After Mrs. M demonstrated to her students how "prior knowledge" and personal experiences can be used in drawing conclusions, she refers back to the worksheet. When she asks them "Do you get the idea of how to do this worksheet?", which indirectly translates into 'Do you know how to draw conclusions?', the question remains unanswered. It is unclear what the impact of Mrs. M's mixed epistemic messages is on her students' understanding of drawing conclusions.

It is important to note that the study was able (a) to identify discrepancies among Mrs. M's espoused beliefs about reading knowledge and the epistemic underpinnings of her enacted beliefs represented in her use of instruction (i.e., epistemic instruction) and educational materials (i.e., epistemic knowledge representations), and (b) to describe the occurrence of mixed epistemic messages. However, the study's design did not permit insights on causal explanations about the relationships among these components; that is, for example, whether, and to what extent the absolutistic underpinnings of the curriculum, textbook, and worksheet influenced Mrs. M's epistemic beliefs and instruction. For this reason, the reciprocal arrows representing causal relationships in Figure 15.3 must be considered hypothetical in nature and must be looked upon cautiously.

Mrs. M states in her interview that "it is explicitly said in the curriculum how to draw conclusions from the text" and "I am fine with the topic and the way it is presented." It could be cautiously hypothesized that her perception of the absolutistic curriculum as an authority for her teaching may have suppressed her personal evaluativist notion of drawing conclusions and resulted in switching between absolutist and multiplist underpinnings of her instruction. Furthermore, it is unclear whether, to what extent, Mrs. M was aware of the epistemic discrepancy among her epistemic beliefs, epistemic instruction, and epistemic knowledge representations of her reading lesson, or not.

DISCUSSION

Teachers' Epistemic Beliefs and Awareness

One interesting finding of this study is the diversity of epistemic beliefs found in the components that constituted the epistemic climate in Mrs. M's classroom (see Table 15.2). The pattern of her epistemic beliefs partly revealed absolutist and evaluativistic beliefs in the 12-Cell Matrix. From a conceptual perspective, these opposing epistemic beliefs conflict conceptually with existing developmental frameworks (e.g., Kuhn, 1999; Perry,

1970) and dimensional frameworks that assume a developmental trajectory of personal epistemology (e.g., Hofer, 2001; Schommer, 1993). However, Mrs. M seemed to hold more fine-grained epistemic beliefs that might be specific to reading knowledge and the context of teaching it (Hammer & Elby, 2002).

From a developmental perspective, the epistemic inconsistencies across all three components (see Figure 15.3) of Mrs. M's epistemic climate appear surprising, as one would assume more consistency. Unfortunately, no insight can be gained by comparing Mrs. M's case with the two English teachers in the Johnston et al. (2001) study. For the purpose of their study, they avoided epistemic discrepancies by purposefully pre-selecting two teachers who were consistent within their epistemic beliefs and across the epistemic underpinnings of their instruction and educational materials. However, Tsai's (2002) empirical study and Patrick and Pintrich's (2001) conceptual paper suggest that this discrepancy might be typical for novice teachers like Mrs. M. Tsai identified that the epistemic beliefs and instruction of science teachers differed in their initial years of teaching and became aligned after several years of teaching. Patrick and Pintrich suggested that novice teachers might experience conflicts between their own epistemic beliefs about a topic and their epistemic beliefs about teaching the same topic to their students. These insights could theoretically explain the occurrence of Mrs. M's mixed epistemic beliefs. That is, alternating between what sources should be used when drawing conclusions—absolutism versus multiplism—might have been a compromise between the absolutistic underpinnings of the mandated curriculum and her own epistemic beliefs at the level of evaluativism.

Based on Mrs. M's statements about the reading curriculum, it could be assumed that she perceived (at least during the interview) it as an authority to guide her teaching. This assumption can be supported theoretically with Benson's research which found that teachers who recognize curricula as a governmental prescription presumably follow the stated learning outcomes more strictly than others. In turn, as Schraw and Olafson (2002) suggest, these teachers are influenced to make choices in their instruction and educational materials that are inconsistent with their own epistemic beliefs.

Another issue that stems from this discussion and is of relevance to teacher education is the question: Was Mrs. M aware of her epistemic beliefs and the discrepancies between them and her teaching? The way she spoke about the curriculum suggests that she was at least aware of the epistemological meaning of the curriculum for her teaching. But if she would have been aware of the discontinuities between her epistemic beliefs and epistemic instruction would she not have somewhat consciously tried to consolidate them more cohesively? Again, this might be a phenomenon that novice teachers might need to work through consciously or not.

What follows is the question, Should teachers, novices or not, receive support in developing their epistemic beliefs and in becoming more aware of the epistemic climate they create in each lesson? Drawing from this study and the reviewed literature, this has implications for teacher education programs. First, teachers' epistemic beliefs seem to develop slowly on their own (e.g., Tsai, 2002). Second, it seems to take several years of teaching experiences for their epistemic beliefs to align with the epistemic underpinnings of their instruction and educational materials (e.g., Tsai, 2002). Third, the level towards which teachers progress in their epistemic development and at which they consolidate the epistemic components of their epistemic climate seems to be left to chance (Feucht & Bendixen, 2010; Patrick & Pintrich, 2001). Therefore, it is pivotal for teachers to be aware of all levels of epistemic development with respect to their own beliefs, their way of teaching, and their epistemic climate, and to develop evaluativistic beliefs of their own. This will permit teachers to consciously and flexibly provide lessons that coincide with the epistemic nature of the topic to be taught and the epistemological level of their students (Feucht, 2010). More specifically, teachers need to gain an understanding of what components might influence the epistemic climate of their classroom and, if inconsistent, that they potentially could send mixed epistemic messages that might be confusing to their students.

Making these goals a part of teacher training and development would help accelerate teachers' epistemic development and target their epistemic knowledge, skills, and attitudes about the epistemic climate in their classrooms. Are these feasible goals? Existing research suggests that teachers' personal epistemologies can be advanced during preservice training (e.g., Brownlee, et al., 2001) and that a more philosophical/didactical approach can help teachers raise their epistemic awareness and make links between their epistemic beliefs and their teaching practice (Feucht & Bendixen, 2010). What is most needed are methodological tools for teachers to assess their epistemic beliefs and to predict and evaluate the epistemic climates of their lessons (Feucht, 2010).

Conceptual and Methodological Issues

Hofer (1997, 2001) called for the integration of different frameworks and the development of mixed-method approaches to better define and measure respectively the construct of personal epistemology. The assessment of epistemic climates requires both integrated frameworks and mixed-method approaches. In other words, to follow the notion of 'the whole is more than the sum of its parts', the research tools employed must be equally complex in their measurement capabilities to assess the conceptual complexity of epistemic climates, it's components and relationships. This became evident in the design and conduct of this study.

The key to unfolding the nature of Mrs. M's epistemic climate was to closely interlock the study's methodological design with its conceptual framework. EMPE and the 12-Cell Matrix were the nuts and bolts of this strategy. First, the EMPE (Figure 15.1) was operationalized as research framework to inform the methodological design of the study. That is, the model provided a theoretical rationale for what components in a classroom lesson would need to be targeted during the data collection to provide sufficient and meaningful data sources to draw an informative picture of the epistemic climate. Several different data sets were collected for each component—teachers' epistemic beliefs, epistemic instruction, and epistemic knowledge presentations—using different methods of data collection. This methodological strategy permitted the generation of more valid evidence through data and method triangulation (see Figure 15.2). For example, the evidence to support the description of Mrs. M's epistemic instruction was identified in two data sources (i.e., data triangulation) which were generated by using two methods, a semi-structured interview and a classroom observation (i.e., method triangulation). This strategy also permitted the flexible selection of appropriate method(s) for the individual components of the model. For example, a semi-structured interview was considered the most suitable technique to collect data about epistemic teacher beliefs for Mrs. M.

Second, the conceptual framework for the study drew on the 12-Cell Matrix (Table 15.1). This provided a more precise definition of personal epistemology by combining the dimensional and developmental approaches, which permitted a systematic representation of epistemic beliefs as epistemic patterns. That is, the matrix informed the systematic analysis and triangulation of each data source in order to understand the epistemic climate as a whole (see Figure 15.3). It is important to note that the 12-Cell Matrix is based on a speculative and untested framework. A different data interpretation may emerge if an alternative scoring scheme were to be used. For this reason, replications of this study should apply the 12-Cell Matrix as the coding scheme.

One limitation of this study was that its design did not permit drawing causal conclusions with respect to influence of the epistemic components on each other or identifying and explaining underlying mechanisms of the (hypothesized) relationships (see Figure 15.1). To help elicit cause/effect and their underlying mechanisms within epistemic climates specifically, and of personal epistemology in general, (more) intervention and micro-genetic research designs are needed to move the field of personal epistemology forward (Feucht, 2010).

CONCLUSION

The study's results and their discussion demonstrate the need for teacher training and development to provide context for teachers to accelerate their epistemic beliefs and to become aware of the nature and influence of the epistemic climate they generate in their lessons. Teachers need to acquire the knowledge, skills, and attitude to become professional custodians of their epistemic climate. As evident with Mrs. M, this cannot be left to chance, but should be considered as an important goal of teacher education. Furthermore, more research should be conducted that informs teacher education. It is essential to conduct more longitudinal research to get a better understanding of how teachers' epistemic beliefs develop over time, intervention research to learn about the effects of different educational programs, and micro-genetic research to shed light on mechanisms that underlie the dynamics of epistemic climates.

REFERENCES

Belenky, M., Clinchy, B., Goldberger, N., & Tarule, J. (1986). *Women's ways of knowing: The development of self, voice, and mind.* New York: Basic Books.
Bendixen, L. D., & Feucht, F. C. (Eds.). (2010). *Personal epistemology in the classroom: Theory, research, and educational implications.* New York: Cambridge University Press.
Bendixen, L. D., & Haerle, F. C. (2005, November). *An interactive measure of children's personal epistemology.* Working session conducted at the Southwest Consortium for Innovations in Psychology in Education (SCIPIE) Inaugural Conference, Las Vegas.
Benson, G. D. (1989). Epistemology and science curriculum. *Journal of Curriculum Studies, 21,* 329–344.
Brownlee, J. (2001). Epistemological beliefs in pre-service teacher education students. *Higher Education Research and Development, 20*(3), 281–291.
Brownlee, J., Purdie, N., & Boulton-Lewis, G. (2001). Changing epistemological beliefs in pre-service teacher education students. *Teaching in Higher Education, 6*(2), 247–268.
Burr, J. E., & Hofer, B. K. (2002). Personal epistemology and theory of mind: Deciphering young children's beliefs about knowledge and knowing. *New Ideas in Psychology, 20,* 199–224.
Feucht, F. C. (2010). Epistemic climate in elementary classrooms. In L. D. Bendixen & F. C. Feucht (Eds.), *Personal epistemology in the classroom: Theory, research, and educational implications* (pp. 55–93). New York: Cambridge University Press.
Feucht, F. C., & Bendixen, L. D. (2008, July). *Epistemological analyses of educational materials: Elementary school books and curricula in English, science, and mathematics.* Paper presented in E. Stahl & D. Kienhues (Chairs/Organizers), Interplay between epistemological beliefs and different media during learning processes. Symposium conducted at the XXIX International Congress of Psychology, Berlin, Germany.
Feucht, F. C., & Bendixen L. D. (2010). Exploring similarities and differences in personal epistemologies of U.S. and German elementary school teachers. *Cognition and Instruction, 28*(1), 39–69.
Fives, H., & Buehl, M. M. (2010). Teachers' articulation of beliefs about teaching knowledge: Conceptualizing a belief framework. In L. D. Bendixen & F. C. Feucht (Eds.), *Personal epistemology in the classroom: Theory, research, and educational implications* (pp. 470–515). New York: Cambridge University Press.
Flick, U. (2002). *An introduction to qualitative research.* London: Sage.
Hammer, D., & Elby, A. (2002). On the form of a personal epistemology. In B. K. Hofer & P. R. Pintrich (Eds.), *Personal epistemology: The psychology of*

beliefs about knowledge and knowing (pp. 169–190). Mahwah, NJ: Lawrence Erlbaum Associates.

Hofer, B. K. (2001). Personal epistemology research: Implications for learning and teaching. *Educational Psychology Review*, *13*, 353–383.

Hofer, B. K., & Pintrich, P. R. (1997). The development of epistemological theories: Beliefs about knowledge and knowing and their relation to learning. *Re. iew of Educational Research*, *67*, 88–140.

Hofer, B. K., & Pintrich, P. R. (Eds.). (2002). *Personal epistemology: The psychology of beliefs about knowledge and knowing*. Mahwah, NJ: Lawrence Erlbaum Associates.

Johnston, P., Woodside-Jiron, H., & Day, J. (2001). Teaching and learning literate epistemologies. *Journal of Educational Psychology*, *93*(1), 223–233.

Kardash, C. M, & Howell, K. L., (2000). Effects of epistemological beliefs and topic-specific beliefs on undergraduates' cognitive and strategic processing of dual-positional text. *Journal of Educational Psychology*, *92*, 524–535.

Khine, M. S. (2008). *Knowing, knowledge and beliefs: Epistemological studies across diverse cultures*. Dordrecht, Netherlands: Springer.

Kuhn, D. (1999). A Developmental Model of Critical Thinking. *Educational Researcher*, *28*(2), 16–46.

Louca, L., Elby, A., Hammer, D., & Kagey, T. (2004). Epistemological resources: Applying a new epistemological framework to science instruction. *Educational Psychologist*, *39*(1), 57–68.

Mason, L. (2003). Personal epistemologies and intentional conceptual change. In G. M. Sinatra & P. R. Pintrich (Eds.), *Intentional conceptual change* (pp. 199–236). Mahwah, NJ: Lawrence Erlbaum Associates.

Muis, K. R. (2008). Epistemic profiles and self-regulated learning: Examining relations in the context of mathematics problem solving. *Contemporary Educational Psychology*, *33*, 177–208.

Olafson, L., & Schraw, G. (2010). Beyond epistemology: Assessing teachers' epistemological and ontological worldviews. In L. D. Bendixen & F. C. Feucht (Eds.), *Personal epistemology in the classroom: Theory, research, and educational implications* (pp. 516–551). New York: Cambridge University Press.

Patrick, H., & Pintrich, P. R. (2001). Conceptual change in teachers' intuitive conceptions of learning, motivation, and instructions: The role of motivational and epistemological beliefs. In B. Torf & R. Sternberg (Eds.), *Understanding and teaching the intuitive mind* (pp. 117–143). Mahwah, NJ: Lawrence Erlbaum Associates.

Perry, W. G., Jr. (1970). *Forms of intellectual and ethical development in the college years: A scheme*. New York: Holt, Rinehart and Winston.

Rosenberg, S. A., Hammer, D., & Phelan, J. (2006). Multiple epistemological coherences in an eighth-grade discussion of the rock cycle. *Journal of the Learning Sciences*, *15*(2), 261–292.

Schommer, M. (1993). Epistemological development and academic performance among secondary students. *Journal of Educational Psychology*, *85*, 406–411.

Schraw, G., & Olafson, L. (2002). Teachers' epistemological worldviews and educational practices. *Issues in Education*, *8*(2), 99–148.

Tsai, C.-C. (2002). Nested epistemologies: Science teachers' beliefs of teaching, learning and science. *International Journal of Science Education*, *24*(8), 771–783.

White, B. C. (2000). Pre-service teachers' epistemology viewed through perspectives on problematic classroom situations. *Journal of Education for Teaching*, *26*(3), 279–306.

16 Teachers' Scientific Epistemological Views, Conceptions of Teaching Science, and their Approaches to Teaching Science

An Exploratory Study of Inservice Science Teachers in Taiwan

Min-Hsien Lee and Chin-Chung Tsai

ABSTRACT

This chapter focuses on issues regarding the relations among inservice teachers' scientific epistemological views, conceptions of teaching science, and their approaches to teaching science. Twenty-five high school science teachers in Taiwan were selected as the subjects of this study. The research data were gathered by means of two instruments: An open-ended questionnaire to explore teachers' scientific epistemological beliefs and conceptions of teaching science, and an inventory to assess their approaches to teaching science. Based on the descriptive data, the relations between teachers' scientific epistemological beliefs, conceptions of teaching science, and their approaches to teaching science were revealed. In addition, the results of the present study show that senior teachers may have inconsistent beliefs regarding scientific knowledge and teaching science (i.e., "traditional" scientific epistemological beliefs but "constructivist" conceptions of teaching science). The results could be interpreted through a cultural lens. The implications for teacher education and professional development regarding inservice teachers are also discussed.

INTRODUCTION

Educational researchers have explored and investigated teachers' beliefs for decades (Pajares, 1992). Moreover, how teachers' beliefs relate to their pedagogical approaches has become an essential issue as perceived by many educational researchers (e.g., Chai, Teo, & Lee, 2010; Tsai, 2007; Waters-Adams, 2006). Teachers hold a variety of beliefs including those about knowing, knowledge, and pedagogy. These beliefs have been shown to have an influence on the ways in which teachers conceptualize and approach teaching (e.g., Bryan, 2003; Pajares, 1992; Tsai, 2007).

An individual's beliefs about knowledge and knowing are often referred to as personal epistemology (Hofer & Pintrich, 1997). Personal epistemology may affect learning in several ways (e.g., Chan, 2003; Hofer & Pintrich, 1997; Liang, Lee, & Tsai, 2010; Tsai, 1998, 1999); that is, in order to keep students engaged in meaningful learning strategies, teachers may need to help them develop mature personal epistemologies. However, teachers may themselves need to hold mature personal epistemologies to guide their pedagogical beliefs in order to foster a learning environment that can promote sophisticated personal epistemologies in students. Several studies have investigated preservice teachers' personal epistemologies and pedagogical beliefs. For example, Chan and Elliott (2004) conducted a relational analysis with Hong Kong preservice teachers, and found that their pedagogical beliefs were driven by their personal epistemologies. Similar findings were also concluded by Chai, Teo, and Lee (2010) who surveyed 718 Singaporean preservice teachers. Maggioni and Parkinson (2008) conducted a review of the research related to teachers' personal epistemologies. They suggested that teachers' personal epistemologies may play a role in their pedagogical practices. In the present study, we explored the relations among teachers' personal epistemologies, pedagogical beliefs, and their pedagogical practices.

Research efforts in science education have explored inservice teachers' personal epistemologies about science (e.g., Abd-El-Khalick & Lederman, 2000; Abell & Smith, 1994) and how these epistemological beliefs relate to teachers' pedagogical practices (e.g., Tsai, 2007; Waters-Adams, 2006). According to Buehl and Alexander's (2001) review, personal epistemology in academic knowledge may be distinct from general knowledge. That is, in the school context, the epistemological beliefs which deal with the beliefs about the nature of school knowledge and knowing may be domain-specific. As suggested by Schwab (1978), academic disciplines have different knowledge structures and epistemological assumptions. That is, personal epistemology may differ by discipline and may be domain-specific. Although many studies have explored the role of students' scientific epistemological beliefs with regards to science learning, relatively less research has focused on the role of teachers' scientific epistemological beliefs regarding science teaching (Tsai, 2007). Teachers' scientific epistemological beliefs are often considered as a significant factor influencing their pedagogical beliefs, and may be related to their teaching approaches (Lederman, 1992).

In recent years, the school system in Taiwan has been strongly influenced by elements of Western philosophy and pedagogy (e.g., constructivism) through educational reform. However, Taiwanese teachers' pedagogical beliefs are traditionally framed by their educational experience and teacher education programs, and such educational experience is shaped and developed by an Eastern culture and/or philosophy (e.g., Confucianism; Jin & Dan, 2004; Yu, 2008). Teachers' beliefs about knowledge and teaching and their approaches to teaching may be potentially shaped by this cultural background. In our previous studies, we have explored students' perceptions regarding the science classroom learning environment (Lee & Chang, 2004) and found that students were able to perceive both student-centered and teacher-centered orientated learning environments. Moreover, we examined students' perceptions of teacher authority in the science classroom in Taiwan and found that students recognized that teachers shared their authority with students in the science classroom (Lee, Chang, & Tsai, 2009). That is, Taiwanese high school students have mixed perceptions concerning both the progressive and traditional features of science learning as defined by science educators. As Taiwanese students tend to show special mixed features of learning science, it is interesting to undertake further investigation of Taiwanese teachers' pedagogical approaches in the science classroom.

The previous literature has established some linkages between teachers' personal epistemologies and their conceptions of teaching (e.g., Chan & Elliott, 2004; Tsai, 2002). However, few of these studies have discussed the relations between science teachers' personal epistemologies (described as scientific epistemological beliefs) and pedagogical beliefs, and how these beliefs may be related to their teaching approaches in science. To address the above issues, in this chapter we propose to explore the relationships among inservice science teachers' scientific epistemological beliefs, conceptions of teaching science, and their approaches to teaching science in Taiwan. In an earlier study, Tsai (2007) investigated the relations among teachers' scientific epistemological beliefs, their views about teaching and learning, and their instructional activities with the sample of 4 Taiwanese science teachers. Based on Tsai's (2007) study, in this chapter, we explored science teachers' conceptions of and approaches to teaching science using a larger sample size.

Personal Epistemology and Scientific Epistemological Beliefs

Researchers previously suggested that epistemological views of academic knowledge may be distinct from beliefs about general knowledge (e.g., Buehl & Alexander, 2001). That is, people's personal epistemology may be domain-specific. In the area of science education, research efforts have been devoted to exploring students' epistemological beliefs about science and scientific knowledge (e.g., Lederman, 1992; Liu & Tsai, 2008). In the last two decades, science education researchers have engaged in much research about the views of the nature of science (NOS; Lederman, 1992, 2007) or scientific epistemological beliefs (Tsai & Liu, 2005). Numerous studies refer to NOS as the development of scientific knowledge, or the epistemology of science. Moreover, Ryan and Aikenhead (1992) suggested that the research on the epistemology of science deals with the issues of the assumptions, values, and conceptual inventions in science; consensus making in scientific communities; and characteristics of scientific knowledge.

With respect to scientific epistemological beliefs, Tsai and Liu (2005) suggested five characteristics of scientific knowledge and its development, including the role of social negotiation in the science community, the invented and creative nature of science, the theory-laden quality of scientific exploration, the cultural impacts on science, and the changing and tentative feature of scientific knowledge. Accordingly, the research on scientific epistemological beliefs has considered the issues of the certainty (e.g., the changing and tentative feature) and developmental process of scientific knowledge (e.g., the invented and creative nature). Moreover, scientific epistemological beliefs also focus on the justification (such as the social role in science: The role of social negotiation) and the process of knowing science (e.g., the theory-laden quality of scientific exploration). The investigation of scientific epistemological beliefs may contribute to a better understanding of the knowledge of school science and how we acquire and validating scientific knowledge. Specifically, we are interested in how scientific epistemological beliefs are related to teachers' conceptions of teaching science.

Teachers' Conceptions of Teaching Science

Personal epistemology is considered to be related to conceptions of teaching and learning. In general, "conceptions" refer to actual experiences, understandings, and conceptualizations that people have of various phenomena (Marton, Dall'Alba, & Beaty, 1993). In this chapter, the "conceptions" of teaching refers to teachers' ideas, understandings, or beliefs about their teaching. Hofer and Pintrich (1997) supported the connections between personal epistemology and conceptions of teaching and learning by suggesting that "beliefs about learning and teaching are related to how knowledge is acquired, and in terms of the psychological reality of the network of individuals' beliefs, beliefs about learning, teaching, and knowledge are probably intertwined" (p. 116). Kukari (2004) also indicated that teachers' personal epistemologies could be considered as "the philosophical basis for teaching and learning" (p. 107).

The term *conception of teaching* is used in the literature to refer to teachers' ideas underlying the descriptions of how they experience the teaching process (Kember, 1997). There have been a number of studies that have emphasized teachers' conceptions of teaching and the associated implications for student learning. A review of 13 articles conducted by Kember (1997) has recognized five dimensions of conceptions of teaching, including the essence of learning and teaching, the roles of student and teacher, the aims and expected outcomes of learning and teaching, the content of teaching, and the preferred styles of and approaches to teaching. Kember (1997) classified all studies in tabular form under five categories: imparting information, transmitting structured knowledge, student–teacher interaction, facilitating understanding, and conceptual change/ intellectual development. Kember (1997) further reduced these categories and suggested a three-level model based on teacher orientation. These were "teacher-centered/content-oriented" and "student-centered/learning-oriented" with an intermediate category labeled as "student–teacher interaction/apprenticeship" (Kember, 1997, p. 264). Following Kember's (1997) review, several studies on conceptions of teaching have found similar categories which also range from teacher-centered/content-oriented to student-centered/learning-oriented (e.g., Boulton-Lewis, Smith, McCrindle, Burnett, & Campbell, 2001; Gao & Watkins, 2001, 2002; Kember & Kwan, 2000; Koballa, Graber, Coleman, & Kemp, 2000). In summary, the research on teachers' conceptions of teaching seems to bear out the existence of two broad teaching orientations ranging from focusing on a teacher-centered/content-oriented to a student-centered/learning-oriented approach, and most conceptions of teaching fall within this continuum (Kember, 1997).

Other studies suggest that conceptions of teaching are discipline- or content-dependent (Koballa et al., 2000; Norton, Richardson, Hartlev, Newstead, & Mayes, 2005; Tsai, 2002). That is, one teacher may have conceptions of teaching science that are very different from those of teaching in general. Trigwell, Prosser, and Taylor (1994) found that the intention of teaching expressed by the majority of university science teachers in their sample focused on transmitting information or on the acquisition of necessary concepts. Norton et al. (2005) found that science teachers tended to place more emphasis on training for future jobs, whereas arts or social science teachers tended to implement interactive teaching. Koballa et al. (2000) studied prospective gymnasium teachers' conceptions of chemistry teaching and identified three conceptions, namely transfer knowledge, problem posing, and interacting with pupils.

Conceptions of teaching are also assumed to be context-dependent (Gao & Watkins, 2001, 2002). Gao and Watkins (2002) claimed that whereas some aspects of teaching conceptions may be consistent across contexts, other aspects may be different among contexts, such as the stage of schooling, major subject, curriculum, and social and cultural backgrounds. Consequently, it is necessary to explore teachers' conceptions of teaching from different cultural backgrounds or in different subject areas. For example, Gao and Watkins (2001, 2002) studied physics teachers' conceptions of teaching in China, and categorized five conceptions, namely knowledge delivery, exam preparation, ability development, attitude promotion, and conduct guidance.

Teachers' Approaches to Teaching Science

In recent years, teachers' approaches to teaching and the conceptions of teaching they hold have been the emphasis of several studies (Bryan, 2003; Eley, 2006; Kember & Kwan, 2000; Laksov, Nikkola, & Lonka, 2008; Postareff & Lindblom-Ylanne, 2008).

In terms of research regarding teachers' approaches to teaching, several studies have investigated university teachers' approaches to teaching, and categorized the teachers' approaches as student-focused and teacher-focused (e.g., Trigwell, Prosser, & Waterhouse, 1999) or as learning-centered and content-centered (Kember & Kwan, 2000). The student-focused and learning-centered approaches stress the student and meaningful learning, whereas the teacher-focused and content-centered approaches emphasize the curriculum material or textbook content. Furthermore, some studies have examined approaches to teaching by applying quantitative methods. Trigwell and Prosser (2004) have developed the Approaches to Teaching Inventory (ATI) to measure the ways in which teachers approach their teaching. The ATI detected two factors: the conceptual change/student-focused approach and the information transmission/teacher-focused approach. In addition, Trigwell and Prosser (2004) found a significant negative correlation between the two factors.

This study further suggests that approaches to teaching, similar to conceptions of teaching, may also be domain-specific. As aforementioned, teachers' approaches to teaching may be influenced by the conceptions of teaching that they hold. Accordingly, one teacher may have approaches to teaching science that are very different from those of teaching in general.

The research on teachers' conceptions of teaching science and approaches to teaching science may potentially contribute to science teacher education and consequently to students' science learning. However, little research literature is found which explores the relationships between science teachers' conceptions of teaching and their approaches to teaching science, especially at the high school level. Hewson and Hewson (1988) were the first to highlight the importance of appropriate conceptions of teaching science for teaching science. Tsai (2002) and Bryan (2003) have also studied the relations between teachers' conceptions of science and teaching science. Specifically, Tsai (2002) found that teachers' conceptions of teaching science may have an impact on their science teaching and how students learn science.

To summarize, scientific epistemological beliefs refer to beliefs about the origin and development of scientific knowledge. Conceptions of teaching (science) are related to the study of teachers' reflections of experiencing teaching (science) (Kember, 1997; Linder & Marshall, 2003). And, the previous literature has established some linkages between teachers' personal epistemologies and their conceptions of teaching (e.g., Chan & Elliott, 2004; Tsai, 2002). However, few of these studies have discussed the relations between science teachers' scientific epistemological and conceptions of teaching science, and how these conceptions may be related to their teaching approaches in science. A better understanding of this association may help teacher education programs to develop and implement instruction that could enhance epistemological development, conceptions of teaching, and approaches to teaching for the professional development of science teachers.

Research suggests that teachers' conceptions of teaching may be driven by their personal epistemologies (e.g., Chan & Elliott, 2004; Tsai, 2007). Accordingly, one purpose of this study is to explore the relation between science teachers' scientific epistemological beliefs and their conceptions of teaching science. However, personal epistemologies and conceptions of teaching may also influence approaches to teaching. Hence, the purpose of this study is to investigate the relationship between personal epistemology, conceptions of teaching, and teaching approaches in the context of teaching science.

THE STUDY

Twenty-five high school science teachers in Taiwan were selected as the subjects of this study using cluster sampling. Eleven of them were female. The population of science teachers was clustered into three demographic areas: northern, central, and southern Taiwan. All of these teachers taught earth science, physics, and/or chemistry at the junior high school or senior high school levels (grades 7 to 12). Their ages ranged from 25 to 48, with the average age being 32.48. All of them had at least a Bachelor's degree in earth science, physics, or chemistry. Their teaching experience ranged from 1 to 24 years, with an average of 7.24 years.

Data Collection

The research data were gathered by means of two instruments: An open-ended questionnaire to explore both teachers' scientific epistemological beliefs and their conceptions of teaching science, and an inventory to assess their approaches to teaching science.

The open-ended questionnaire consisted of two parts: The first exploring teachers' conceptions of teaching science, and the second investigating teachers' scientific epistemological beliefs. The questions were modified from those used in Tsai's (2002) study. Whereas the questions mainly investigated the nature of scientific knowledge, participants' beliefs about the nature of knowing science could also be identified through their responses. The open-ended questions are presented below:

1. Scientific epistemological beliefs: If someone asks you "what is science?" what will you tell him or her? What are the main characteristics of scientific knowledge? What are the differences between scientific knowledge and other kinds of knowledge?
2. Conceptions of teaching science: In your view, what is teaching science? What makes the most successful science teaching? Could you describe what an ideal science teaching environment would look like? Why? Is there any difference between teaching science and non-science subjects? Why?

To assess the teachers' approaches to teaching science, all participants completed the Approaches to Teaching Inventory-science subject (ATI-s; Lee, Tsai, Changa & Liang, 2009). The ATI-s was modified from the Approaches to Teaching Inventory (ATI; Trigwell & Prosser, 2004). The original ATI has two scales, the student-focused approach and the teacher-focused approach. In this study, the item description of ATI-s was revised to encompass science related content. The ATI-s in the current study, much like the ATI, also consists of two scales (i.e., six items regarding the student-focused approach and five items for the teacher-focused approach). The student-focused approach measured the extent to which teachers focused on students' conceptual change and conducted student-focused strategies (i.e., I feel that the assessment in science subjects should be an opportunity for students to reveal their conceptual change in science). On the other hand, the teacher-focused approach assessed to what extent teachers focused on information transmission and conducted teacher-centered strategies (i.e., I feel it is important that the science subject should be completely described in terms of specific objectives relating to what students have to know for formal assessment items).

The ATI-s was presented in a 5-point Likert mode, ranging from "always" to "never". The "always" response was assigned a score of 5, whereas the "never" response was assigned a score of 1. The reliability coefficient of the student-focused approach was 0.73 and of the teacher-focused was 0.72, suggesting sufficient reliability in examining teachers' approaches to teaching science.

Data Analysis

The process of analyzing the open-ended responses involved examining the evidence and sorting the descriptive data to present patterns (Bogdan & Biklen, 1998). Two main categories of responses, based on Tsai's (2002) and Boz and Uzuntiryaki's (2006) study, were used to describe teachers' scientific epistemological beliefs and conceptions of teaching science. The "constructivist" category views scientific knowledge as deriving from scientists' reasoning, as not being the absolute truth, and that teaching science helps students construct knowledge. The "traditional" category perceives scientific knowledge as correct answers or established truths, and views teaching science as transferring knowledge. A description of the constructivist/traditional dichotomy is presented in Table 16.1 for science teachers' scientific epistemological beliefs and conceptions of teaching science. Table 16.1 also provides sample quotations of written responses for each category.

To ensure the credibility of this analysis, another researcher was asked to analyze a subset of representative sentences coded from the participants' responses to the open-ended questionnaire, and the inter-coder agreement for this analysis was 87%. In addition, the discrepancies were discussed case by case, and final agreements were achieved.

Table 16.1   Framework for Categorizing Teachers' Scientific Epistemological Beliefs and Conceptions of Teaching Science

	Description	Quotation of written responses
Scientific epistemological beliefs		
Constructivist	Scientific knowledge derives from scientists' reasoning. Scientific knowledge is tentative, evolving, and it is not the absolute truth.	Scientific knowledge is uncertain. Scientific knowledge is developed by the collaboration of scientists and through the negotiation of the science community (ST02).
Traditional	Scientific knowledge originates from outside the self and resides in external authorities. Scientific knowledge refers to the absolute truth.	Scientific knowledge is a collection of the facts. Scientific knowledge is unchallengeable (JT04).
Conceptions of teaching science		
Constructivist	Science is best taught by helping students construct knowledge, make interpretations, and providing authentic experiences.	Teaching science needs to help students connect scientific knowledge with real life (JT01). Teaching science needs to firstly understand students' prior knowledge, and to provide real life problems for thinking about and exploring (ST01).
Traditional	Science is best taught by transferring knowledge from teacher to students. Teachers highlight the students' ability to prepare for tests.	Teaching science is transferring basic content knowledge from the textbook (JT05). Sometimes, we need to ask students to memorize the scientific concepts, formulas, and symbols (JT18).

In addition, according to the qualitative nature of the present study and the small sample size, this study uses descriptive data to illustrate the responses of the participants in the ATI-s.

FINDINGS

Analysis of Written Responses for Scientific Epistemological Beliefs and Conceptions of Teaching Science

Table 16.2 reports teachers' scientific epistemological beliefs and their conceptions of teaching science according to the aforementioned framework.

Table 16.2 Teachers' Scientific Epistemological Beliefs and Conceptions of Teaching Science

	Constructivist	Traditional
Scientific epistemological beliefs	4 (16%)	21 (84%)
Conceptions of teaching science	13 (52%)	12 (48%)

As shown in Table 16.2, 84% of the teachers held "traditional" scientific epistemological beliefs, whereas 16% of them expressed "constructivist" epistemological beliefs regarding science. Similar findings were also found by Tsai (2002) in that only 11% of teachers in his study were identified as having "constructivist" beliefs about science. In contrast, with respect to conceptions of teaching science, about half of the teachers held "constructivist" conceptions.

To further understand the association between teachers' written responses regarding scientific epistemological beliefs and conceptions of teaching science, Table 16.3 represents the result of each category across the two beliefs system. As shown in Table 16.3, 40% of the teachers were identified as being in the 'traditional' category for beliefs about scientific knowledge and teaching science. However, 44% of the teachers hold traditional scientific epistemological beliefs but have constructivist teaching conceptions. In particular, only 2 teachers held constructivist beliefs about scientific knowledge and 2 teachers held constructive beliefs about teaching science. Few teachers had framed the "constructivist" philosophy about the epistemology of science and science teaching.

The present study found that about half of the teachers held consistent beliefs concerning scientific knowledge and teaching science (48%). However, we also found that about half of the teachers held inconsistent beliefs about scientific knowledge and teaching science (52%). Actually, most of those teachers with inconsistent beliefs held traditional scientific epistemological beliefs with constructivist conceptions of teaching science (44%). Elements of Western philosophy and pedagogy (e.g., constructivism) have been introduced into the Taiwanese school system in recent years. However, Taiwanese teachers' beliefs about teaching are framed by their educational

Table 16.3 Association between Teachers' Scientific Epistemological Beliefs and Conceptions of Teaching Science

Scientific epistemological beliefs	*Conceptions of teaching science*	
	Constructivist	*Traditional*
Constructivist	2 (8%) *Consistent*	2 (8%) *Inconsistent*
Traditional	11 (44%) *Inconsistent*	10 (40%) *Consistent*

experience and teacher educational program which are embedded in an Eastern culture and philosophy (e.g., Confucianism; Jin & Dan, 2004; Yu, 2008). Thus, those teachers possessing inconsistent constructivist teaching conceptions may be shaped by the educational environment which encourages constructivism (i.e., teaching science is to help students construct knowledge) while still embracing traditional epistemological beliefs concerning science (i.e., scientific knowledge is certain).

The Associations among the Categories of Scientific Epistemological Beliefs, Conceptions of Teaching Science, and their Responses to the ATI-s

Table 16.4 presents sample teachers' mean scores on the ATI-s, the descriptive results of science teachers' years of teaching, and the means of the sub-scales of ATI-s grouped by their categories of scientific epistemological beliefs and conceptions of teaching science. Regarding the result of all participants' mean scores on the ATI-s, there were no differences between their responses to the student-focused and teacher-focused approaches to teaching science.

With respect to teachers' scientific epistemological beliefs, the descriptive data suggest that junior teachers (5.25 years of teaching) tend to have constructivist scientific epistemological beliefs (as shown in Table 16.4). As aforementioned, elements of constructivism have been introduced into the Taiwanese school system in recent years. Thus, in contrast to the senior teachers who were educated in the traditional educational system, the junior teachers may have been educated in this progressive educational system and thus tend to embrace constructivist scientific epistemological beliefs. The teachers holding constructivist scientific epistemological beliefs tended to score relatively high on the student-focused approaches and lower on teacher-focused approaches than teachers with traditional scientific epistemological beliefs did. The results seem to indicate that teachers' student-focused approaches to teaching science may relate to their constructivist scientific epistemological beliefs.

Furthermore, Table 16.4 also shows the descriptive results of science teachers' years of teaching, and the means of the sub-scales of ATI-s grouped by their categories of conceptions of teaching science. These descriptive data seem to show that teachers with constructivist conceptions of teaching science tend to have more years of teaching experience (9.39 years of teaching) and to score relatively highly on both student-focused (3.46 per item) and teacher-focused approaches (3.42 per item) to teaching science than teachers with traditional conceptions of teaching science.

Conceptions of teaching may stem from the teachers' experiences of teaching (Kember, 1997). In general, it might be expected that senior teachers with more exposure to traditional teaching than junior teachers might hold more traditional conceptions of teaching. This was not the case in

Table 16.4 Science Teachers' Years of Teaching, and Mean Scores With Standard Deviation on the ATI-S by Scientific Epistemological Beliefs and Conceptions of Teaching Science

	Years of teaching	ATIs Student-focused approach (M, SD)	ATIs Teacher-focused approach (M, SD)
All participants	7.24	3.29 (0.59)	3.29 (0.54)
Scientific epistemological beliefs			
Constructivist	5.25	3.38 (0.94)	2.90 (0.26)
Traditional	7.62	3.27 (0.53)	3.35 (0.55)
Conceptions of teaching science			
Constructivist	9.39	3.46 (0.54)	3.42 (0.56)
Traditional	4.92	3.10 (0.60)	3.13 (0.50)

our data, with experienced teachers describing constructivist conceptions of teaching science. It is possible that the more experienced teachers may be more adept at political correctness than junior teachers, and thus more likely to acknowledge and support the constructivist curriculum guidelines which are now part of Taiwanese educational reform in science and life technology education (MOE, 2004).

However, whereas these teachers described constructivist conceptions of teaching they described a mix of both student-focused and teacher-focused approaches to teaching science. That is, teachers not only focused on students' conceptual change, but also stressed the memorizing of scientific formulas. In our previous studies, we also found that Taiwanese high school students perceived both student-centered and teacher-centered features in their science learning environment (Lee & Chang, 2004; Lee, Chang, & Tsai, 2009). The reason for the teachers with constructivist teaching conceptions still expressing a mix of both student-focused and teacher-focused teaching approaches may stem from the Taiwanese educational climate which emphasizes high-stakes examinations at the school and national level. To this end, the traditionally teacher-focused approaches may be quite effective for enhancing students' achievement in such examinations. Accordingly, it seems reasonable to find that teachers tend to embrace mixed approaches to teaching science (i.e., student-focused and teacher-focused approaches).

Furthermore, according to the means of the sub-scales of ATI-s grouped by teachers' categories of scientific epistemological beliefs and conceptions of teaching science, the results seem to reveal that in comparison to teachers' scientific epistemological beliefs, their conceptions of teaching science tend to relate more to their teaching approaches. As shown in Table 16.4, with respect to the means of student-focused approaches, the difference between "constructivist" and "traditional" categories were greater in relation to conceptions of teaching science (3.46 versus 3.10) than for their scientific epistemological beliefs (3.38 versus 3.27). As described earlier, teachers' conceptions of teaching science were framed by their past educational experiences and their training in the teacher education program. Pratt (1992) also assumed that teachers' conceptions of teaching could be viewed as different categories of ideas underlying their descriptions of how they experience the teaching process. Consequently, rather than teachers' scientific epistemological beliefs which reflect their beliefs about the nature of knowledge in science, teachers' conceptions of teaching science which reflect how they experience the teaching process, to some extent, seem to be more related to their approaches to teaching science. Nevertheless, this claim needs to be further verified.

CONCLUSION

This is an exploratory study which aims to investigate the relations among science teachers' scientific epistemological beliefs, conceptions of teaching science, and their approaches to teaching science. It should be noted that, according to the limited sample size and the descriptive nature of the present study, a follow-up study is needed to conduct a large-sample study which employs rigorous statistical methods to examine these relationships.

Based on the descriptive data provided by the present study, three major findings can be summarized. First, the present study found that about half of the teachers held consistent beliefs concerning scientific knowledge and teaching science (48%). This seems to reveal that the teachers' pedagogical beliefs may be driven by their epistemological beliefs. However, half of the teachers were found to have inconsistent beliefs regarding scientific knowledge and teaching science (52%). This result may stem from the socio-cultural background in Taiwan. As suggested by Lee, Chang, and Tsai (2009), the learning environment in Taiwan may lie in the transition between traditional teacher-centered and constructivist orientation. The traditional teacher-centered feature of pedagogy cannot be abandoned, whereas the constructivist philosophy of education is introduced through educational reforms. In this situation, it seems reasonable to find teachers who hold inconsistent beliefs regarding scientific knowledge and teaching science.

Second, based on the descriptive data represented in Table 16.4, the results of the present study seem to indicate that teachers with constructivist scientific epistemological beliefs and conceptions of teaching science are more likely to embrace student-focused approaches to teaching science. Similar findings were indicated by Kang and Wallace (2005) who investigated secondary teachers' epistemological beliefs and instructional practices. The present result, to some extent, supports the suggestion that teachers' scientific epistemological beliefs and conceptions of teaching science may have an influence on their approaches to teaching science. However, this claim also needs to be further verified.

Third, according to Table 16.4, the results of the present study seem to indicate that teachers who are categorized as having traditional scientific epistemological beliefs (7.62 years of teaching) and who are categorized as having constructivist conceptions of teaching science (9.39 years of teaching) tend to have many more years of teaching experience. Such results imply that senior teachers may have inconsistent beliefs regarding scientific knowledge and teaching science (i.e., traditional scientific epistemological beliefs but constructivist conceptions of teaching science). As aforementioned, having inconsistent beliefs may be due to the learning environment in Taiwan which may lie in the transition between traditional teacher-centered and constructivist orientation. On the other hand, perhaps, the strong emphasis on the constructivist pedagogy by the new curriculum guidelines for science and life technology education in high schools (MOE, 2004) may have influenced the teachers to provide the politically correct responses to the questions regarding teaching conceptions.

IMPLICATIONS FOR PROFESSIONAL DEVELOPMENT

In this chapter, we have initially generated a profile of scientific epistemological beliefs, conceptions of teaching science, and the approaches to teaching science of inservice teachers in Taiwan. This profile, to some extent, seems to support the suggestion that teachers' pedagogical practice may be driven by both their conceptions of teaching and their personal epistemologies (e.g., Boz & Uzuntiryaki, 2006; Kang and Wallace, 2005; Tsai, 2002). Moreover, the profile of conceptions of teaching and personal epistemologies seems to contribute to the implementation of a constructivist learning environment. Accordingly, science educators and teacher educators may need to help inservice teachers to develop sophisticated beliefs about scientific knowledge and pedagogical beliefs; in particular they may need to help senior teachers who may be more likely to possess inconsistent beliefs about science and teaching.

To successfully enhance teachers' constructivist scientific epistemological beliefs, science educators not only need to implement appropriate professional development programs, but also need more time and continuous efforts for teachers to make improvements (Tsai, 2007). Mulhall and Gunstone (2008) suggested that programs which aim to successfully enhance teachers' pedagogical practice and their beliefs about scientific knowledge may need to explicitly embed and integrate the history and philosophy of science. Tsai (2005) has employed a science education course which covers the philosophy of science, instruction in students' alternative conceptions, and theories of conceptual change, and found that the teachers changed their beliefs about scientific knowledge after completing the course. Consequently, to enhance inservice teachers' sophisticated beliefs about scientific knowledge and pedagogical beliefs, teacher education and professional developmental programs for inservice teachers may create workshops which consist of instruction about the history and the philosophy of science.

ACKNOWLEDGMENTS

The funding of this research project is supported by the National Science Council, Taiwan, under grant number NSC 97–2511-S-011–003-MY3 and NSC 99–2511-S-011 -002.

REFERENCES

Abd-El-Khalick, F., & Lederman, N. G. (2000). Improving science teachers' conceptions of nature of science: a critical review of the literature. *International Journal of Science Education, 22*, 665–701.

Abell, S. K., & Smith, D. C. (1994). What is science? Preservice elementary teachers' conceptions of the nature of science. *International Journal of Science Education, 16*, 475–487.

Bogdan, R. C., & Biklen, S. K. (1998). *Qualitatively research for education: An introduction to theory and methods.* Boston: Allyn and Bacon.

Boulton-Lewis, G. M., Smith, D. J. H., McCrindle, A. R., Burnett, P. C., & Campbell, K. J. (2001). Secondary teachers' conceptions of teaching and learning. *Learning and Instruction, 11*, 35–51.

Boz, Y., & Uzuntiryaki, E. (2006). Turkish prospective chemistry teachers' beliefs about chemistry teaching. *International Journal of Science Education, 28*, 1647–1667.

Bryan, L. A. (2003). Nestedness of beliefs: examining a prospective elementary teacher's belief system about science teaching and learning. *Journal of Research in Science Teaching, 40*, 835–868.

Buehl, M. M., & Alexander, P. A. (2001). Beliefs about academic knowledge. *Educational Psychology Review, 13*, 325–351.

Chai, C. S., Teo, T., & Lee, C. B. (2010). Modelling the relationships among beliefs about learning, knowledge, and teaching of pre-service teachers in Singapore. *The Asia-Pacific Educational Researcher, 19*, 25–42.

Chan, K. W. (2003). Hong Kong teacher education students' epistemological beliefs and approaches to learning. *Research in Education, 69*, 36–50.

Chan, K. W., & Elliott, R. G. (2004). Relational analysis of personal epistemology and conceptions about teaching and learning. *Teaching and Teacher Education, 20*, 817–831.

Eley, M. G. (2006). Teachers' conceptions of teaching, and the making of specific decisions in planning to teach. *Higher Education, 51*, 191–214.

Gao, L. B., & Watkins, D. (2001). Identifying and assessing the conceptions of teaching of secondary school physics teachers in China. *British Journal of Educational Psychology, 71*, 443–469.

Gao, L. B., & Watkins, D. (2002). Conceptions of teaching held by school science teachers in P. R. China: Identifying and crosscultural comparisons. *International Journal of Science Education, 24*, 61–79.

Hewson, P. W., & Hewson, M. G. (1988). An appropriate conception of teaching science: A view from studies of science learning. *Science Education, 72,* 597–614.

Hofer, B. K., & Pintrich, P. R. (1997). The development of epistemological theories: Beliefs about knowledge and knowing and their relation to learning. *Review of Educational Research, 67,* 88–140.

Jin, S.-H., & Dan, J.-W. (2004). The contemporary development of philosophy of education in mainland China and Taiwan. *Comparative Education, 40,* 571–581.

Kang, N.-H., & Wallace, C. S. (2005). Secondary science teachers' use of laboratory activities: Linking epistemological beliefs, goals, and practice. *Science Education, 89,* 140–165.

Kember, D. (1997). A reconceptualisation of the research into university academics' conceptions of teaching. *Learning and Instruction, 7,* 255–275.

Kember, D., & Kwan, K. P. (2000). Lecturers' approaches to teaching and their relationship to conceptions of good teaching. *Instructional Science, 28,* 469–490.

Koballa, T., Graber, W., Coleman, D. C., & Kemp, A. C. (2000). Prospective gymnasium teachers' conceptions of chemistry learning and teaching. *International Journal of Science Education, 22,* 209–224.

Kukari, A. J. (2004). Cultural and religious experiences: Do they define teaching and learning for pre-service teachers prior to teacher education? *Asia-Pacific Journal of Teacher Education, 32,* 96–110.

Laksov, K. B., Nikkola, M., & Lonka, K. (2008). Does teacher thinking match teaching practice? A study of basic science teachers. *Medical Education, 42,* 143–151.

Lederman, N. G. (1992). Students' and teachers' conceptions of the nature of science: A review of the research. *Journal of Research in Science Teaching, 29,* 331–359.

Lederman, N. G. (2007). Nature of science: Past, present, and future. In S. K. Abell & N. G. Lederman (Eds.), *Handbook of research on science education* (pp. 831–880). Mahwah, NJ: Lawrence Erlbaum Associates.

Lee, M.-H., & Chang, C.-Y. (2004). Development and exploration of the earth science classroom learning environment instrument (in Chinese). *Chinese Journal of Science Education, 12,* 421–443.

Lee, M.-H., Chang, C.-Y., & Tsai, C.-C. (2009). Exploring Taiwanese high school students' perceptions of and preferences for teacher authority in the earth science classroom with relation to their attitudes and achievement. *International Journal of Science Education, 31,* 1811–1830.

Lee, M.-H., Tsai, C.-C., Chang, C.-Y., & Liang, J.-C. (2009). *The relationships between Taiwanese high school science teachers' conceptions of learning science and their approaches to teaching science.* Paper presented at the Association for Science Teacher Education (ASTE) Annual Meeting, Hartford, CT.

Liang, J.-C., Lee, M.-H., & Tsai, C.-C. (2010). The relations between scientific epistemological beliefs and approaches to learning science among science-major undergraduates in Taiwan. *The Asia-Pacific Education Researcher, 19,* 43–59.

Linder, C., & Marshall, D. (2003). Reflection and phenomenography: Towards theoretical and educational development possibilities. *Learning and Instruction, 13,* 271–284.

Liu, S.-Y., & Tsai, C.-C. (2008). Differences in the scientific epistemological views of undergraduate students. *International Journal of Science Education, 30,* 1055–1073.

Maggioni, L., & Parkinson, M. (2008). The role of teacher epistemic cognition, epistemic beliefs and calibration in instruction. *Educational Psychology Review, 20,* 445–461.

Marton, F., Dall'Alba, G., & Beaty, E. (1993). Conceptions of learning. *International Journal of Educational Research*, 19, 277–299.

Ministry of Education [MOE]. (2004). *The 10–12 grades science and life technology curriculum standards*. Ministry of Education, Taiwan.

Mulhall, P., & Gunstone, R. (2008). Views of physics held by physics teachers with differing approaches to teaching physics. *Research in Science Education*, 38, 435–462.

Norton, L., Richardson, J. T. E., Hartley, J., Newstead, S., & Mayes, J. (2005). Teachers' beliefs and intentions concerning teaching in higher education. *Higher Education*, 50, 537–571.

Pajares, M. F. (1992). Teachers' beliefs and educational research: Cleaning up a messy construct. *Review of Educational Research*, 62, 307–332.

Postareff, L., & Lindblom-Ylanne, S. (2008). Variation in teachers' descriptions of teaching: Broadening the understanding of teaching in higher education. *Learning and Instruction*, 18, 109–120.

Pratt, D. D. (1992). Conceptions of teaching. *Adult Education Quarterly*, 42, 203–220.

Ryan, A. G., & Aikenhead, G. S. (1992). Students' preconceptions about the epistemology of science. *Science Education*, 76, 559–580.

Schwab, J. J. (1978). Education and the structure of the disciplines. In I. Westbury & N. J. Wilkof (Eds.), *Science, curriculum, and the liberal education* (pp. 229–272). Chicago: University of Chicago Press.

Trigwell, K., & Prosser, M. (2004). Development and use of the approaches to teaching inventory. *Educational Psychological Review*, 16, 409–424.

Trigwell, K., Prosser, M., & Taylor, P. (1994). Qualitative differences in approaches to teaching first year university science courses. *Higher Education*, 27, 74–84.

Trigwell, K., Prosser, M., & Waterhouse, F. (1999). Relations between teachers' approaches to teaching and students' approaches to learning. *Higher Education*, 37, 57–70.

Tsai, C.-C. (1998). An analysis of scientific epistemological beliefs and learning orientations of Taiwanese eighth graders. *Science Education*, 82, 473–489.

Tsai, C.-C. (1999). "Laboratory exercises help me memorize the scientific truths": A study of eighth graders' scientific epistemological views and learning in laboratory activities. *Science Education*, 83, 654–674.

Tsai, C.-C. (2002). Nested epistemologies: Science teachers' beliefs of teaching, learning and science. *International Journal of Science Education*, 24, 771–783.

Tsai, C.-C. (2007). Teachers' scientific epistemological views: The coherence with instruction and students' views. *Science Education*, 91, 222–243.

Tsai, C.-C., & Liu, S. Y. (2005). Developing a multidimensional instrument for assessing students' epistemological views toward science. *International Journal of Science Education*, 27, 1621–1638.

Waters-Adams, S. (2006). The relationship between understanding of the nature of science and practice: The influence of teachers' beliefs about education, teaching and learning. *International Journal of Science Education*, 28, 919–944.

Yu, T.-L. (2008). The revival of Confucianism in Chinese schools: A historical-political review. *Asia Pacific Journal of Education*, 28, 113–129.

Conclusion

17 Teachers' Personal Epistemologies and Teacher Education
Emergent Themes and Future Research

Gregory Schraw, Joanne Brownlee, and Donna Berthelsen

ABSTRACT

This chapter summarizes the responses to four questions in each of the chapters in this volume. The questions addressed the use of a conceptual framework that guides the chapter, issues of domain-generality, how personal epistemology relates to teaching, and how personal epistemologies change. We concluded that all of the chapters discussed the distinction between constructivist and transmission teaching practices, while suggesting that there are many inconsistencies in understanding the relationship between the nature of beliefs and teachers' practices regardless of the relative sophistication of teachers' personal epistemologies. We also summarized a multi-component instructional model for calibrating teaching practices based on suggestions in each of the chapters, and made four suggestions for future research, including the need for an integrated theory that accounts for the development and manifestations of personal epistemology in the classroom, the generalizability of findings across different measurements, a set of guidelines to promote teacher epistemological change, and an explicit instructional model that explains the development and calibration of beliefs and practices.

The goal of this volume was to examine the relationship between teachers' personal epistemologies and teacher education. Sixteen different chapters addressed one or more aspects of this issue. Although each of the chapters addressed different aspects of teachers' personal epistemologies, a number of common themes are apparent across the chapters. We believe it is useful to articulate these themes in greater detail to provide a better retrospective understanding of this volume, as well as a better prospective framework for future research and changes to teacher training programs.

We divide this chapter into two main sections. The first section addresses four key questions about the nature of teachers' personal epistemologies that were discussed in the introductory chapter as part of a larger set of questions. These questions focus on how to conceptualize these beliefs as explicit models; whether beliefs are domain-specific or domain-general; how beliefs are related to teaching; and how beliefs change over time. We provide a summary of each chapter in terms of these four questions. The second section proposes four general suggestions for future research based on the studies reported within this volume.

FOUR QUESTIONS ABOUT TEACHERS' PERSONAL EPISTEMOLOGIES

Question 1 examined how each chapter situated its discussion of teachers' personal epistemologies in terms of four conceptual models of epistemology. Figure 17.1 provides an overview of these models, which have been discussed in detail elsewhere (Hofer, 2001; Muis, 2004), as well as individual theories representative of each model. Using the terminology in Chapter 1 (Brownlee, Schraw, & Berthelsen, this volume), we refer to these models respectively as *epistemological development* (King & Kitchener, 1994; Kuhn, 1991; Perry, 1970), *epistemological beliefs* (Hofer, 2004; Schommer, 1990), *epistemological theories* (Bendixen & Rule, 2004; Schraw & Olafson, 2008), and *epistemological resources* (Hammer & Elby, 2002).

Models of epistemological development focus on the development of a personal epistemological framework that changes across three or more general stages, typified by the absolutist, subjectivist, and evaluativist views described by Brownlee, Schraw et al. (this volume). These stages span a

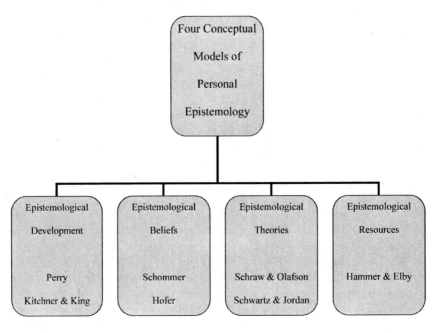

Figure 17.1   Conceptual models of personal epistemology.

range from *naive* to *sophisticated* personal epistemologies. A number of similar developmental models evolved in the 1980s, due in part to the continuing legacy of Piagetian developmental psychology. These models have been criticized, however, in terms of whether development is strictly stage-like and whether stages are domain-general.

An alternative perspective arose during the 1990s which we refer to as the epistemological beliefs paradigm. These models focus on how personal epistemology consists of a set of independent, multidimensional beliefs which influence learning. Schommer (1990) was the first to describe personal epistemologies as a set of multidimensional beliefs, which consisted of five separate dimensions she referred to as *certain knowledge* (i.e., absolute knowledge exists and will eventually be known), *simple knowledge* (i.e., knowledge consists of discrete facts), *omniscient authority* (i.e., authorities have access to otherwise inaccessible knowledge), *quick learning* (i.e., learning occurs in a quick or not-at-all fashion), and *innate ability* (i.e., the ability to acquire knowledge is endowed at birth). In contrast, Hofer (2004) proposed an alternative system, which focused on four separate beliefs, subsumed under two general belief dimensions referred to as *the nature of knowing* and *the process of knowing*. Although Hofer referred to her system as theory-based, we categorize it here as a beliefs-based model because it focuses on four belief dimensions rather than an integrated epistemological theory that subsumes these beliefs. The "nature" dimension included two beliefs labeled *certainty of knowledge* (i.e., the degree to which one sees knowledge as fixed versus fluid and changeable) and *simplicity of knowledge* (i.e., the degree to which knowledge is viewed as individual facts versus complex, interrelated concepts). These beliefs are similar to those proposed by Schommer (1990). The "process" dimension included two factors called *source of knowledge* (i.e., the extent to which credible knowledge is self- or other-generated) and *justification of knowing* (i.e., the rules and criteria that individuals use to evaluate knowledge claims). These beliefs differ from Schommer's (1990) framework in that they focus on cognitive processes used to evaluate knowledge claims, rather than beliefs about the "content" of knowledge per se.

A more recent framework is the *epistemological theories* paradigm, which focuses on general theories of knowledge that differ along a continuum of naïve to sophisticated world views. These models assume that an individual's personal epistemology is comprised of multiple beliefs that develop together as an integrated set of beliefs that comprise a unified belief system (Bendixen & Rule, 2004; Olafson, Schraw, & VanderVeldt, 2010). For example, Schraw and Olafson (2008) used the term *epistemological worldview* to refer to an individual's collective beliefs about the nature and acquisition of knowledge, which they contrasted to an *ontological world view*, which included an individual's collective beliefs about the nature of reality and being. In this volume, Schwartz and Jordan use a continuum-based model on the distinction between *pathognomonic* and *interventionist* beliefs. Several other researchers have used the term *personal epistemology* (Brownlee, Purdie, & Boulton-Lewis, 2001; Brownlee & Berthelsen, 2006) with regard to an epistemological worldview that includes one's collective beliefs, attitudes, and assumptions about the acquisition, structure, representation, and application of knowledge.

Another recent perspective is the *epistemological resources* paradigm, which envisions personal epistemology as context specific set of epistemological resources, rather than developmental stages, or a set of individual beliefs (Hammer & Elby, 2002). In this view, children as well as adults construct multiple ways of knowing that vary depending on the domain, the specific context of learning, as well as the socio-cultural setting and affordances that are relevant to the learning situation. One of the main goals of this framework is to suggest that personal epistemologies are highly variable between and within individuals depending on context. Learners may invoke different resources at varying times throughout a learning task and shift epistemological perspectives before, during, or after critical environmental changes. Hammer and Elby (2002) view the other models described above as *unitary* in that they view beliefs as relatively fixed and unchangeable within a particular context, whereas their own account suggests that individuals hold multiple epistemological stances, characterized by fine-grained epistemological resources, that are activated or deactivated as a function of situational constraints.

Several chapters in this volume combine two or more models into a hybrid analysis to examine the development of individual beliefs (Feucht, this volume; Marra & Palmer, this volume; Schraw et al., this volume). For example, Feucht (this volume) examines the change in four beliefs (i.e., stability and structure of knowing, source and justification of knowing) across three developmental levels (i.e., absolutist, multiplist, and evaluativist). These chapters attempt to integrate two theories for the purposes of articulating the process of epistemological change and explaining empirical findings, but do not attempt to provide a broader theoretical unification that integrates two fundamentally different theories. Nevertheless, we believe theoretical unification is a worthwhile goal that we return to later in this chapter.

Table 17.1 provides a summary of how each chapter aligns itself with the four models shown in Figure 17.1. Most authors utilize either a beliefs or a developmental model. Belief-based models are evenly divided between the systems proposed by Schommer (1990) and Hofer (2004). Approximately one quarter utilize a developmental perspective, focusing on the distinction between absolutist, multiplist, and evaluativist perspectives. Another one quarter adopt some type of personal theories model to explain how beliefs "in toto" are related to teaching practices and teacher change. At least two chapters use what we refer to as hybrid models that focus on the role of individual beliefs across multiple developmental stages (Feucht, this volume; Marra & Palmer, this volume).

Table 17.1 Responses to the Four Core Questions in Each Chapter

Chapter	Q1: What is the model used to conceptual personal epistemologies?	Q2: Are personal epistemologies domain-specific or domain-general?	Q3: How are teachers' personal epistemologies related to teaching?	Q4: How do personal epistemologies change?
2. Yadav et al.	Overview of developmental, beliefs, and theories models.	Overview of domain-general and domain-specific perspectives.	Evidence that show personal epistemologies related to practice, but are inconsistent. Many preservice teachers show naive personal epistemologies.	Explicit reflection that emphasizes relativistic nature of education. Need longitudinal research as teachers go through preservice courses and into practice.
3. Tillema	Beliefs model based on Schommer (1990).	Unspecified, although consistent with domain-general.	Teachers face a variety of dilemmas that are resolved in different ways based on personal epistemologies.	Reflection on classroom dilemmas. Select a *deliberate action* to resolve dilemma. Resolution of dilemma changes personal epistemologies.
4. Strømsø & Bråten	Beliefs model based on Hofer (2001).	Unspecified, although consistent with domain-general.	*Transmission versus facilitation* beliefs lead to direct instruction versus constructivist teaching styles.	Reflection and conceptual change via discussion of conflicting beliefs. Explicit effort to calibrate beliefs and teaching practices.
5. Brownlee, Edwards et al.	Developmental model based on absolutist, multiplist, and evaluativist stances.	Unspecified.	Sophisticated beliefs lead to constructivist practices based on autonomous and peer learning, whereas naive beliefs lead to direct instruction, observation, and modeling.	Modeling, reflection on, or evaluation of practical strategies. Social interaction that promotes *self-authorship* of beliefs.
6. Walker et al.	Hybrid: Beliefs model to measure pre–post beliefs; developmental model for interviews.	Unspecified, although consistent with domain-general.	Transition from *reproductive* to *constructivist* classroom practices.	Increased understanding that knowledge is relative. Integration of otherwise discrete beliefs and teaching practices. Modeling and reflection on sophisticated beliefs.
7. Bendixen & Corkill	Beliefs model based on Schommer (1990).	Unspecified, although consistent with domain-general.	Unspecified.	Diaries and reflective tasks to increase awareness of beliefs. Explicit discussion of beliefs.

(continued)

Table 17. (continued)

Chapter	Q1: What is the model used to conceptual personal epistemologies?	Q2: Are personal epistemologies domain-specific or domain-general?	Q3: How are teachers' personal epistemologies related to teaching?	Q4: How do personal epistemologies change?
8. Fives	Focus on belief development (implicit to explicit) over a semester.	Unspecified.	Explore students' beliefs. Encourage student-centered involvement.	Recognize personal epistemology as a developing rather than static belief system. *Microtransformations that affect belief filters.*
9. Marra & Palmer	Developmental (Perry, 1970; King & Kitchener, 1994).	Domain-specific.	Intentional (discussion, reflection, content discussion) and unintentional (team collaboration) strategies.	Collaborative reflection and discussion of teacher beliefs on pedagogical choices and potential *disconnect* with student beliefs.
10. Schraw et al.	Theories model based on Schraw & Olafson (2008).	Domain-general.	Realist beliefs to direct instruction; relativist beliefs to student-centered reflection and problem solving.	Discussion, reflection, and action research based on connecting beliefs and practices. Calibration of beliefs and practices.
11. Weinstock & Roth	Beliefs model based on Hofer (2001).	Unspecified, although consistent with domain-general.	Teachers' relativistic epistemologies promote teacher perspective-taking, higher student autonomy, and multiple viewpoints.	Reflection and perspective-taking.
12. Tabak & Weinstock	Developmental model based on absolutist, multiplist, and evaluativist stances.	Unspecified.	Classroom interactions affect *epistemological socialization.* Recitation fosters absolutist views; inquiry fosters relativist views.	Discussion and reflection on the consequences of different pedagogical practices. Use of classroom *adjudication processes.*

13. Valinides & Angeli	Beliefs model based on Schommer (1990).	Unspecified, although consistent with domain-specific.	Not discussed.	Promote *guided* ill-defined problem solving. Encourage disagreements and group-based discussion and resolution.
14. Schwartz & Jordan	Personal theories (Jordan et al., 2009) using *Pathognomonic-Interventionist* interview.	Unspecified, although consistent with domain-specific for students with disabilities.	Amount and quality of interaction with students, cooperative groupings, allotment of time, attitudes towards inclusion, teacher empathy.	Promoting awareness of underpinnings of beliefs about knowledge and learning on teaching and students.
15. Feucht	Hybrid: Beliefs (Hofer, 2001) and developmental (Kuhn, 1999) models.	Unspecified.	Absolutist beliefs lead to emphasis on skills, step-by-step instruction, rules.	Promote explicit awareness of beliefs and epistemic development and calibration of beliefs and practices.
16. Lee & Tsai	Personal theories (*constructivist* versus *traditional*).	Domain-specific (i.e., beliefs about science).	Traditional teachers focus on transfer of knowledge, skills, and memorization; constructivists focus on exploration and student-based inquiry.	Promote constructivist pedagogy and conceptual change. Help teachers calibrate beliefs and practices about teaching.

Collectively, Table 17.1 reveals two main points. One is that researchers continue to utilize a variety of theoretical models to pose and address research questions. Studies interested in factors that affect the development and change of epistemological thinking often rely on developmental models, whereas studies interested in how specific beliefs affect teaching practices utilize beliefs models. In this volume, studies that focused on the relationship between specific beliefs and teaching practices typically were cross-sectional in nature rather than longitudinal. A second point is that the theoretical landscape shows signs of diversifying rather than unifying. For example, the epistemological theories and resources models are relatively recent additions to the literature and represent new ways to understand personal epistemology, rather than substantive additions to existing models. Although these models make rich contributions to the existing literature, it is becoming increasingly unclear how researchers might reconcile and integrate the four models in Figure 17.1 into a unified theory that accounts for all epistemological phenomena.

Question 2 addresses whether teachers' personal epistemologies are domain-specific or domain-general. Domain-specific beliefs are those that apply within a specific domain of study such as mathematics, science, or literacy education, whereas domain-general beliefs are assumed to cut across a variety of academic disciplines. Previous research has supported domain-specific (Fives, this volume; Lee & Tsai, this volume; Muis, 2004), domain-general (Schraw et al., this volume), and hybrid views that propose an important role for both specific and domain-general beliefs (Hofer, 2004; Olafson & Schraw, 2006). Yadav et al. (this volume) provide a detailed discussion of this issue, as well as a compelling rationale why both domain-specific and domain-general beliefs may affect teaching practices and teacher change.

Table 17.1 suggests two important conclusions. One is that most researchers believe there is an important effect on teacher learning, teaching, and intellectual change that is attributable to domain-general epistemological beliefs. Indeed, many earlier models of personal epistemology, but especially developmental models, reported that general beliefs affected reasoning and problem solving regardless of problem type or domain (King & Kitchener, 1994; Kuhn, 1991). One advantage of domain-general theories, in our opinion, is that they subsume a variety of individual beliefs that frequently reveal the same trajectory of change over time. Nevertheless, it also is clear that beliefs differ across domains in terms of their importance to each domain, as well as the "prevailing epistemology" within that domain. For this reason, our second conclusion is that domain-specific and domain-general beliefs likely both contribute to teachers' thinking and practices within a specific domain. Although the chapters in this volume discuss this inter-relationship, none of the chapters directly addresses the relative contribution or importance of domain-specific versus domain-general beliefs. We suggest that researchers consider better ways to accommodate the specificity of beliefs into theoretical models and explanations of teacher developmental change.

Question 3 addresses how teachers' personal epistemologies are related to classroom practices. This question is of central importance to the present volume for both theoretical and practical reasons. Theoretically, it is important to establish whether there is a discernable link between personal epistemologies and teaching practices, as well how these practices affect student learning. Practically, it is important to identify differences, especially as a function of more or less sophisticated personal epistemologies, and identify how these beliefs are related to different curricular and pedagogical decisions in the classroom.

Brownlee, Edwards et al. (this volume) provided a summary of previous research on the relationship between teachers' personal epistemologies and classroom teaching and learning outcomes. It is fair to say that most research has focused on the relationship between personal epistemologies and teaching practices, whereas little research has directly addressed the relationship between teachers' personal epistemologies and student learning. Several generalizations seem appropriate. One is that teachers with sophisticated personal epistemologies are more likely to promote ill-structured problem solving and reflective thinking in their classroom, as opposed to basic skills and transmission of core facts and concepts. Second, teachers with sophisticated personal epistemologies are more likely to utilize strategies that focus on building personal meaning and organizing ideas that are linked to prior knowledge. These classrooms tend to be characterized by what Muis (2004) refers to as *availing* epistemologies that support constructivist approaches to learning in the classroom.

Notwithstanding the contribution of previous research, there is much we do not know about the relationship between personal epistemologies and teaching. Chapters in the present volume make a variety of claims about this relationship, but it is important to bear in mind that most of these studies do not overtly measure the relationship between personal epistemologies and teaching practices, or focus empirically on a narrower range of practices to which they generalize. Thus, we believe the relationships presented across the chapters and summarized in Table 17.1 are provisional in nature and require additional research.

A comparison of chapters in Table 17.1 suggests two general conclusions. One is that all of the chapters postulate an important distinction between constructivist and transmission teaching practices. Table 17.2 summarizes some of the key differences in these approaches with respect to epistemological development, beliefs, and classroom practices. Perhaps the most important assumption is that constructivist teaching reflects a more sophisticated level of epistemological development compared to transmission teaching. In this view, constructivist teaching is characterized by an evaluativist epistemology, whereas transmission teaching is characterized by absolutist epistemology. Importantly, this conclusion is consistent with

Table 17.2   A Comparison of Constructivist Versus Transmission Beliefs and Practices

	Constructivist Teaching	Transmission Teaching
Developmental Stage	Characterized by evaluativist stance	Characterized by absolutist stance
Epistemological Beliefs	Sophisticated beliefs (more explicit awareness)	Naïve beliefs (less explicit awareness)
Teacher Practices: Pedagogy	Student-centered approach which emphasizes collaborative learning, teacher scaffolding and independent work, leading to domain-general application of critical thinking skills	Teacher-centered approach which emphasizes acquisition of core facts and concepts, mastery of basic procedures, leading to automated application of domain-specific skills
Teacher Practices: Curriculum	Higher order thinking and evaluation skills based on reasoned application of first-order skills (i.e., domain knowledge and procedures)	Mastery of first-order domain knowledge and procedures

previous research findings, which reported that evaluativist epistemologies are related to higher level reasoning, use of evidence, and counterarguments, compared to less sophisticated reasoning characterized by absolutist epistemologies (King & Kitchener, 1994; Kuhn, 1991).

Constructivist teaching also is associated with more sophisticated individual epistemological beliefs such as the complexity and changeability of knowledge (Feucht, this volume; Tillema, this volume). Many of the chapters in this volume focus on the relationship between one or more specific beliefs and teaching practices. Generally speaking, teachers who utilize constructivist classroom practices are more likely to believe that knowledge is complex, malleable, constructed by the knower, and important to the extent that it provides a means to the intellectual end of *informed, critical reasoning and evaluation*. In contrast, teachers who utilize transmission practices are more likely to believe that knowledge is fixed, transmitted intact from experts to novices, unchanging in scope and nature, and important in and of itself, rather than as a means to a higher intellectual end. Most chapters also make the critical assumption that constructivist-oriented teachers have greater explicit awareness of their beliefs than transmission-oriented teachers, and therefore are better able to reflect on their beliefs and incorporate them into classroom practice. However, it is important to note that this assumption has not been tested in many cases and requires further empirical investigation.

Constructivist and transmission teachers are assumed as well to differ in terms of pedagogical and curricular choices. For example, constructivist teachers focus on a student-centered classroom in which the student is expected to construct meaning and a higher order understanding using teacher, peer, and autonomous support. Indeed, Weinstock and Roth (this volume) directly investigated this question and reported a link between constructivist practices on the one hand, and student ratings of autonomy and perspective-taking on the other. This type of instruction emphasizes ways in which students can construct meaning in a manner that promotes sophisticated thinking outside the classroom. Ideally, constructivist teaching over time should lead to the development of a broad set of domain-general, self-regulatory skills that prepare the student for the intellectual demands of the post-education settings.

A second main conclusion is that there are many inconsistencies in understanding the relationship between the nature of beliefs and teachers' practices regardless of the relative sophistication of teachers' personal epistemologies (Yadav et al., this volume). Several previous studies have demonstrated that there is a gap between teachers' espoused beliefs and their teaching practices. This gap appears to be robust across all teachers regardless of their beliefs (Olafson et al., 2010; Ozgun-Koca & Sen, 2006; White, 2000). Most chapters in this volume address this issue directly or indirectly, suggesting that the best way to eliminate this problem, and promote better *calibration* between beliefs and practices, is to increase explicit awareness of the nature of beliefs and use this awareness to plan and justify teaching practices. Indeed, we return to this important question latter in this chapter when discussing directions for future research.

Question 4 concerns the development and change in teachers' personal epistemologies. Unfortunately, very little is known about this topic, although a large number of previous studies have reported that teachers' beliefs often do not change substantially over time prior to inservice experiences to address change, and often do not change in the long run even with extensive inservice experience (Ozgun-Koca & Sen, 2006). Even though sophisticated personal epistemologies are an important goal for teacher education programs, most teachers appear to enter the profession with relatively naïve personal epistemologies. Overall, research suggests that teacher education programs frequently do not help preservice teachers develop sophisticated personal epistemologies in preparation for effective teaching (White, 2000). However, some researchers have reported change in beliefs following an in-depth intervention (Marra, 2005; Maggioni & Parkinson, 2008) or across time within a teacher education program (Walker et al., this volume).

Brownlee, Schraw et al. (this volume) suggested that preservice teachers require four separate skills that prepare them for effective classroom teaching: Build knowledge for teaching; have access to knowledge systems; hold personal epistemologies that influence what they gain from teacher education courses; and be able to make decisions in ill-defined contexts. One way to develop these skills is to focus on personal epistemologies in teacher education. Teacher educators must understand the nature of preservice teachers' personal epistemologies and the specific teaching and learning strategies and environments that help to promote more sophisticated personal epistemologies. Consistent with all of the chapters in this volume, these goals may be reached by providing a variety of constructivist-oriented experiences to preservice (and inservice) teachers in order to promote change in personal epistemologies.

Table 17.1 suggests that constructivist pedagogy relies on a multi-component instructional process (Marra, 2005; Olafson et al., 2010). Component 1 is to promote explicit awareness of personal epistemological beliefs, which frequently are implicit, as well as developing a personal theory that incorporates these beliefs. That is, teachers must first construct some type of explicit beliefs. A variety of chapters discuss activities designed to achieve these ends, including identification of teaching dilemmas (Tillema, this volume), collaborative discussion of dilemmas (Marra & Palmer, this volume; Yadav et al., this volume), diaries (Bendixen & Corkill, this volume), action research (Schraw et al., this volume), and expert modeling (Walker et al., this volume).

Component 2 is to promote in-depth reflection about individual epistemological beliefs and theories with the intent to change or modify beliefs over time. This approach is consistent with a long tradition of reflective change and practice (Schon, 1983), which argues that explicit awareness (i.e., mindfulness) of beliefs is the most crucial step towards development of beliefs and conceptual change. One advantage of reflection is to identify what Fives (this volume) refers to as *belief filters,* which often lead to faulty understanding of classroom events due to biases and misconceptions. Moreover, reflection is a critical component in what Brownlee, Edwards et al. (this volume) refer to as *self-authorship,* which occurs when individuals examine beliefs to make informed judgments in the context of one's identity and interdependent social relationships.

Component 3 is to identify inconsistencies and gaps between one's beliefs and intended classroom practices (White, 2000). Tillema (this volume) discusses the role of identifying potential or actual *teaching dilemmas* that may be caused by inconsistencies between belief and action. Dilemmas or discrepancies may be brought to explicit awareness in part by disagreements and guided group-based discussion of problems (Valinides & Angeli, this volume). A variety of chapters suggest that inquiry-based discussion of *disconnects* may help to resolve dilemmas and promote conceptual change among teachers (Lee & Tsai, this volume; Marra & Palmer, this volume; Schwartz & Jordan, this volume).

Component 4 is to promote integration among epistemological beliefs and classroom practices, which a number of chapters refer to as *calibration* of beliefs and practice (Lee & Tsai, this volume; Feucht, this volume; Walker et al., this volume). Tillema (this volume) discusses the importance of *deliberate action* based on resolution of dilemmas as a means for achieving calibrated classroom practice. Schraw et al. (this volume) proposed a

4-step process based on action research and reflection in order to reach calibrated practice. Tabak and Weinstock (this volume) and Weinstock and Roth (this volume) also discuss the role of reflective discussion as a vehicle for achieving developmental change and calibrated practice.

At their core, all of the chapters in this volume emphasize the role of reflection and discussion on conceptual change and the development of beliefs and calibrated practice. These strategies are consistent with much of the writing on conceptual change and teaching practice (Murphy & Mason, 2006). In addition, there is evidence that reflective practice helps students reflect on their own personal epistemologies, which facilitate learning (Lidar, Lundqvist, & Ostman, 2005; Schon, 1983). Indeed, most studies of teachers' personal epistemologies recommend that students should participate in explicit reflection on such beliefs. Yet research clearly suggests that beginning preservice teachers, in particular, and all teachers, in general, need help both in reflection on practice and opportunities to reflect on practice in their busy lives (Brownlee, Schraw, & Berthelsen, this volume). For this reason, we believe it is imperative to infuse discussion and reflection into teacher training to the fullest extent possible to promote rich explicit personal epistemologies (Kienhues, Bromme, & Stahl, 2008; Maggioni & Parkinson, 2008), as well as better calibration between beliefs and practices.

SUGGESTIONS FOR FUTURE RESEARCH

We make four suggestions for future research based on themes and motifs spanning the 16 chapters in this volume. These include the need for an integrated theory that accounts for the development and manifestations of personal epistemologies in the classroom, the generalizability of findings across different types of measurements, a better articulated set of guidelines to promote teacher epistemological change, and an explicit instructional model that explains the development and calibration of beliefs and practices.

Figure 17.1 summarized four different conceptual models of teachers' personal epistemology that differ with respect to development, beliefs, theories, and resources. Although beyond the scope of this chapter, each of the four models holds a number of elements in common, but especially the notion that teachers differ primarily with respect to the sophistication of the personal epistemologies. Yet each of the models focuses on a unique aspect of epistemology such as development versus individual beliefs that comprise a personal theory. There is no comprehensive model to date that explains the inter-relationship of beliefs to theories and how they develop over time in a manner that affects a teacher's epistemological resources (Brownlee et al., this volume; Yadav et al., this volume). However, there have been a number of recent attempts to develop models that explain multiple aspects of epistemological phenomena (Brownlee, 2003; Bendixen & Rule, 2004).

We believe it is theoretically and practically important to create an integrated model of personal epistemology that explains how beliefs and theories develop over time to increase a teacher's resources in the classroom. Ideally, such a model would differentiate beliefs, explain how beliefs are aligned with an integrated personal epistemological (and ontological) theory, how personal theories develop (e.g., across discrete stages), what factors shape and facilitate development, and how epistemological resources increase as a function of development. Although we understand the complexity of such a theoretical task, we believe that research is of limited value until a centralized theory can be developed and used as a touchstone for evaluating and integrating research findings.

A second suggestion for future research is to improve the measurement of epistemological phenomena, by codifying definitions and how these phenomena are assessed. Researchers have used at least six different measurement strategies for assessing epistemological beliefs and theories, including multi-item questionnaires; interviews; vignettes that characterize prototypical epistemological world views; essays, journals, and storyboards; concept maps (Ozgun-Koca & Sen, 2006); and multi-dimensional scaling of epistemological and ontological relativism. Although we applaud the use of multiple measures that can be used to make convergent inferences, they nevertheless raise questions regarding the construct and criterion related validity of these measurements, as well as their inter-relationships (Schraw & Olafson, 2008). It is unclear at times whether the measurement strategies used in contemporary epistemological research measure the same constructs and whether findings reported by different researchers using different measurement strategies are comparable.

We suggest that researchers devote more attention to what we refer to as a lack of *universal measurement design principles*, by which we mean using a measurement strategy in a consistent manner across studies to enhance the generalizability of findings. There are at least four ways this might be accomplished. One way is thorough definition of constructs being investigated and the domain of study. This includes some statement regarding the domain-generality of the construct. A second way is through content consistency, by which we mean using the same items on a questionnaire or structured interviews as other researchers to cross-validate findings. One strategy would be to use two separate self-report questionnaires with a common set of linking items. A third way is to use consistent administration procedures such as order of presentation, instructions provided to participants, amount of time to complete the assessments, and conditions under which the data is collected. A fourth way is through consistent use of scoring procedures. Indeed, we were struck by the fact that rubrics were poorly described in the research and rarely the same across studies. Structured interviews typically differed and used very different coding schemes. For all of these reasons, it may be difficult to generalize across studies, even those using similar methodology and measurement strategies.

A third goal of research should be to specify a set of guidelines to promote teacher epistemological change during teacher training. Chapters in this volume suggest at least seven important strategies, including discussion, reflection (Brownlee & Berthelsen, this volume; Tabak & Weinstock, this volume), action research (Schraw et al., this volume), dilemmas and conflicts (Marra & Palmer, this volume; Tillema, this volume), diaries and journals (Bendixen & Corkill, this volume), and collaborative in-class experiences that help students develop an explicit awareness of their personal epistemologies. Each of these strategies has particular strengths that complement the strengths of other strategies. Some strategies such as reflection (Schraw et al., this volume; Walker et al., this volume) appear to be especially important and useful in terms of promoting explicit awareness of beliefs and theories. Other strategies such as identifying conflicts and dilemmas (Strømsø & Bråten, this volume; Tilemma, this volume; Valinides & Angeli, this volume) may be particularly useful after beliefs are made explicit in order that preservice teachers can work through these dilemmas and generate a set of potential solutions.

We believe that future research should attempt to expand this set and to investigate whether these strategies are optimally effective when used in a specific instruction sequence. For example, none of the chapters in this volume examined whether viewing videos or movies of real-life classroom situations can be used to clarify teachers' personal epistemologies, even though recent advances in technology open up a variety of opportunities for use in teacher training, especially when using real-life classroom environments to articulate emerging preservice teacher beliefs and teaching practices. Similarly, we believe that some strategies such as examining dilemmas and conflicts may be most useful as a precursor to discussion, reflection, and collaborative problem solving.

A fourth goal of research should be to develop and test an explicit instructional model that facilitates the development and calibration of beliefs and teaching practices. Figure 17.2 shows a hypothetical model that we derived from a number of the chapters included in this volume. We emphasize that this model is a hypothetical hybrid, even though we believe it provides a reasonable starting point for future research. We use this model as an example of what a better theoretically articulated model might look like. The development and refinement of such a model could be used profitably as a template for preservice (and perhaps inservice) teacher development.

Figure 17.2 includes a 5-stage sequence intended to integrate activities described in many of the chapters in this volume. Stage 1 focuses on the articulation of class content and activities that are aligned to course objectives. This stage provides an opportunity for class instructors to set objectives in conjunction with student goals. Stage 2 provides an initial opportunity for students to engage in discussion, reflection, modeling, and proposed action research in order to establish a meaningful explicit connection between personal epistemological beliefs and potential teaching practices. Stage 3 includes

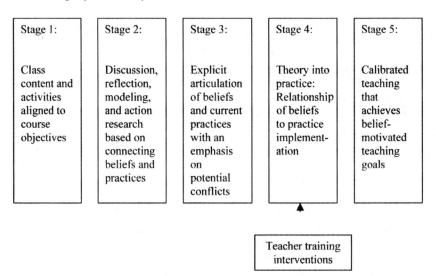

Stage 1:	Stage 2:	Stage 3:	Stage 4:	Stage 5:
Class content and activities aligned to course objectives	Discussion, reflection, modeling, and action research based on connecting beliefs and practices	Explicit articulation of beliefs and current practices with an emphasis on potential conflicts	Theory into practice: Relationship of beliefs to practice implement-ation	Calibrated teaching that achieves belief-motivated teaching goals

Teacher training interventions

Figure 17.2   A hypothetical instructional sequence model that fosters calibrated teaching.

explicit clarification of beliefs and teaching practices with an emphasis on potential conflicts. Stage 3 also provides an excellent opportunity for formal instruction based on readings and teacher modeling. Stage 4 introduces the integration of theory into practice, whereby students may begin to clarify the relationship between their personal beliefs and teaching practices. We view this stage as especially critical in the development of calibrated teaching and recognize the ongoing, dynamic nature of this process as it gradually unfolds. In addition, Stage 4 may be a particularly auspicious time to introduce instructional interventions such as dilemmas (Tillema, this volume), conflicts between beliefs and classroom constraints imposed by school curriculum or pedagogical mandates (Fives, this volume; Kienhues et al., 2008), or conceptual change pedagogy (Lee & Tsai, this volume; Strømsø & Bråten, this volume). Finally, Stage 5 attempts to promote calibrated teaching that integrates personal beliefs and practices. Ideally, this would include school-based interventions with preservice teachers that draw on their experiences in the classroom. This could be accomplished using videos of classroom experiences, journals, action research projects, and collaborative discussions outside the context of the classroom (Schraw et al., this volume).

Collectively, these four directions for future research would benefit our conceptual and practical understanding of the interplay between personal epistemologies and teaching practices. We strongly believe it would benefit researchers to develop an explicit model that integrates the change in epistemological beliefs across developmental stages, articulating factors that promote development. In addition, there is a crucial need for an explicit model of calibrated teaching that articulates and evaluates ways in which teachers develop explicit beliefs that are aligned to curricular and pedagogical strategies. Last, we emphasize the importance of providing clear definitions of salient constructs, as well as guidelines for measuring and interpreting these constructs.

SUMMARY

We examined common themes are across the chapters in this volume. Each of the chapters addressed four questions which focused on how to conceptualize personal epistemologies; whether beliefs are domain-specific or domain-general; how personal epistemologies are related to teaching; and how they change over time. We summarized the four models shown in Figure 17.1 and concluded that the theoretical models used to understand personal epistemology appear to be expanding and diversifying rather than converging towards a unified theory. We also discussed the relative contributions of domain-specific versus domain-general beliefs. Table 17.1 summarized a variety of ways in which personal epistemologies affect teaching strategies, and enumerated strategies for changing personal epistemologies, including discussion, reflection, journals, diaries, peer dialogues, and modeling. Collectively, the chapters suggested that constructivist epistemologies lead to better teaching and that the lack of calibration between beliefs and practices often creates dilemmas and challenges for teachers.

We made four suggestions for future research, which included the need for an integrated theory of personal epistemology in the classroom, the generalizability of findings across different types of measurements, a set of guidelines to promote teacher epistemological change, and an explicit instructional model that explains the development and calibration of beliefs and practices.

We argued that the development of an integrated model of personal epistemology would help to unify research findings, which frequently utilize different research models and data-collection methods that make comparisons and synthesis difficult. We argued further that a unified model would help to promote our understanding of how to change beliefs. Towards this end, Figure 17.2 provided a tentative model based on a number of suggestions made across the chapters, which emphasize the need for explicit articulation of personal epistemological that are calibrated with teaching practices.

REFERENCES

Bendixen, L. D., & Rule, D. C. (2004). An integrative approach to personal epistemology: A guiding model. *Educational Psychologist, 39,* 69–80.

Brownlee, J. (2003). Changes in primary school teachers' beliefs about knowing: A longitudinal study. *Asia-Pacific Journal of Teacher Education, 31*(1), 87–98.

Brownlee, J., & Berthelsen, D. (2006) Personal epistemology and relational pedagogy in early childhood teacher education programs. *Early Years, 26,* 17–29.

Brownlee, J., Purdie, N., & Boulton-Lewis, G. (2001). Changing epistemological beliefs in pre-service teaching education students. *Teaching in Higher Education, 6,* 247–268.

Hammer, D., & Elby, A. (2002). On the form of a personal epistemology. In B. K. Hofer & P. R. Pintrich (Eds.), *Personal epistemology: The psychology of beliefs about knowledge and knowing* (pp. 169–190). Mahwah, NJ: Lawrence Erlbaum Associates.

Hofer, B. (2001). Personal epistemology research: Implications for learning and teaching. *Educational Psychology Review, 13,* 353–384.

Hofer, B. (2004). Exploring the dimensions of personal epistemology in differing classroom contexts: Student interpretations during the first year of college. *Contemporary Educational Psychology, 29,* 129–163.

Jordan, A., Schwartz, E., & McGhie-Richmond, D. (2009). Preparing teachers for inclusive classrooms. *Teaching and Teacher Education, 25,* 535–545

Kienhues, D., Bromme, R., & Stahl, E. (2008). Changing epistemological beliefs: The unexpected impact of a short-term intervention. *British Journal of Educational Psychology, 78,* 545–565.

King, P. M., & Kitchener, K. S. (1994). *Developing reflective judgment.* San Francisco: Jossey-Bass.

Kuhn, D. (1991). *The skills of argument.* New York: Cambridge University Press.

Kuhn, D. (1999). A developmental model of critical thinking. *Educational Researcher, 28,* 16–26.

Lidar, M., Lundqvist, E., & Ostman, L. (2005). Teaching and learning in the science classroom: The interplay between teachers' epistemological moves and students' practical epistemologies. *Science Education, 90,* 148–163.

Maggioni, L., & Parkinson, M. (2008) The role of teacher epistemic cognition, epistemic beliefs, and calibration in instruction. *Educational Psychology Review, 20*(4), 445–461.

Marra, R. (2005). Teacher beliefs: The impact of the design of constructivist learning environments on instructor epistemologies. *Learning Environments Research, 8,* 135–155.

Muis, K. (2004). Personal epistemology and mathematics: A critical review and synthesis of research. *Review of Educational Research, 74*(3), 317–377.

Murphy, P. K., & Mason, L. (2006). Changing knowledge and beliefs. In P. A. Alexander & P. H. Winne (Eds.), *Handbook of educational psychology* (2nd ed., pp. 305–325). Mahwah, NJ: Lawrence Erlbaum Associates.

Olafson, L. J., & Schraw, G. (2006). Teachers' beliefs and practices within and across domains. *International Journal of Educational Research, 45,* 71–84.

Olafson, L. J., Schraw, G., & VanderVeldt, M. (2010). Consistency and development of teachers' epistemological and ontological world views. *Learning Environments Research, 13,* 243–266.

Ozgun-Koca, S., & Sen, A. (2006). The beliefs and perceptions of pre-service teachers enrolled in a subject-area dominant teacher education program about "effective education." *Teaching and Teacher Education, 22,* 946–960.

Perry, W. G. (1970). *Forms of intellectual and ethical development in the college years.* New York: Holt, Rinehart and Winston.

Schommer, M. (1990). Effects of beliefs about the nature of knowledge on comprehension. *Journal of Educational Psychology, 82,* 498–504.

Schon, D. A. (1983). *The reflective practitioner.* New York: Basic Books.

Schraw, G., & Olafson, L. (2008). Assessing teachers' epistemological and ontological worldviews. In M. Khine (Ed.), *Knowing, knowledge, and beliefs: Epistemological studies across diverse cultures* (pp. 25–44). Amsterdam: Springer.

White, C. (2000). Pre-service teachers' epistemology viewed through perspectives on problematic classroom situations. *Journal of Education for Teaching, 26,* 279–305.

Contributors

EDITORS' BIOGRAPHIES

Joanne Brownlee is an associate professor in the School of Early Child-hood, QUT, Australia. Her current research, funded by two Australian research Council grants, investigates early childhood professionals' personal epistemologies and the impact of such beliefs about knowing and learning on teaching. This research is important because there are implications for such beliefs on caregivers' practice, and subsequent quality, in child care. She has also been awarded a total of 11 University (QUT) research grants that have focused on personal epistemology in teacher education. She has an extensive publication profile in the area. She has also co-edited the text *Participatory Learning and the Early Years* (2009, Routledge).

Gregory Schraw is a Barrick Distinguished professor of educational psychology at the University of Nevada, Las Vegas. Dr. Schraw holds a Ph.D. in learning and an M.S. in applied statistics. He has published widely research articles and books in both the areas of human learning and testing. He teaches statistics, human measurement, research methods, and evaluation courses at UNLV, and serves on eight editorial boards. He is the recipient of several teaching and research awards, as well as the American Psychological Association's early career achievement award. He currently serves on the Nevada Technical Advisory committee which oversees the state testing programs, several Institute of Educational Science evaluation panels, and recently served 3 years on the NAEP Technical Working Group.

Donna Berthelsen is a professor in the School of Early Childhood at Queensland University of Technology. She is a developmental psychologist engaged in research that focuses on children's early learning, early childhood education programs, and the transition to school. She is Education Design Team Leader in the national Longitudinal Study of Australian Children, funded by the Australian Government, and a principal investigator in the Early Home Learning Study, funded by the Victorian Government. The outcomes of her research inform social and educational policy and practice. Donna is a member of the editorial boards of the *Early Childhood Research Quarterly* and the *International Journal of Early Childhood*.

CHAPTER AUTHOR BIOGRAPHIES

Dr. Charoula Angeli is associate professor of instructional technology at the University of Cyprus. She has undergraduate and graduate studies at Indiana University—Bloomington, United States (B.S. in computer science, 1991; M.S. in computer science, 1993; and Ph.D. in instructional systems technology, 1999). Her research interests include the utilization of educational technologies in K–12, the design of computer-enhanced curricula, educational software design, teacher training, teaching methodology, online learning, and the design of learning environments for the development of critical thinking skills and epistemological beliefs.

Lisa D. Bendixen is an associate professor in the Department of Educational Psychology at the University of Nevada, Las Vegas, United States. Her research interests focus on the educational implications of personal epistemology theory and research pertaining to student learning and instruction including cross-cultural influences on teachers and teacher education. In addition to 18 refereed journal publications and book chapters, and numerous national and international conference presentations on the topic, she has co-edited the book *Personal Epistemology in the Classroom: Implications for Research, Theory and Practice* (2010, Cambridge).

Gillian Boulton-Lewis is currently an adjunct professor in the School of Design at the Queensland University of Technology and Professor of Teacher Education at the University of the South Pacific in Fiji. Her research interests are in learning and its implications for education across the lifespan. Her recent research involvement is focused on moral development in early childhood, aging and learning, and sustainable communities for seniors. She has published widely and been involved with a large number of funded research projects.

Ivar Bråten is a professor of educational psychology in the Department of Educational Research at the University of Oslo, Norway. He is a leader of the doctoral concentration in language development, text comprehension, and literacy within the National Graduate School in Educational Science, and head of the Research Group on Text Comprehension—Development, Instruction, and Multiple Texts at the Faculty of Education, University of Oslo. He is currently directing the project Multiple-Documents Literacy, funded by the Norwegian Research Council, investigating epistemic cognition, source evaluation, and intertextual processing when students read multiple documents containing conflicting scientific information. He has published widely in high-quality international research journals and currently serves on the editorial boards of the *Educational Psychologist, Reading Research Quarterly,* and *Learning and Instruction.*

Alice J. Corkill is an associate professor in the Department of Educational Psychology at the University of Nevada, Las Vegas, United States. Dr. Corkill's research interests include working memory, intelligence, interference, and metacognition. Dr. Corkill is the associate editor of *Educational Psychology Review* and serves on the editorial boards of the *Journal of Educational Psychology* and *Learning and Individual Differences.* Her work has been published in the above journals as well as in other distinguished journals such as *Acta Psychologica.*

Angela Edwards is a master of education student and research assistant in the Centre for Learning Innovation at Queensland University of Technology, Australia. Angela has a background as a teacher and director in child care. Her research background includes a focus on the development of early childhood practitioner's professional identity as they move into professional practice. She has experience with qualitative analysis of epistemological beliefs data and qualitative coding of epistemological interviews.

Beryl Exley is a senior lecturer in language and literacy studies within the Faculty of Education at the Queensland University of Technology, Australia. Her 2005 doctoral thesis examined teachers' knowledge bases for new times. She continues to research in the area of teacher education with a special focus on primary education. Beryl has published in edited collections with Routledge, Oxford University Press, and Continuum. Her contact details are b.exley@qut.edu.au

Florian C. Feucht is an assistant professor of educational psychology at the University of Toledo, Ohio. Dr. Feucht holds a Ph.D. in educational psychology (United States) and a Ph.D. in empirical Didaktiks (Germany). In his scholarship, he focuses on the nature of epistemic climates in learning settings and how it pertains to student learning and teacher professional development. Dr. Feucht conducted a variety of classroom and cross-cultural research studies around the world and successfully published his empirical and conceptual work in peer-reviewed journals, book chapters, and a monograph. He recently co-edited the book *Personal Epistemology in the Classroom. Theory, Research, and Implications for Practice* (2010, Cambridge).

Helenrose Fives is an associate professor of educational foundations at Montclair State University, NJ, United States. Dr. Fives's research lies at the intersection of teachers' beliefs and practices, with an emphasis on understanding the interrelationship between teachers' beliefs (specifically self-efficacy, epistemological, and ability beliefs) and the processes of teaching and learning to teach. An examination of how these beliefs develop and are shaped through life experiences and preservice preparation may offer salient avenues for teacher development and preparation. She has been awarded four University research grants to support her investigation into teachers' beliefs and preservice preparation and with a team of colleges was awarded a large U. S. Department of Education grant to develop a preservice preparation program. She has a sound publication record including 13 peer-reviewed publications in print, 5 book chapters in print, and over 40 refereed presentations at international conferences.

Mauricio Herron is a Fulbright Grantee enrolled as a graduate student in educational psychology in the Department of Educational Studies at Purdue University. Currently, he is working on a research project about preservice teachers' epistemological beliefs and pedagogical practices across different domains with Ala Samarapungavan and Aman Yadav. Since 2006 he has been working as a professor in the Department of Education and the Department of Psychology at Universidad del Norte, Colombia. He was also granted with two consecutive "Joung Researchers" scholarships (2005, 2006) from Colciencias, Colombia, and has participated as co-researcher in two research projects (2004, 2006) on university students' conceptions about learning, both sponsored by Universidad Del Norte. He has three publications in referred Colombian journals.

Anne Jordan is a professor emerita at the University of Toronto, Canada. She is the author of four books, including a recent electronic text published by Wiley Canada and accessible by internet, on inclusive education for classroom teachers. She conducts research in elementary classrooms on teachers' beliefs and practices and is the author of over 50 scholarly articles.

Min-Hsien Lee holds a Ph.D. degree (2009) at the National Taiwan Normal University, Taiwan. He is currently an assistant professor at Graduate Institute of Engineering, National Taiwan University of Science and Technology, Taiwan. His research interest deals with student and teacher beliefs in relation to learning and teaching science.

Rose M. Marra is an associate professor in the School of Information Science and Learning Technologies at the University of Missouri. Her research interests include gender equity issues, the epistemological development of college students, and promoting meaningful learning in web-based environments. She is PI of the NSF-funded Assessing Women and Men in Engineering (AWE) and Assessing Women in Student Environments (AWISE) projects, the National Girls Collaborative Project (NGCP), and a recent recipient of the Betty Vetter Award for Research.

Lori Olafson is an associate professor in the Department of Educational Psychology at the University of Nevada, Las Vegas. Her current research interests focus on the relationship between moral reasoning and epistemological beliefs, and on the epistemological and ontological beliefs of preservice and inservice teachers.

Betsy Palmer is an associate professor of adult and higher education and educational research and statistics at Montana State University. She conducts research on college student outcomes and university teaching, particularly focused on student epistemology, non-traditional pedagogies, and multicultural education. She also collaborates with engineering colleagues to research educational practices in engineering education. She is currently a Co-PI on the NSF funded Prototyping the Engineer of 2020: A 360-degree Study of Effective Education grant.

Guy Roth is a lecturer in the Department of Education at Ben-Gurion University of the Negev. His research and writing focus on antecedents and consequences of autonomy supportive and autonomy suppressive (controlling) behaviors of parents, teachers, and principals. He teaches courses in educational leadership, motivation, and research methods. He has published in leading psychology and education journals such as *Developmental Psychology*, the *Journal of Educational Psychology*, and the *Journal of Personality*.

Ala Samarapungavan, Ph.D. is a professor of educational psychology and interim head of the Department of Educational Studies at Purdue University. She is interested in how people think and learn in knowledge rich domains. Her research projects focus on epistemic reasoning and learning in science from childhood through adulthood. Professor Samarapungavan's research is funded by grants from the US Department of Education's Institute of Education Sciences and the National Science Foundation.

Eileen Schwartz spent many years as a teacher, special educator, and consultant in inclusive practices for students with disabilities. After retiring from the school system, she undertook her doctorate, completing in 2009 with a thesis on teachers' epistemological beliefs and how these relate to teaching practices.

Helge I. Strømsø is a professor of higher education in the Department of Educational Research at the University of Oslo, Norway, where he is also heading the university's faculty and curriculum development program. His research interests include personal epistemology, self-regulated learning, text comprehension, and the use of information and communication technology in higher education. He has published articles in international peer reviewed journals in all of these areas. For the past several years, he has been working on a project funded by the Norwegian Research Council, focusing on the relationship between university students' epistemic beliefs and their comprehension of complex science topics.

Iris Tabak (B.S.E., computer engineering; Ph.D., learning sciences) is a senior lecturer in the Department of Education, Ben-Gurion University of the Negev, Israel, and past chair of the Learning, Instruction & Technology program. Dr. Tabak's research and writing focus on complex reasoning in naturalistic settings, and on the role of identification, forms of knowledge, and multiple interacting agents in this process. Her work on teacher practice examined which moves not only facilitate mastery of science but empower learners to participate in science. As a principal investigator in a project funded by the Seventh Framework of the European Commission, she studies how to support everyday evidence-based health care decisions, and how to adapt and share learning technologies across countries to increase curricular capacity (CoReflect). Dr. Tabak was president of the International Society of the Learning Sciences (ISLS), and a recipient of the AERA Division C Jan Hawkins Award. She serves on the editorial board of *Educational Psychologist*, and is an associate editor of the *Journal of the Learning Sciences* (JLS).

H. H. (Harm) Tillema (Ph.D.) is a senior lecturer, specialized in teacher education and human resource development. Currently, he is affiliated at Leiden University (The Netherlands). He has contributed to several funded research and consultancy projects in the areas of teacher professional learning and competence development of personnel in organizations. His consultancy work in teacher education and his internationally published research have resulted in several conceptual artifacts for expertise development in areas of teacher professional development and (student) teacher learning. This includes powerful training interventions, such as study teams, as well as contributions to assessment (for learning), teacher team learning, and audit evaluations of practice teaching interventions. His main interest enabled him to design solutions for professional practice, based on research in which conceptualization and validation of constructed artifacts have high priority. As a counselor to several projects, both commissioned and granted, he has sought to qualify himself as a coach and critical friend to teacher educators and student teachers, as well as Ph.D. students. In his research work he has been internationally oriented within several projects and research studies.

Chin-Chung Tsai holds a Bachelor of Science degree in physics from National Taiwan Normal University, Taiwan. He received a Master of Education degree from Harvard University and a Master of Science degree from Teachers College, Columbia University. He completed his doctoral study also at Teachers College, Columbia University, 1996. From 1996–2006, he joined the faculty at Institute of Education, National Chiao Tung University, Hsinchu, Taiwan. He is currently a chair professor at Graduate Institute of Digital Learning and Education, National Taiwan University of Science and Technology, Taiwan (e-mail cctsai@mail.ntust.edu.tw). He is now also the co-editor for the journal *Computers & Education*. His research interests deal largely with epistemological beliefs, science education, and Internet-based instruction. In the past 5 years, he has published more than 50 papers in English-based international journals.

Nicos Valanides is associate professor of science education at the University of Cyprus. He has undergraduate studies at the Aristotelian University of Thessaloniki (B.A. in physics, 1969; and B.A. in law, 1985), and graduate studies at the American University of Beirut (teaching diploma, 1980; and M.A. in education: teaching sciences, 1981) and at the University of Albany, State University of New York, SUNY—Albany (M.Sc. in instructional supervision, 1986; and Ph.D. in curriculum and instruction and educational research, 1990). His research interests include teacher training, methodology of teaching and curricula for science education, the development of scientific reasoning and epistemological beliefs, science-and-technology literacy, the utilization of ICT in science education, blended learning, and the design of educational interventions and learning environments. He has published significantly in referred journals and has extensive experience and expertise with research projects funded by European Union.

Michelle VanderVeldt is an assistant professor in the Department of Elementary and Bilingual Education at California State University, Fullerton. Her research interests focus on examining epistemological and ontological beliefs, exploring civics education through active citizenship projects, and investigating effective mathematics instruction.

Sue Walker (Ph.D.) is a senior lecturer in the School of Early Childhood and a researcher within the Centre for Learning Innovation at QUT. Her research foci include early years teachers' epistemic beliefs and teaching practice, child outcomes in relation to inclusive early childhood education programs, early intervention, and the transition to school. She is currently a chief investigator on two Australian Research Council Discovery Grants investigating early years teachers' epistemic beliefs and beliefs about moral learning and the outcomes for young children with developmental disabilities across the transition to school. Dr. Walker teaches courses in early childhood development and research methods.

Michael Weinstock is a lecturer in the Department of Education at Ben-Gurion University of the Negev. He has served as the chair of the school psychology program and teaches courses in educational psychology and cognitive, moral, and epistemological development. Dr. Weinstock's research and writing focus on epistemological development and everyday reasoning. As the principal investigator of a project funded by the Israeli Science Foundation he is studying cultural differences in adolescents' epistemological beliefs, argument norms, and personal and intellectual values. He was also the principal investigator of a project funded by the Israel Foundation Trustees researching the role of academic and social contexts in postsecondary epistemological development. He serves on the editorial boards of *Learning and Instruction* and *Educational Psychologist.*

Chrystal Whiteford is a Ph.D. student and research assistant in the Centre for Learning Innovation at Queensland University of Technology, Australia. Her research background includes a focus on social-emotional and learning competence in the early years for children with special health care needs, preservice teachers' personal epistemological beliefs, and the moral development of young children. She has experience with statistical analysis of epistemological beliefs data and qualitative coding of epistemological interviews.

Annette Woods is a senior lecturer in the Faculty of Education at the Queensland University of Technology, Australia. Her research interests include literacies, curriculum, pedagogy, and assessment, and social justice. She is currently working on large grants related to teachers' use of curriculum documents, literacy reform through digitisation of the curriculum in low SES schools, and an evaluation of large scale project aimed at improving school-based outcomes for Indigenous students. She has publications across a range of journals and collections including a recent chapter on policy and adolescent literacy in the *Handbook of Adolescent Literacy.*

Aman Yadav (Ph.D.) is an assistant professor in the educational psychology program in the Department of Educational Studies at Purdue University. His current research focuses on the use of video cases in teacher preparation and professional development. His research also focuses on the role of epistemological beliefs in preservice teacher education and how those beliefs change over the course of a program. Dr. Yadav has 11 refereed publications, 3 book chapters, 7 conference proceedings, and 27 conference papers since 2000.

Index